'This book is rich in detail not only of events but of the people and places and interactions leading to them. Yet it has a comprehensive sweep – encompassing contemporary inter-state relations as well as theory, history, domestic politics, interests, perceptions, identity and much more. This is a must-read for any student, scholar, or practitioner interested in Southeast Asia and its project of regional community building.'

Aileen Baviera, *Asian Center, University of the Philippines, Manila*

'Regional integration is no easy business – especially in the Southeast Asian context! However, Dr Roberts' book provides an excellent analysis that enables readers to understand this complex process. The book also provides valuable insights and analysis on the challenges ahead. It is a highly balanced book about ASEAN and a must read to anyone who wants to better understand Southeast Asia.'

Rizal Sukma, *Executive Director, Centre for Strategic and International Studies (CSIS), Jakarta*

'This outstanding volume covers key debates within the regional organization as it moved to adopt the ASEAN Charter and weathered criticism following the entry of Myanmar/Burma. It will also be useful to students of regionalism and globalization because of its empirical analysis of the imperatives for regional integration through ASEAN and its awareness of the limitations arising from inter-state competition and divergent domestic capabilities within its member states which impact on efforts to create an ASEAN identity.'

Barry Desker, *Dean of the S. Rajaratnam School of International Studies, Nanyang Technological University, Singapore*

ASEAN Regionalism

This book examines the key motivations for and challenges to greater regional integration in Southeast Asia. It demonstrates how security and economic concerns – domestic, regional and international – have either contributed to, or detracted from, an increased level of unity and cooperation in ASEAN. It also explores how the patterns of interaction and socialization generated by these issues, together with the nature of domestic political systems, have affected the emergence of common values, norms and interests.

Extensive fieldwork in all the ASEAN countries – including interviews and surveys – contributes to a fresh and empirically grounded assessment of ASEAN's effectiveness in responding to domestic and regional security and economic concerns. It also explores the extent to which the patterns of interaction and socialization generated by these issues have contributed to greater cooperation and institutionalization through common norms, values and interests. It covers a full range of issues confronting ASEAN at present (including the ASEAN Charter and Myanmar) as well as likely future developments.

Christopher B. Roberts is Senior Lecturer, National Security College, Australian National University.

Routledge security in Asia Pacific series

Series Editors: Leszek Buszynski
International University of Japan
and
William Tow
Australian National University

Security issues have become more prominent in the Asia Pacific region because of the presence of global players, rising great powers, and confident middle powers, which intersect in complicated ways. This series puts forward important new work on key security issues in the region. It embraces the roles of the major actors, their defense policies and postures and their security interaction over the key issues of the region. It includes coverage of the United States, China, Japan, Russia, the Koreas, as well as the middle powers of ASEAN and South Asia. It also covers issues relating to environmental and economic security as well as transnational actors and regional groupings.

1 **Bush and Asia**
America's evolving relations with East Asia
Edited by Mark Beeson

2 **Japan, Australia and Asia-Pacific Security**
Edited by Brad Williams and Andrew Newman

3 **Regional Cooperation and Its Enemies in Northeast Asia**
The impact of domestic forces
Edited by Edward Friedman and Sung Chull Kim

4 **Energy Security in Asia**
Edited by Michael Wesley

5 **Australia as an Asia Pacific Regional Power**
Friendships in flux?
Edited by Brendan Taylor

6 **Securing Southeast Asia**
The politics of security sector reform
Mark Beeson and Alex J. Bellamy

7 **Pakistan's Nuclear Weapons**
Bhumitra Chakma

8 **Human Security in East Asia**
Challenges for collaborative action
Edited by Sorpong Peou

9 **Security and International Politics in the South China Sea**
Towards a co-operative management regime
Edited by Sam Bateman & Ralf Emmers

10 **Japan's Peace Building Diplomacy in Asia**
Seeking a more active political role
Lam Peng Er

11 **Geopolitics and Maritime Territorial Disputes in East Asia**
Ralf Emmers

12 **North Korea's Military-Diplomatic Campaigns, 1966–2008**
Narushige Michishita

13 **Political Change, Democratic Transitions and Security in Southeast Asia**
Mely Caballero-Anthony

14 **American Sanctions in the Asia-Pacific**
Brendan Taylor

15 **Southeast Asia and the Rise of Chinese and Indian Naval Power**
Between rising naval powers
Edited by Sam Bateman and Joshua Ho

16 **Human Security in Southeast Asia**
Yukiko Nishikawa

17 **ASEAN and the Institutionalization of East Asia**
Ralf Emmers

18 **India as an Asia Pacific Power**
David Brewster

19 **ASEAN Regionalism**
Cooperation, values and institutionalization
Christopher B. Roberts

ASEAN Regionalism

Cooperation, values and institutionalization

Christopher B. Roberts

LONDON AND NEW YORK

This edition published 2012
by Routledge
2 Park Square, Milton Park, Abingdon, Oxon OX14 4RN

Simultaneously published in the USA and Canada
by Routledge
711 Third Avenue, New York, NY 10017

Routledge is an imprint of the Taylor & Francis Group, an informa business

First issued in paperback 2013

British Library Cataloguing in Publication Data
A catalogue record for this book is available from the British Library

Library of Congress Cataloging-in-Publication Data
Roberts, Christopher B.
ASEAN regionalism: cooperation, values and institutionalisation/
Christopher B. Roberts.
p. cm. – (Routledge security in Asia Pacific series; 19)
Includes bibliographical references and index.
1. ASEAN. 2. Regionalism–Southeast Asia. 3. Southeast Asia–Foreign relations. I. Title. II. Series: Routledge security in Asia Pacific series; 19.
DS520.A873R64 2012
341.24′73–dc23

2011019784

ISBN: 978-0-415-49001-6 (hbk)
ISBN: 978-0-415-85664-5 (pbk)
ISBN: 978-0-203-18104-1 (ebk)

Typeset in Times
by Wearset Ltd, Boldon, Tyne and Wear

Contents

Figures and tables

Figures

Tables

Preface

The writing of this book has been a consequence of several fortuitous events. I commenced a PhD dissertation in 2004 under the supervision of Professor James Cotton at the Australian Defence Force Academy campus of the University of New South Wales (Canberra). While I was always very fortunate to start a PhD programme under the supervision of such an eminent professor – together with the support of a full scholarship (Australian Postgraduate Award) – the opportunity to undertake significant and original research arose when I became one of the first recipients for the Australian government's inaugural Endeavour Australia Cheung Kong Award. The generous bursary associated with the award, together with some additional research grants and a further award from UNSW, enabled me to undertake extensive fieldwork in all the ASEAN nations. These activities were further aided by the kind hospitality and visiting appointments at Singapore's S. Rajaratnam School of International Studies and the Institute of Southeast Asian Affairs. This enabled me to live in Singapore and I utilized Singapore as a very cost effective base to travel to the remaining ASEAN nations. Consequently, I was able to conduct more than 150 interviews, 100 elite level surveys and a further 819 surveys in seven languages at the grassroots level.

Singapore served as an exceptional locality to conduct PhD fieldwork from but S. Rajaratnam School of International Studies also played a pivotal role in launching my formal academic career through an appointment as a Research Associate in 2007 and then as a Post-Doctoral Fellow in 2008. Throughout my time in Singapore, I was exposed to many highly creative minds and leading experts in the field whilst simultaneously being immersed in an environment where a strong publication rate was not only expected but was also the norm. Consequently, my connections throughout Southeast Asia continued to deepen and my own publication record significantly expanded. I have since been able to bring the knowledge I gained from Singapore back to Australia where I have applied them for the purpose of further publications, including this book, together with my teaching at the University of Canberra.

As a consequence of the aforementioned events, together with new developments in Southeast Asia, the present manuscript could not be completed to my satisfaction until 2011. While I have remained consistent with my key contentions, new explanatory and contextual layers have been added to the manuscript including a greater emphasis on the domestic variables to regionalism – an aspect that is all too often 'black boxed' in the literature. The addition of new case studies, issues and updates also reflect my fervent hope that this manuscript will be informative to the reader and also spark further debates and research about how to overcome the challenges to greater regionalism, cooperation, stability and peace in Southeast Asia. For my own part, I hope that the insights from this manuscript, including the survey and interview material, will also serve as a significant platform from which I will conduct further research. Importantly, my recent appointment as a Senior Lecturer at the National Security College – within the Australian National University – has provided me with a new and exciting institutional 'home' through which I hope to continue to develop the theories, ideas and key contentions that are contained in the pages that follow.

Acknowledgements

First and foremost, I would like to thank Professor James Cotton for his excellent supervision during my PhD, the dissertation of which provided an earlier incarnation of the present study. He has been a true mentor in every sense of the word and this book could not have been completed in the absence of his guidance. I am also deeply indebted to Professor Mark Turner for providing me with the support and time necessary to complete the manuscript. I am also extremely grateful to four other professors – Carl Thayer, John Ravenhill, Leszek Buszynski and Bill Tow – for their friendship and guidance over the years. I would also like to thank the University of New South Wales at the Australian Defence Force Academy for providing an 'Australian Postgraduate Award Scholarship', a further two research grants, and for the UNSW 'Business Services Travel Award'. Here, I am also very grateful for the constant support and encouragement provided by the head of the School of Humanities and Social Sciences – Professor David Lovell. I am equally indebted to the Australian government for selecting me for the 'Endeavour Australia Cheung Kong Award' and for providing an associated bursary that funded a significant portion of the research. Without these sources of financial assistance it would not have been possible to undertake field trips to all ten of the ASEAN countries. My research was also significantly aided by the kind hospitality provided by RSIS during a sixteen-month stay as a visiting associate, followed by a postdoctoral fellowship, and by ISEAS during a seven-month stay as a visiting associate. In this regard, I would like to thank both Ambassador Barry Desker and Ambassador Kesavapany for their kind hospitality and invaluable assistance.

Many other people have provided their valuable time and assistance in the compilation of this study. Of these, I would like to begin by expressing my sincere gratitude to Professor Don McMillen and Associate Professor Peter Wicks for their supervision, kindness and support during the completion of an MA (Asian Studies) programme between 2001 and 2002; they played a key role in showing the way into a university career. Since this time, a number of other individuals stand out in the provision of invaluable support and guidance both during and outside work hours. Such individuals include, but are not limited to, my good friends Dr Brendan Taylor, Dr Debbi Elms, Dr Edwin Jurriens, Dr Richard Carney and Dr Manoj Gupta. Many others who have played a valuable role in this work over the years including Associate Professor Ralf Emmers, Mr Sng Seow Lian, Professor Hugh

White, Associate Professor Leonard Sebastian, Associate Professor Joseph Liow, Associate Professor Tan See Seng, Dr Hiro Katsumata, Professor K. S. Nathan, Dr Stephen Leong, Dr Bantarto Bandoro, Professor Des Ball, Mr Barry Wain and especially General Pham Tuan and his family. Of equal importance has been the guidance and support I have received from the scholars and administrative staff of both the University of Canberra and the University of New South Wales at the Australian Defence Force Academy. In particular, I would like to thank Professor Peter Dennis, Mrs Shirley Ramsay, Mrs Sheila Wood, Mrs Rebecca Zhang, Dr Craig Stockings, Dr Taufiq Tanasaldy, Mrs Bernadette McDermott, Mrs Sandra Mason, Mrs Marilyn Anderson Smith, Mrs Jo Muggleton, Dr Frank Cain, Professor Robin Prior, Ms Elvira Berra, Ms Danica Robinson, Dr Minako Sakai, Dr Jian Zhang and Dr Paul Tickell. I would also like to thank the many others who have provided invaluable support, inspiration and guidance during the course of the PhD.

Equally important is my appreciation of the hundreds of policy makers and scholars throughout Southeast Asia who freely provided their time and knowledge during the course of interviews and the compilation of the survey data. Similarly, my thanks to the 819 citizens of Southeast Asia who participated in the communal level survey sample and to all those who assisted with the translations and the survey work in the capital cities of most of the ASEAN countries. In relation to the survey work, I would like to specifically thank Mrs Fiona Cotton for her assistance in organizing a pilot test of my two survey designs with military officers from Southeast Asia studying at the Australian Defence Force Academy. In the context of my interview data, I am equally grateful to Mr John McFarlane as this book could not have been completed in its current form without his most gracious generosity in sharing his many contacts in Southeast Asia. In relation to the very helpful feedback I received towards the end of completing the book I am also especially grateful for the guidance and help provided by Ms Susan Cowan, two anonymous reviewers and Peter Sowden from Routledge.

On a more personal note, I would also like to thank my parents for all their support and love over the years. I am also extremely fortunate to have some long-standing friends who have stood by me through thick and thin and these include Ingrid Neilson and Gerard Pauley. Many other friends, teachers and work colleagues have been a source of inspiration over the years and some of these include Sister Lucy Kert, Father Peter Quilty, Lisha Kayrooz, Paul and Jacqui Hughes, Shelton Bond, Robyn Culley and many more. I would also like to thank my cousin, David Cameron, for his long-term support and understanding. I am also deeply indebted to my wife's family for not only understanding the demands of my profession, but for having so warmly embraced me as a part of their family. To my late grandmother, Mrs Lillian Campbell, I will always think of you, as you always believed in me and supported me; I will always remember the inspiration and love you provided to all those who knew you. Last, but by no means least, this book could never have been completed without the infinite love and support of my dear wife Le Thi Thu Huong – it is to you and our baby girl Lily that I dedicate this work.

Abbreviations

ACD	Asian Cooperation Dialogue
ACSC	ASEAN Civil Society Conference
ADB	Asia Development Bank
AEC	ASEAN Economic Community
AFTA	ASEAN Free Trade Area
AICHR	ASEAN Intergovernmental Commission on Human Rights
AIPMC	ASEAN Inter-Parliamentary Myanmar Caucus
AMDA	Anglo-Malayan Defence Agreement
AMM	ASEAN Ministerial Meeting
AMMTC	ASEAN Ministerial Meeting on Transnational Crime
APA	ASEAN People's Assembly
APEC	Asia-Pacific Economic Cooperation
APR	Asia-Pacific Roundtable
APT	ASEAN Plus Three (ASEAN 10+3)
ARF	ASEAN Regional Forum
ASA	Association of Southeast Asia
ASC	ASEAN Security community
ASCC	ASEAN Socio-Cultural Community
ASEAN	Association of Southeast Asian Nations
ASEM	Asia–Europe Meeting
ASG	Abu Sayyaf Group
ASOE	ASEAN Senior Officials on the Environment
ASP	ASEAN Surveillance Process
ASPAC	Asian and Pacific Council
BSA	bilateral swap arrangement
CEP	Comprehensive Economic Partnership
CEPT	Common Effective Preferential Tariff Scheme
CLMV	Cambodia, Laos, Myanmar and Vietnam
CMIM	Chiang Mai Initiative Multilateralism
CSBM	Confidence and Security Building Mechanism
CSCA	Council for Security and Cooperation in Asia
CSCAP	Council for Security and Cooperation in the Asia-Pacific
CSCE	Council for Security and Cooperation in Europe

CSIS	Centre for Strategic and International Studies (Jakarta)
CSO	civil society organization
DPV	Democratic Party of Vietnam
DRV	Democratic Republic of Vietnam
DSM	Dispute Settlement Mechanism
EAEC	East Asia Economic Caucus
EAEG	East Asia Economic Group
EAS	East Asia Summit
EDSM	Enhanced Dispute Settlement Mechanism
EEZ	Exclusive Economic Zone
EOI	export-oriented industrialization
EPG	Eminent Persons Group
ERAT	Emergency Rapid Assessment Team
EU	European Union
F	free (survey response)
FDI	foreign direct investment
FPDA	Five Power Defence Arrangement
FTA	free trade agreement
GAM	*Gerakan Aceh Merdeka* (Free Aceh Movement)
GDP	gross domestic product
ICJ	International Court of Justice
ICRC	International Committee for the Red Cross
IMF	International Monetary Fund
INTERFET	International Force for East Timor
IOI	Import Orientation Industrialization
IR	International Relations
ISA	Internal Security Act
ISIS	Institute for Security and International Studies
LPRP	Laotian People's Revolutionary Party
Maphilindo	Malaysia–Philippines–Indonesia
MINDEF	Ministry of Defence (Singapore)
NAFTA	North American Free Trade Agreement
NAM	Non-Aligned Movement
NF	not free (survey response)
NLD	National League for Democracy (Myanmar)
NGO	non-governmental organization
OCHA	UN Office for the Coordination of Humanitarian Affairs
PAP	People's Action Party (Singapore)
PF	partly free
PICC	Paris International Conference on Cambodia
PITF	Political Instability Task Force
PKI	*Partai Komunis Indonesia* (Indonesian Communist Party)
PMC	ASEAN Post-Ministerial Conference
PONJA	Post-Nargis Joint Assessment Team
PPP	purchasing power parity

PRK	People's Republic of Kampuchea
PSSR	political and security sector reform
R2P	Responsibility to Protect
ROO	Rules of Origin
RTA	Regional Trade Agreement
SAPA	Solidarity for Asian People's Advocacy
SEAARC	Southeast Asian Association for Regional Cooperation
SEAFET	Southeast Asian Friendship and Economic Treaty
SEANWFZ	Southeast Asia Nuclear Weapons Free Zone
SEATO	South East Asia Treaty Organization
SIT	Social Identity Theory
SLOC	Sea Lanes of Communication
SLORC	State Law and Order Restoration Council, Myanmar
SOM	Senior Officials Meeting
SPDC	State Peace and Development Council
TAC	Treaty of Amity and Cooperation
TCF	Trillion Cubic Feet
TCG	Tripartite Core Group
TNI	*Tentara Nasional Indonesia*
UMNO	United Malays National Organisation
UN	United Nations
UNEP	United Nations Environmental Program
UNESCO	United Nations Educational, Scientific and Cultural Organization
UNGA	United Nations General Assembly
UNODC	United Nations Office of Drugs and Crime
UNSC	United Nations Security Council
UNTAC	United Nation's Transitional Authority of Cambodia
UNTAET	United Nations Transition Authority on East Timor
US	United States
USDA	Union Solidarity and Development Association (Myanmar)
USDP	Union Solidarity and Development Party (Myanmar)
VPA	Vientiane Plan of Action/Vientiane Action Program
WB	World Bank
ZOPFAN	Zone of Peace, Freedom and Neutrality

Introduction

By the turn of the millennium, a complicated mix of regional events and global uncertainties had significantly challenged the modus operandi, values and prestige of the Association of Southeast Asian Nations (ASEAN). Consequently, a growing proportion of the region's political elite came to accept that the pursuit of security, stability and economic development would require greater political cooperation and integration between the ASEAN members. For the more democratic states, this realization impelled a growing sense of urgency regarding the need to transform the underlying values and norms of the Association and, in the process, deepen the level of supranational institutionalization currently extant. Negotiations subsequently culminated in an ASEAN Charter as well as a formal proposal to establish an integrated 'security community', 'economic community' and 'socio-cultural community'. While key components in these institutional blueprints have emulated constructivist ideas, the specific proposal for a security community reflects more than half a century of scholarly work on the subject. As a security community can only exist where armed conflict between the members would no longer be foreseeable, the realization of ASEAN's goals would result in a level of cooperation and international integration akin to the European Union (EU). Given the political, economic and ethno-religious diversity of Southeast Asia, such institutionalized regionalism will be no easy feat.

Despite the above caveats, ASEAN's regionalist aspirations are both promising and extraordinary in nature. The veritable increase to cooperation, stability and security inherent in the realization of these goals provides added incentive to undertake fresh empirical and theoretical investigation. Consequently, this book assesses the prospects for success by weighing the motivations and benefits of regionalism against the challenges and limitations of historical memories, competing interests and a diversity of values in Southeast Asia. In the pursuit of this task, the book examines the level of regionalism to date and how political, security and economic concerns have variously contributed to, or detracted from, regional unity and cooperation. Further, the book seeks to ascertain the extent to which patterns of interaction (socialization) and institutionalization (in the supranational sense) have generated common values, a harmonization of interests and foreign policy coordination. As a complement to this, the analysis also examines the preconditions for, and triggers of, increased political, economic and socio-cultural integration. In line with the scholarly literature, the ultimate outcome of such regionalist processes, as aspired by ASEAN, would be the establishment of a security community.[1]

Regionalism and ASEAN: bridging the divide between policy and theory

Recent scholarship has come to view regionalism as a 'strategic goal of region building, of establishing regional coherence and identity'.[2] Because of this, 'regionalism' has been frequently cited in the literature as denoting both a 'policy' and a 'project', thereby enabling its application and interchangeability with ASEAN's own project for a security community.[3] In other words, a security community represents the *ideal* outcome of a successful regionalist project. The concept of a 'security community' has been largely accredited to the work of Karl Deutsch and his associates back in 1957[4] and led to the creation of sociological liberalism as a distinct school of thought.[5] While some have claimed that this concept represented the first substantive challenge to the realist paradigm,[6] the importance Deutsch placed on considerations such as *power* implied a more eclectic framework with the opportunity to accept some of the contentions of the neo-realist and neo-liberal paradigms. Deutsch also asserted that a security community could only exist where there are 'dependable expectations of peaceful change'.[7] According to Deutsch, the existence of such 'expectations' will most likely arise whenever two or more states become integrated to the extent that there is an overall sense of community, 'which in turn, creates the assurance that they will settle their differences short of war'.[8] Therefore, the 'community of states' that form a security community abide by norms of peaceful conduct and in fact anticipates a stable peace. Deutsch articulated his framework in the following manner:

> A security community is a group of people which become 'integrated'.... By integration we mean the attainment, within a territory, of a 'sense of community' and of institutions and practices strong enough and widespread enough to assure, for a 'long' time, dependable expectations of 'peaceful change' among its population.... By sense of community we mean a belief on the part of the individuals in a group that they have come to agreement on at least this one point: that common social problems must and can be resolved by processes of 'peaceful change'.... By peaceful change we mean the resolution of social problems, normally by institutionalized procedures, without resort to large-scale physical force.[9]

The policy documents surrounding ASEAN's aspiration to forge a security community, together with ASEAN's blueprints for regionalism more broadly, reflect Deutsch's definition of a security community. For example, the proposal for a security community was initiated by the Indonesian Foreign Ministry (*Deplu*) and, as a policy document, it was remarkably conceptual in nature due to the input of Indonesian scholars including Rizal Sukma from the Centre for Strategic and International Studies (CSIS) in Jakarta. The *Deplu* proposal, entitled 'Towards an ASEAN Security community', virtually replicated Deutsch's language where, for example, the paper stated that through the establishment of a security community the members will come to share 'expectations of peaceful change' and 'rule out the use of force as a means of problem-solving'. Such linkages between ASEAN's notion of a security community and the Deutschian concept can also be seen in ASEAN's Bali Concord II. The document represents the outcome of Deplu's initial proposal and describes a future 'ASEAN community' that will not only be built on the emergence of a 'security community' but that will also be strengthened by the 'closely intertwined and mutually reinforcing pillars of an 'economic community' and a 'socio-cultural community … for the purpose of ensuring durable peace, stability and shared prosperity in the region.'[10]

Deutsch's notion of a security community is also evident in the declaration in the Bali Concord II that the ASEAN 'members shall rely exclusively on *peaceful processes* in the *settlement of intra-regional differences* and regard their security as fundamentally linked to one another and bound by geographic location, common vision and objectives'. The ASEAN declaration further argues that these goals will be realized by moving 'ASEAN's political and security cooperation to a higher plane'. More broadly, constructivist influences are also evident where, for example, the Bali Concord II aspires to explore 'innovative ways to increase its security and establish modalities … which include, *inter alia*, the following elements: *norm-setting* approaches to conflict resolution and post-conflict peace building'.[11] As Jones and Smith assert, the Bali Concord II 'redescribes the Treaty of Amity and Cooperation in language that could be found in many undergraduate course outlines in international relations'.[12] The establishment of the three pillars of the ASEAN Community was initially scheduled for 2020 but this date was later brought forward to 2015.[13]

The conceptual connections described above are indicative of how key scholars have markedly influenced regional policy making, language and perceptions.[14] Problematically, however, the influence of security community frameworks, and constructivism more generally, has been criticized for being too ambiguous, overly subjective and, in the context of Southeast Asia, often lacking sufficient linkages between theory and empirical evidence.[15] Nonetheless, Donald Emmerson suggests that if the key propositions to a security community can be empirically tested, applied and accepted as a general theory, then there is the possibility of the concept gaining additional relevance as a policy goal (normative project) by 'governments, international organizations, social movements and other relevant bodies throughout the world'.[16] In this context, the book also represents an important contribution as the conceptual developments concerning regionalism, integration and security communities in this study have been designed to contribute towards such an outcome.

In line with the goals above, the concept and relevance of a security community framework in this book has been strengthened through an overarching focus on 'regionalism' because the associated 'new regionalism' literature delivers important insights concerning the benefits of intensified political, economic and socio-cultural cooperation within a spatially defined area.[17] Likewise, integration theories represent a central pillar of the analysis as they contribute to an understanding of the processes behind such a phenomenon including the gradual transfer of sovereignty from state to supranational structures (institutionalization).[18] While some positivistic scholars have accurately highlighted the continued centrality of both *states* and *geography* in regional affairs,[19] recent 'new regionalism' literature has adopted a more multidimensional approach including a consideration of trade patterns, shared environmental effects and shared cultural identities. These developments tie in with the contributions of constructivism, sociological liberalism and neo-liberal institutionalism. These schools of thought, to varying degrees, have emphasized a 'normative interest in integration through various-order bringing schemes' eventually culminating in regional organization (institutionalization).[20] Thus, the analysis of both material and ideational factors within this book has been guided by a constructivist interpretation of integration theory, including the contention that, in addition to increased cooperation and institutionalization between states, regionalism also assists in a gradual homogenization of values.

Research rationale and methodology

Given a lack of consensus concerning how ASEAN should be characterized and the extent to which it has contributed to regional order,[21] the present study also provides a new perspective through intensive fieldwork involving in-depth interviews and survey work at the elite and grassroots levels. These research activities were designed to examine the fundamental characteristics of the international relations of the ASEAN states (among other things) and to assess how these features correspond with the implementation of greater regionalism in Southeast Asia. To this end, the author has conducted more than thirty field-trips to all the ASEAN countries. For the purpose of this study, hundreds of interviews and meetings were held with members of government, academia, political dissidents, journalists and relevant NGOs. Due to the political culture of some governments within the region, *inter alia*, some of the political elite interviewed for the book requested that their comments be cited without attribution. To the extent that is possible, references to each interview will at least indicate the interlocutor's field of work, country and approximate position.

Given the high-level access gained by the author to various interlocutors (e.g. from Deputy Foreign Ministers through to the Secretary-General of ASEAN), a semi-structured interview approach was deemed the most appropriate for the purpose of complementing the standardized survey-work in the study. In the case of the latter, because the actual perceptions of the people of Southeast Asia have never been tested on a region-wide basis, two sets of surveys were developed.[22] The first survey design had a set of questions specifically targeted towards the elite of Southeast Asia. Within this survey design, the questions assumed a purposive sample of regional elite who held a reasonable level of knowledge concerning Southeast Asia. As with the interviews, over three years of fieldwork was required to obtain the survey sample of 100 elites.

As indicated by Figure I.1 below, thirty-eight of the elite survey respondents were from an academic background while thirty-eight were government officials. While the respondents came from all ten countries, there were a number of limitations to the sample. The authoritarian nature of some regimes meant that the elite samples within Myanmar and Brunei were particularly small. While three participants responded from Myanmar (with two of these from government), only one person responded from Brunei (government). While the sample from Singapore was significantly larger, all attempts to get a response from members of the political elite (government) were refused and resulted in 'return to sender' post and emails that indicated that the author's correspondence had been monitored.[23] Nonetheless, greater time and resources would have undoubtedly helped to mitigate some of these problems. Despite these challenges, political elites from all the remaining countries did participate in the survey.

For the purpose of carrying out the investigative tasks of the book, a second survey was also designed. This survey utilized a grassroots (communal) sample of respondents and assumed little to no knowledge about the region. Due to the oppressive nature of the military dictatorship in Myanmar, the communal level sample for Myanmar was not conducted 'in country'. As an alternative, a small sample of surveys was conducted with primarily blue-collar Myanmarese workers in Singapore. Beyond Myanmar, the communal samples were conducted in seven different languages (English, Laotian, Khmer, Vietnamese, Bahasa Indonesia, Tagalog and Thai) and, for the purpose of comparative analysis, the

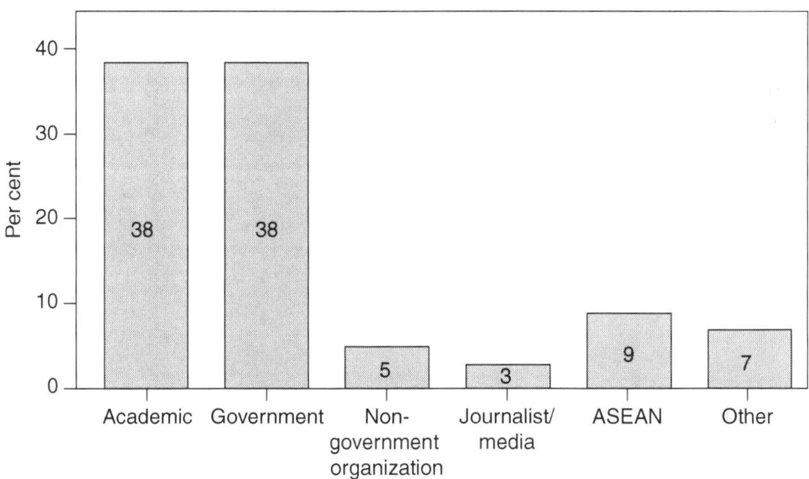

Figure I.1 Category of work (elite sample) (source: compiled by author).

majority of the survey samples came from the capital city of each ASEAN state.[24] Furthermore, most of the participants were randomly approached in the street and token gifts to the value of approximately $1 were offered as a gesture of appreciation. In most cases, postgraduate students were employed by the author to conduct the survey to overcome any potential language difficulties. In all cases, translations were conducted by native speaking postgraduate students and, where possible, cross-checked by other native speakers at the university. In total, 819 communal level surveys were completed and the proportion from each country is listed in Figure I.2 below.

It is important to recognize that neither the elite level survey nor the communal level survey designs were random in nature. The elite level survey is best described as a 'purposive sample'. The communal level survey, by contrast, can be more accurately described as a 'cluster sample' where the majority of the participants were sampled in a semi-random fashion within each capital city but the selection of the location (e.g. the capital city of each ASEAN country except Myanmar) was performed on a purposive basis.[25] Further, while the survey samples were reasonably large for the purpose of the present study, the aggregated data that has been extracted from the surveys should be interpreted as a set of rudimentary indicators regarding regional perceptions and attitudes. Having said this, the contribution of the elite survey sample is significant as the security community proposal is an 'elite' project and the participants in the survey ranged from senior foreign ministry officials, to defence officials, to senior scholars and relevant non-governmental organization (NGO) groups and journalists. Further, because some of the questions in the two survey designs were the same, components of each sample have served as an important check, or control, against the other sample and *vice versa*. Nonetheless, the research conducted for the

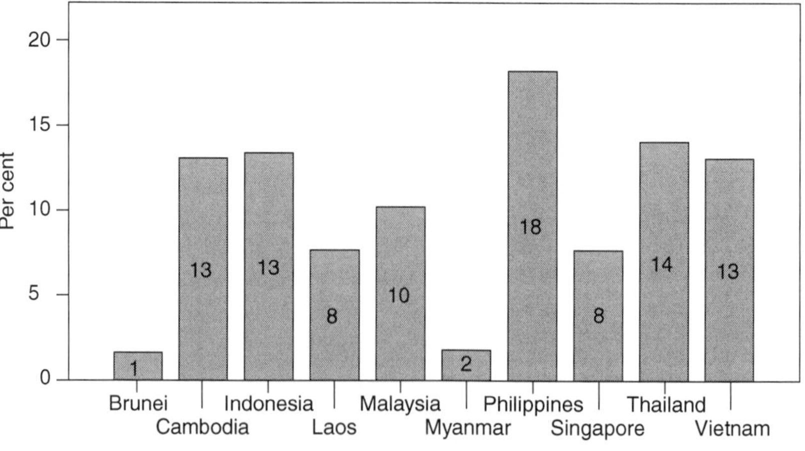

Figure I.2 Citizenship (communal level sample) (source: compiled by author).

book may serve as a valuable baseline for further, more representative, survey work regarding the perceptions and attitudes of the people and political elite of Southeast Asia. While such research will be expensive and time consuming, subsequent and additional insights concerning the nature of regional relations will be highly valuable and may also contribute to future foreign policy formulation.

Structure of the book

As ASEAN has aspired to forge an institutionalized form of regionalism akin to a security community, the next chapter provides a framework to assist in understanding the processes and dynamics associated with this integrated state-of-affairs. The framework accepts that various patterns of inter-state behaviour predicted by realism may be prominent at low levels of integration but suggests that a shift towards the patterns of behaviour predicted by neo-liberal institutionalism can become more prominent at higher integration. To this end, the chapter utilizes constructivist insights to demonstrate the processes that contribute to higher integration and any associated changes to the nature of inter-state relations. This approach provides an understanding of how the emergence of collective identities reduces the security dilemma and increases the likelihood of cooperation and interaction based on absolute gain. The chapter then examines other key factors with the potential to enable the realization of ASEAN's regionalist project as well as how such outcomes would affect the nature of state behaviour (e.g. common values, cooperation and institutionalization). The extent to which the enablers of integration have generated common values, greater cooperation and deeper institutionalization is, in turn, evidence of the degree to which the region has become integrated.

The second chapter examines the early causes and constraints to cooperation and regionalism in Southeast Asia. As explained in the first chapter, the existence of a region entails more than mere geographical propinquity and, therefore, the chapter commences by examining the claim that Southeast Asia can be recognized as an identifiable region. Despite the lack of mutual identification and trust that was a consequence of Southeast Asia's history, the analysis subsequently demonstrates that a combination of domestic volatility and exogenous threats necessitated a process of reconciliation with a sufficient convergence of interests to facilitate the formation of ASEAN and other regionalist developments including the Zone of Peace, Freedom and Neutrality (ZOPFAN). Finally, the chapter contextualizes how Southeast Asia's history has shaped the emergence of common norms collectively known as the 'ASEAN Way' – e.g. non-interference and consensus-based decision-making.

Chapter 3 follows by examining ASEAN's performance through to the third decade. The chapter commences with an analysis of how the Cold War dynamics of the time, including Vietnam's invasion of Cambodia, helped to strengthen the range and depth of the common interests and norms shared between the ASEAN members and that these developments eventually provided ASEAN with a collective diplomatic voice on the international stage. However, while these challenges contributed to the development of a relative identification between the ASEAN states, the chapter demonstrates that ASEAN's regionalist aspirations were simultaneously constrained by competing strategic assessments and continued interstate tensions. Nonetheless, the end of the Cold War provided new opportunities and challenges. Thus, the second half of the chapter examines how ASEAN responded to an increasingly uncertain world through the pursuit of greater economic integration, the institutionalization of processes for exogenous engagement and the enlargement of the Association to embrace all the nations of Southeast Asia. While these developments increased the level of interaction and socialization between regional elites, they were also a consequence of strategic and economic uncertainty at the regional and global levels.

Through several case studies, Chapter 4 examines how a range of domestic, regional and extra-regional security and economic issues have challenged multilateral cooperation and the continued efficacy of the ASEAN Way. The case studies examined include the haze, the economic crisis, territorial disputes and the continuation of domestic insurgencies – including increased violence in Southern Thailand and its impact on relations with Malaysia. While full-scale armed conflict in relation to any of these security issues remains highly improbable, the case studies indicate the extent of mistrust and competitive behaviour that persists in Southeast Asia along with the ineffectiveness and impracticality of the ASEAN Way in resolving controversial issues. Further, the manner by which some Southeast Asian states have responded to issues that involve a significant conflict of national interests at the interstate level has also been indicative of the limited sense of mutual identification that is to be expected at low levels of integration.

One consequence of membership expansion has been to increase the diversity of values, interests, capacities and political systems (structures) that exist within ASEAN. However, such diversity has also been exacerbated by the process of political change in some of the ASEAN states. Consequently, Chapter 5 examines how political change has affected the interests, norms and values of some ASEAN states. To this end, political developments in Thailand, the Philippines and Indonesia, together with the impact of these developments on their foreign policies, represent the key focus of the analysis. Among other things, the chapter demonstrates how shifts towards or away from democratic systems of governance affect the nature of foreign policy formulation. Further, changing political values in some member-states have challenged the ASEAN Way and pushed ASEAN towards a new phase of regional engagement. Consequently, the final section examines how these developments contributed to Indonesia's proposal for a security community together with some controversial, but more specific, proposals including a regional peacekeeping force.

The gradual process of democratization in some of the ASEAN members has increased a divide in the regional values espoused by different ASEAN members. In this regard, the dictatorship in Myanmar represents the most oppresive end of Southeast Asia's political spectrum and the question of how to respond to the crisis of governance in the country has now become one of the most difficult diplomatic challenges facing ASEAN. Because of the significance of this issue, Chapter 6 discusses the Myanmar case study at length. This chapter examines how Myanmar has challenged ASEAN's cohesion and cooperation as well as the Association's international stature. The chapter commences with an analysis of ASEAN diplomacy vis-à-vis Myanmar since the turn of the century. Based on these developments, the chapter demonstrates the extent to which Myanmar's membership has further challenged ASEAN's traditional norms including 'non-interference'. The final section then examines how ASEAN reduced some of the pressure for normative change by depoliticizing the delivery of aid in response to Cyclone Nargis and assesses the implications for the November 2010 elections for ASEAN regionalism.

Chapter 7 builds on the previous analysis through a critical assessment of the institutional outcomes of ASEAN's regionalist blueprints including the ASEAN Charter and the Human Rights Commission. The first section also includes an analysis of why ASEAN has been relatively more successful in the realm of economic cooperation and integration. The analysis in the second section builds on the insights in the previous section, as well as the chapters before it, by further utilizing the interview and survey data, together with other primary and secondary sources, for the purpose of investigating the level of perceptual convergence and/or divergence in terms of political interests and values as well as perceptions of trust and amity in the region. In other words, the section examines the perceptual and attitudinal factors that explain the limitations to political institutionalization and integration. The final section more significantly focuses on the communal level survey data for the purpose of assessing the implications for regionalism at the grassroots level. The chapter notes the continued challenge of distrust and that the level of integration within ASEAN has been limited by a normative divide that has been driven by competing democratic and authoritarian values.

The conclusion assesses the status of regionalism and integration in Southeast Asia and returns to the conceptual framework to assess how political, economic and socio-cultural integration can be advanced in the future. The analysis suggests that before significant integration can develop between the states of Southeast Asia, adequate levels of state capacity, together with a sufficient compatibility of values contributing to a convergence of interests, must first emerge. An equalization of the level of state capacity throughout Southeast Asia is important because this affects not only a state's interests but also the resources available to contribute to regionalist efforts. Based on the analysis in the preceding chapters, the conclusion also outlines how common interests also emerge because of similar political values. While similar values – together with any associated norms of behaviour – may emerge through several decades of socialization, intra-state developments such as economic growth and democratization significantly shape the values espoused by each of the ASEAN member-states. A greater level of compatibility and complementarity between the economies and political systems of Southeast Asia will also assist ASEAN to overcome the problematic levels of mistrust currently extant throughout Southeast Asia. However, the mitigation of historical animosities and suspicions will also require a heightened prevalence of practices of reciprocity and a demonstrated willingness to sacrifice national interests for the collective good of the region. The study demonstrates that the level of mutual identification and integration in Southeast Asia has not yet progressed to a point that would ensure consistent adherence to such behaviour.

1 Security, cooperation and identity in international relations

ASEAN has declared an intention to pursue several regionalist goals including greater 'integration', a 'common vision and objectives', higher 'political and security cooperation', and the establishment of intramural relations where its 'members shall rely exclusively on peaceful processes in the settlement of intra-regional differences'.[1] Consequently, this chapter provides a theoretical framework for understanding the variables, processes and challenges that are interdependent with the realization of ASEAN's goals. In this context, the chapter also investigates the feasibility of domestic and regional security as well as supranational institutionalization. Empirically, the accomplishment of ASEAN's objectives would coincide with the existence of security community and such a state of affairs would be unlikely to exist in the absence of adequate mutual identification between the states and communities of the region; such mutual identification, in turn, entails a compatibility of values. While the concept of a security community represents an important element of the framework developed in this chapter, the chapter places equal emphasis on the concept of *regionalism* while also offering a remodelled version of *integration theory*. In the case of regionalism, the term is conveniently compatible with the broad array of ASEAN's visions for the future including, but not limited to, ASEAN's 'security community' proposal. Meanwhile, a unique interpretation of the *behavioural effects* of integration has been developed to explain transitions from competitive regional orders (at low integration) to cooperative regional orders (at high integration). As will be seen, this approach provides an eclectic application of relevant international relations theories (such as realism, liberalism and constructivism) as well as a formula for when the behaviour predicted by the different International Relations (IR) paradigms will dominate the international affairs between a collection of states.

Regionalism, behavioural transitions and security communities

While regionalism has sometimes been confused with *regionalization*, the latter is the 'dependent variable' that can be more accurately defined as a *process* denoting the outcome of either regionalist policies or other forces from *below* and *within* the region.[2] Therefore, the 'process of regionalization fills the region with substance such as economic interdependence, institutional ties, political trust, and cultural belonging'.[3] When considered from this perspective, regionalization is at least partially synonymous with integration. While the book recognizes the utility of 'regionalization' as a general descriptive tool, the term *integration* is more advantageous in that it can be applied to different units of analysis and at different levels including elites, people, communities, states, regions and/or the international system. As with both regionalism and regionalization, the concept of integration is contested but the definition by William Wallace is particularly suitable for the purpose of its application in this study. According to Wallace, integration represents 'the creation and maintenance of intense and diversified patterns of interaction among previously autonomous units. These patterns may be partly economic in character, partly social, partly political: definitions of political integration all imply accompanying high levels of economic and social interaction'.[4] Given that regionalism can be considered as a policy and a project, the successful realization of ASEAN's security community project would represent the *outcome* of adequate transnational integration.

Regionalism naturally entails the existence of a region. According to Shaun Breslin, such a region would normally be 'formalized … with officially agreed membership and boundaries that emerge as a result of intergovernmental dialogues and treaties'.[5] However, and as noted in the introduction to this study, since the mid-1990s a new wave of regionalism ('new regionalism') has emerged that represents a cognitive shift away from interpreting regions as a 'given' towards an understanding of regions being 'constructed and reconstructed in the process of global transformation'.[6] According to this perspective, the social construction of both *collective identities* and of *regions* is viewed as being entwined through a mutually constitutive and reinforcing relationship.[7] Thus, just as the formation of transnational communities between states constructs and defines regions, a sense of mutual belonging in a region socializes states or communities into the formation of a collective identity.[8] Here, a community can be understood as a 'human association in which members … wish to cooperate to realize common objectives'.[9] Such communities are built through the emergence of a collective identity and identity is defined as a sense of belonging to some type of citizenship or population. This sense of 'belonging' may simultaneously exist at multiple levels including the local, state, transnational, regional and/or global.[10] Socialization (or social learning), in turn, can be understood as a process that nurtures behaviour to encourage conformity to social expectations as encapsulated by the collective identity of a community.[11] More simply, people learn the way of life, culture and norms of their community.[12]

While notions of community and identity play an important role in understanding regionalism and the processes of integration, the suggestion by some scholars that there is a need to more exclusively seek out 'imagined or cognitive regions' to 'free security studies from their territorial shell'[13] has been criticized by others who believe that the jettisoning of territory is premature and that the idea of post-nationalism is a bridge too far.[14] Key works by Thompson, Buzan, Lemke and Lake, validate such contentions through their continued emphasis on the role of proximity while also adopting a neo-functionalist approach in connection with 'interactions' (transactions) and the 'flows that bind'. Thus, Southeast Asia would not be a region if the security flows – of threats or friendship – do not demonstrably bind its entire expanse.[15] Given the empirical realities that exist in Southeast Asia, a more appropriate balance would be a requirement for sufficient geographical propinquity and interdependence, a degree of autonomy and distinctiveness from the global system (so that it 'refracts' the power of that system), and an appreciation of whether the people themselves (together with outside parties) *perceive* the region to exist.[16] Such an approach retains sufficient flexibility whilst simultaneously complementing and maintaining a compatibility with the notion of 'integration' as developed here and applied in the remaining chapters.

Regional order and complex integration

The analysis within this chapter does not intend to suggest that it is necessary to choose between rationalism (i.e. realism and some strands of liberalism) and constructivism or that certain behaviours predicted by each of the approaches never take place. As Lebow argues, '[a]ll three paradigms are relevant because there is more to the international system than is captured by a single paradigm'.[17] Therefore, the eclectic nature of this framework draws the question as to when states will exhibit the attributes of one school of thought compared to another. Here, Muthiah Alagappa provides some insight through his interpretation of order. Alagappa argues that 'order is not [necessarily] an ideal or ultimate condition but a matter of degree. Spanning a spectrum, it ranges from total disorder that is associated with the law of the jungle to the rule of law associated with a cohesive political community in which most people obey the law'.[18] In this sense, the concept of a regional order can be interpreted in a similar fashion to Barry Buzan's concept of a regional security complex where Buzan recognizes that variations in amity and enmity mean that the characterization of a security complex can range from a conflict formation to a security regime to a security community.[19] The problem with both of these approaches is that they do not adequately account for why and how transitions in inter-state behaviour may occur. Further, the two approaches, together with a large proportion of the 'new regionalism' literature, incorrectly paint 'integration theories' as an 'other' where, in reality, it is actually impossible to fully separate or distinguish 'new regionalism' from the old regionalism of the Karl Deutsch and Ernst B. Hass varieties.[20] Consequently, the analysis below seeks to complement the notion of *order* by developing a preliminary outline of processes behind integration together with the impact of deepening integration (regionalization) on international relations.

As Figure 1.1 illustrates, and in line with the conceptual approach developed in ASEAN's security community proposal, this study introduces the concept of *complex integration* to describe the dynamics behind economic,

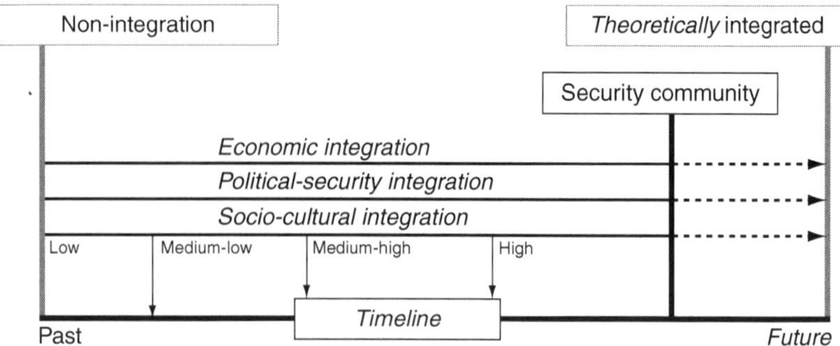

Figure 1.1 The spheres of complex integration (source: author).

political-security, and socio-cultural integration.[21] This concept has also been developed with the aim of drawing out the structure and forms of regional order as well the order in which the processes of integration can be expected to take place. Each of these integrative spheres is interdependent and mutually reinforcing with the remaining two spheres. While both political-security integration and economic integration can be issue specific, socio-cultural integration can apply to different tiers of analysis (e.g. the elite or communal levels) and is partly substantiated by the emergence of adequate collective identification. When the three fields of integration have *advanced to the level of high-integration then the collection of states can be said to constitute a security community.*

The dotted portions of the timelines that lie beyond the security community benchmark do not follow a particular timescale but represent the *grey area* that exists between the level of integration necessary to constitute a security community and the *theoretical abstraction* of being integrated. The notion that the states of a security community can be 'integrated' is considered a theoretical abstraction because, in reality, there can be no end to how much individuals, communities and states can be integrated into some kind of transnational entity: whether economically, politically and/or socio-culturally defined. Further, it is not possible to become fully integrated where there is no discernable distinction between either the institutions and identities of individual units of analysis or the identity and institutions of the security community itself. In other words, the processes of complex integration are considered continuous and never entirely complete.

Figure 1.2 outlines the aspects of complex integration that sketch the likely pathways through which a group of states may evolve from non-integration to relative integration. In this context, because of either elite-driven initiatives (top-down) or communal-driven processes (bottom-up), a collection of states can advance along the spectrum of integration depicted by the figure. Recalling that regionalism can be conceived as a policy and a project, such an approach is in line with a broad consensus in the 'new regionalism' scholarship.[22] In this context, references to 'elite-driven' processes, as opposed to 'state-driven' processes, have been deliberate. This approach acknowledges a broadening of the range of international actors with the capacity to exercise *agency* beyond the 'state' (i.e. pluralism); it also recognizes the possibility that certain initiatives may be driven by pockets of elite, within the states of the grouping, that may include a pivotal influence by agents ranging from state leaders to individual government ministries or even interest groups outside the government.

While both the *elite* and *communal* push–pull integrative processes can influence each other and/or evolve at the same time, it is likely that one set of processes will be more dominant than the other. Further, regardless of which is the dominant process (whether elite or communal driven), the secondary group of processes can either assist or detract from the primary group. In the example of ASEAN, and regardless of whether or not all the ASEAN states wholeheartedly commit to the project of a security community in the future, the secondary 'communal-driven' process may in fact act to inhibit the pace of integration due to inter-community tensions and rivalry – e.g. as a consequence of cultural, religious and nationalistic divides. Nonetheless, should ASEAN progress along the spectrum of complex integration then, as later chapters will substantiate, elite-driven integration is likely to represent the dominant process within Southeast Asia.

While the economic sphere of elite-driven integration (Figure 1.2) is likely to advance at the fastest pace, the emergence of economic integration will require a degree of consensus, cooperation and mutual identification between the political elite of the grouping. Further, the increased frequency of social transactions associated with economic integration may also accelerate the process of socialization and thereby reinforce the collective identity of the political elite within the grouping of states. Thus, the integrative process ultimately causes, and/or is a consequence of, a number of empirical events.[23] Such events include the gradual movement towards increased cooperation; a gradual homogenization of values; a gradual transfer of authority towards supranational institutions such as ASEAN; and finally, the establishment of a transnational civil society including the construction of new forms of political community as exemplified in the European Union.[24]

Figure 1.3 illustrates that neo-realist behaviour (the *logic of consequences*) is more dominant at low levels of integration. However, at high levels of integration states alternatively seek intra-mural cooperation on the basis of absolute gains where the *logic of appropriateness* dominates. Further, whether at the elite or communal levels, or a combination of the two, the transitions toward higher integration are explained by various concepts including interdependence theory, socialization and the neo-functionalist notion of 'spill over'. Should the level of complex integration be so low that all three of the pillars of integration would be better characterized as 'fragmented', then there will be a high risk of negative interaction (enmity) along the lines depicted by Alexander Wendt's Hobbesian model.[25] Here, realist predictions concerning a power and security dilemma will largely apply and such a dilemma is particularly interdependent with

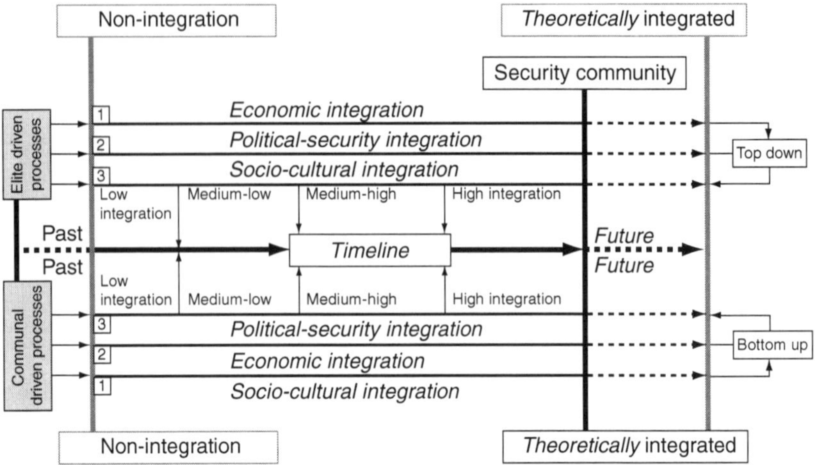

Figure 1.2 The processes behind complex integration (source: author).

considerations of proximity as evidenced by recent hostilities between Cambodia and Thailand (see Chapter 4). Thus, where a low level of complex integration exists then increases to a state's economic and military capacity leave other states comparatively less secure. While the exercise of self-help, combined with the pursuit relative gains (in the security, political and economic fields) will dominate regional relations, significant enmity at a region-wide level will be unlikely. In other words, the 'war of all against all' suggested in Wendt's Hobbesian model is unlikely to occur in practice despite the fact that, in the socio-cultural sphere, there will be little to no collective identification.[26] Nonetheless, the sceptical predictions by neo-realism concerning the feasibility of cooperative endeavours will likely prevail as any *limited* examples of cooperation will be primarily driven by hegemonic states or a temporary convergence of interests on specific issues (i.e. limited functional cooperation).

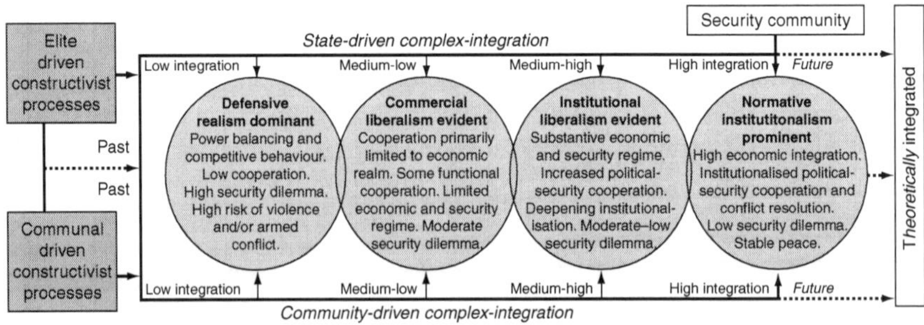

Figure 1.3 The impact of integration on transnational behaviour (source: author).

As states move along the spectrum of complex integration (to a medium–low level) then the nature of the regional order begins to transcend the competitive self-help system that had hitherto been dominant. In its place, the regional order evolves to become more in line with the behaviour expected by *commercial liberalism*. As implied by the name, a convergence of interests in the economic sphere starts to emerge leading to the formation of limited economic regimes as the region's political elite seek 'free trade and a market or capitalist economy as a way towards peace and prosperity'.[27] In the political-security sphere, a degree of norm-governed behaviour will start to emerge but this is primarily confined to the notion of a limited security regime.[28] However, the constraints of the realist model largely remain in place as far as cooperation is concerned although some tentative experiments in functional cooperation may start to become evident over time. Nonetheless, the security dilemma will remain relatively high and the level of collective identification is also limited; although a degree of mutual understanding has started to emerge as a consequence of economic interaction.

At a medium–high level of integration, the world view associated with institutional liberalism becomes more prevalent where, in addition to more institutionalized forms of economic cooperation, a full economic and security regime will emerge leading to cooperative institutions in the political-security sphere. As the level of institutionalization continues to deepen, the security dilemma is further reduced due to rising levels of political and economic interdependence where the material cost of conflict is increased. Further, the major contentions associated with neo-liberal regime theory – e.g. the reduced risk of non-compliance or cheating through institutionalized cooperation – will also become more pertinent, thereby providing an auxiliary set of factors to reduce the security dilemma further.[29]

Through rising interdependence the frequency of cooperative endeavours also increases by necessity. Consequently, the region's elite become increasingly socialized into a 'collective identity' leading to an increased prevalence of the 'forms' of behaviour to be expected from a sociological form of liberal institutionalism – herein labelled normative institutionalism.[30] Such a label is appropriate because, as stated in the introductory chapter, new regionalism maintains a normative interest in integration through various order bringing schemes usually culminating in regional institutionalization.[31] For example, evidence of the emergence of this kind of order occurred in 2009 when the European Union ratified the Lisbon Treaty. This treaty accorded greater supranational institutionalization to the European Union through, *inter alia*, a Charter of Fundamental Human Rights, a strengthened role for the European Parliament and enhanced mechanisms for collective foreign policy formulation.[32] Such developments can only be understood through a consideration of both material and ideational motives and influences. Further, it is only through the incorporation of ideational considerations – including the salience of the type of norms necessitated by dependable expectations of peaceful change – that we can understand how and when the behaviour associated with (and predicted by) normative institutionalism will dominate.

Within a normative institutional order, the security dilemma is all but mitigated and an *integrative peace*, followed by a *stable peace*, emerges amidst a community of states that is now likely to be governed by a high level of supranational institutionalization.[33] Such a relationship is reinforced by the central tenets of liberal institutionalism where regional elites have largely substituted the pursuit of relative gains with cooperative arrangements based on assessments of absolute gain. Moreover, regime theory explains how this transition is facilitated; cooperation is not problem-free but the formation of institutions will be reinforced by the provision of *loyalty* and *resources* where such institutions are interpreted as benefiting the interests of the relevant actors.[34] Further, 'rather than existing on the basis of deterrence and power balancing, the [integrative] peace becomes more significantly attributable to the identification of mutual interests, interdependence, joint problem-solving and norm-governed behaviour.... Although not as far-reaching as stable peace, integrative peace is characterized by trust rather than distrust'.[35] At the highest feasible level of complex integration, the security dilemma is all but mitigated and a security community will exist. Based on these assertions, the evolution of a group of states to become a security community can be understood as the process of integration whereas a group of states that are already a security community have progressed to the point of being close to 'integrated'. Thus, when a group of states and communities have become integrated then a community of states has been formed. Consequently, the discussion below outlines the defining characteristics of a security community while later sections detail the causation behind transitions towards more cooperative relations.

Security communities and supranationalism at high integration

Because the end goal of a security community is to bar the possibility of transnational conflict, much of the security community literature has neglected economic and security issues pertaining to the domestic and international tiers of analysis.[36] However, as Katzenstein and Sil note, employing a broader understanding of security that 'focuses on the primacy of economic growth and its interconnectedness with social stability, societal order, and regional peace and stability' is in line with a 'regionwide consensus' and the empirical evidence proffered by the region since the end of the Cold War.[37] Consequently, this study also emphasizes the importance of domestic security and this approach ties in well with ASEAN's concept of comprehensive security; a concept that provides a broad umbrella covering all traditional and non-traditional security issues.[38] Nonetheless, it is important to recognize that '*dependable expectations of peaceful change*' represents the defining element to a security community and thereby the end goal (and end result) of the evolutionary process of complex integration. In the context of 'peaceful change', Deutsch's emphasis on the resolution of social problems without resort to large-scale physical force entails a continued role for a traditional definition of security. Vayrynen defines such security in the following terms:

> [As a] low past, present and future probability of using serious coercive force between or within nations. Coercion can be both military and economic in nature as both of them can inflict major damage and pain on the targeted people. Peace is broken, and the security community unrealized in the region, if people are subjected to physical destruction and suffering. In other words, peace and security mean, ultimately, freedom from coercion and its threats.[39]

In contrast to other security community frameworks, Vayrynen's definition should be utilized as a threshold test for the existence of a security community. In circumstances where this threshold test is not satisfied then this would bar any finding of a security community. However, once the application of this test has been satisfied, or where the application of the test would be shrouded in ambiguity, then the broader notion of comprehensive security (incorporating considerations of domestic stability) can then be applied to assist in the delineation of whether or not a security community exists. In other words, while the continuation of traditional security threats bars a finding of a security community, the absence of these threats does not necessarily translate into a finding that a security community does exist.

In the context of Deutsch's requirement for sufficient integration, the 'habits' of peaceful change should be entrenched to an extent that would preclude the declaration of a security community between states that might form an overnight 'alliance' only to be reneged upon the next day.[40] Given these considerations, there should be a degree of consistency and evolution towards a situation of *anticipated* and *actual* peace between the nations analysed. Thus, social problems would normally need to be resolved through 'institutionalized procedures' including explicit and/or implicit restrictions on how, when and where a state can employ coercive military and/or economic measures. Naturally, such conditions would be 'marked by the absence of a competitive military build-up or arms race involving their members'.[41] Further, the prevalence of either strategic ties and formal alliances or normative prohibitions against conflict is directly proportional to the degree of integration that subsists between and throughout the states of a community. Thus, broadly speaking, dependable expectations of peaceful change can be said to prevail when a group of states are able, as a minimal task, to resolve the substance of all intra-mural traditional security threats. Further, there needs to be sufficient political-security integration to (a) support such security and (b) evidence adequate collective identification.

At a sufficient level of complex integration, the processes and outcomes above will signify the emergence and prevalence of other behaviours and values. For example, the 'prevalence of mutually compatible self-images of the states participating in the process, up to the point of developing a common identity and mutual expectations of shared economic and security gains', represent preconditions to the existence of a stable peace.[42] These outcomes would also be reinforced by substantial intra-mural trust, practices of 'reciprocity', and an entrenched sense of community including a 'we-feeling'.[43] Under such conditions, a regional organization would be empowered by the pooling of sovereignty. Consequently, Jewellord Singh has argued that ASEAN's regionalist project will not become feasible until its members demonstrate a willingness to pool a significant level of sovereignty and to create mechanisms to 'force members to comply and to prevent backtracking'.[44] While institutions can exist in an informal sense – e.g. a regime comprised of norms and informal rules governing behaviour in particular areas[45] – a security community would normally be evidenced by supranational institutionalization (i.e. pooled sovereignty). Aside from coinciding with high complex integration (normative institutionalism), such institutionalization is further important because it facilitates the creation of coherent rules-based mechanisms designed to address economic, political and security issues.

From a constructivist perspective, the deepening of institutionalization can also reinforce patterns of cooperation by developing similarities through the socialization of regional norms and principles. Thus, Joseph Nye argues that institutions help 'create a climate in which expectations of stable peace develop'.[46] Further, institutionalized regionalism can also aid the consolidation of state-building and democratization, control oppressive behaviour by states and institutions, and also facilitate greater transparency and accountability.[47] Meanwhile, considerations of both 'scope' and 'depth' determine the extent to which ASEAN has been 'institutionalized'. While 'scope' concerns the number of areas that have been institutionalized, depth is determined by (a) the extent to which expectations of appropriate behaviour have converged (i.e. commonality); (b) the extent to which these expectations are clearly specified in binding rules (i.e. specificity); and (c) the extent of 'autonomy' granted to the organization (e.g. ASEAN) for the purpose of determining its rules.[48]

Institutionalization also links with the earlier mentioned process of complex integration where, for the purpose of this study, *integration* is concerned with 'how and why states voluntarily mingle, merge, and mix with their neighbours so as to lose several factual attributes of sovereignty'.[49] Such integration, together with the increased interdependence that ensues, acts to reduce the number of policy options that can be viewed as aggressive by increasing the material and ideational costs of conflict and war – which, in a circular fashion, links back to the core definition of a security community. Thus, Deutsch maintains that a key outcome of integration is the 'maintenance of peace'[50] and it is the centrality of 'peace' within the concept of *integration* that provides a direct link to regionalism and ASEAN's pursuit of a security community.[51]

Integration also provides a bridge between 'security' and 'community'. For example, a security community cannot form without the transnational integration of the mindsets of state actors to form a largely 'common' viewpoint vis-à-vis security and economic issues of a transnational nature. Thus, the emergence of high complex integration and supranational institutionalization coincides with the establishment of a 'mutual aid society' complete with some sort of collective security system, leading to a 'post-sovereign system' where its supranational institutions are supported by common transnational and national institutions.[52] As the next section will demonstrate, the level of cooperation and institutionalization to be expected within a security community will first require an adequate compatibility of values and structures and such an outcome is conditional upon adequate collective identification in the first place. Again, while the absence of any individual element of the criteria above would not necessarily bar the existence of a security community, their absence would render the finding of a security community, in any meaningful sense of the term, all the more improbable. While Zhiqun Zhu may summarize Deutsch's work as 'no security community, no integration',[53] a more accurate statement would be *no security community, inadequate integration.* Therefore, the study proposes that a 'security community' can be more appropriately defined as *a transnational grouping of two or more states whose sovereignty is increasingly institutionalized (amalgamation) and whose people maintain dependable expectations of peaceful change.*[54]

The dilemmas of identity and determinants of cooperation

The previous section outlined some of the major conceptual aspects behind an understanding of regionalism and the eventual outcome of a security community. Importantly, it suggested that regionalization can be characterized as an 'integrative process' where the level of complex integration determines the nature of the regional order and the type of behaviour to be anticipated in international relations. In building on these considerations, the present section paves the way for an understanding of the major processes behind, and preconditions to, the realization of ASEAN's regionalist goals. This section also seeks to discern how various ideational, material, global, regional and domestic factors interrelate with one another and potentially contribute to complex integration and the formation of a stable peace. Understanding the processes and pathways towards high complex integration not only equips the analyst with an ability to foresee many of the obstacles to regionalist endeavours, but can also assist with the development of insights concerning how to resolve such obstacles. The likelihood of ASEAN successfully responding to these obstacles is a separate issue and one that will be addressed in the concluding chapter of this study.

While a nation-state's identity is constituted by a range of economic, geographic, domestic, social and cultural factors,[55] the collective identity of a state (i.e. socio-cultural integration) is most strongly influenced by the *combined memories of history.*[56] This contention is made because all of these factors can be understood, to one degree or another, through the lens of history; as Katzenstein argues, '[h]istory is a process of change that leaves an imprint on a state and its society's identity'.[57] However, the construction of these identities is an ongoing process where the 'domestic norms and values are formed and reformed by contact with the external world.'[58] Here, it is important to note that norms and values are not the same. Leszek Buszynski distinguishes between the two in the following manner:

> While norms are regulative and involve expectations about correct behaviour the term 'value' is a wider concept which embraces emotional attachments ranging from basic nationalism through to the highest principles. Values refer to the beliefs, customs and principles which are important for an identity. Certain situations may stimulate strong emotional responses if core values relating to identity such as lifestyle and communal and religious beliefs are under threat. Such values may strongly motivate decision-makers but do not constitute norms by strict definition.[59]

At the level of the state (or at least those elite with the capacity to act), an understanding of 'identity' is important because, as Alexander Wendt has argued, the interests of an agent/state are informed by the agent/state's identity.[60] A basic comprehension of the role of identity (and thereby the fundamental interests of the state) is further important because it informs when an agent/state is likely to 'perceive a particular norm as salient'.[61] Here, however, an important caveat is necessary; despite the contentions of Wendt and others that the state has its own personality with the capacity to act (agency),[62] it is argued that the branches (institutions) of a state will not always be homogenous in nature. For example, this caveat is particularly applicable where the state had a fractured identity or, in other words, falls short of having integrated to the point of a nation-state. Under such circumstances, the interests of a state will be more difficult to ascertain. Ascertaining the 'interests' that will prevail during interactions with the relevant elite from other states will be dependent on a subjective analysis demarcating the group of elite that have the dominant capacity or power to act in connection with the issue at hand.

The important role that history performs links back to the concept of socialization which, in turn, builds on the *transactionalist approach* developed by Deutsch over sixty years ago. This approach utilized a wide range of indicators to assist with developing an understanding of the level and pace of socio-cultural integration. These indicators include 'international trade, mail flows, student exchanges and travel'.[63] A modern version of this approach would include the internet and its social media components such as email, Yahoo Messenger, Skype, Google Talk, ICQ, Facebook, Twitter, blogs and various other discussion forums and chat communities. Direct and numerous interactions (transactions) between different communities over an *extended timeframe* 'socialize' the different identities in a manner where *elements* of the 'part' evolve into the collective identity of the group (i.e. socio-cultural integration). Thus, as stated earlier, socialization becomes part of the 'process of learning to conform one's behaviour to social expectations'.[64] This is not to suggest that the emergence of a 'collective identity' fully replaces any or all of the individual socio-cultural identities (co-cultures); to the contrary, the idea is that these individual identities may eventually become socially compatible with one another to an extent that there might emerge an *identifiable* collective identity. This process of socialization leads to the formation of regulative norms that, in the present context, depict the standards of behaviour that the *society* of a given state expects its leaders to uphold – domestically and internationally.[65]

The question of how norms and values can be changed is examined by various social theories on structure and agency. In the case of structure, an eclectic interpretation would recognize that structures are shaped by power, technology and geography as well as institutions, political systems and norms.[66] Much of the recent literature on regionalism has particularly focused on the role of the latter variable – norms. In this context, while the 'norms of the social group are the structures that determine behaviour and constitute agent identity',[67] the agent has the capacity to 'self-consciously' seek to construct new norms that might potentially enhance the incentives for specific forms of behaviour and even affect the very structure of society itself.[68] Thus, in the case of agents, they are the actors in politics who have the power to exercise and display choice, reflexivity, learning and transformative capacity. In this context, the process of the transfer of norms, whether consciously or unconsciously, occurs mainly at the agent level.[69] In summary, the collective identity of a state arises from the sum-total of historical interaction (including ideas, learning and socialization)[70] at both the domestic and international levels. As will be demonstrated, the nature of a state's collective identity affects its propensity to enter into cooperative arrangements.

Collective identities are interdependent with trust and different states will be hesitant to agree to cooperative arrangements in the absence of trust.[71] The development of trust between states and/or communities entails a compatibility of values that does not conflict with the political and ideational survival of the other state and/or community to which interaction takes place. In the absence of any such political and/or ideational friction, positive interaction on a frequent basis will contribute to at least some degree 'of identification with the other because without such association actors would be self-contained and devoid of any ... basis for common action'.[72] The existence of trust is central to the constituent elements of a community (e.g. in the form of reciprocity and altruism) as well as the formation of dependable expectations of peaceful change. In addition to these considerations, Waltz adds that ideological values (ideational factors) represent a 'system of meaning that entails the distinction between self and other in the definition of threat'.[73] This is because, particularly in the case of a robust nation-state, norms and values influence the core existence of self – the identity of the state. Therefore, both ideational survival and political survival represent key factors in the formation of a state's national interests – whether declared or otherwise.[74]

In the absence of trust (low complex integration), the security dilemma is higher leading to greater military expenditure and there is a lower occurrence of cooperation and cooperative arrangements. The greater sense of predictability (together with reduced perceptions of risk) to stem from the existence of trust and a transnational collective identity also reduces the perceived costs of cooperation and integration at the political, security and economic levels. In order to better understand the basis for distinguishing between those who are perceived as a 'threat' and those actors a state can 'trust' it is necessary to consider recent developments within social psychology concerning Social Identity Theory (SIT). While the relationship of *identity* to security community frameworks has already been discussed, recent theories concerning identity have facilitated an improved understanding of the conditions that inform how and why states will relate to each other in particular ways. To this end, SIT has been applied by various international relations theorists for the purpose of understanding not only *whether international conflict will be likely*,[75] but the causal properties behind when *two or more states will seek to cooperate.*

Because it is possible to conceive of identity as understanding oneself relative to others, it follows that a state or community's *social identity* is also constructed through its relationship with others.[76] Within the large body of literature on SIT, it is clear that the concept of 'social identity' or 'social group' plays an important role between all sets of relations – whether that of the individual, the group or the state. As with the notion of a *collective identity*, the 'social group' is defined as 'one that is psychologically significant for the members, to which they relate themselves subjectively for social comparison and the acquisition of norms and values'.[77] In this context, SIT argues that individuals and communities that fit within the umbrella of a collective identity will attach a strong sense of importance to their membership of that social group. These groups utilize their acquired norms and values for the purpose of comparing and evaluating their sense of 'self' with other social groups comprising of contrasting identities. In other words, communities of all types (including security communities) tend to draw boundaries around themselves in order to 'differentiate between themselves and outsiders'. Thus, the theory argues that once actors identify themselves as part of the same group then they will interact, trade and bargain with each other in terms of absolute gain. However, when dealing with actors who are identified, consciously or unconsciously, as being outside the 'grouping' then how they interact, trade and bargain will be conducted on the basis of relative gain. According to Hemmer and Katzenstein, these 'findings have been consistent across studies even with the flimsiest and most arbitrarily defined groups'.[78]

Identity is a relative phenomenon. The notion of a *relative differentiation* between groups is aptly explained by Trine Flockhart:

> What actually happens is that identities are constructed through complex constellations of 'we-groups' in a system of social groups consisting of the 'Self'/'We', placed in a hierarchical system between the 'Other' and what I call the 'Significant We'. The 'Other' defines what the 'Self'/'We' is not and what it seeks to distance itself from, whereas the 'Significant We' is as important (perhaps even more so) for the construction of identities, as is the other.[79]

For example, in the context of democratic norms transfer within Europe, the European Union could be conceptualized as the 'Significant We'. Here, the 'other' would be represented by the contrasting communities perceived as displaying core values at variance from those of the EU. The importance of the *Significant We* has been evidenced by a myriad of social psychology studies illustrating a fundamental desire to associate and assimilate with compatible groups (i.e. those that demonstrate a compatible collective-identity) based on several factors: existential distress, uncertainty reduction, and desires for inclusion, belonging and self-esteem.[80] Of these factors, self-esteem has received the most attention; this is not to suggest that it is because individuals and/or communities consciously seek self-esteem that they associate with a group but, rather, that they remain with the group where such 'association' provides '*collective* self-esteem' through that social group's achievements.[81] These findings are relevant to ASEAN because if membership does not provide adequate self-esteem then the members will either leave the group or be less influenced by its leadership and normative values.[82]

Due to the propensity for political elites to identify with the collective identity of their own nation and to imbue their 'national identities with positive value', when 'such positivity is challenged, leading to ... consequential,... relative comparisons with ... salient external nations', there is a heightened risk that a state will promote *competition* leading to 'the rivalry of two or more groups for limited material or symbolic purposes'.[83] The risk of such competition is also determined by the degree of internal consolidation in the context of state-building (weak or strong states), together with nation-building (nationally incongruent or congruent), and the two issues link directly with the security dilemma. For example, a strong state that is nationally congruent typically seeks the status quo in its international relations. However, a strong state that is nationally incongruent has been found to have a higher likelihood of aggression in its foreign relations. Meanwhile, 'weakness but congruence' risks a frontier state with a higher propensity for undertaking boundary and territory wars; however, national incongruence within a weak state can result in civil war or even foreign intervention in the case of a failed state.[84]

Regardless of the level of internal consolidation and/or structure of the state, the occurrence of competition is a necessary precondition to the initiation of conflict. Furthermore, the development of 'We' identification and 'Other' hostility is 'progressive and contingent rather than necessary and inevitable'.[85] Thus, conflict represents the last stage in a four-stage process where the transition from stages one to two is taken as automatic but the transition between stages two and three and between stages three and four are progressive and contingent. It is at the juncture of these later stages that social comparison takes place (where the identity and national interests of a state are challenged) and, moreover, competition will only arise at the lower levels of complex integration where such comparisons are salient, consequential and zero-sum.[86] Further, in order for conflict to take place the 'agents' must not view each other as either a 'We' or 'Significant We': the challenge for ASEAN therefore becomes how it can develop enough trust and esteem to create a collective identity or, alternatively, a *Significant We*.

The practicalities of cooperation: transnational challenges and common interests

In relation to security cooperation and its connection with a security community, Amitav Acharya has suggested that security community frameworks are more about the prevention of war than the development of security cooperation between states.[87] Yet the European Union, as the only regional order approaching the status of a security community, has sought security cooperation as well as formal organizations, associations, and political institutions in its pursuit of security.[88] While the processes taking place within the European Union are a consequence of a multitude of factors and motivations, the greater interdependence that has stemmed from integration has also dramatically increased both the material and ideational costs of future armed conflict.[89] Nonetheless, Acharya does concede that the level of diversity extant within Southeast Asia has challenged the establishment of multilateral institutions and cooperation.[90] At one level, the extent of such diversity is summarized by Donald Weatherbee who states that

> beyond the macro-geographic unity of the latitude–longitude box, there are few qualities that we usually associate with a world region to be found in Southeast Asia … [as there is no common] race, ethnicity, language, religion, culture, and history such as we find in the Arab World, Western Europe, or, with the exception of Brazil, Latin America.[91]

However, for the elites of Southeast Asia, structural differences in relation to the political systems and economies of the region also represent major obstacles to cooperation in all spheres. As later chapters will substantiate, this diversity has impeded collective identity formation (socio-cultural integration) and interest harmonization (political-security and economic integration).

Despite the challenges above, issues of common concern can drive a convergence of interests and thereby facilitate cooperation (foreign policy coordination) and complex integration between the states of a regional grouping. While intramural traditional security threats constitute the threshold test to the existence of a security community and such formations are 'ultimately built from within',[92] extra-mural security challenges are also relevant as the occurrence of *collective responses* from the region provide insights concerning the level of identity convergence. Second, as Ganesan notes, the actions and policies of external powers and institutions can have a unifying role where, for example, 'it is interesting … that much of ASEAN's ideological convergence derived from external forces and structures'.[93] Thus, the second and third chapters highlight how the threat of communism contributed to regionalist policies that eventually led to the formation of ASEAN. In the absence of this common threat the history of ASEAN could have been very different.

As far as the risk of inter-mural threats and coercion are concerned, the existence of a hegemon can drive a degree of unity that can lead to the pursuit of greater regionalism.[94] For example, states may pursue a *collective balance of power* to create a 'just equilibrium' vis-à-vis potential or actual external coercion.[95] Under such circumstances, the maintenance of a balance of power could also drive increased levels of interest harmonization (in connection with some foreign policy issues) thereby advancing ASEAN's project for greater regionalism. Further, military alliances or other forms of security coalitions that are formed to address security externalities 'reflect in the first place, the differences between or commonality of its member's values and identities'.[96] In other words, a consideration of these intramural responses to exogenous challenges assists in an assessment of the degree to which foreign policy interests have converged and such convergence also indicates elite-level socio-cultural integration (collective identity formation). Consequently, this approach provides a conceptual linkage between *empirical assessments* of 'security' and 'community' that, in turn, help to facilitate a richer level of insight regarding the driving forces behind complex integration.

Regionalism, together with the level of cooperation necessary to deepen it, can also be driven by the effects of globalization – including the economic and technological spheres. In the case of the former, the economic aspects of globalization have enhanced the vulnerability and sensitivity of states to the economic policies (positive or negative) of other major economies and economic actors.[97] Thus, Chapter 5 details how greater global interdependence contributed to the collapse of the Indonesian economy (including the Suharto regime) and the disintegration of consensus vis-à-vis regional macroeconomic policies. The new wave of economic cooperation that followed between the ASEAN members is reflective of a desire to combat the insecurity generated by globalization which, in turn, drives a desire to seek 'collective action in the form of regional integration, to foster formal, institutionalized cooperation alongside the informal cross-border initiatives emerging through public and/or private activity under micro-regionalism'.[98]

In the context of the globalization of technology, rapid developments in this sphere have also meant that the security and sovereignty of a state can be increasingly penetrated by factors ranging from weapons proliferation to the internet and associated dissent.[99] Thus, globalization has contributed to the proliferation of both traditional and non-traditional (comprehensive) security threats that affect the state. For example, the opportunities for business provided by globalization, such as the revolution in information technology and communications, the porousness of state borders (thus allowing for ease of entry and exit by *people*, *goods*, *capital* and *information*), and the accompanying economic and political changes, have also provided the same opportunities for transnational criminal organizations.[100] However, common security challenges, whether of a traditional or non-traditional nature, can help to facilitate a convergence of interests between a community of states. Thus, the emergence of non-traditional 'security concerns like drug trafficking, terrorism and pandemics – such as HIV/AIDS – leads to the realization that threats to a country's security cannot be addressed unilaterally; to the contrary, successful responses require cooperation through the creation of transnational regimes.[101]

Shared comprehensive security problems also generate additional social transactions reinforcing the socialization process that takes place between state actors. Again, these social transactions facilitate a sense of collective identity leading to attempts to resolve additional comprehensive security threats resulting in a kind of circular process akin to certain developments concerning cooperation and institutionalization in ASEAN – as elaborated in later chapters. Here, the linkages between non-traditional security and the maintenance of an adequate level of traditional security have been addressed by the neo-functionalists and complex interdependence theories. These schools of thought advocate the notion of 'spill-over' between *low politics* (non-traditional security) and *high politics* (traditional security). This belief holds that 'exchanges and cooperation among independent state actors in areas of "low politics", such as economics and trade, could incrementally create common stakes among them in areas of "high politics" '.[102] Further, the level of insecurity associated with these transnational security concerns may also be sufficient to generate common interests leading to functional cooperation even when there may be significant deficits in terms of a compatibility of values. Despite the limitations of these early and often transient experiments in cooperation, their occurrence potentially contributes to positive spillover effects in terms of the socialization of new norms and values as well as, in the longer term, collective identify formation.

The preconditions to cooperation: internal consolidation and common values

Beyond the earlier consideration of the potential causes behind conflict, considerations of capacity and domestic stability are also interdependent with the emergence of cooperation and, eventually, supranational institutionalization. In the case of the former, a state must first develop the capacity to adhere to, and benefit from, regional commitments – whether in the economic, political and/or security spheres. As Louise Fawcett states, a low capacity is 'an impediment to cooperation, and will, along with the nature of the regional and international environment, crucially affect the success or failure of any regionalist project'.[103] For example, the pace of economic liberalization and open regionalism that Singapore is comfortable with may be economically and/or socially destabilizing for the less developed economies in Laos or Myanmar. In terms of domestic stability, where a state has only recently come into existence – and its people, therefore, remain divided by ethnicity, religion and/or language – then it is likely that a significant proportion of a state's resources will be devoted to the process of nation-building (defined below). The greater the number of domestic challenges that exist and shape the national interests of a state, the more this deflects from formulations of the national interest that are conducive to, or compatible with, regionalist endeavours. In order to overcome these challenges, each of the states that are privy to the regionalist project must first internally consolidate.

A state is considered to have achieved internal consolidation when it has developed a *reasonable* capacity to respond to international and domestic challenges including any major sources of instability and insecurity. Thus, a country wracked by civil war, insurgencies or collapsing economic institutions cannot be said to have consolidated internally. The conditions necessary to achieving internal consolidation can alternatively be understood through the realization (consolidation) of a state's national interests. According to Reynolds, the national interests can be generalized as a series of goals, the most important being 'state survival, wealth maximization and promotion of values'.[104] In building on a combination of empirical research together with an examination of relevant theories, the realization of these goals can be achieved through internal consolidation based on (a) nation-building, (b) political and security sector reform (PSSR) and (c) efficient economic management.

Nation-building encompasses policies that increase the number of common elements in social communication to build social cohesion and collective identify formation amongst the communities within the territorial confines of the state.[105] From the perspective of the state, nation-building is important for the purpose of generating domestic security – sometimes referred to as 'state-building' – and the end goal is the creation of a nation-state where there is a shared identity.[106] This state-of-affairs exists where the inhabitants of a state consider themselves members of one nation as constituted by the state, that is to say, members of a 'Significant We'.[107] Under these circumstances, the challenges to domestic security are reduced. Such security, together with economic development, is complemented by a process of state-building through PSSR.[108] In the case of political sector reform, the purpose is to consolidate an efficient, capable and diverse bureaucracy that has the capacity to effectively carry out government policy and deliver public goods – such as education, health care and economic development. Meanwhile, security sector reform represents the aim of the state to secure 'armed, uniformed forces that are functionally differentiated, professional forces under objective and subjective civilian control, at the lowest functional level of resource use'.[109] The emphasis on the lowest functional level of resource use also applies to political sector reform and is aimed at freeing resources in the direction of economic management and nation-building.

PSSR is also interdependent with, and complemented by, effective economic management that results in economic development. For the original ASEAN members, a 'focus on economic development since about the mid-1960s' has played a significant role in facilitating both domestic stability and a degree of legitimacy for the elites in power.[110] Further, economic development helps to equip the state with the resources necessary for both PSSR and nation-building. Such resources can be utilized for the education and professionalization of the military, police and other related organs of government. Adequate wages and professional training can further limit the level of corruption in a state and assist in the maintenance of a separation of powers. Of equal importance is the increased ability to resolve domestic security problems. This is important because 'endemic state weakness shifts the focus of security from inter-state, lateral pressure toward intrastate, centrifugal challenges – secessionists, terrorists, militias and others'.[111] Under such conditions, the security dilemma becomes internally focused resulting in disengagement or even disassociation with the processes behind complex integration. Weak security sectors also have implications for cooperation in terms of both regional and international assistance. Here, 'there has been a growing awareness in the development and aid communities that not only do "repressive or corrupt security structures undermine the stability crucial to maximizing the benefits of aid programmes" but also that positive reform of the security sectors can provide a catalyst for wider "good governance" and democratization programmes'.[112]

The nature of the problems addressed by PSSR has positive implications for a state's nation-building policies such as the capacity to provide services like a secular education. *Inclusive* nation-building policies, when combined with adequate PSSR and sound economic management, should provide sufficient internal consolidation for the state (including social cohesion and collective identity formation) leading to the creation of a stable nation-state.[113] Such an outcome has a reciprocal effect by facilitating more resources to allow for an outward orientation of a state's national policy resulting in heightened regional participation, cooperation, and complex integration. Nonetheless, in an increasingly globalized world, a key challenge of the ASEAN states will be the ability to manage open regionalism (a stated goal of ASEAN) whilst simultaneously building social structures and protective mechanisms that can cope with, and benefit from, both regional and global markets.

Components of the framework in this chapter – such as PSSR and 'inclusive' nation-building policies – have implied a degree of interdependence between regionalism and democratic values. Certainly, the key suppositions of social identity theory, including the emergence of a 'Significant We' (e.g. ASEAN), in the very least, necessitate a commonality of values. This is because common values lead to collective identification and this helps facilitate interest harmonization. In the absence of adequate interest harmonization and mutual identification, the task of coordinating policies becomes highly difficult, if not impossible, to accomplish. While Deutsch suggested that a commonality of 'main values' would be sufficient,[114] other scholars, such as Zhiqun Zhu, find it less probable that different countries could share similar value systems and expectations in the absence of similar political and economic systems.[115] The emergence of democratic structures has also been said to be relevant to the existence of a stable peace as articulated by the Kantian notion of a 'democratic peace'. Here, the Kantians refer to the empirical record to justify their argument that 'democracies are significantly less likely to fight wars with each other'.[116] According to this perspective, the types of structures and institutions typically inherent in liberal democracies impose normative and legal-procedural constraints on the decision-making process thereby creating a more predictable strategic environment. Further, democratic governments tend to be more economically liberal, generating further economic interdependence which, in turn, detracts from the efficacy of applying coercive and or violent measures in foreign relations.[117]

Beyond the issue of amity versus enmity, a growing number of regionalist scholars argue that consolidated democracies serve as preconditions to political and security integration.[118] According to this perspective, the outcomes of regionalist projects between democratic governments (cooperation and institutionalization) are reinforced through more frequent and regularized interactions; the deepening and broadening of the processes of socialization (in a manner that better accommodates the concerns of civil society); and a broadening of the agenda for regional institutions (due to a reduced concern with the issue of sovereignty).

Democracy also reinforces and builds upon these outcomes by generating greater transparency, understanding, trust, regional stability, conflict resolution and foreign policy innovation.[119] These contentions have also been supported by other studies that have demonstrated that democratic governments have historically been more willing to enter into cooperative arrangements.[120] Further, the development of the political and institutional capacity necessary to the advanced stages of regionalism (i.e. a security community) has also been more prevalent within democratic societies.[121] As Miller states, 'only among liberal democracies is the security dilemma sufficiently reduced to allow the states to surrender a part of their sovereignty without the fear that today's partner may become tomorrow's enemy'.[122]

Democratization, however, has yet to be universally accepted as a positive or necessary force for domestic stability and regionalism.[123] In the context of domestic stability, recent reports from the Political Instability Task Force (PITF) provide insightful accounts of how the most stable forms of government are typically either full democracies or full autocracies. Meanwhile, the states that are most likely to suffer from political instability are those undertaking a transition from autocracy to democracy.[124] Benson and Kugler provide a further caveat by arguing that the degree of governance rather than the form of government is more important.[125] Some of the region's political elite, such as Mahathir bin Mohamad, Lee Kuan Yew and Kishore Mahbubani, have also critiqued the applicability of democracy by arguing, through the lens of cultural relativism, that Western notions of democracy are not compatible with 'Asian values'.[126] However, as later chapters will indicate, such values may not extend between the narrow club of political elites (and those patronized by them) with an interest in maintaining the *status quo*.

Other debates concerning the impact of democracy center around the issue of causation; for example, an alternative explanation for the democratic peace thesis 'might be that liberal states tend to be wealthy, and therefore have less to gain ... by engaging in conflicts than poorer authoritarian states'.[127] Nonetheless, such criticism can be turned in on itself by utilizing it as an example of the multifaceted benefits to be expected from democratization; as noted above this has already been done by the Kantians who include notions of economic interdependence as a component of their theory. Furthermore, while democratic values may not serve as a precondition to a stable regional order, Barry Buzan argues that their presence signifies a 'huge asset'.[128] Nonetheless, given the lack of consensus regarding the utility and impact of democracy in connection with regionalism, later chapters will continue to seek further insight concerning the impact of different regimes types on the nature of foreign policy and any related tendency to commit to regionalist measures in the context of Southeast Asia.

The characteristics of regionalism and regionalization in summary

This chapter has provided an eclectic theoretical framework that has recognized and embraced components from the major IR paradigms. Moreover, it suggested that the occurrence of the different models of behaviour predicted by these schools of thought is determined by the level of complex integration. While complex integration maintains certain conceptual similarities with regionalization, it can apply between just two or more states and involves integration in the socio-cultural, economic, and political-security fields. Importantly, the chapter noted the role of constructivism in explaining transitions from one type of order to another. Hypothetically, these regional orders could range from a conflict formation (i.e. low complex integration) through to a security community (i.e. high complex integration). In the case of the latter, security communities represent a form of normative institutionalism due to an intricate blend of elements from constructivism and neo-liberal institutionalism. More specifically, a security community was defined as a '*transnational grouping of two or more states whose sovereignty is increasingly institutionalized (amalgamation) and whose people maintain dependable expectations of peaceful change*'. The existence of dependable expectations of peaceful change, in turn, necessitates substantial cooperation and supranational institutionalization. In the absence of supranational institutionalization (i.e. pooled sovereignty), the coordination of cooperation will be weak and the implementation of agreements between the members of the community will remain low. Finally, the onset of the interconnected components of high complex integration discussed in the chapter represents a natural consequence of the emergence of trust, common values and collective identify formation.

As will be evidenced by later chapters, the substantial additions to the theoretical framework provided in this chapter do not necessarily entail an assessment that ASEAN is, or will be, a security community. Thus, this framework is also different from some earlier works on the subject in its attempt to develop a conceptual toolkit designed to *critically* measure the impediments to regionalization. The approach undertaken by the remaining chapters is also designed to seek further insights on the root causes behind instability and the potential for conflict in Southeast Asia. Furthermore, in as far as the community components of the framework are concerned, the analysis is limited to the types of ideational attributes, processes, and policies that form the collective identity of the state (when it is a nation-state) or the communities within the state. To this end, the analysis in the remaining chapters will be founded on the basis of concrete historical settings with the aim of ascertaining the collective ideational qualities of states, and how these attributes impact on transnational collective identity formation and on the spillover effect of security community formation. Therefore, and as a first step in applying the conceptual framework above, the next chapter begins with a consideration of how the region's history has affected the nature and extent of interaction between the Southeast Asian states along with the major events that eventually contributed to the creation of ASEAN in 1967.

2 The rise of Southeast Asia and the search for regional order

Today, Southeast Asia is one of the most diverse regions on earth. Nevertheless, one of the earliest common influences to drive a convergence of identities within the region (limited as that may be) was the mutual impact of colonialism and the volatile process of achieving independence that followed. While some of the Southeast Asian states were reluctantly 'pushed' together in the face of domestic and international volatility, the identities of other states have been *pulled* apart as a consequence of the Cold War and associated great power competition between the United States and the Soviet Union. Nonetheless, and despite periods of conflict and antagonistic regional relations, several Southeast Asian states eventually sought a modus vivendi in their intramural relations. This working arrangement emerged in the hope that 'limited collaboration' might better equip these states to overcome some of the causes behind the volatility of individual states and thus enhance the viability of the regimes in power. As will be seen, and despite several abortive attempts at multilateralism, the result was the formation of the Association of Southeast Asian Nations (ASEAN) in 1967.

This chapter commences by outlining, first, the empirical basis for the claim that Southeast Asia can be recognized as an identifiable region. The chapter then outlines the circumstances that eventually motivated the political elite, in several of the Southeast Asian states, to pursue a regional order that embraced, at least rhetorically, multilateralism as a building block in the common pursuit of stability and economic advancement. The chapter then follows with an assessment of the imperatives behind the formation of ASEAN together with the nature of the institutional order established by its formative instrument – the Bangkok Declaration. The final section of the chapter analyses the performance of ASEAN during its early years. While ASEAN was initially limited in both its form and intent, the chapter reveals that ASEAN's formation coincided with a significant improvement (relatively speaking) to the original members' intramural relations.

From colonialism to independence to the beginnings of regionalism

Some scholars have suggested that there was a pre-colonial notion of 'Southeast Asia as a region'.[1] However, the actual label of 'Southeast Asia' can only be traced as far back as the works of German writers in the late nineteenth century.[2] Further, while the region started to be recognized by some scholars from 1941 onwards,[3] it was first formally labelled *Southeast Asia* during the Pacific War against Japan, which led to the establishment of Lord Louis Mountbatten's Southeast Asia Military Command in 1943.[4] It was only from this time that the notion of 'Southeast Asia' started to become a familiar term. Despite criticisms that this approach falls into the trap of a narrowly 'realist' and 'Eurocentric' fallacy,[5] the elite-level survey indicated that the Southeast Asian elite by and large also perceive the region to be a modern construction. Thus, when asked, 'Do you believe that the notion of Southeast Asia is a centuries old phenomenon?', 64.9 per cent answered 'no' only, while 22.3 per cent responded 'yes' and 12.8 per cent held 'no opinion'. Recalling Patrick Morgan's definition of regionalism in the previous chapter, together with the new regionalist literature in general, such perceptions are highly informative. As respected historian Milton Osborne writes,

> [f]or the most part,... neither the foreigners who worked in Southeast Asia before the Second World War, whether as scholars or otherwise, nor the indigenous inhabitants of the countries of Southeast Asia, thought about the region in general terms. The general tendency to do so came with the Second World War when, as a result of military circumstances, the concept of a Southeast Asian region began to take hold.[6]

In reality, the modern state formations of Southeast Asia – with the exception of Siam (later Thailand) – were primarily constituted through colonialism. During the height of the colonial period and prior to 1941, Southeast Asia had been divided up between France, the Netherlands, Portugal, Britain and the United States.[7] A further consequence of colonialism was to obstruct the emergence of an indigenous region-wide identity. From the perspective of Ali Alatas, Indonesia's longest serving Foreign Minister, at the time of independence, and at least through to the formation of ASEAN, the 'former colonies knew more about Europe than ... their neighbours'.[8] Nonetheless, the ease with which Japan expelled the foreign powers from Southeast Asia raised initial hopes that independence was at hand. While various promises, ranging from local autonomy to independence through to Japan's proposal to implement a 'Greater East Asia Co-Prosperity Sphere', were soon revealed to be mere propaganda, Japanese discourse and the events of the Second World War ensured that the process of decolonization could not be suppressed in the years that followed.[9] Nevertheless, for a brief period after the Second World War colonial authority was reasserted. Of the European powers, the Dutch controlled the Indonesian archipelago; the English ruled Malaya (later Malaysia), Singapore, Brunei and Burma (later Myanmar); and the French held sway over the Indochina sub-region. The United States, for its part, regained temporary control of the Philippines but had previously agreed to grant independence in 1946.[10]

For some of the modern-day Southeast Asian nations, nationalist sentiments and the struggle for independence from colonialism provided one of the earliest – albeit extremely limited – common-identity-building experiences.[11] Nonetheless, such sentiments were not organized or coordinated beyond the boundaries of each individual state. In the case of Indonesia, and similar to the Philippines, the Indonesians had begun their struggle for independence during the pre-war era, a struggle with which they succeeded in 1949.[12] Meanwhile, the United Kingdom, weakened by the Second World War, granted independence to Burma in 1948. Nearly a decade later, in 1957, independence from Britain followed for Malaya and in 1963 the British decolonized Singapore and British North Borneo (Sabah and Sarawak) by incorporating them with Malaya into the new 'Federation of Malaysia'. While the Kingdom of Brunei 'reluctantly' gained independence from Britain in 1983, independence did not come so easily for the Indochinese states: Laos, Cambodia and Vietnam.[13] The independence of Myanmar, the Indochinese states, and their eventual membership in ASEAN, will be examined in detail in the next chapter.

As various Southeast Asian states gained independence, new internal and external security problems came to the fore. At the traditional level of security analysis, the global bipolar divisions that emerged between communism and capitalism (exacerbated further by the United States (US) policy of containment) acted to cleave Southeast Asia through the creation of two antagonistic camps.[14] These camps were constituted by Indochina in the north and the future ASEAN-5 in the south.[15] However, during these early years, animosity was no less evident in the 'south'. Consequently, the experience of colonialism – to varying degrees – contributed to a worldview that saw the international system as deeply predatory.[16] Thus, in 1963, Indonesian President Sukarno initiated a policy of *konfrontasi* (confrontation) against Malaysia in an attempt to prevent the merger of Sabah and Sarawak into the Malaysian federation – a decision that Sukarno maintained was a 'neo-colonialist' plot to perpetuate British influence in the region. Meanwhile, relations in the 'south' were further complicated by the Philippines pressing its territorial claim to Malaysian controlled Sabah and Singapore's ejection from the Federation of Malaysia in 1965. As Yuen Foong Khong reflects, peace in Southeast Asia 'seemed anything but likely' at the time.[17]

Interestingly, each of the newly independent Southeast Asian states faced similar domestic challenges – including the formidable challenge of nation-building – whilst simultaneously consolidating state power.[18] In Indonesia, the Sudanese and other non-Javanese communities were protesting against Javanese rule while Singapore's membership in the Federation of Malaysia had aggravated an alternative set of ethnic tensions that contributed to the onset of race riots in Singapore in 1964.[19] This was an event that had been exacerbated by long-term economic imbalances between the Chinese and Malay ethic groups leading to further large-scale riots and violence in both Malaysia and Singapore in May 1969.[20] Several of the Southeast Asian governments were also fighting various insurgencies fuelled by ethnicity, religion and/or contending ideologies (e.g. communism). In the case of Burma, for example, during the 1950s the government lost control of much of its territory to several insurgent groups (e.g. the Burmese Communist Party); the challenge became so significant that even the capital city (Rangoon) soon came under the threat of falling to opposition forces.[21]

Malaya, which later became the Federation of Malaysia in 1963, also had to contend with what became known as 'The Emergency'. The Emergency was a British declared state of emergency in response to armed opposition from the Communist Party of Malaya.[22] These domestic insurgencies also became entwined with the Cold War dynamics of the time due to their sponsorship, in some instances, by other communist regimes such as China.[23] Meanwhile, the United States provided clandestine support to insurgencies within Indonesia.[24] Given the colonial history endured by the region, these insurgencies were also a concern as they invited external intervention of the kind that occurred in the case of the Federation of Malaysia.[25] Under such conditions many scholars characterized the region as anything but stable; some scholars even considered Southeast Asia to be a 'cultural shatter belt' that was not only diverse and fragmented but also balkanized.[26]

The search for a new beginning: limited regionalism amidst fragile relations

Due to these internal and external challenges, the maintenance of stability and the consolidation of power (domestically) became the primary strategic goals.[27] Thus, during the years that followed the non-communist states of Southeast Asia 'came to share an almost religious belief in the effects of rapid economic growth in diffusing the sources of social and political discontent within their societies'.[28] However, in order to achieve these goals, the region's leaders first had to create a stable environment for such development and economic progress to take place. It is with these state interests in mind that, in the wake of independence and through to the time of ASEAN's formation, several multilateral initiatives were launched. While these early and often abortive attempts at regionalism were designed to address and constrain challenges to Southeast Asian security, they also reflected an underlying recognition of the necessity for some form of institutionalized cooperation to tackle these challenges.

In reaction to the involvement of China in the Korean War, the defeat of the French in Vietnam and emergence of the 'domino theory', the United States collaborated with the United Kingdom to create the *Southeast Asia Collective Defence Treaty* (Manila Pact) on 8 September 1954. For the United States, the creation of the pact was a component of its Cold War strategy to contain communism.[29] In February 1955, the treaty became institutionalized in structure when a council meeting in Bangkok approved the establishment of the *Southeast Asian Treaty Organization* (SEATO).[30] SEATO was largely unsuccessful as Thailand and the Philippines were the only regional members.[31] From the standpoint of Indonesia, Singapore and Malaysia, the organization's extra-regional origin conflicted with an emerging policy preference of resisting *overt* external influence and enmeshment in great power machinations. On this basis, they refused to become members.[32] Moreover, US policies backfired in both Indonesia and Burma (now Myanmar). In the case of Myanmar, the nationalist Kuomintang forces that were resident in the country's Eastern Highlands –

financed and supported by Thailand and the United States – not only violated the country's sovereignty (thus inviting interference from the People's Republic of China) but also verified the virtue of non-alignment and international isolation – a policy that remained for decades to come. In the case of Indonesia, the US strategy of tying aid to mutual security frameworks brought down a 'West-leaning government' because of a leftist-nationalist backlash in 1958.[33]

Meanwhile, the enthusiasm SEATO received from the Thai and Filipino governments exemplified the diversity of interests, threat perceptions and alignments then extant in Southeast Asia during the early years of independence. Moreover, the intramural behavioural patterns predicted by low complex integration (defensive realism) were evident as Thailand and the Philippines sought to pursue a collective balance of power against their neighbours. In the case of the Philippines, its leadership had become strongly anti-communist because of the many challenges to domestic stability faced by the country. Thus, the Philippine government had already concluded a 1947 Military Bases Agreement (providing the US with the use of more than ten facilities) and in 1951, this agreement was followed by a mutual defence pact. Thailand, already fearful of the strategic threat of the increasingly strong Viet Minh (a communist movement to depose colonial rule in Vietnam), was further alarmed by various Viet Minh incursions into Cambodia and Laos between 1953 and early 1954. While Bangkok quickly volunteered to become the seat of SEATO because of these events, Thailand soon became disenchanted with the treaty due to perceptions that SEATO had reacted inadequately and indecisively to further developments in Laos.[34] Here, the ineffectiveness of the organization's response over Laos was, in retrospect, more significantly a consequence of different threat perceptions between both the regional and extra-regional SEATO members including, in the case of the latter, divisions between the UK and the US.[35]

As a consequence of regional suspicions concerning these security developments, Indonesia hosted the April 1955 'Asian–African Conference' in Bandung, Indonesia. The Bandung conference provided an early indication of Indonesia's aspiration to be the natural leader of Southeast Asia and the 'chairman' of the third world as represented, eventually, by the Non-Aligned Movement (NAM).[36] The Bandung conference was attended by several Southeast Asian governments including the communist Democratic Republic of Vietnam (DRV) together with the neutral governments of Indonesia, Myanmar, Laos and Cambodia as well as America's allies – the Philippines, Thailand and South Vietnam. Given the character of many of the participants, together with the history of greater Asia, the conference was governed by both anti-imperialist and non-aligned themes.[37] Nevertheless, it represented a significant development partly because twenty-nine countries attended the deliberations – including the People's Republic of China – and also because it was the first Southeast Asian inspired initiative to seek greater amity (mutual understanding) and cooperation.[38] Most significantly, however, the conference was important for entrenching further the legal-procedural norms of *international society* within Southeast Asia.[39]

Traditionally, the norms of international society, as initiated in Europe by the Council of Constance (1415),[40] and further entrenched by the Peace of Westphalia (1648), include *rex est imperator in regno suo* (all leaders are equal and independent of one another); *cuius regio, eius religio* (no right to intervene in internal affairs because of religion); and third, the concept of a 'balance of power' (i.e. the prevention by any means of a power rising and dominating others).[41] More contemporarily, the norms of international society (alternatively understood as the 'Westphalian international system') have evolved to include the principle of non-interference and the pacific settlement of disputes as enshrined in the Charter of the United Nations.[42] The influence of these norms can be seen in Table 2.1; these are the agreed upon principles of the final Bandung communiqué 'by which nations should practice tolerance and live in peace with one another as good neighbours and develop friendly cooperation'.[43]

The region's readiness to accept the standard norms and principles embraced by international society was not only a consequence of volatile states struggling for security (both domestic and regional) but also from ideals that can be attributed to a history of socialization through colonial rule. Thus, it was during the colonial era that the European powers cemented into being aspects of the region's norms for the purpose of introducing and sustaining viable legal and administrative structures. Nonetheless, and as Haacke indicates, the overarching 'legal-procedural norms' – as outlined by the principles of Bandung and eventually adopted by the region's elites – emerged both in consequence of the 'imposed socialization' of the colonial powers as well as through common and 'interlocking struggles for recognition'.[44]

Furthermore, the struggle for recognition endured by most of the newly independent participants led to the non-intervention concept beyond the standard norms of international society to embrace the idea that great power intervention, for the purpose of power-balancing, was no longer acceptable.[45] As will be seen, the principle of non-interference (together with the other principles emboldened

Table 2.1 The Bandung Principles

1. ***Respect for*** *fundamental human rights and for* ***the purposes and principles of the charter of the United Nations***
2. ***Respect for the sovereignty and territorial integrity*** *of all nations*
3. *Recognition of the equality of all races and of the* ***equality of all nations*** *large and small*
4. *Abstention* ***from intervention or interference in the internal affairs of another country***
5. *Respect for the right of each nation to defend itself, singly or collectively, in conformity with the charter of the United Nations*
6. *(a) Abstention from the use of arrangements of collective defence to serve any particular interests of the big powers*
   (b) Abstention by any country from exerting pressures on other countries

Source: author. Principles of the Bandung at: http://fds.oup.com/www.oup.co.uk/pdf/bt/cassese/cases/part3/ch18/1702.pdf.

within Table 2.1) would later become a central component of ASEAN's normative framework, which is alternatively known as the ASEAN Way. Furthermore, while the ASEAN Way would enable the pursuit of divergent approaches to nation-building by individual governments, the common goals that seemingly motivated each of these approaches were *regime survival* and *domestic stability* – the former being dependent on the latter. Nonetheless, the norms that would eventually be enshrined in the ASEAN Way have continued to be routinely violated by the ASEAN members.[46]

Over time, other attempts at constructing regional and extra-regional security bodies and alliances included the Anglo-Malayan Defence Agreement (AMDA), the Asian and Pacific Council (ASPAC), Malaysia–Philippines–Indonesia (Maphilindo), and the Association of Southeast Asia (ASA). The AMDA was formed in 1957 by Britain, New Zealand and Australia together with Singapore, Malaysia and the British Borneo territories. In 1971, the arrangement was succeeded by the Five Power Defence Arrangement (FPDA).[47] In contrast to the Philippines and Thailand, the alternative security arrangements sought by Singapore and Malaysia reflected their colonial history with the British. The agreement was also significant for enabling military assistance from the Commonwealth during *konfrontasi*. Unlike SEATO, the FPDA survived the end of the Cold War and the member countries continue to undertake annual joint military exercises.[48] Meanwhile, in contrast to SEATO and the FPDA, the stated purpose of ASPAC (a South Korean initiative) was 'consultation on economic and cultural matters'.[49] Nonetheless, when ASPAC was formed in 1966 the United States branded it as the 'bulwark of anti-Communist solidarity in Asia' thereby undermining its legitimacy from the outset.[50] The Southeast Asian members were Malaysia, the Philippines, Thailand and South Vietnam, while the remaining members consisted of South Korea, Taiwan, Japan, Australia and New Zealand. The Council never moved beyond a few modest and carefully written statements and eventually expired seven years after its inception, following an improvement to relations (rapprochement) between the United States and China.[51]

The ASA and the Maphilindo, by contrast, were both significant for being completely regional initiatives with a membership totally indigenous to Southeast Asia. The ASA, with the eventual goal of promoting regional economic cooperation, was inaugurated on 31 July 1961 with just three members – Thailand, the Philippines and Malaysia. Both the Philippines and Malaysia had initially favoured a deeply institutionalized structure modelled on the European Economic Community (now the European Union) but Thailand was against anything more than a loosely articulated and non-binding form of intergovernmentalism. The Malaysian and Philippine governments pragmatically accepted Thailand's preferences because, first, it was necessary to maintain Thai participation and, second, the two countries hoped this loosely structured formula would be more likely to entice other Southeast Asian states to join;[52] the organization later proved to be unsuccessful in this second goal.

Interestingly, negotiations for the ASA had in fact been initiated as far back as 1959 when a previous reincarnation, the Southeast Asian Friendship and

Economic Treaty (SEAFET), had been proposed by the Prime Minister of Malaysia, Tunku Abdul Rahman.[53] There were, however, three further problems with SEAFET and later the ASA. First, in proposing the treaty the Tunku alienated Indonesia by refusing to incorporate and/or express support for the principles of Bandung, by then a cornerstone of Indonesian foreign policy. Second, the Indonesians resented Malaysia's attempt at regional leadership, something Sukarno increasingly viewed as an Indonesian right.[54] Finally, and again in contrast to the underlying philosophy behind the Bandung conference, the Tunku habitually 'displayed an unfortunate tendency to mention regional economic and cultural cooperation in the same breath as he lamented the evils of communism and encouraged an ever-vigilant opposition to it'.[55] Thus, despite many statements by the Tunku that he had no intention for SEAFET to develop into a collective security or defence pact, Indonesia (and others) remained suspicious of its intended purpose together with the strategic alignment of its proposed members. Accordingly, they were not in favour of the proposal.[56] Due to these problems, and a continued divide in threat perceptions, Indonesia did not join SEAFET and it soon ran into difficulties over a dispute between Malaysia and the Philippines concerning Sabah which, in turn, provided the final death knell to the institution.[57]

Unlike SEAFET, the stated goal of the Maphilindo was to provide an open-ended non-institutionalized framework for regional consultation on issues of common concern through the 'spirit of consensus'.[58] Importantly, the Maphilindo invoked certain Bandung principles that sought to develop the notion of regional resilience by avoiding collective defence agreements that would serve the interests of foreign powers. In so doing, the Manila accords that established the Maphilindo 'had Sukarno's fingerprints all over it'.[59] Proclaimed in August 1963, the Maphilindo comprised Malaysia, the Philippines and Indonesia but was abandoned a month later due to various animosities by the Philippines and Indonesia over the formation of the Federation of Malaysia which, at the time, consisted of Malaya, Singapore, Sabah and Sarawak.

In the case of Indonesia, and since the declaration of martial law in 1957, the political orientation of the Sukarno-led government became increasingly leftist to the point where, eventually, the government opened a parliamentary role for the Indonesian Communist Party (PKI). Consequently, under Sukarno's leadership, Indonesia's earlier principle of non-alignment gradually evolved to become a fight against neo-colonialism and Western imperialism along a 'Jakarta–Phnom Penh–Hanoi–Beijing–Pyongyang axis'.[60] Because of this background, when the proposal for a new Federation of Malaysia was announced by Malaysia in May 1961, Sukarno quickly responded by denouncing the planned territory as an artificial creation of the colonial powers.[61] He further argued that the maintenance of Malaysia's links to Britain – and the Anglo-Malaysian Defence Arrangement in particular (FPDA) – provided additional evidence of a neo-colonialist plot to maintain power in the region. Moreover, Sukarno interpreted the far reaching Federation of Malaysia as a physical security threat to Indonesia that 'cut traditional links in the Malay world'.[62]

Given Indonesia's threat perceptions, Sukarno reoriented Indonesia's policy of *konfrontasi* (confrontation), which had been previously applied against the Dutch vis-à-vis its control of Irian Jaya (West Papua), to be applied against the Federation of Malaysia. In an attempt to undermine the legitimacy of the Federation, and later an independent Singapore, his policy incorporated a combination of diplomatic coercion (e.g. the severing of diplomatic ties) as well as armed confrontation (e.g. the supply of arms to Malaysian militants).[63] The failure of *konfrontasi* soon became apparent following the involvement of foreign forces in support of the Malaysian Federation together with the election of Malaysia as a non-permanent member in the United Nations Security Council (UNSC).[64] Indonesia responded to the latter development by taking the unprecedented step of withdrawing its membership from the United Nations.[65]

The Philippines, for its part, objected to plans for Sabah (then known as North Borneo) to be incorporated into the new Federation of Malaysia and, in 1962, officially laid claim to sovereignty over Sabah. The Philippine government argued that Sabah was an inseparable segment of its own territory due to it having been under the fief of the Sultan of Sulu.[66] Despite the Sultanate being centred within the Philippines, Sabah was incorporated in the Federation of Malaysia in September 1963.[67] The Maphilindo subsequently collapsed and diplomatic relations between Kuala Lumpur, Manila and Jakarta were terminated. While some claim that the primary purpose of the Maphilindo was to 'establish a diplomatic framework that would facilitate the peaceful resolution of disputes about Malaysia's border',[68] others argue that the initiative 'was in fact a diplomatic device through which the Philippines and Indonesia sought to frustrate or delay the creation of the Malaysian Federation'.[69]

Shifts in the equation? The rationale behind the formation of ASEAN

By the mid-1960s, the limitations to *konfrontasi* and Sukarno's 'exercise in political pyrotechnics' had become painfully obvious.[70] Aside from failing to undermine Malaysia's legitimacy in international society, Indonesia had also alienated several Western governments, neglected its struggling economy, and breached key international norms including the non-use of force; norms that Indonesia itself had led a reaffirmation of at the Bandung conference. *Konfrontasi* also provided early evidence of the mutual dependency and vulnerability of the Southeast Asian States as Indonesia's economic sanctions against Malaysia had been 'almost as painful to Indonesia as its intended target'.[71] However, Sukarno and his government did not wish to lose face and so Indonesia initially resorted to further coercive measures with the effect of prolonging the policy. Subsequently, a number of Indonesian military raids between August and September 1964 (involving a total of more than two hundred soldiers and paratroopers) took place on the southern tip of peninsular Malaysia in the towns of Pontian and Labis. Moreover, some believe that the occurrence of further race riots in Singapore was provoked by foreign military agents from Indonesia.[72]

In the wake of these events, Sukarno secretly approached the Tunku about the possibility of a meeting with a view to ending *konfrontasi* in return for a 'face saving' plebiscite on the future of Sabah and Sarawak. The Tunku reacted coolly and Sukarno soon had to deny claims by Kuala Lumpur that he had attempted to end his 'crush Malaysia' campaign. Consequently, armed military incursions by Indonesia into Malaysia and Singapore resumed.[73] Despite the continuation of violence, some of the region's leaders understood that Sukarno was prepared to end *konfrontasi* so long as it could be done in a way that did not weaken him domestically – both in terms of popular opinion and in terms of his position vis-à-vis the PKI. As a result, the Philippine government sounded out the possibility of negotiating a resolution under the umbrella of an Afro-Asian Commission.[74] However, in the end, this diplomacy was rendered unnecessary due to domestic developments where, on 30 September 1965, several officers backed by the PKI were allegedly involved in an attempted coup.[75] Given this new opportunity to resolve the crisis, the Philippines quickly sought support from Thailand and Malaysia to revive the ASA in the hope that they could entice Indonesia to become its fourth member. Sukarno, who at this point was steadily losing executive power and authority to General Suharto, did not acquiesce to the idea.[76] In the wake of the attempted coup – in which Sukarno was implicated – the country was embroiled in a violent nationwide anticommunist campaign that resulted in the deaths of many thousands – some suggest millions – of alleged communist sympathizers and ethnic Chinese.[77] Given Indonesia's mounting internal security dilemma, the government initially lacked the *capacity* and the *will* to lead any initiatives for a new or expanded regional organization.

Amidst a decline in Sukarno's health, Suharto acquired executive authority for Indonesia in March 1966. Sukarno, who three years earlier had been made 'president for life', surrendered all his remaining powers eleven months later in February 1967.[78] These developments created a new opportunity to reinvigorate efforts to not only end *konfrontasi* but to also contemplate a new organization for regional cooperation between the capitalist states. Thus, just two months after Suharto obtained executive control, both Indonesia and Malaysia declared an end to the conflict at a conference in Bangkok on 28 May 1966. Then, on 11 August 1966, the two countries signed the *Bangkok Accord* that had earlier been negotiated by Malaysia's Deputy Prime Minister (Tun Abdul Razak) and Indonesia's Foreign Minister (Adam Malik). The *Bangkok Accord*, together with a series of 'secret letters' between Sukarno and the Tunku (at the behest of Suharto), enabled a resumption of diplomatic relations between the two countries. However, this tentative modus vivendi was conditional upon a face-saving poll of the public's will in both Sabah and Sarawak;[79] a vote was held in 1967 where the people opted to remain part of Malaysia. Subsequently, full diplomatic relations between the two countries were restored on 31 August 1967.[80]

Back in May 1966, when Malik and Razak had met to negotiate a treaty between Malaysia and Indonesia, Thailand's Foreign Minister, Thanat Kohman, had also been present and had discussed with his foreign ministry counterparts (Malik in particular) the possibility of greater regional cooperation.[81] While not directly involved in the discussions, and still under the shadow of President Sukarno, General Suharto was in a position to 'decisively' influence the dialogue by pressing for a pragmatic foreign policy 'based on regional cooperation and domestic economic development'.[82] Thus, in consultation with Indonesia, Thailand drafted and presented its proposal for a Southeast Asian Association for Regional Cooperation (SEAARC). In recognition of the sensitivities of Indonesia, the proposal had the potential to bring Indonesia into a regional organization without producing an appearance that Indonesia had asked to join.[83] However, before the prospective members could agree to the proposal, two major difficulties in the drafting of the organization had first to be overcome.

The first difficulty was that the initial SEAARC proposal stated the member states were in agreement that 'foreign bases are temporary in nature and should not be allowed to be used directly or indirectly to subvert the national independence of Asian countries' and 'that arrangements of collective defence should not be used to serve the particular interest of any big powers'.[84] These two clauses proved highly controversial as the Philippines, Malaysia, Singapore and Thailand all had security relationships with major exogenous powers. The Philippines, for its part, argued that it would rather avoid any mention of 'security related issues' than be forced into a position of having to accept the two components advocated within the SEAARC statement. As the exclusion of any security framework was unacceptable to Indonesia, a series of complex negotiations followed and a compromise was eventually reached.[85] While the final version of the agreement maintained that 'foreign bases are temporary', there was no prohibition 'against arrangements of collective defence ... [that might serve] ... the interests of the big powers'.[86]

The second difficulty pertained to the revival of the ASA. The Malaysian government had engineered its formation and was, moreover, hesitant to abandon an organization that was already in existence and functioning. However, Indonesia viewed the ASA to be anti-communist, anti-Indonesian and closely aligned with the West. This, together with Indonesia's role in NAM, rendered the option of joining the ASA politically unacceptable.[87] Negotiations continued and the Thai blueprint eventually morphed into a face-saving proposal to establish the Association of Southeast Asian Nations (ASEAN), on 8 August 1967, that still followed the loose structure and security premises of the ASA.[88] Thus, at the inaugural meeting of ASEAN, Tun Abdul Razak declared '[w]e, in Malaysia, are extremely happy that the ideals and aspirations which led to the establishment of ASA six years ago, have now grown and have gathered another form and wider import in the birth of ASEAN today'.[89]

The five members of the Association at its inception were Indonesia, Malaysia, the Philippines, Singapore and Thailand. At the time, both Myanmar and Cambodia refused to join the Association.[90] The establishment of this grouping was by no means a natural or logical development. In addition to the level of distrust generated by *konfrontasi*, each of the members maintained diverging security interests (and perspectives) that had also contributed to regional enmity. In the case of the Philippines and Malaysia, for example, the crisis over competing claims for Sabah had not been resolved and diplomatic relations had only recently been restored – partly as a consequence of a change of leadership in the Philippines.[91] Meanwhile, relations between Singapore and Malaysia were equally troublesome as Singapore had been ejected from the Federation of Malaysia due to irreconcilable differences over politics and diverging approaches to problematic race relations.[92] Even in the case of Thailand, its government maintained a degree of apprehension over the possibility that Malaysia might want to regain the Malay territories in Southern Thailand that had been arbitrarily separated through colonial intervention. Malaysia was similarly distrustful of Thailand as it felt that Bangkok was not particularly cooperative in combating the Malayan Communist Party, which had retreated to pockets along the border in the 1950s.[93] Hence, the actual ability of these governments to come together for the purpose of even a limited mechanism for dialogue (if not cooperation) reflected the enormous sense of vulnerability felt by each of the members in terms of the security environment they faced at the time.[94]

The 'Bangkok Declaration' and the early structures of ASEAN

ASEAN's formative instrument was the 'ASEAN Declaration', alternatively known as the 'Bangkok Declaration'. In line with the historical imperatives behind the organization's foundation, the 'second' of the declared intentions is to promote 'regional peace and stability' through an 'abiding respect for justice and the rule of law in the relationship among countries of the region and adherence to the principles of the United Nations Charter'.[95] Nonetheless, references to collaboration and mutual assistance on political and security issues, along with the need for regional reconciliation, were deliberately avoided in the enabling declaration.[96] Instead, the Declaration's 'first' official aspiration was the promotion of social, cultural, and economic development and cooperation. Meanwhile, points three through seven of the declaration reiterated similar ideals concerning functional cooperation as well as enhanced trade links, the promotion of Southeast Asian studies and the need to maintain 'close and beneficial cooperation with existing international regional organizations'. The limited and open ended nature of references to 'regional peace and security' can be understood through several considerations, including a continued lack of trust between the member-states, a desire to protect each country's sovereignty and the fear of hostile reactions from either Vietnam or China.[97] Thus, the ASEAN leaders repeatedly and expressly denied that ASEAN was a security alliance or security organization.[98]

Given the constraints to regionalism that existed at the time of ASEAN's inception, it is unsurprising that the Bangkok Declaration is humble both in its intent and the institutional structures it established. The declaration contains less than two pages of print and did not include any programme for 'transforming objectives into realities'. Furthermore, to the extent that it referred to economic and socio-cultural cooperation, there were no 'concrete steps' for implementation.[99] Additionally, the limited nature of the region's investment in the Association's establishment was evidenced by the fact that the signatories to the Declaration were not ASEAN leaders but, rather, deputy leaders, foreign ministers and a 'secretary of Foreign Affairs' from the Philippines. In terms of structure, while the document envisions regular meetings of the ASEAN Economic Ministers and other subordinate committees, the highest policy-making body was an annual meeting of foreign ministers. Problematically, therefore, the Bangkok Declaration contained no provision for meetings between the heads of government and, subsequently, the ASEAN leaders did not meet for a further ten years.

As noted above, the Association adopted the practical goals and institutional format of the ASA. However, at Indonesia's insistence, the Association also adopted the declaratory aspirations of the Maphilindo.[100] Therefore, regional scholars such as Kusuma Snitwongse have interpreted the language of the Bangkok Declaration – including the members' 'stability and security from external interference' – as an elite move to deepen the salience of the acceptable normative rules governing the ASEAN Way. Rhetorically, the normative rules governing regional interaction have traditionally been (i) consensus based decision-making; (ii) a respect for national sovereignty; and (iii) the non-interference in the domestic affairs of others.[101] Such an interpretation is supported by the Declaration's reference to the principles of the United Nations Charter which, among other things, includes the principle of non-interference. However, as will be seen in the next chapter, the behaviour of the member states most significantly reflected this normative ideal when faced by common external threats. Further, the limited periods of cohesion that ASEAN enjoyed during its early decades were simultaneously driven and restricted by the bipolar cleavages of the Cold War. Regardless of the limitations of the Bangkok Declaration, the formation of the Association was at least important for establishing a culture of consultation – whether that be at a karaoke bar or at a golf course.[102]

Aside from the 'official' imperatives behind ASEAN's foundation – and despite the highly tangible nature of the various threats to security that afflicted the Southeast Asian states at the time – there remains some debate over whether the creation of ASEAN can be primarily attributed to domestic, regional and/or extra-regional motives. In reality, different interpretations of Southeast Asia's political history may reflect the distinctive worldviews that have been socialized within the territorial confines of each state. For example, one senior member from Indonesia's foreign ministry argues that 'ASEAN was a solution in its own merit to … the problem of bilateral conflict',[103] whereas a senior member from Singapore's Ministry of Defence (MINDEF) argues that ASEAN merely 'brought a few countries together in the face of external threat'.[104] Scholars such as Bunn Nagara add to the diversity of opinion on the matter by arguing that the formation of ASEAN was primarily a response to the threats posed by domestic insurgencies and a desire, vis-à-vis *konfrontasi*, 'that the future should not be a repeat of the past'.[105] Donald Weatherbee adds to this list that a 'desire to intensify and regularize … political contacts in a multilateral setting' was further impelled by an escalation of the Vietnam War and the need to integrate Indonesia into a collaborative regional order as opposed to one that saw Indonesia acting as a potential hegemon.[106]

The extent to which this diversity of opinion reflects differences in the level of an understanding of ASEAN (and Southeast Asia) by individuals, communities, and states is considered further in later chapters. In the meantime, however, it is important to state that the common glue facilitating the formation of ASEAN was a pragmatic assessment by the ruling elite of how the aforementioned challenges might affect their ability to govern fragile states. In the context of these concerns, it was the disruptive potential of the many actual and potential disputes within Southeast Asia that, by 1967, had resulted in a recognition that unless the five governments established some form of organized dialogue to mitigate competition and future interstate conflict, then they would either fail or be delayed in their endeavours towards internal consolidation – particularly economic development and nation-building. Thus, as Michael Leifer suggests, 'regional co-operation was not intended to serve the interest of common security through the projection of common power but through the mitigation and management of conflict and attendant economic development'.[107] However, as will be seen, the maintenance of good relations between the Southeast Asian states has proven to be much more difficult than much of the founding rhetoric would indicate.

ASEAN's performance: the early years

Yuen Fong Khong has argued

> that the sense of collective identity central to the building of security communities did not originate from intensive economic interaction or interdependence. The lack of success in economic cooperation during ASEAN's first decade was more than made up by achievements in political security cooperation. It is here that the inklings of a regional consciousness or solidarity may be found.[108]

However, in reality, the ability of the ASEAN member-states to operate collaboratively through the structure of ASEAN during the Association's formative years was strongly hampered by the continuation of internal instability and the emergence of a world increasingly polarized between the two superpowers – the Soviet Union and the United States.[109] Further, such collaboration was also impeded by the continuation of hostile relations and several potential initiators of conflict within the region. Given these impediments, it is not surprising that in the course of ASEAN's first decade of operation the Association struggled to achieve anything of significance concerning cooperation, integration or institutionalization. The challenge of intra-regional conflicts, such as *konfrontasi*, has already been noted; however, further impediments to trust, cooperation and institutionalization remained. While an 'in principle' reconciliation between Indonesia and Malaysia was necessary prior to the formation of ASEAN, the residual effects of *konfrontasi* did not entirely dissipate until later. For example, Indonesia and Malaysia did not re-establish full diplomatic relations until a month after the formation of ASEAN. Meanwhile, the bilateral tensions extant between Malaysia and the Philippines, as well as between Singapore and Malaysia, also had to be attended to before ASEAN could move ahead with even a minimal level of cooperation and collaboration.

For example, the Corregidor Affair between the Philippines and Malaysia transpired in March 1968. The Philippine government, under the leadership of President Marcos, had sought to pursue its claim to Sabah by funding and assisting a training camp for an intended Sabah separatist rebellion in Corregidor. While the full facts of the affair have never been confirmed, in March 1968 a Filipino Muslim recruit reported to the governor of the Cavite province that he had survived a massacre of the intended rebels; a massacre that had been precipitated by a mutiny over demands for back-pay.[110] Soon thereafter, the Malaysian government arrested twenty-six Filipinos carrying small-arms and explosives on a Malaysian island some thirty kilometres north of Sabah.[111] The Corregidor Affair is significant in that it gave rise to ASEAN's only example of preventative diplomacy at 'an intra-mural level'. Here, President Suharto intervened at the second ASEAN Ministerial Meeting (AMM), in August 1968, and proposed a cooling off period between Manila and Kuala Lumpur.[112] However, despite his efforts, a month later the Philippine Congress passed a resolution (later endorsed by President Marcos) reaffirming the Philippine claim to Sabah. Not only did the two countries re-suspend diplomatic relations, but all ASEAN meetings were cancelled until May 1969.[113] The dispute has not yet been resolved and, therefore, continues to impede their relations as well as the overall sense of community and cohesiveness in ASEAN.[114]

Meanwhile, in the years that followed Singapore's separation from Malaysia, through to well after ASEAN's formation, Singapore–Malaysia relations remained openly hostile and completely contrary to the 'spirit of equality and partnership' enunciated in the Bangkok Declaration.[115] Moreover, by early 1968, just six months after ASEAN's establishment, 'the two sides were at a point of treating each other in terms and policies more alien than their attitudes towards other countries'.[116] The many factors that contributed to the fractious relationship between Singapore and Malaysia included the feasibility of a common market and a common currency; the dissolution of joint stock companies such as Malaysia–Singapore airlines; threats over the supply of potable water from Johor (Malaysia); debates over the control of a Malaysian railway line, a Malay regiment and a Malaysian naval base in Woodlands; the use of Israeli military advisors leading to the adoption of an Israeli-style doctrine of 'forward defence'; as well as various territorial disputes.[117]

As touched on earlier, a further issue that negatively affected their bilateral relations was the escalation of ethno-religious divisions and the distinctive policies adopted in response to them. Not only were these ethno-religious divides inseparably linked to the factors considered in the preceding paragraph, but they were also interdependent with the diverging nature of the two countries' developmental strategies and conflicting approaches to nation-building and social development within their multi-ethnic societies.[118] The strategy behind

Singapore's plans for development was significantly informed by the sense of vulnerability that had emerged from a perception that it was a 'Chinese island in a Malay sea'.[119] The Singapore leadership initially reacted with an abrasive and competitive tone that included 'scathing comparison[s] with its neighbours'.[120] In response, Malaysian policy makers and academics alike continue to draw reference to the '*kiasu*' (afraid to lose) mentality of the Singaporeans and view this as the basic source of Singaporean verbal provocations.[121] Thus, according to a high-profile academic in Malaysia, the problematic nature of dealing with Singapore has been exacerbated by a sense of paranoia (or, in his words, 'Israeli defence force mentality') that there are 'threat[s] everywhere' and this has meant that, through a 'Forward Defence' plan, Singapore is constantly ready and prepared to invade the Southern Malaysian state of Johor over such issues as water-resources or, potentially, religion.[122] However, a reprieve for the future of ASEAN emerged when relations between Malaysia and Singapore improved following a change of leadership in Malaysia. Prime Minister Tunku Abdul Rahman was replaced by Tun Abdul Razak following a loss of confidence by the politically dominant United Malays National Organisation (UMNO).[123]

Limited progress in the face of international change: ZOPFAN

Greater cordiality had emerged between the ASEAN members by the 1970s and such cordiality had been driven by leadership change as well as several international developments with significant bearing on Southeast Asia's regional order. For example, both Singapore and Malaysia had been forced to rethink their security alliances when Britain announced plans to accelerate its withdrawal from Southeast Asia and all territories east of Suez. Then, in 1969, and in response to growing domestic opposition to the Vietnam War, President Nixon issued the Guam (Nixon) doctrine, a doctrine that effectively limited the military involvement of the United States in Southeast Asia. Meanwhile, in the same year, the Soviet Union expressed an interest in the region through its proposal for an Asian 'collective security system' and the re-emergence of China had become a particular concern for some of the ASEAN members, as were the potential consequences of the Vietnam War spreading into Cambodia, Laos and beyond (i.e. the domino theory). Further, the ASEAN members found it increasingly necessary to retune their development strategies to take advantage of the increased magnitude of the Japanese economy. Moreover, broader adjustments in macroeconomic policy had also become increasingly necessary (and difficult) due to the uncertainty generated by rapid and sometimes volatile shifts in global trade and economic structures.[124] These events and uncertainties contributed to an ASEAN-wide consensus concerning the need for greater regional cooperation and some form of collective security based on the realization that they could no longer rely on the major powers for their own security.

As a consequence of the evolving geo-strategic environment faced by the region, ASEAN agreed to the Declaration for a Zone of Peace, Freedom and Neutrality (ZOPFAN) in 1971. Aside from a reassessment of extra-regional security dependencies – including a subsequent goal to construct a non-threatening regional security order independent of the United States – ZOPFAN represented the reinvigoration of Indonesia's vision for a regional order free from foreign interference as seen in the Bandung, the Maphilindo, SEAARC and the Bangkok Declaration.[125] Given these considerations, ZOPFAN expressed a desire to remove all foreign bases from the soil of the ASEAN member states. However, ASEAN never really moved beyond an expression of intent as the document was not binding in nature, it contained no concrete steps or dates for implementation and was sufficiently ambiguous to allow each of the ASEAN members to develop their own unique interpretation of the agreement.[126] Furthermore, the ongoing Cold War (together with a continued divergence of security perspectives) meant that Thailand and the Philippines were reluctant to dispense with US bases and the security they offered; meanwhile Singapore was hesitant to give up the power balancing approach that continues to represent a central pillar of its foreign policy.[127]

The limitations of ZOPFAN notwithstanding, the declaration was significant for representing a political compromise by Malaysia when it abandoned its neutralization policy. According to Malaysia, neutralization involved the pursuit of guarantees from the great powers that they would not pursue their disputes in Southeast Asia. The problem was that this policy relied on exactly what Indonesia was trying to avoid: continued dependence on foreign powers for security in return for a guarantee of neutrality by the ASEAN states. As Indonesia perceived itself as a leader within the Non-Aligned Movement (NAM) – and given Indonesia's role in the formulation of the Bandung Principles – the pursuit of regional security via the Malaysian formula was not acceptable.[128] Therefore, aside from the preamble, the final declaration contained just two clauses, with the most significant (but ambiguous) component stating that the ASEAN states were determined to 'secure the recognition of, and respect for, Southeast Asia as a *Zone of Peace, Freedom and Neutrality*, free from any form or manner of interference by outside Powers'.[129] Nevertheless, a perceived association with Malaysia's policy of 'neutralization', *inter alia*, led to opposition by China and Vietnam, including Vietnamese allegations that ZOPFAN represented another example of American imperialism.[130]

The ZOPFAN declaration was, however, more historically significant as a marker of the normative direction that the ASEAN states were heading and, perhaps, also of the initiative's effect on the salience of these norms. Similar to the Bangkok Declaration, the ZOPFAN initiative articulated the continued desire of the ASEAN states to abide by the principles of the United Nations Charter. However, the preamble of the ZOPFAN document moved beyond the wording of the Bangkok Declaration by stating explicitly that the most 'worthy aims and objectives of the United Nations' were 'the principles of respect for the sovereignty and territorial integrity of all states, abstention from threat or use of force, peaceful settlement of international disputes, equal rights and self-determination and non-interference in affairs of States'.[131] The gradual solidification of these normative values in the Bangkok Declaration, ZOPFAN, and later instruments, is partially explained by their consistency with the Suharto (New Order) regime's philosophy and policy of national resilience (*ketahanan national)* that emerged in the late 1960s.[132]

National resilience is understood as the pursuit of national stability, independence and sovereignty on the basis of national development. Such national development covers all the social, cultural, ideological, political and economic aspects of nation-building. According to the philosophy of national resilience, the security of the state is also considered dependent on an environment that is unhampered by external and domestic security threats. Reflective of an empirical connection with the concept of *internal consolidation*, the ASEAN members believed that when a state overcame internal issues (e.g. the dangers of subversion) then it would become a more viable entity where insurgencies and ethnic separatism would be prevented from 'infecting neighbouring states'.[133] This reasoning also evolved into a consensus that the greater stability generated by national resilience would also contribute to 'regional resilience'. In turn, the pursuit of regional resilience would also support 'national resilience' through the creation of stable sets of inter-mural relations that would enable the ASEAN members to divert more resources towards economic development.[134] Thus, the ASEAN states have traditionally adhered to a conviction that each member is in the best position to decide its specific path to national resilience. However, this philosophy has also enabled sometimes brutal nation-building policies with the knowledge that other ASEAN members will not respond with any public denunciation.[135] Given the above goals and practices, it becomes somewhat less surprising that the ASEAN states found it necessary to repeat their reference to the principle of 'non-interference' (or a paraphrase thereof) four times within the ZOPFAN document.

Conclusions

The existence of Southeast Asia as a distinct region was largely a consequence of the strategic dynamics of the Second World War and, in particular, the establishment of Lord Louis Mountbatten's Southeast Asia Military Command. The fact that Southeast Asia only became an identifiable region during the course of the twentieth century was further verified by the perceptions of elites from Southeast Asia (the elite level survey) together with the fact that, prior to independence, the differences between the indigenous communities of Southeast Asia far outweighed the similarities. Consequently, there never existed a precolonial regionwide identity. To the extent that interactions have occurred between the Southeast Asian communities, such interactions (transactions) were frequently antagonistic. While colonialism and the mutual struggles for independence that ensued represented one of the few common experiences in Southeast Asia, Southeast Asia's colonial past did not always represent a common force for mutual identification. Here, colonialism also split ethno-religious communities through the arbitrary delineation of borders, it exacerbated the diversity of religion through the introduction of Christianity (e.g. the Philippines), and contributed to divergent strategic alignments (and dependencies) in line with each of the original ASEAN members' former 'colonial masters'. Thus, between the time of independence and through to the formation of ASEAN, many of the Southeast Asian elite knew more about their former rulers than they did about their own neighbours.

Notwithstanding the limitations to socio-cultural integration above, the region underwent a period of rapid and sometimes tumultuous transition following independence. During this period, foreign powers imposed an ideological basis for a division in the region's identities – capitalism in the 'South' and communism in the 'North'. Meanwhile, the two superpowers (the Soviet Union and the United States), together with an emerging power (China), vied for regional influence. Consequently, some of the early attempts to undertake regionalist projects were either explicitly driven by these Cold War cleavages (e.g. SEATO) or were alternatively suspected of being a part of them (e.g. ASPAC and the ASA). With the exception of the FPDA they all failed. Other attempts at regionalism also failed, such as the Maphilindo, due to intra-regional hostilities. Nonetheless, a mutual desire for regime survival in the face of common challenges (domestic and transnational) eventually contributed to greater collaboration and the pursuit of a more sustainable regionalist project between the capitalist states in Southeast Asia. In the absence of such a modus vivendi, the capitalist states believed that that regional hostility and distrust would continue unabated and thereby detract from the level of internal consolidation (national resilience) necessary for regime survival. The collaboration that followed culminated in the formation of ASEAN in 1967.

Beyond the overarching strategic concerns of the original members of ASEAN, each state had more specific motivations for joining the Association. Singapore, while remaining intensely suspicious of Malaysian and Indonesian motives, hoped that membership would help consolidate a national and regional identity for the country and Lee Kuan Yew, Singapore's Prime Minister, also hoped that membership would reinforce recognition of Singapore's sovereignty.[136] The Philippines similarly viewed ASEAN as a means of creating a new region-wide identity that would help it escape a perception that it remained a 'trans-Pacific appendage to the United States'.[137] Meanwhile, Thailand saw the formation of ASEAN as a potential basis of 'collective political defence' that could eventually alleviate its security dependence on the United States.[138] Malaysia, for its part, hoped that ASEAN would provide a vehicle to mend regional relations and that ASEAN would provide an opportunity for it to become more independent in its security relations which, in the process, would fill the vacuum left by the retreat of the colonial powers.[139] Finally, Indonesia viewed ASEAN as an opportunity for regional reconciliation, as a chance to exercise regional leadership, and as an opportunity to reduce the ability of external powers to interfere in the affairs of Southeast Asia (regional resilience).[140] Again, even at the individual state level of analysis, the *end goal* underpinning the motivations behind ASEAN's formation was primarily intramural, having stemmed from the specific necessity of enhancing the level of domestic stability through economic development and regional cooperation.[141]

The history of the region indicates a very low level of complex integration between the ASEAN states through to the time of the Association's formation. Thus, the establishment of ASEAN necessitated a modus operandi akin to Indonesia's philosophy of 'unity in diversity' where the principles of non-interference, state sovereignty and consensus-based decision-making were central to what became known as the 'ASEAN Way'. Furthermore, given the previously noted consensus that each state should decide its own pathway to obtaining national resilience, any cooperation between the member-states was to be at all times mutually beneficial and of mutual interest with an absolute assertion of sovereignty as well as an unqualified right of veto. Consequently, both ASEAN's formative instrument, the Bangkok Declaration, together with ZOPFAN four years later, were undemanding, lacked any binding commitments, and avoided supranational institutionalization. Given these humble beginnings, ASEAN's project to forge a security community represents a significant evolution in the purposes and institutional design of ASEAN. Whether or not ASEAN can muster the level of collaboration and cooperation necessary to realize such goals will continue to be considered and critiqued throughout the remaining chapters. Meanwhile, the next chapter will follow on from this chapter by reviewing the institutional performance of ASEAN through to its third decade.

3 ASEAN through to the third decade

Institutional responses and expansion

In building on the analysis of the previous chapter, this chapter evaluates the historical performance of ASEAN through to the immediate years after the collapse of the Soviet Union and the end of the Cold War. In carrying out this task, the first section examines ASEAN's performance during the Cold War and illustrates that, despite an initial period of distrust and animosity, exogenous issues and threats eventually induced a convergence of interests. The ASEAN states responded to this through greater collaboration including the presentation of a more unified diplomatic voice within international society. Furthermore, to the extent that ASEAN has contributed to a region-wide identity, the section demonstrates how a nascent elite-level *collective identity* was tentatively seeded by the second decade of ASEAN's existence. During this period, the ASEAN members discovered the utility of exercising a collective diplomatic voice and this was applied against a common external threat – Vietnam's occupation of Cambodia.

While the second section outlines how ASEAN survived the Cold War with a heightened sense of self-confidence and international stature, the emerging multi-polar world order has generated greater unpredictability and, eventually, created a new set of challenges for ASEAN. ASEAN responded through a multi-pronged approach that attempted to deepen the level of regional cooperation, expand ASEAN's membership to embrace all of Southeast Asia, and sought to expand its diplomatic voice through the establishment of the ASEAN Regional Forum. Nonetheless, ASEAN continued to struggle with the coordination of foreign policies and remained vulnerable to the influence (and interference) of extra-regional actors. Most significantly, the diversity of the region meant that the Association continued to avoid any significant form of regional institutionalization and legally binding arrangements.

Institutional progress amidst external volatility

The first ASEAN summit of national leaders was held at Bali in 1976 and was partly motivated by concern over a possible communist 'domino effect' following the successful reunification of Vietnam and communist victories in Laos and Cambodia in 1975.[1] However, the Bali Summit also reflected a growing belief in, if not occurrence of, the need for foreign policy coordination and regional institutionalization. The Summit led to the creation of the ASEAN Secretariat together with an agreement over the *Treaty of Amity and Cooperation* (TAC) and the *ASEAN Concord*. These agreements followed more than two years of negotiations with the decision for a Secretariat, together with an initial proposal by the Philippines for an actual Charter, having been previously agreed to at the seventh ASEAN Ministerial Meeting (AMM) held in Jakarta in May 1974.[2] While neither the TAC nor the ASEAN Concord represented an actual legal charter, collectively the documents are significant for acknowledging the mutual interdependence of security and for further embedding, at least rhetorically, ASEAN's norms including the concept of sovereign equality, freedom from external coercion, the peaceful settlement of disputes and the renunciation of force against one another.[3]

In the case of the ASEAN Concord, its primary focus was on the economic aspects of security through four areas of cooperation: basic commodities (food and energy in particular); industrial projects and plants; trade liberalization; and joint approaches to global economic problems.[4] In addition, the instrument was also important for expanding ASEAN's modus vivendi to an *in principle* consideration of political cooperation as well as cooperation in the economic and socio-cultural fields.[5] In relation to security, and given the organization's concerns about Vietnam and China, the Concord condoned continued military cooperation on a 'non-ASEAN basis' but rejected the potentiality of such cooperation on an ASEAN basis due to concerns (among other things) about hostile reactions from Vietnam and China. Thus, the document reiterated ASEAN's endorsement of ZOPFAN but this was now more specifically expressed as an 'aspiration' rather than a corporate objective. The ASEAN Concord is further important for formally endorsing *national resilience* and *regional resilience* as ASEAN goals.[6]

In the context of the TAC, it is important for being open to accession by non-Southeast Asian states. The TAC also affirms the notion of 'non-interference in the internal affairs of one another' as a core principle.[7] At one level, this norm has assisted in the continuation of the sometimes brutal nation-building policies adopted by some ASEAN states in the pursuit of national resilience. However, for smaller states such as Singapore, the principle of non-interference had been rendered all the more important because of events such as Indonesia's invasion of Timor Leste the previous year. The TAC also endorsed and codified several subsidiary norms, principles and purposes including:

> Mutual respect for the independence, sovereignty, equality, territorial integrity, and national identity of all nations; The right of every state to lead its national existence free from external interference, subversion or coercion; Settlement of differences or disputes by peaceful means; Renunciation of the threat or use of force; Effective cooperation among themselves.[8]

In the context of non-interference, Articles 14 and 15 of the TAC also provide for a latent contradiction – the possible formation of a High Council for the purpose of dispute resolution.[9] The idea of a High Council was put forward by the Philippine government but it has never been invoked by the ASEAN members. Furthermore, there is an escape clause (Article 16) where no party to a dispute will be bound by the High Council unless they first agree to take part in such mediation.

As mentioned, Laos, Cambodia and South Vietnam had all 'fallen' to communism by the end of 1975. Of these countries, the newly reunified Vietnam was by far the most militarily powerful, with the potential to seek and sustain regional hegemony. Due to a continued divergence in threat perceptions and strategic alignment, together with an inability to influence events within Indochina, ASEAN initially sought a 'policy of accommodation' with Vietnam.[10] Thus, in mid-1975 the Association proposed the establishment of cooperative relations (but not membership) with communist Indochina.[11] However, Vietnam quickly rebuffed ASEAN's call for a 'friendly and harmonious' relationship and instead tried to publically discredit the organization. Thus, Vietnam denounced the Bali Summit and called for ASEAN's termination.[12] Given further hostile rhetoric, some ASEAN members became suspicious that Vietnam was supporting other revolutionary movements within ASEAN territory.[13] Vietnam also continued to object to ZOPFAN and, at the 1976 NAM conference in Colombo, it blocked the inclusion of the ZOPFAN principles in the final communiqué whilst submitting a counterproposal for 'genuine neutrality'.[14] Two years later, at the June 1978 UN Special Session on Disarmament, Vietnam alienated ASEAN further by 'reinvigorating its own vision for regional order through a proposed Zone of *Genuine* Independence, Peace and Neutrality.[15]

Over time, Vietnam adopted a more nuanced diplomatic approach by attempting to build its bilateral relationships with certain ASEAN members.[16] Then, in 1977, Vietnam dropped its 'stick' and signalled a willingness to be more hospitable towards ASEAN as a multilateral institution. In late 1978, this 'peace offensive' peaked with a September to October tour of the ASEAN states by Prime Minister Pham Van Dong. However, prior to his arrival, extensive consultations took place between the ASEAN governments in order to ensure a unified ASEAN position.[17] Accordingly, when Vietnam pushed for a new regional order based on *bilateral* treaties of friendship, all the ASEAN members declined Vietnam's offer of a non-aggression treaty.[18] This unity was indicative of the growing cohesiveness of ASEAN in the face of the 'common' external threats. However, these early displays of solidarity were tested on 25 December 1978 when – just two months after Vietnam had pledged to 'scrupulously respect each other's independence, sovereignty, and territorial integrity' in the region – Hanoi occupied Cambodia.[19]

The height of solidarity: early ASEAN responses to the invasion of Cambodia

In retrospect, the diplomatic olive branches offered by Vietnam – including its non-aggression treaties – represented strategic components of an overall plan to respond militarily to what it saw as an emerging threat to Vietnamese security – Cambodia.[20] Moreover, Hanoi's refusal to engage ASEAN multilaterally had been designed to divide the members over strategic issues in the hope that it could weaken ASEAN solidarity and thereby prevent a collective response to its actions in Cambodia.[21] Aside from Vietnam's own strategic motivations for entering Cambodia – including 'self-defence' and a sense of vulnerability vis-à-vis China – Vietnam's overthrow of the genocidal Khmer Rouge in Cambodia served an arguably humanitarian purpose.[22] Nonetheless, ASEAN solidarity held and the Association quickly indicted Vietnam for breaching the principles of 'territorial sovereignty and non-interference in the internal affairs of another state'.[23] While ASEAN lacked the capacity and intention to physically eject Vietnam from Cambodia, it did manage to rely on the use of collective diplomacy for the purpose of diplomatically isolating Vietnam in the United Nations and denying international recognition of the People's Republic of Kampuchea (PRK) – the Vietnamese-installed government in Cambodia.[24]

The early phases of the Cambodia crisis represented the most successful period of collective diplomacy in the Association's forty-five year history. ASEAN's mobilization of international diplomatic support, together with its backing for armed Khmer resistance, significantly increased the political and economic costs for the Vietnamese military to remain in Cambodia. These achievements brought international respect to the Association and they marked a turning point where its diplomatic voice was enlarged from economic affairs to an influence over major security issues; a goal that was initially envisioned in the Bali Summit agreements.[25] As a consequence of this 'collective-political defence with an extra-mural point of reference', Michael Leifer has suggested that ASEAN maintains some utility as a 'diplomatic community'.[26] Notwithstanding these achievements, ASEAN's early responses to the Cambodian issue more significantly reflected a common concern about vulnerability to external interference rather than a common identity or political cohesion. Thus, Michael Leifer argues that aside from 'the credibility of the Association being called into question', '[t]he member governments were conscious, therefore, of the implications of endorsing, even by default, a precedent which might be applied in the future to one of their number.'[27] Nonetheless, there has been a tendency by some regional scholars to exaggerate regional solidarity and their analysis has at times neglected to acknowledge the continuation of divergent strategic perceptions in relation to both security threats and economic challenges regardless of whether they are intra-mural or extra-mural in nature. Thailand's response to the Cambodian issue provides a case in point.

Despite continued distrust of China, Thailand's sense of vulnerability as a frontline state during the conflict led to a limited alliance between Thailand and China. Consequently, Thailand permitted the Chinese military to enter its territory to provide military assistance to the Khmer Rouge.[28] Moreover, this alliance evinced a judgement by the Thai government that the level of threat generated by the Cambodia crisis rendered any consideration of 'ASEAN cohesion' a secondary issue in its foreign policy calculations.[29] Thailand's alliance with China, the aim of which was to balance against and contain Vietnam and the Soviet Union, peaked with a one month long punitive attack by China against Vietnam's northern border in February 1979. Unofficial Thai support for the attack was intended to weaken Vietnam and thereby avert future incursions by the Vietnamese military across Thailand's border with Cambodia. However, the deterrent value of the action was undermined when the Chinese forces performed feebly against the Vietnamese defenders.[30] Meanwhile, China's attack of Vietnam heightened the distrust of China held by other ASEAN members and also raised concerns about the potential escalation of Soviet support for Vietnam. Consequently, ASEAN pressured Thailand to join an ASEAN declaration that called for 'countries outside [the] … region to exert utmost restraint and to refrain from any action which might lead to escalation of violence and the spreading of the conflict'.[31]

Meanwhile, and contrary to Thailand's approach, Indonesia and Malaysia were primarily concerned about the growing military strength of China and viewed Vietnam as a counterbalance to a potentially hegemonic China. The two countries responded to these threat perceptions through the Kuantan statement in March 1980. The statement was engineered outside the collective diplomacy of ASEAN by Indonesia and Malaysia and this breach generated divisions between the ASEAN members. The Kuantan statement was grounded in the philosophy of the ZOPFAN and thereby acknowledged the security concerns of Vietnam in Indochina (i.e. China) whilst simultaneously calling for an end to Soviet influence vis-à-vis Hanoi.[32] Because the statement emerged out of differences in strategic perceptions, it never became a part of ASEAN's official position due to strong objections from Thailand and Singapore.[33] Nevertheless, and despite a temporary reconciliation between the ASEAN members over the Association's 'official position',[34] the rift between the ASEAN members continued to grow during the next three years and eventually spilled into the public domain at the 1983 NAM Summit in New Delhi.

During the NAM Summit, both the Malaysian and Vietnamese foreign ministers privately met to discuss the possibility of informal talks outside the official 'International Conference of Cambodia' formula. They agreed on a 'five plus two' formula where the ASEAN states would meet with Vietnam and Laos as a two party block.[35] While Singapore and Indonesia supported the initiative, it floundered over strong Chinese objections that in turn led to opposition by Thailand.[36] For Indonesia, the loss of an opportunity to resolve the Cambodian crisis, and China's interference with ASEAN's diplomacy, was difficult to tolerate. The Indonesian leadership, moreover, believed that ASEAN could not benefit from bringing about the collapse of Vietnam as such an event would invite further Chinese influence in Cambodia and could indefinitely entrench the Russians in Vietnam. Given these considerations, Indonesia sent its military chief to Hanoi, in February 1984, to unilaterally initiate its own channels for dialogue with Vietnam. Meanwhile, ASEAN attempted to hide this breach in solidarity through a policy for 'dual track diplomacy' that retrospectively appointed Indonesia as its official 'interlocutor' with Vietnam.[37]

Indonesia's unilateralism eventually resulted in a breakthrough when Jakarta announced a plan for two informal meetings. The first informal meeting took place in July 1988 and the second in February 1989.[38] However, soon after the first meeting, Thailand's military leadership announced an intention to turn the Indochinese 'battlefields into marketplaces'; this announcement constituted a complete about-face in its Indochina policy. Rather than consult ASEAN about the policy, Thailand immediately entered into direct dialogue with Vietnam, Laos and Cambodia (the People's Republic of Kampuchea) with the promise of economic benefits through cross-border trade.[39] The Thai Prime Minister also invited the new head of the PRK government, Prime Minister Hun Sen, to Bangkok. Not only did the invitation occur just a month before the second set of ASEAN negotiations with Hanoi, but the Prime Minister's actions also provided de facto recognition and added legitimacy to the PRK government that further undermined ASEAN's diplomatic efforts.[40] Nonetheless, the second set of negotiations between ASEAN and Hanoi faltered over whether the PRK should be dismantled prior to elections and there was also disagreement concerning the structure and functions of an international body to oversee the elections and any transition of power that would follow.[41]

ASEAN's inability to finalize a settlement to the crisis resulted in an enlargement of the peace process to nineteen nations – including France and Australia – at the Paris International Conference on Cambodia (PICC). However, Indonesia maintained a key role as the conference's chair. The first session of the conference ended in a deadlock and, in its wake, the agenda for a resolution to the crisis was seized by the five permanent members of the United Nations Security Council (UNSC). Eventually, the UNSC secured a final Peace Accord but this was primarily a consequence of dramatic changes in the great-power dynamics of the time rather than any intra-regional diplomacy. The Soviet Union and the Cold War were in their final days and the Soviet President, Mikhail Gorbachev, sought to normalize relations with China in an effort to rebuild the Soviet economy. Once the Sino-Soviet element of the Cambodian crisis had been removed, it was far easier to form a Great Power consensus over the terms of settlement.[42] Consequently, on 18 August 1990 the five permanent members of the UNSC adopted a framework agreement for a comprehensive settlement and this agreement was endorsed two months later, on 15 October 1990, by the United Nations General Assembly (UNGA). Despite an official end to the Third Indochina War, the continuation of resistance from the Khmer Rouge meant that it would be several more years before the United Nation's Transitional Authority of Cambodia (UNTAC) installed nation-wide peace.

The 1992 Singapore Summit: new directions for a new era

The ASEAN members were keenly aware that a key element of what had driven their unity, namely, common threat perceptions, had dissipated with the conclusion of the Cambodia issue and the end of the Cold War. Consequently, in order to ensure the continued utility of ASEAN it became necessary to seek a new modus vivendi. In the context of ASEAN's self-declared aspirations this would not be too difficult. The Cambodian issue may have occupied the minds of the ASEAN leadership for more than a decade, but the formation of ASEAN had also been motivated by the necessity for greater regionalism in order to address common *intramural* challenges. In this sense, ASEAN simply returned to its original *raison d'être* by pursuing national and regional resilience through enhanced intramural cooperation. Thus, the leader's statement at the fourth ASEAN summit in Singapore (January 1992) pledged 'to move towards a higher plane of political and economic cooperation'. Additionally, the Association institutionalized itself further by strengthening the role of the ASEAN Secretariat including the conferral of 'ministerial status' to the 'Secretary-General of ASEAN'. The member-states also increased their diplomatic investment in ASEAN by committing to undertake a formal Heads of Government meeting at least every three years together with informal gatherings in the interim.[43] The Declaration was also notable for reaffirming the Association's desire to welcome the remaining Southeast Asian states to accede to its Treaty of Amity and Cooperation (TAC).

The Singapore Summit provided a further reaffirmation of the desirability of ZOPFAN and, as a tangible step towards its realization, declared a goal to establish a Southeast Asian Nuclear Weapon Free Zone (SEANWFZ). While SEANWFZ had been mooted as early as 1971,[44] the end of both the Cambodian conflict and the Cold War, together with the removal of US bases, had generated a comparatively better environment to reinvigorate, negotiate and implement the treaty. Thus, at the 25th AMM, the Association reconvened a Senior Officials Meeting (SOM) 'working group' to move toward a final proposal for the treaty and, on 15 December 1995, the ASEAN members acceded to the SEANWFZ.[45] However, as Leifer asserts, the treaty was primarily 'symbolic' as the signatories continued to allow foreign powers to bring nuclear weapons and nuclear powered transport into their respective territories.[46] Moreover, while the treaty prohibited the manufacture, storage or testing of nuclear weapons (or allowing foreign states to use their territory for these activities), such agreement was not difficult as the signatories lacked the intention and capacity to pursue such activities.[47] Nevertheless, the United States and China were initially suspicious of SEANWFZ. In the case of the US, it was needlessly concerned about the passage of its nuclear warships and aircraft. However, in the case of China, its primary concern was related to an already emerging dispute in connection with the South China Sea (see Chapter 4).

The Singapore Summit was also notable for announcing an agreement to establish an ASEAN Free Trade Area (AFTA) by 2007.[48] The proposal for AFTA built on the Common Effective Preferential Tariff Scheme (CEPT), a programme that had been agreed to earlier in the year and now represents a key source of elite-driven economic integration. Such policies were necessary as intra-ASEAN trade had remained marginal – at less than 15 per cent of total trade – despite previous attempts to deepen such trade.[49] While some hailed AFTA as a 'landmark agreement', it was hedged with conditions, qualifications, and escape clauses so that the domestic pain that liberalized trade might cause could be minimized.[50] AFTA notwithstanding, the ability of the ASEAN states to implement *tangible* steps for cooperation and integration continued to be limited by the competing interests entailed by political, economic and socio-cultural diversity. Not only did an incompatibility of interests between the ASEAN members generate a problematic paradox for regionalization, but also such diversity soon threatened the facade of unity that ASEAN had sought to portray internationally.

Public divisions between the ASEAN members soon emerged over how to achieve deeper economic and political cooperation and integration. During the two year lead-up to the Singapore Summit, Malaysia had attempted to establish the East Asian Economic Group (EAEG) which, due to extra-mural resistance, was later modified to an East Asian Economic Caucus (EAEC). The EAEC effectively proposed a protectionist block that did not include the United States or any regional neighbours such as Australia or New Zealand.[51] At the time, Malaysia had responded very negatively to an Australian initiative establishing the Asia-Pacific Economic Cooperation (APEC) forum in 1989.[52] Despite arguments by Malaysian Prime Minister Dr Mahathir bin Mohamad that the EAEC was a necessary response to the increasingly protectionist policies of the EU and the US, some of the ASEAN members rejected its exclusionary nature.[53] Rather than denote the next stage in ASEAN regionalism, the EAEC was notable for symbolizing the divisions in economic policy that had emerged between the ASEAN members. Some ASEAN elite, in retrospect, have attributed these divisions, including a lack of economic leadership, as having weakened ASEAN centrality thereby enabling outside powers to form institutions such as APEC. ASEAN, in an attempt to regain the ground it had lost, eventually agreed to disagree and simply declared that the Malaysian proposal should be studied further. Eventually, a face-saving formula emerged at the 1993 ASEAN Ministerial Meeting with the proposal establish the EAEC as 'a caucus within APEC'.[54] Nonetheless, in the context of the later ASEAN Plus Three meetings – the 'Plus Three' being China, South Korea and Japan (Chapter 7) – Mahathir 'may have had the last laugh' when he stated that 'we would be very happy if we stopped hiding behind this spurious title and called ourselves the East Asia Economic Group'.[55]

Membership expansion – insights and implications

ASEAN's membership expanded over time. Indeed, the eventual embrace of all the Southeast Asian states as members of ASEAN (with the notable exception of Timor Leste) had been a goal of the Association's founding fathers from the outset. For example, ASEAN had informally approached Myanmar and Cambodia about membership at the time of the Association's formation. However, the two countries declined due to their membership in NAM and the associated bipolar cleavages generated by the Cold War.[56] Nonetheless, despite the potential challenges of membership expansion, certain ASEAN elite believed that a larger ASEAN would enhance its ability to exercise a diplomatic voice that, as

Michael Leifer later assessed, would be 'greater than the sum of its parts'.[57] In particular, ASEAN hoped that the exercise of an expanded diplomatic voice would enhance its capacity to balance against, and influence, other larger powers in the Asia-Pacific including India, Japan and China.[58]

A further rationale behind membership expansion was the desire to pursue the formation of a unified economic (and perhaps political) block under the auspices of an 'ASEAN-10'. The looming economic blocs of Europe (the EU) and the Americas (the North American Free Trade Agreement, NAFTA) provided further motivation as there was the fear that Southeast Asia could, in the future, be afflicted by ruinous trade restrictions.[59] Enlargement was also considered to work well with ASEAN's ambitions for economic integration, as symbolized through AFTA, and an associated desire to increase investment incentives. An early indication of ASEAN's intention to establish a more integrated regional community (i.e. a human association whose members are bound by a collective identity, Chapter 1), together with its justification of an enlarged ASEAN-10, was echoed by the then President of the Philippines, Fidel Ramos, who stated that 'progress towards a *Southeast Asian community* would add considerable weight to ASEAN – in its influence in the world and in dealing with big powers'.[60]

The realization of an Association of Southeast Asian Nations with a region-wide constituency commenced with the membership of Brunei in 1984. Brunei's membership in ASEAN also marked an important point of reconciliation as Brunei had endured turbulent relations with Malaysia following the refusal of its Sultan to join the Federation of Malaysia.[61] However, beyond Brunei, membership expansion remained impossible until after the Cold War when the final historical constraint to enlargement was removed through the resolution of the Cambodian conflict. The ASEAN members subsequently proceeded with the formalities necessary to enable the remaining Southeast Asian states to join ASEAN. In 1995, Vietnam became the first CLMV country (Cambodia, Laos, Myanmar and Vietnam) to become a member. For Vietnam, ASEAN membership had become necessary as the economic costs of the war in Cambodia, together with the failure of socialist economic policies within Vietnam, had severely weakened the nation and its Communist party. Consequently, the Vietnamese government, at the sixth national congress, adopted a new policy of pursuing market-driven economics under the banner of *doi moi* (renovation).[62] The adoption of *doi moi* marked a shift in the values and goals of Vietnamese government in a manner that rendered its domestic and foreign policies more compatible with the ASEAN member-states and the overarching 'economic' precepts embraced by the Association.[63]

For similar reasons Laos was also able to become a member in 1997. The ruling Laotian People's Revolutionary Party (LPRP) remains a fully fledged communist party that – as with the regime in Myanmar – maintains a strong grip on power with little space for dissent. Nevertheless, in 1986, Laos also began experimenting with free market reforms (but with relatively less commitment than Vietnam) and, following the end of the Third Indochina War, the party's leadership became more open to the idea of ASEAN membership together with the international recognition and aid such membership could potentially generate.[64] While Myanmar acquired membership in 1997, and Cambodia in 1999, significant controversy surrounded the admission of both countries. In the case of Cambodia, some ASEAN states were concerned about political instability; whereas with Myanmar, there were concerns about its record of human rights abuse.

Cambodia had been expected to join ASEAN in 1997 with Myanmar and Laos. In preparation, Cambodia acceded to ASEAN's Treaty of Amity and Cooperation (TAC) in 1995, attended the AMM as an observer, and also joined the ASEAN Regional Forum (ARF). However, Hun Sen, originally under Vietnam's patronage, had started to adopt increasingly draconian measures to consolidate his power including the expulsion of an 'anti-corruption' Finance Minister from parliament and the imprisonment of the Foreign Minister on false 'conspiracy to assassinate' charges.[65] Then, just a few weeks before Cambodia's scheduled admission into ASEAN, Hun Sen instigated a violent coup against his coalition partner, the FUNCINPEC Party. The event marked a turning point in the debate surrounding Cambodia's admission as the timing of the coup was highly embarrassing for ASEAN and, moreover, demonstrated Hun Sen's disregard for the Association's interests.[66] The subsequent 'un-ASEAN-like squabble ... over admitting Cambodia to the Association' resulted in an indefinite delay of its admission.[67]

ASEAN initially continued to recognize the head of FUNCINPEC, Prince Norodom Rannaridh, as a joint-leader in the Cambodian government and put forth a proposal for a caretaker government to oversee scheduled elections in 1998. Hun Sen, however, dismissed the ASEAN proposal and 'bluntly told the organization to stay out of Cambodia's internal affairs'.[68] Despite a compromise agreement being reached between Hun Sen and ASEAN, where Hun Sen would hold elections in May 1998 and ASEAN would, in return, cease to demand the restoration of Prince Rannaridh to power, the East Asian financial crisis (1997–98) undermined ASEAN's political leverage. Consequently, Hun Sen reneged on his agreement whilst attacking ASEAN for preaching to Cambodia about democracy and issues of human rights when it could not even look after its own affairs.[69] In any event, Hun Sen's power was further consolidated and, on 30 April 1999, Cambodia became the most recent member of ASEAN. Since Cambodia's membership in ASEAN, the federal politics of Cambodia have not improved. Dr Chap Sotharith, a former academic, now working for Prime Minister Hun Sen, describes the sentiment of the ruling elite in the following manner:

> Hun Sen can ensure that security is good with no internal fighting and no coup d'état. However, there is a dilemma between democracy and authoritarianism. For example, there is a strong authoritarian element in both Malaysia and Singapore but it is because of this that the two countries are stable. Democracy destabilizes the country.... We are a weak state and we need stability more than anything else.[70]

In the case of Myanmar, its leadership attempted to end decades of diplomatic isolation by approaching Jakarta, in 1987, about the possibility of membership in an attempt to end decades of diplomatic isolation. However, the Indonesian response was not particularly enthusiastic and it indicated that it might only be prepared to provide 'observer status'.[71] In 1988, the issue was temporarily set aside following massive nationwide protests against the regime that garnered world attention. Nonetheless, and given the regime's refusal to accept the election result, along with several more years of instability with transnational consequences, first Thailand, and then ASEAN, started to reconsider their relations with Myanmar. While the policies of ASEAN concerning Myanmar are discussed in Chapters 5 and 6, the discussion below examines the initial reasoning behind the decision to admit Myanmar as a member.

Some of the motives behind Myanmar's admission dated back to when ASEAN first approached Myanmar about joining the Association and included 'geographic proximity, cultural similarities and [a] comparable security situation'.[72] Further, following the fall of the communist bloc, new opportunities *and* new challenges emerged. For example, the previous 'ideological divide' between the original ASEAN members and CLMV countries had been removed resulting in the earlier-mentioned Thai proposal to convert the Indochinese 'battlefields into marketplaces'. However, concerns about a possible 'China threat' lingered and these fears were compounded by China's growing military liaison with Myanmar. Consequently, some of the member-states hoped that the admission of Myanmar into ASEAN would lessen the country's dependence on China and thereby weaken China's influence.[73] ASEAN was further motivated by resistance from Western nations as the ASEAN leaders did not want to seen to bow to Western pressure. As discussed in Chapter 5, some members strongly defended the decision to admit Myanmar as a member of ASEAN on the basis that interaction through 'constructive engagement', rather than exclusion, would help improve the situation in Myanmar.[74] As General Jose Almonte, former advisor to President Ramos, stated in interview:

> There were real requests from outside the region to prevent Myanmar's membership in ASEAN but for us the issue of inclusion transcends human rights considerations. At [the] formation [of ASEAN] the original idea was one Southeast Asia and this was instructed by the gradual balkanization of the region since the sixteenth century as a consequence of colonization.[75]

The expansion of ASEAN also bore an obligation to support the political infrastructure of the new members and to facilitate an improved capacity to comply with the administrative, political and normative responsibilities of membership. The challenges in so doing were immense and were aptly exemplified through the problems of language and communications that ASEAN then faced in bringing the new members into the fold. As General Almonte states, 'in Laos only 32 people [spoke] English, not enough to join the hundreds of meetings we in ASEAN organize every year' and so ASEAN had to resolve the problem by bringing government officials from Laos, Vietnam and Cambodia to other members, such as the Philippines, to teach them English in preparation for membership.[76] However, while the original ASEAN members undertook such 'training and assistance programs', the advent of the economic crisis in midst of membership expansion took 'its toll on the commitment of the ASEAN-6 to the newer members' and the assistance provided became less than what was needed.[77]

As illustrated in Table 3.1, the economic gaps that existed at the time of membership enlargement were not significantly reduced during the decade that followed. Further, the gross domestic product (GDP) per capita (purchasing power parity, PPP) of three of the original ASEAN economies – the Philippines, Thailand and Indonesia – had not yet surpassed their pre-financial crisis levels of 1997. The advent of the crisis, together with a continued divide in the level of wealth, not only tested the ideal of *equality* in ASEAN's economic decision-making process, but also raised further questions over the level and extent of assistance that should be provided along with the extent to which 'special dispensations' should be afforded to ASEAN's so-called 'second-tier members'.[78] The issue of special dispensations had specific relevance to AFTA as membership expansion had not only complicated the approach to its implementation but had also prolonged the proposed schedule for its realization. Furthermore, the CLMV countries were (a) hesitant to grant most-favoured-nation status to their ASEAN counterparts; (b) delayed the finalization of lists for the Common Effective Preferential Tariff (CEPT) programme; and (c) have often failed to meet deadlines regarding tariff reductions along with the removal of non-tariff barriers.[79]

The impact of membership expansion on regional solidarity, cooperation and integration has also received significant scholarly interest based on a perception that inadequate long-term socialization rendered interest harmonization and policy coordination all the more difficult. According to this perspective, a degree of mutual identification between the original ASEAN members had evolved as a

Table 3.1 Shifts in ASEAN GDP per capita (PPP) ($)

Country	*Per capita GDP–PPP (1997)*	*Per capita GDP–PPP (2007)*
Singapore	24,600	49,900
Brunei	18,000	51,000
Malaysia	11,100	14,500
Thailand	8,800	**8,000**
Indonesia	4,600	**3,600**
Philippines	3,200	**3,200**
Vietnam	1,700	2,600
Myanmar	1,190	1,900
Laos	1,150	2,000
Cambodia	715	1,900

Source: author, based on statistics located at http://strategicasia.nbr.org.

coincidence of history through a 'shared anti-communist ideology, experiences with communist insurgency, and security bonds with the west'.[80] However, the new CLMV members had endured a different set of historical memories and processes of socialization. An example of a continued differentiation in the identities between the Indochina countries and first tier ASEAN members occurred soon after the financial crisis. In this instance, the heads of government from Vietnam, Laos and Cambodia attended a separate meeting in Vientiane in October 1999 where, as Leifer summarized, '[t]hey stressed the need to further strengthen their *traditional solidarity* which recalled the political polarization of Southeast Asia during the height of the Cambodian conflict during the 1990s'.[81] In part, the meeting had been called because the CLMV countries were disillusioned with ASEAN as they had expected that membership would not only provide collateral benefits in terms of 'internal stability and economic development', but would also produce greater 'political credibility and legitimacy'.[82] The economic crisis, however, weakened the capacity of ASEAN to deliver on these fronts. As membership enlargement has weighed heavily on cooperation and institutionalization within ASEAN, the material and ideational effects of enlargement will continue to be assessed at appropriate junctures in the remaining chapters. In the meantime, the next section examines the motivations behind, and consequences of, another form of expansion: institutionalized engagement beyond Southeast Asia.

Exogenous engagement: from dialogue partners to the ASEAN regional forum

The extra-regional security and economic challenges faced by the ASEAN states during and after the Cold War also rendered it increasingly necessary to extend the Association's diplomatic voice beyond Southeast Asia. Thus, through the institutionalization of formal structures for engagement, it was initially hoped that ASEAN could secure better access to global markets while collectively balancing against (and influencing) the impact (and behaviour) of major powers ranging from the United States and Europe to China and Japan. In this context, one of the first initiatives for extra-regional engagement was the establishment of the ASEAN Post-Ministerial Conference (PMC) in 1978. The PMC is a collective forum where the ASEAN members meet with their 'official dialogue partners'. These dialogue partners include Australia, Japan, New Zealand, Canada, the Republic of Korea, China, India, Russia and the United States.[83] In 2004, the Indonesian Chair of ASEAN introduced a change of format in an attempt to encourage more open dialogue between the participants. Consequently, ASEAN now meets with each of the dialogue partners individually (referred to as the PMC 10+1) before a more multilateral retreat and a dinner with all the ASEAN members and all the dialogue partners in attendance.

Given the importance of the vast import and export markets in Europe, ASEAN also established the ASEAN–EU Ministerial Meeting and, with some overlap, several Asian states sought to further advance their dialogue with

Europe through the establishment of Asia–Europe Meeting (ASEM) in 1996. ASEM, however, is not a specific ASEAN institution as membership on the Asian side initially included China but excluded Myanmar (an ASEAN member) due to international controversy surrounding human rights in the country. Nonetheless, today the ASEM countries represent 60 per cent of global trade and 60 per cent of the global population.[84]

Over time, the imperatives for enhanced extra-regional engagement and dialogue grew. In part, this was a consequence of a perception that the emerging security order was less stable;[85] a security order that was no longer determined by the hegemonic competition of the Cold War. Given this, some ASEAN elite were concerned that the allegiance of individual states would become more fluid as the foreclosure of the Cold War meant that there was no longer a clearly defined threat around which the broader Asia-Pacific region 'could organize regional alliances'.[86] Moreover, political elites were concerned that the dominance of traditional restraints against the coercive actions of other major powers – such as China in the South China Sea – was at risk as a result of systemic changes in power and hierarchy. Finally, the ASEAN states were also concerned about their increased vulnerability to extra-regional economic and security developments as a consequence of a more globalized and interdependent world.

Given the nature of these concerns, ASEAN realized that it would not be possible to achieve regional resilience through the pursuit of isolation from extramural influences. Rather, and in the best possible scenario, the Association could seek to manage how these forces interacted with, and influenced, Southeast Asia.[87] ASEAN responded to these concerns through a number of strategies. First, the ASEAN states hoped to develop a mechanism to maintain US engagement in the region to balance against rising Chinese power. Second, the ASEAN members hoped to engage China via a functional commitment to a comprehensive network of multilateral relations.[88] Third, it was hoped that such engagement would socialize China into more benign conduct along the lines of the ASEAN Way. Finally, the ASEAN states hoped to speak with a single diplomatic voice on extra-regional issues and, to the extent that this was possible, the ASEAN states would also be able to exercise greater leverage and leadership on political and security issues with an extra-regional bearing. Given these imperatives, ASEAN has launched several initiatives for extra-regional engagement including the ASEAN 10+3 (APT), the 'Asian Cooperation Dialogue' (ACD), the East Asia Summit (EAS) and the ASEAN Regional Forum (ARF). Of these initiatives, the ARF has been widely considered to represent the key institution for security dialogue beyond Southeast Asia through to the turn of the century. Moreover, the ARF also provides an interesting case study of the interplay between regional and extra-regional forces.

Prior to the formation of the ARF the viability of ASEAN's aspiration to be a leader in regional engagement, consultation and dialogue had been threatened through a number of competing proposals to address the many security issues that afflicted the Asia-Pacific. For example, in 1986, President Mikhail Gorbachev broached the idea of a Pacific Ocean security conference that would be loosely based on the Helsinki Conference prototype. During the next few years, several other non-ASEAN proposals for extra-regional security dialogue also emerged. For example, Australia's Foreign Minister Gareth Evans recommended the creation of a Council for Security and Cooperation in Asia (CSCA) that would be loosely modelled on the Council for Security and Cooperation in Europe (CSCE). While the ASEAN states rejected the initial proposal, the proposal led to the establishment, in 1993, of the less formal, but highly active, Track 2 Council for Security Cooperation in the Asia Pacific (CSCAP).[89] Meanwhile, the ASEAN-ISIS network, another Track 2 dialogue, eventually convinced ASEAN of the utility of expanding its PMC framework into a more institutionalized regional security forum. However, Japan, South Korea and Australia pre-empted ASEAN's plans by publicly suggesting exactly what ASEAN was going to announce – the use of the PMC as an enlarged mechanism for security dialogue.[90] The announcement caught ASEAN off-guard and reservations about the proposal were subsequently expressed by some ASEAN elite.[91]

Nonetheless, pressure to establish a security forum embracing the Asia-Pacific continued to mount and so ASEAN was forced to seize the initiative before other powers intervened. In so doing, the ASEAN members hoped that they could take the driver's seat so 'that they could channel rather than resist the momentum'.[92] Therefore, the ASEAN members decided to formally accept the 'Japanese proposal' a few days later adding that 'it is already a reality that security has become a proper topic for discussion within the PMC'.[93] The ASEAN states subsequently reached a formal agreement to create the ASEAN Regional Forum (ARF) at the Twenty-Sixth ASEAN Ministerial Meeting and Post-Ministerial Conference held in Singapore on 23–25 July 1993. The official purpose of the ARF is to 'foster … dialogue and consultation on political and security issues of common interest and concern'.[94] The ARF has since been characterized as an 'embryonic venture in multilateralism' involving an annual assembly of Foreign Ministers from each of its members.[95] Today, the ARF members include all the Southeast Asian states along with the United States, Canada, Russia, New Zealand, the European Union and a further fourteen states from the greater Asia-Pacific: Bangladesh, Sri Lanka, China, India, Japan, Mongolia, New Zealand, North Korea, Papua New Guinea, Pakistan, Russia, South Korea, Timor-Leste and the United States.

At the inaugural meeting of the ARF, held in Bangkok on 25 July 1994, ASEAN quickly sought to claim a proprietary role in the ARF; the speeches by the ASEAN leaders were therefore notable in the degree to which they focused on the centrality of ASEAN in the future of the ARF.[96] Further, the Chairman's Statement referred to the 1992 Singapore Summit as the declaratory origin of the initiative and confirmed the endorsement of Brunei Darussalam (by this time the sixth ASEAN member) as the Chair of the next ARF meeting. In the lead-up to the second ARF meeting, ASEAN worked on a concept paper detailing both the purposes of the ARF and plans for its future institutional development. The final paper was presented at the ARF meeting and sought to reinforce a 'pivotal role' for ASEAN including a declaration that 'ASEAN had undertaken the obligation to be the primary driving force of the ARF'.[97] While the remaining dialogue partners accepted ASEAN's leadership in the ARF, recent calls by Australia and Japan for new regional institutions have further challenged ASEAN centrality.[98]

The second ARF meeting adopted most of the recommendations made by the ASEAN Concept Paper concerning the normative and institutional structure of the ARF. Mirroring the process of consultation within ASEAN itself, one of the paper's guidelines for future meetings included the statement that 'they will be based on prevailing ASEAN norms' and therefore 'decisions should be made by consensus after careful and extensive consultations'.[99] The Concept Paper also confirmed that there should be an annual Ministerial Meeting for the ARF and that such meetings would occur immediately after the ASEAN Ministerial Meeting (AMM). The meetings were to be chaired by the host country on a rotating basis (the ASEAN Chair) as per the ASEAN system; non-ASEAN states would not chair the ARF. The concept paper argued against the establishment of a Secretariat and further recommended that any institutionalization of the forum should be avoided during the early phases of its existence. Not only was the substance of these recommendations adopted at the second meeting of the ARF, but the normative and operational framework proposed by ASEAN was actively supported by China because the absence of any legally binding commitments enabled China to benefit from engagement without any significant risk of pressure to either its domestic or foreign policies.

The acceptance of the ASEAN Way – including non-interference and the peaceful resolution of disputes – as a requirement for membership in the ARF was championed by some to be a successful confidence and security building measure (CSBM) that would moderate the risk of armed conflict within the greater Asia Pacific.[100] Further, the development of CSBMs more broadly has been an area where the ARF has been noted for its success. By 2000 the broad range of CSBMs included:

> [T]he distribution of Defence Policy Statements; the publication of defence White Papers; the preparation of annual submissions to the United Nations Register of Conventional Arms and the circulation of member submissions to ARF members; engagement in bilateral security dialogues, high-level defence contracts, and defence training exchanges since 1995; and participation in arms control, disarmament, and non-proliferation activities such as Comprehensive Test Ban Treaty, Chemical Weapons Convention, Convention on Conventional Weapons, Biological Weapons Convention, and Nuclear Non-Proliferation Treaty.[101]

Beyond these CSBMs, Prime Minister Mahathir proclaimed that ASEAN's institutions had successfully engaged China.[102] During the early years of the ARF, however, such engagement was not without disadvantages. For example, a further recommendation in ASEAN's original Concept Paper concerned the implementation of a three-stage process in security multilateralism involving mechanisms and institutions for the implementation of (a) CSBMs, (b) preventative diplomacy and (c) conflict resolution procedures.[103] However, the engagement of China necessitated certain concessions and one of these was a modification (no doubt symbolic) of the third and final goal for the institutionalization of the organization – namely, the development of conflict resolution procedures – towards the more ambiguous and less institutionalized goal of an 'elaboration of approaches to conflict'.[104] Further, the ARF is structurally designed to function on an ad hoc basis in order to accommodate resistance by China to the institutionalization of ARF's activities.[105] Thus, while Shaun Narine surmises that 'the ARF may represent a non-traditional, diplomatic approach toward managing a traditional security problem, in this case the emergence of a rising, revisionist power in China',[106] the next chapter details how China has continued to apply coercive measures in regard to territorial disputes within the Southeast China Sea. Aside from undermining the credibility of China and its 'peaceful rise', such developments raise questions about the extent to which the ARF has socialized its non-ASEAN counterparts into the norms of good conduct and peaceful relations.

Aside from China and the South China Sea, the ARF also avoids any discussion of other core security issues including the Taiwan Straits and the North Korean nuclear crisis. Paul Dibb argues that a contributory factor to this failure concerns the absence of an annual meeting of defence ministers.[107] However, the annual Shangri-La Dialogue, while not a part of the ARF framework, does involve defence ministers from the Asia-Pacific countries who have met annually since June 2002. Further, the Southeast Asian defence ministers (except Myanmar) did at least meet for the first time in May 2006 as a consequence of institutional developments within ASEAN.[108] Nonetheless, the absence of such dialogue within the ARF, together with the occurrence of new regional crises, has contributed to growing questions about the continued relevance of the ARF. Already various political elites, such as Jusuf Wanandi and Barry Desker, have called for a broadening of ARF leadership by inviting non-ASEAN members to co-chair the meeting. They argue that this would provide external powers with a greater stake in ensuring the success of the regional organization. Barry Desker adds that further initiatives could include the development of an ARF Secretariat; the de-linking of the ARF meeting from the AMM and PMC; and the elevation of the ARF to include summit meetings that would incorporate the participation of the leaders of all the member countries.[109]

Other weaknesses in the structures and regional effects of the ARF can also be seen. While the CSBMs above have made a contribution to trust and security in the Asia-Pacific region, several limitations remain as they neither include 'measures that seriously expose the capabilities of military hardware and software, nor those that necessitate significant policy coordination among the militaries of the member states'.[110] Further, the ARF has failed to progress beyond the first phase of confidence building to the implementation of preventative diplomacy or an elaboration of any substantive approaches to conflict. The negative consequences of ASEAN's attempts to be accordant with Chinese concerns have been compounded by an already existent aversion to supranational institutionalization; a preference system that is a natural consequence of diverging political systems and the interdependent principles of the ASEAN Way. Thus, despite the achievement of bringing China into a multilateral forum, the ARF has been criticized as little more than a 'talk shop' for great powers to have informal discussions about whatever is important to them at the time.[111] Four parallel criticisms of the ARF include: the difficulty of policy coordination due to the diversity of membership; its ASEAN-style reliance on consensus based decision-making; the associated effects of limited institutionalization; and the way in which it defines political stability, human rights and regional security.[112] A contrary criticism has been that a focus on peripheral and uncontroversial issues has, ironically, rendered it easier to reach a consensus and thereby maintain an 'aura' of success.[113] Moreover, while the utility of the ARF as a forum for dialogue is evidenced by its survival nearly two decades from its inception, the creation of the East Asia Summit – together with the planned expansion to include the US and Russia – has now endangered any political relevance the ARF had hitherto retained.

Conclusions

Some regional scholars have reviewed the period covered by this chapter and argued that the ASEAN Way has made a significant contribution to regional security and economic development. As noted in the previous chapter, the ASEAN Way *did* represent a necessary foundation to the Association's modus operandi due to the strategic, political, economic and socio-cultural diversity of the region. Moreover, such diversity has been exacerbated through membership expansion. Conveniently, and perhaps even necessarily, the ASEAN unity in diversity approach – which stems from the norm of consensualism – allowed for, and indeed justified, the existence of a variety of regimes ranging from semi-authoritarian to military dictatorships.[114] The Philippines and its catch cry chant of 'people power' was viewed as an exception – even an aberration – to the normative values of the region. In truth, however, economic growth and the associated 'performance legitimacy' such growth delivers represented the key foundation to the security of both the region and its governments.[115] Thus, the Singapore Summit, via the proposal for AFTA, effectively cemented economic cooperation and integration as an official component of ASEAN's agenda.

Despite some initial hostility between Singapore and Malaysia as well as between the Philippines and Malaysia, the Bali summit was notable for (i) the adoption of the TAC, (ii) in principle support to the idea of political cooperation, and (iii) the creation of the ASEAN Secretariat. Nearly two decades later, the Singapore Summit increased the corporate investment in ASEAN by, *inter alia*, strengthening the ASEAN Secretariat and committing to more frequent formal and informal ASEAN Summits. However, these initiatives were also notable for the extent to which they demonstrated a continued aversion to the pooling of any sovereignty in the collective institutions of ASEAN. Moreover, the continued practice of consensus-based decision-making has further negated the evolution of any substantive supranational institutionalization. Consequently, the lowest common denominator in ASEAN's membership has always dictated the pace of cooperation, institutionalization and integration due to an implicit right of veto. Further, various breaches of ASEAN's norms – such as Indonesia's invasion of Timor Leste and the delay in Cambodia's membership – have revealed that the ASEAN members would only abide by the ASEAN Way when such adherence coincided with their respective national interests.[116]

The chapter also analysed the overarching behavioural patterns that underpinned the strategic outlook of the ASEAN states. Through the examples of the Cambodian settlement, the regional response to the end of the Cold War, and the evolution of the ARF, the chapter evidenced the continued and inseparable interdependence of ASEAN with the outside world. The strategic dynamics surrounding the Cold War period, together with the 'communist threat' (domestically and internationally), contributed to some common values and helped to drive a degree of mutual identification leading to one of the stronger periods of diplomatic unity in the history of ASEAN. Nevertheless, ASEAN's utility as a diplomatic community was short-lived due to diverging threat perceptions and strategic interests. Various clashes in strategic alignments were first evident in relation to Thailand's limited alignment with China; an alignment that was to the discontent of the remaining ASEAN members including, in particular, Malaysia and Indonesia. The divergent threat perceptions held by Indonesia and Malaysia soon led towards alternative policies (e.g. the Kuantan Statement) in the pursuit of a limited recognition of the strategic interests of Vietnam for the purpose of balancing against China. Thus, despite some scholarly contentions that the period covered by this chapter reflected a high point in ASEAN unity, low complex integration has in practice rendered interest harmonization and policy coordination an infrequent and transient event.

The limitations to regional resilience were also evident in the context of the ASEAN Regional Forum. While the creation of the ARF, along with the maintenance of a proprietary role within it, reflects positively on the diplomatic effectiveness of ASEAN (relative to its humble beginnings), it must also be recognized that the development of the ARF was primarily a 'reactive' response to the ambitions and initiatives of exogenous actors – such as Japan and Australia. Further, some of the initial aspirations for institutionalization and conflict resolution within the ARF had to be moderated due to, *inter alia*, a growing influence by China and its desire to maintain the *status quo* regarding the procedural norms of ASEAN. Given these events, ASEAN attempted to marginalize the influence of foreign powers but the outcomes were primarily symbolic in nature – e.g. ZOPFAN and SEANWFZ. Further, by the turn of the century, ASEAN's engagement with foreign powers reflected a growing recognition that ASEAN could no longer seek to deny their influence but could, at best, hope to guide the manner by which such powers interacted and cooperated with ASEAN and its member-states.

In summary, the first three decades of ASEAN's existence were significant for several diplomatic achievements (particularly Cambodia), the expansion of

ASEAN's membership and the engagement of foreign powers through institutions such as the ARF. However, the period was also marked by strategic disunity, divergent foreign policies and an absence of any significant political and security cooperation or institutionalization. Nonetheless, the political elite largely benefited from the ASEAN Way as it not only enabled the coming together of an extremely diverse group of states but also provided the necessary space for states to focus on internal consolidation at a time when they lacked the resources to commit to any significant regionalist project. Perversely, the ASEAN Way also provided the freedom to focus on internal consolidation without fear of external intervention, with the result that ASEAN has not affected the quality of governance in the region. In this context, the avoidance of any institutional role for ASEAN in the domestic affairs of its members has exacerbated a schism in the region's values including human rights and democracy. Thus, as will be detailed in later chapters, ASEAN eventually passed a crossroad where, as far as regional cooperation, institutionalization and complex integration were concerned, its modus operandi became more burden than benefit. In the meantime, the next chapter most significantly examines the level of ASEAN cohesion over controversial security issues and the extent to which any dependable expectations of peaceful change are associated with such cohesion. Such analysis is important because, as Mark Beeson states,

> what is arguably [ASEAN's] … greatest potential claim to fame – the absence of war between member states since its inauguration – may owe as much to the widely noted general decline in the level of inter-state conflict as it does to anything ASEAN itself may have done.[117]

4 Testing ASEAN cohesion

Security and economic challenges

During the last two decades, many other uncertainties and challenges with a more specific impact on Southeast Asia and its immediate neighbourhood have arisen. While some of these challenges have been associated with regional transformations in strategic relations and alliances, more tangible difficulties have also arisen in the context of economic management, domestic stability and other comprehensive security issues, including environmental degradation and pollution, transnational crime and human security. While it is not possible to cover all the issues that afflict ASEAN and its security environment, the present chapter provides a broad sample of some of the most problematic issues to have recently affected the comprehensive security of Southeast Asia. Consequently, the first section provides a synopsis of the nature of Southeast Asian responses to territorial disputes. In the first example, a recent dispute concerning the Preah Vihear Temple demonstrates how both history and domestic volatility continue to adversely affect regional relations. The section then examines recent hostility between Malaysia and Indonesia concerning their competing claims in the Sulawesi Sea. The final issue covered by the section concerns the South China Sea. While the ASEAN members initially attempted to coordinate collective responses through the multilateral framework of ASEAN, the section outlines how China has managed to exploit ASEAN disunity over controversial economic and security issues. The latter two case studies are also significant for demonstrating the limits to regional solidarity when competing economic interests are at stake.

The second section proceeds with an analysis of regional cohesion and cooperation concerning the challenges of terrorism and insurgency. While the 'common' threat of terrorism provided a convergence of interests leading to various cooperative endeavours – such as the sharing of intelligence – ASEAN has not collectively responded to regional insurgencies due to the sensitivities of the political elite as well as the localized nature of each dispute. Moreover, the chapter reveals how these insurgencies are interdependent with considerations of ethnicity and religion, which have, in turn, exacerbated regional animosities. The propensity for regional governments to follow contradictory pathways in the formulation of foreign and economic policy is also demonstrated through an analysis, in the third section, of the 1997 'haze' and economic crisis. In the context of these two issues, a lack of *reciprocity*, and the propensity of individual ASEAN members to draw negative interstate or inter-community comparisons (SIT), has also negatively affected regional cohesion, trust and cooperation. However, the final section analyses how the financial crisis, together with considerations of domestic instability and non-traditional security issues, eventually galvanized regional thinking in the context of economic cooperation and limited institutionalization. While certain challenges to regional cohesion remained, a level of coordination and cohesion emerged that had previously been avoided.

Territorial issues and the South China Sea

By the close of 2009, broader Asia accounted for nearly one-third (113) of the world's 365 domestic and international conflicts.[1] While Southeast Asia, as the subject of this study, continues to be plagued by both domestic and transnational conflicts, there has been some progress in recent years concerning the resolution of several conflicts. At the domestic level, for example, the next chapter analyses how democratic reforms in Indonesia contributed to a resolution of a longstanding insurgency in Aceh. Other insurgencies, however, continue, including those in the Southern Philippines and Southern Thailand. In the context of several transnational territorial disputes, two longstanding conflicts between Indonesia and Malaysia were successfully addressed through the International Court of Justice (ICJ) in 2002. Here, the ICJ ruled in favour of Malaysia concerning its sovereignty over Pulau Litigan and Pulau Sipadan. Singapore and Malaysia have also had some long-standing territorial disputes that they both submitted to the ICJ, and in May 2008 the ICJ awarded sovereignty over Middle Rock to Malaysia while sovereignty over Pedra Branca was awarded to Singapore. In the case of a third claim, sovereignty over the South Ledge was split between Malaysia and Singapore in line with their territorial waters. However, both the ICJ rulings were incomplete in that they did not determine how the territorial waters around the claims would be delimited. While the willingness of Indonesia, Malaysia and Singapore to resolve their disputes through the ICJ represents a positive development for the region, the means of resolution also demonstrates the continued inability of ASEAN to resolve regional disputes – particularly in the realm of traditional security issues. Further, Table 4.1 illustrates that many more territorial disputes remain unresolved in the region.

In recent years, the most significant quarrel involving *actual* armed conflict concerns a longstanding dispute between Thailand and Cambodia over the *Preah Vihear* Temple and surrounding territory. In mid-July 2008, the UN Educational, Scientific and Cultural Organization (UNESCO) conferred World Heritage status on the temple, leading to a nationalist backlash in Thailand. From the Thai perspective, an earlier decision by the French to locate the temple within Cambodia's territory was 'both unjust and illegal'; moreover, the outcome reflected the ability of the French colonial authorities to impose an 'unequal treaty' on Thailand at the time.[2] Despite this background, Thailand's Prime Minster, Samak

Table 4.1 Non-exhaustive list of regional transnational disputes

Transnational dispute	*Disputants*	*Further information*
Doi Lang	Myanmar and Thailand	Border dispute
Gulf of Thailand	Thailand, Cambodia and Vietnam	Cambodia objected to a settlement between Thailand and Vietnam
Paracel Islands	Vietnam and China	Maritime dispute
Pedra Branca Lighthouse	Singapore and Malaysia	Despite the ICJ ruling, sovereignty over the surrounding territorial waters has yet to be resolved
Preah Vihear Temple	Cambodia and Thailand	Border dispute
Sabah	Philippines and Malaysia	The Philippines maintains a dormant claim
Spratly Islands	China, Vietnam, Malaysia, Philippines	Maritime dispute
Sulawesi/Celebes sea	Malaysia, Indonesia	Maritime dispute
Further territorial disputes	Including Malaysia and Thailand, Malaysia and Singapore, Thailand and Laos, Vietnam and Cambodia, Myanmar and Thailand.	Some of these disputes are in the process of being resolved through bilateral initiatives establishing committees for territorial demarcation

Sundaravej, had indicated that his government would not oppose such an outcome and his Foreign Minister, Noppadon Pattama, had signed a joint communiqué with Cambodia providing Thailand's support over the issue. However, opponents of both Samak and Noppadon (namely the People's Alliance for Democracy) viewed them as proxies for ousted Prime Minister Thaksin Shinawatra and this resulted in a crisis of legitimacy for the Samak government. Thus, domestic instability in Thailand soon led the Samak government and its successor – headed by Prime Minister Abhisit Vejjajiva – to exploit Thai nationalist sentiments for domestic political gain. The resulting chaos directly contributed to several armed skirmishes and the death of between twelve and eighteen Thai and Khmer soldiers between 2008 and 2010.[3]

The first military incident occurred on 15 July 2008 when Thai troops were arrested by the Cambodian military as they attempted to cross into territory around the *Preah Vihear* Temple. During the episode, a Thai solider was injured by a landmine. Within two days, 600 Khmer soldiers and 400 Thai soldiers had amassed along their respective borders. Following the arrival of further reinforcements, including Thai artillery, an exchange of fire between both sides occurred on 3 October resulting in a number of wounded. A further skirmish occurred on 14 October but this time three Khmer soldiers were killed while seven Thais were wounded.[4] A further exchange of fire occurred on 2 April 2009 killing at least two soldiers and, despite claims of a de-escalation of the conflict, a further skirmish occurred on 24 January 2010 where the Cambodian army reportedly launched RPG rockets in response to Thai fire; there were no reported injuries or deaths from this incident.[5] At the time of writing, armed confrontations had continued through to 2011 including a February 2011 exchange of artillery fire that led to the loss of five lives and the evacuation of thousands of civilians.[6]

The Preah Vihear situation was further aggravated when Prime Minister Hun Sen later appointed Thaksin Shinawatra as Cambodia's economic advisor. The episode affected ASEAN's image as Hun Sen announced Thakin's appointment at an ASEAN leader's summit in Thailand; this simultaneously caused embarrassment for ASEAN and also provided a further example that highlighted the level of difficulty that lay ahead in realizing the type of regional order that ASEAN has envisioned. Importantly, ASEAN's attempts to resolve the issue, together with a unilateral attempt by Indonesia, have been consistently rejected. Further, Cambodia has since acquired new equipment including ground-to-air missiles, constructed new roads, 'sown fresh minefields and deployed thousands of troops in newly built villages'.[7]

Given the vast superiority of Thailand's military forces, some of Hun Sen's more provocative actions may be explained by the fact that economic interdependence between Thailand and Cambodia has been a one-sided affair. In 2009, Thailand exported US$1.58 billion of goods to Cambodia whereas Cambodia's exports to Thailand accounted for only US$77.73 million.[8] Huns Sen's actions may also reflect the realist paradigm through a rational and strategic calculation that Thailand cannot afford to undertake a military response due to its structural vulnerability to international markets and diplomatic pressure. For example, a loss of investor confidence and a further decline in tourism would be devastating to the Thai economy. Nonetheless, Thailand's historical rhetoric and relations with Cambodia have deeply affected trust and affinity between the two countries. Thus, as illustrated by Figure 4.1, when the communal level survey (written in Thai) asked the Thai participants to view a list of Southeast Asian countries 'and rank them on a numerical scale between the country you trust the most (1) and the country you trust the least (10)', 91 per cent of the eighty-one Thai respondents indicated a rank of between 6 and 10 (trust the least).

A further dispute that has recently brought two ASEAN members to the brink of conflict involves competing claims by Indonesia and Malaysia over the Ambalat offshore oil block in the Sulawesi (Celebes) Sea. High stakes are involved due to the natural resources in the region with one Indonesian geographer estimating that just one of the nine sections of the Ambalat sub-region contains 764 million barrels of oil and 1.4 trillion cubic feet (TCF) of gas.[9] Given these competing economic interests, on 3 March 2005 Indonesian President Susilo Bambang Yudhoyono ordered his military to secure Indonesian sovereignty over the disputed area. The gunboat diplomacy that ensued – including the deployment of several naval vessels and four F16 fighter jets from Indonesia

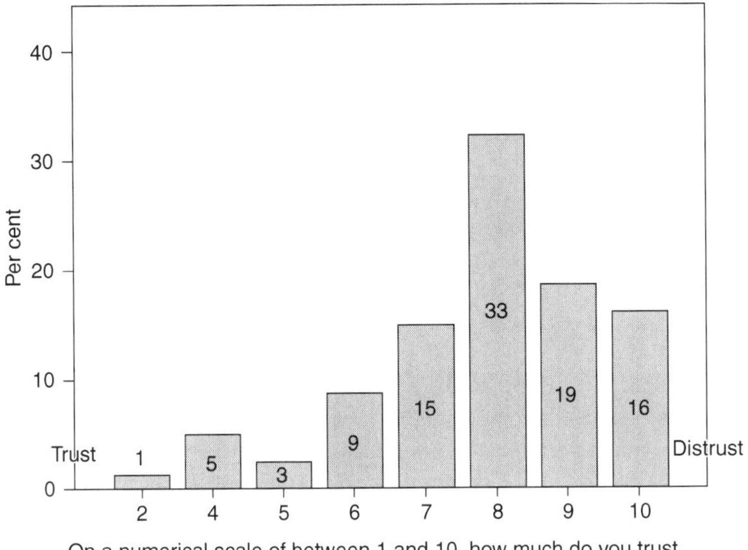

Figure 4.1 Thai perceptions of trust: Cambodia (source: author).

against two naval vessels by Malaysia – risked armed conflict between the two countries.[10] Not only did anger quickly flood the local media, but at one point during the incident a crowd gathered outside the Malaysian embassy in Indonesia and shouted the historical *konfrontasi* catch cry of 'Crush Malaysia'.[11] The dispute continued and in August 2009 Navy Chief of Staff Admiral Tedjo Edhy Purdijato informed the press that 'for the security in Ambalat six warships remained in place to anticipate possible infiltration by ships from Malaysia. Navy personnel are ready to intercept in case a foreign ship is infiltrating'.[12] The level of hostility that is implicit in such statements contrasts sharply with the statements of political elite alleging that ASEAN is a 'happy family', a 'friendly community' of nations or that the Association has been a 'blessing for regional security'.[13]

As with the Preah Vihear example, Admiral Tedjo's statement is also indicative of the adverse role that historical memories and animosities continue to play within Southeast Asia. For example, a month later groups of vigilantes took to the streets in Jakarta reportedly in search of Malaysians to impale on sharpened bamboo poles. The incident stemmed from erroneous allegations that Tourism Malaysia had used 'stolen' images of a traditional *Pendet* dance from Bali in its advertising.[14] Despite the religious and cultural similarities between Malaysia and Indonesia, causation can again be traced to historical (negative) nation-building policies that have driven consequential and relative comparisons between the two countries (i.e. social identity theory, Chapter 1). However, it is interesting to note that the Malaysian Foreign Minister had earlier tried to reduce tensions over the issue when he declared that ‘both sides agree that the situation should be cooled down and wish to use an entirely diplomatic approach’, adding that ‘[s]ince long ago a spirit to resolve to solve [such problems] cooperatively has been apparent among ASEAN’s members’.[15] There appears to be pattern in the region where, on balance, foreign ministry officials tend to be more conciliatory in their statements while defence officials appear to be more willing to verbalize their distrust of neighbouring ASEAN states. As indicated in the previous chapter, annual ministerial meetings between the Defence Ministers only commenced in 2006 whereas the Foreign Ministers have been interacting since ASEAN’s inception. The outcomes of such patterns will be further analysed in the context of the survey results on perceptions of trust and conflict in Chapter 7.

As observed by James Cotton, the most crucial traditional security issue in Southeast Asia concerns the territorial claims in the South China Sea.[16] Due to the landlocked nature of the South China Sea, it has been referred to as a ‘geopolitical lake’ and a significant component of its strategic significance pertains to its role as a Sea Lane of Communication (SLOC). In connecting with the Straits of Malacca, Lombok and Sunda, the South China Sea SLOC is one of the world’s busiest waterways with over 100,000 merchant ships and 3.96 billion barrels of oil passing through its waters annually.[17] The second element to the South China Sea’s strategic significance pertains to the immense wealth of natural resources in its waters including a rich combination of fertile fishing beds, natural gas, oil and minerals. Over five million tons of fish are extracted from the area each year and this represents 25 per cent of the protein requirements of Southeast Asia’s 596 million people. Further, Chinese scholars have speculated, somewhat optimistically, that there exist between 105 billion and 213 billion barrels of oil in the area.[18] Additionally, these sources estimate a further 2,000 trillion cubic feet (TCF) of natural gas and 900 tcf within the territorial confines of the Spratly Islands alone.[19] By the turn of the millennium, the sum-total of all these resources had been estimated to be worth over US$1 trillion – a figure that is now likely to be far higher given the current price and shortage of hydrocarbon resources.[20]

It is in light of this strategic importance that official Chinese objections over the SEANWFZ treaty (Chapter 3) can be better understood. Aside from the land covered by the established territorial borders of each signatory, the ambit of the treaty also includes each country’s continental shelves and a 370 kilometre Exclusive Economic Zone (EEZ). Consequently, the Chinese government was concerned that its own claims to the maritime sub-region might be prejudiced should it accede to SEANWFZ. As indicated by Figure 4.2, the problem was further compounded by the fact that Taiwan, Vietnam, the Philippines, Brunei and Malaysia are all claimants to either all or parts of the waters, shoals, reefs and islands (including the Paracel and Spratly islands) within the South China Sea. The de facto embroilment of Indonesia can be added to this list as the Chinese claim reaches as far South as Indonesia’s own Exclusive Economic Zone, continental shelf and the Natuna Gas Field.[21]

Figure 4.2 Competing claims in the South China Sea region (source: © the Government of the United States of America. www.eia.doe.gov).

Meanwhile, the most noteworthy and volatile outcome to stem from the strategic significance of the South China Sea has been the manner in which individual territorial claims have been hotly defended in recent decades. Thus, amidst regional competition and the pursuit of relative gains (low complex integration), skirmishes have occurred between the Philippines and Vietnam (1998 and 1999) and between Taiwan and Vietnam (1995). Meanwhile, larger scale confrontations have taken place between China and Vietnam (1974, 1988, 1992, and 1994) as well as China and the Philippines (1995, 1996, 1997 and 1999).[22] The bloodiest conflict over the islands occurred between China and Vietnam in 1988 when Chinese and Vietnamese forces clashed at Fiery Cross Reef near Johnson Island. During the hostilities, the Vietnamese lost up to three vessels and seventy-seven crew members.[23] While the occurrence of hostile actions has declined in frequency during the past decade, the level of competition and diplomatic maneuvering to maximize each claimant's share over the discovery of any potential resources has not.

In 1992, China reasserted its claim to exclusive sovereignty over the entire sub-region by passing a new *Law of the Territorial Sea and Contiguous Zone of the People's Republic of China.* ASEAN sought to avoid both an escalation of hostilities on the matter and the alienation of China which, by this time, had become a highly important trading partner for the ASEAN block. Thus, ASEAN called for the exercise of restraint through its *Declaration on the South China Sea.* In its attempt to 'seize the political agenda', the declaration effectively put Beijing on notice that a 'unified ASEAN position was emerging from which ASEAN would view the bilateral issues through regionalist eyes'.[24] Furthermore, the declaration reiterated various ASEAN principles including the 'non-use of force' along with the 'resolution of disputes by peaceful means'. The declaration also urged the claimants, 'without prejudicing the sovereignty and jurisdiction of countries having direct interests in the area', to explore greater cooperation in several fields – such as 'navigation' and cooperation against 'piracy' and 'illicit drugs' – but, notably, did not discuss the exploration of natural resources. Finally, the declaration also reiterated ASEAN's aim to have all parties accept and abide by the principles of the TAC as a basis for establishing a regional 'code of international conduct'.[25] While the ASEAN members agreed to the declaration, the Association was not successful in its attempt to acquire China's acquiescence to the declaration – the PRC had other plans.

In 1995, China occupied a small set of islands called Mischief Reef that are also claimed by the Philippines. China's occupation of Mischief Reef was well within the Philippines' EEZ but diplomacy was the only course of action available because of the low capacity of the Philippines navy. To ASEAN's credit, the Association was quickly able to muster a degree of solidarity over the issue by censuring China for its actions and reiterating its call for restraint based on the spirit of its *Declaration of the South China Sea.*[26] However, these early displays of ASEAN unity did not immediately alter China's behaviour as, one year later, the Philippine navy reportedly engaged in a ninety-minute battle with three Chinese navy vessels and China has continued to upgrade its facilities.[27] From the perspective of one analyst, the withdrawal of US navy forces from Subic Bay was likely to have contributed to the growing assertiveness of China.[28] Jeanie Henderson also suggests that 'the timing of the move also seemed calculated to capitalize on ASEAN's difficulties at the time of the economic crisis' – an event that is analysed later in the chapter.[29]

In the wake of these developments, a growing sense of disunity developed amongst the ASEAN claimants over negotiations for the implementation of an actual 'Code of Conduct'. Further, China was duly able to provoke such disunity by exploiting ASEAN's incapacity to resolve divisions generated by their mutually contradictory claims.[30] Thus, by 2002, negotiations for a 'Code of Conduct' had stalemated and in its place the claimants signed a non-binding communiqué known as the *Declaration on the Conduct of Parties in the South China Sea*. As regional analyst Barry Wain explains, 'disunity developed on the ASEAN side between Vietnam and Malaysia. … In the end, you had the sad spectacle of China, which initially rejected the ASEAN approach to a code of conduct, being more enthusiastic about the final declaration than the ASEAN side'.[31] Consequently, in August 2003, China forged a deal with the Philippines (which Vietnam reluctantly joined later) for petroleum exploration in the area. The lack of solidarity that resulted in this bilateral, and later trilateral, approach has left other claimants, such as Malaysia, out in the cold.

Meanwhile, beyond the Sulawesi Sea and South China Sea issues, the possible emergence of Chinese hegemony in the region also has implications for ASEAN's security community proposal. Amidst China's almost uninterrupted economic growth, averaging close to 10 per cent per annum, China was able to increase its military expenditure by 238 per cent between 2000 and 2007, including a 17.8 per cent increase for the 2007 fiscal year.[32] These increases, combined with the type of weaponry and armaments that China has acquired, evidence an intention to obtain blue water naval capacity. While such actions do not necessarily prohibit dependable expectations of peaceful change in Southeast Asia (as it is an actor exogenous to the grouping), China has mustered the potential to splinter any sense of collective identity in ASEAN's elite-level strategic relations. Such influence was most recently demonstrated when China managed to keep the South China Sea dispute off the agenda of the October 2009 ASEAN Summit and, according to diplomats, the issue 'barely surfaced in [the] informal sessions' that followed; China continues to state that it will only discuss the issue on a bilateral basis.[33]

China's self-declared 'territorial ambitions' should have highlighted the necessity of a united front between the ASEAN members; however, the past few years have been more notable for ASEAN-wide disunity on the issue. Vietnam, for example, only agreed to the earlier mentioned joint exploration with China and the Philippines because, according to one Vietnamese foreign ministry official, it felt it could no longer expect solidarity and support from ASEAN.[34] Meanwhile, Vietnam had already started to hedge its bets by improving its relations with both India and the US and has recently permitted several visits by US Navy ships; the most recent visits being from the USS *Blue Ridge* and USS *Lassen* to the central Vietnamese port of Da Nang (November 2009). Further, in December 2009, Vietnam finalized an agreement with Russia to purchase six Kilo-class submarines. By contrast, both Thailand and the Philippines have recently entered into various agreements to increase military and economic cooperation with (and greater aid from) China.[35] Meanwhile, ASEAN's engagement with Myanmar has not prevented a closer political and military alignment with China[36] – a challenge that will be discussed further in the next two chapters.

Nonetheless, despite concerns privately expressed by many political elite in interview, Figure 4.3 indicates that more than 64 per cent of the respondents in the 'elite level survey' believed that the ASEAN members would unite at the diplomatic level to condemn China should it forcibly occupy further islands in

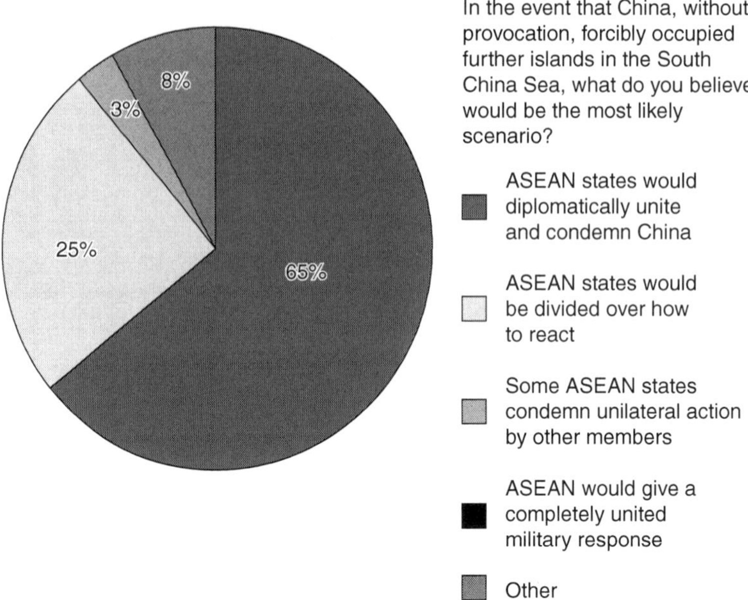

Figure 4.3 Perceptions of unity in the event of Chinese coercion (source: compiled by author).

the maritime region. Interestingly, and reflective of the perceived limitations to the potential security role for ASEAN (and its member's military capabilities), not one of the respondents felt that the 'ASEAN member countries would [or could] be completely united in ... [providing] a military response against China's occupation'. Still, given the vast resources and the subsequent stakes involved in the South China Sea, the absence of any significant conflict to date is encouraging. The extent to which this outcome can be further accredited to the ASEAN Way and *dependable expectations of peaceful change* (e.g. as symbolized by the 'non-use of force' principle) will continue to be a subject of analysis.

Terrorism and insurgency in Southeast Asia

The political, military and strategic realignments taking place in Southeast Asia are not only a consequence of increased Chinese hegemony but are also an outcome of terrorism and its influence on global security. For Southeast Asia, moreover, terrorism is a transnational force that has affected virtually 'every dimension of Southeast Asia's multilateral interactions' including the strategic, political, economic and cultural realms.[37] The substantial impact of terrorism on the region's strategic security architecture has been interdependent with both US actions in connection with its 'war on terror' and regional 'reactions' to these policies – whether by states, communities or terrorist organizations. Further, despite the fact that the US designated Southeast Asia as the second front on terror,[38] there is a perception that the US largely neglected Southeast Asia and that China quickly moved to fill the subsequent power vacuum by enhancing its diplomatic, political and security relations.[39] Further, the previous Bush administration's 'with us or against us' approach polarized both the political elite and the communities of Southeast Asia to a degree that had not been seen since the pinnacle of the Cold War. Bush's policies also had the associated risk of exacerbating already existent divisions in identity that have been a consequence of different social and religious histories throughout Southeast Asia.

In Singapore and Malaysia for example, the continuation of discontent within the Malay, Indian and Chinese ethnic minority groups means that the risk of future identity-based conflict should not be underestimated.[40] Limited episodes of such conflict involved Indian protestors in Malaysia between 2007 and 2008[41] and during the course of 2009 various Christian churches in Malaysia were burned down because of protests by some Muslims against the use of the word 'Allah'.[42] Terrorist acts also have the potential to fuel religious and ethnic-based animosities. For example, had Singapore and Malaysia failed to arrest twenty-one militants in December 2001 (who were planning 'to detonate seven truck bombs at American, British, Australian and Israeli targets in Singapore') then the subsequent loss of life and damage to local economies could have panned out negatively for race relations within and between the two countries.[43] In this regard, Lee Kuan Yew, former Prime Minister and current Minister Mentor of Singapore, has warned about the growing separateness between the country's Islamic and non-Islamic communities.[44] The divisive nature of terrorism, together with how states have responded to the issue, was further verified in a recent survey conducted by the *Straits Times*. Within this survey 39 per cent of Malaysians chose the word 'hate' to describe their feelings towards the US and 83.5 per cent expressed a negative attitude towards America.[45] Given these perceptions, the divisive potential of terrorism and the 'war on terror' becomes readily apparent when one also considers the strength of US security relations with the Philippines, Singapore, and Thailand together with the hard-line approach of the latter to Muslims in its 'Southern' provinces.

Despite the actual and potential divisions generated by the 'war on terror', the survey work conducted within the region, as partially displayed by Figure 4.4, indicates a relatively unified perception (at both the communal and elite levels) that terrorism is a concern for the world and/or the countries of Southeast Asia.[46] Here, the Bali bombings likely contributed to the convergence of these threat perceptions together with the sense of urgency demonstrated by the elite-level interviews concerning the need to combat terrorist organizations and their cells. At the communal level of analysis, perceptions concerning the region-wide interdependence of terrorism were likely strengthened by actual attacks on Southeast Asian soil and the associated consequences regarding several relatively tangible issues such as trade, investor confidence, tourism, employment and personal security.

The need for internal consolidation in Southeast Asia – whilst simultaneously addressing the challenges of state legitimacy and, in some instances, democracy

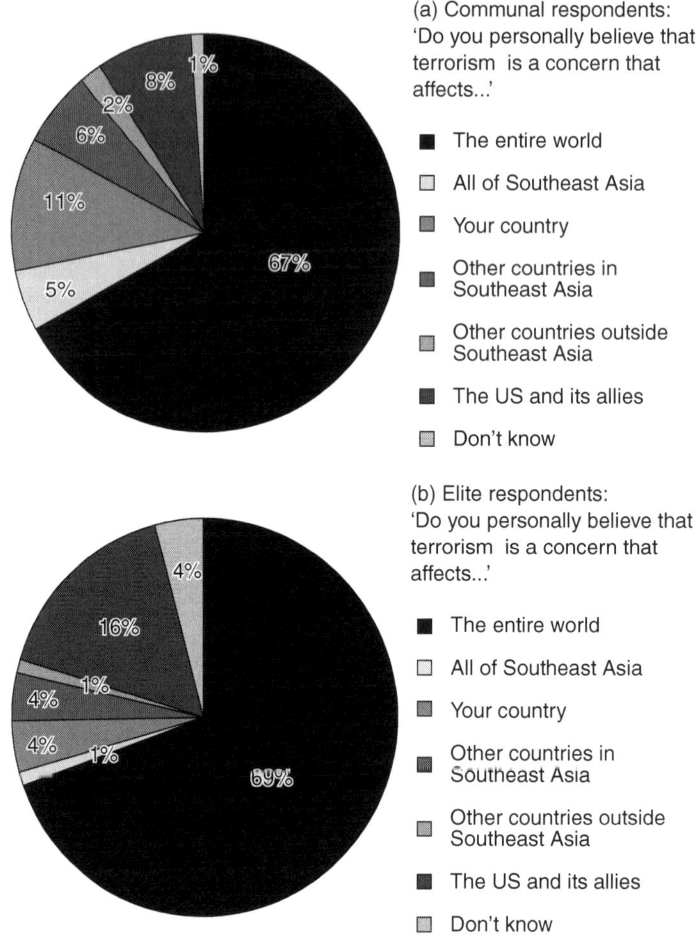

Figure 4.4 Communal and elite perceptions regarding terrorism (source: compiled by author).

– can be seen in that it is the *weaker* and *poorer* states that have had to struggle the most with both terrorism and the insurgencies that these terrorist groups have sometimes exploited.[47] Moreover, poor domestic security, the absence of secular education, high unemployment and low standards of living, all contribute to the appeal of radical terrorist ideology. The ethnic violence that might ensue from increased terrorist and insurgency activity adds to this vicious cycle and further detracts from the capacity of individual states to look beyond their borders and implement initiatives for heightened regional cooperation, security and economic development. Meanwhile, regardless of the linkages between transnational terrorist organizations and insurgencies, the latter have often engaged in 'a range of militant activities, including conventional and guerrilla warfare', many of which have been described as 'terrorist activity'.[48] In the case of Indonesia, and in the wake of the economic crisis and the instability that followed, the country also had to contend with other terrorist attacks in its capital along with several hotspots for religious and/or ethnic based violence in various other locations within the country such as the Maluku Islands, Madura in Kalimantan and central Sulawesi.[49]

The relevance of terrorism to Malaysia, by contrast, is predominately limited to a concern that the country continues to serve as a source of Islamic militancy rather than a victim of it.[50] The Philippines, meanwhile, continues to suffer from both communist (e.g. the New People's Army) and Islamic (e.g. Moro Islamic Liberation Front and the Abu Sayyaf Group) insurgencies. Further, in Laos there remain occasional but limited occurrences of violence by ethnic minority groups with the most recent episode involving an alleged, albeit foiled, plot by Hmong Rebels to purchase weaponry from US companies (including Stinger surface-to-air missiles) in an attempt to usurp the Communist government in Laos.[51] In the case of Myanmar, while it has not yet been a major source of terrorist activities beyond its own borders (despite claims to the contrary by its government), the country has endured more than half a century of civil war and insurgency. Finally, and since the commencement of the US 'war on terror', the separatist movement in Southern Thailand has re-emerged (involving an estimated 3,000 militants) and generated large-scale violence.[52] Further, by the beginning of 2007, the violence in Southern Thailand had become so pervasive that the newly installed military government declared that it was considering the implementation of *Sharia Law* in the predominantly Malay (Muslim) provinces of Yala, Narathiwat and Pattani.[53] This proposal also represented an attempt to provide a 'softer image' following the harsh approach undertaken by the former Thaksin government where, in one instance, eighty-four Thai Muslims were killed as a result of suffocation whilst being detained in overcrowded military trucks.[54]

Relations between Thailand and Malaysia

The violence in Southern Thailand has also affected Thailand's relations with Malaysia. Here, colonialism resulted in territorial boundaries being drawn that, in this instance, split the Malay communities between Malaysia and Southern Thailand.[55] Thus, according to James Wise, a former Australian High Commissioner in Kuala Lumpur, when the eighty-four Muslims were killed in Southern Thailand 'the depth of feeling was very high' within the political elite of Malaysia and the Malaysian government immediately called for its Foreign Minister to hold talks in Bangkok.[56] However, the abrupt and highly defensive responses by Prime Minister Thaksin, together with a general distrust of Malaysia by the Thais – including allegations by Thaksin that the militants in Southern Thailand were being trained in jungle hideouts in Kelantan Malaysia[57] – led to a further deterioration of relations.

In response to public expressions of 'shock' and subsequent 'denials' by the Malaysian government over the claims, the Thai government, a few days later, announced that it had photographic 'proof' of the Malaysian camps.[58] Despite the photos being exposed in the media as nothing more than 'old sports-day school photos from Thailand's southern Pattani Province',[59] and Thaksin later backing away from these allegations claiming that they had been distorted by the media,[60] the official position maintained by some members of the political elite in Thailand is that there remains *bone fide* evidence of the Malaysian government's complicity in supporting insurgents in southern Thailand. Thus, according to one Major-General in the Thai police force,

> right now we know Malaysia is supporting insurgents. Their Minister of Defence came out and all these people were meeting in Langkawi, we had photographs that they were doing it. Were they supporting it [at the meeting]? We don't know, maybe indirectly, but they knew because we had photographs and so they didn't come out and say anything [in response].[61]

By August 2005, the heavy-handed nature by which Thai security forces had responded to the insurgency problem under Thaksin's leadership also resulted in 131 Thai Muslims fleeing across the border into Malaysia and declaring themselves 'refugees'. Malaysia was hesitant to force the refugees to return to Thailand under circumstances where, as the Malaysian Foreign Minister described, there is 'no denying that the situation in Thailand is still not safe, it is still not stable'.[62] Thaksin's response was very hostile and he also declared that Malaysia's acceptance of the refugees represented 'interference in the domestic affairs of Thailand'.[63] The Malaysian Government responded by stating that 'we will not release them to Thailand except if we have an assurance that their human rights are not being infringed upon by the Thai government' and that any final decision about the Thai refugees by Malaysia would be based on the rule of law and the principles of human rights.[64]

The delicate balance between Thailand's treatment of Malays and the level of security extant within Southern Thailand became even harder to maintain following accusations that Thailand was spying on Malaysia (October 2005),[65] plans to end dual citizenship by Thailand (October 2005),[66] and the detention of six Malaysian soldiers who (allegedly) crossed into a southern province of Narathiwat in Thailand (February 2006).[67] According to Anthony Davis, an in-country researcher for *Jane's Intelligence*, by August 2005 relations between Thailand and Malaysia had declined to their worst level in the two nations' history.[68] Such tensions subsequently spilled into other spheres including military cooperation where, according to one Thai Major-General, even the pretence of diplomatic cordiality was abandoned during one meeting at the *Akademi Tentera Malaysia* (Military Academy of Malaysia) leading to the temporary cancellation of a military officer exchange programme between the two countries.[69] Regardless of the authenticity of such allegations, the occurrence of these comments is indicative of a lack of trust and mutual identification between the political elite of the two countries. Thus, when the communal survey respondents from the two countries were asked 'On a numerical scale of between 1 and 10 how much do you trust Thailand/Malaysia?', 62 per cent of the Thai respondents provided a rank of between 1 and 4 (the trust end of the spectrum), but only 35 per cent of the Malaysian respondents (the subject of Thai allegations) ranked Thailand within the same range of trust.

Counterterrorist cooperation in ASEAN

ASEAN has concluded several agreements in response to the threat of 'transnational terrorist networks'. At the November 2001 ASEAN Summit, just two months after the 11 September attacks in New York, ASEAN issued its 'Declaration on Joint Action to Counter Terrorism'. The declaration emphasized the need to strengthen 'comprehensive' cooperation against terrorism at the bilateral, regional and international levels.[70] Several months later, in May 2002, a special Foreign Minister's Meeting indentified several specific areas for functional cooperation including extradition, airport security, bomb detection, the formation of national anti-terrorist units and the sharing of intelligence.[71] The eighth ASEAN Summit added to this list by proposing measures against money laundering and the financing of terrorism.[72] Later, in negotiating the November 2004 Vientiane Action Program, the ASEAN states agreed to work towards 'concluding an ASEAN Mutual Legal Assistance Agreement, an ASEAN convention on counter terrorism, and the establishment of an ASEAN extradition treaty as originally envisioned in the 1976 Declaration of ASEAN Concord'.[73]

While ASEAN has forged other agreements regarding counterterrorism efforts and activities, the Association continues to avoid more contentious issues (such as domestic insurgencies) and the ASEAN Way remains a challenge for the implementation of the Association's commitments due to an absence of legally binding commitments or mechanisms for enforcement. For example, while a decision for intelligence sharing at an ASEAN Foreign Ministers meeting in 2002 was described as a 'watershed' for ASEAN cooperation, only Malaysia, Indonesia and the Philippines joined the agreement. As James Cotton states, 'Thailand decided the proposal merited further study, and Singapore refused at that stage to participate'.[74] Despite such problems, several interlocutors have contended that intelligence sharing has been one of the strongest areas of cooperation in relation to both terrorism and transnational crime. However, they add that such cooperation has primarily been limited to the bilateral level.[75]

Anti-terrorist cooperation has also emerged in connection with extra-regional organizations and actors. Aside from a number of initiatives within APEC and the ARF (including agreement to freeze the financial assets of terrorist organizations), the United Nations adopted a 'broad-based series' of counterterrorism obligations as articulated by Resolution 1371 in 2001.[76] While the US may have neglected other aspects of regional engagement, its role in the Philippines demonstrates that it has entrenched itself as the most significant sponsor of counterterrorist efforts in Southeast Asia. The role of the US commenced in January

2002 when it sent 1,200 troops in support of Filipino operations against the Abu Sayyaf Group (ASG). Later, in December 2002, an additional 150 US special forces were sent to the Philippines for the purpose of training the Philippine military in counterterrorist operations.[77] Counterterrorist cooperation between the two countries has also involved the coordination of joint airstrikes by the US and Philippine air forces against a cluster of municipalities in Southern Maguindanao – e.g. November 2004, January 2005 and April 2005.[78] Further, in 2005 the US doubled its aid to the Philippines. While the Philippines' relationship with the US did not appear to be a significant problem in the regional interviews, there may be less tangible consequences at the communal level including those indicated in the earlier-mentioned *Straits Times* survey.[79] In any event, the fact that the most significant assistance has come from outside the region indicates the current limitations to regional resilience and an associated capacity for the ASEAN states to manage their own security. Nonetheless, the next chapter outlines how continued dependence on exogenous powers has also motivated some of the ASEAN states to enhance ASEAN regionalism for the purpose of greater domestic and regional resilience.

The regional 'haze' and the financial crisis

In 1997 the massive fires that swept through Sumatra and Kalimantan – known as the 'haze' – exemplified the limitations to environmental management as well as limited capacity for multilateral cooperation. The wall of smoke that followed spread from Indonesia to as far as Singapore, Malaysia, Brunei and parts of Thailand, the Philippines and Australia. In the wake of the 'haze', an estimated two million square miles or eight million hectares – an area roughly 120 times the size of Singapore – was burnt out.[80] By the time the crisis reached its peak in 1998, the level of air pollution in Sarawak (East Malaysia) had reached critical levels and, at its worst, the residents of Kuching, for example, could not see more than a few meters in the middle of the day.[81] Further, the financial loss to industries such as tourism and air travel, along with ascertainable and immediate health costs, has been variously estimated at $1 billion,[82] $4.5 billion[83] and $9 billion.[84] While the extent of destruction to forest and plantation resources can also be estimated, the consequences in other areas – such as the impact on endangered species (e.g. the orangutan communities), the impact of increased erosion and the deterioration of sanitary water for human consumption – have been far harder to calculate. However, as outlined below, significant challenges also emerged for ASEAN in relation to regional solidarity and the ASEAN Way. While incidents of the 'haze' have since reoccurred, the 1997–98 episode was the most acute in terms of economic costs and life-threatening health consequences.[85]

ASEAN had been attempting to address the problem of 'transboundary pollution' for two decades. The 'ASEAN Environment Program 1' in 1977 represented the first initiative. Several other agreements then followed, including the ASEAN Senior Officials on the Environment (ASOEN) in 1989, the Kuala

Lumpur Accord on Environment and Development in 1990 and various statements of intent at Singapore Summit in 1992. According to ASEAN, the cumulative effect of all these declarations was to identify the 'issue of transboundary pollution' as being 'among the major environmental concerns of ASEAN'.[86] Nonetheless, following an episode of the 'haze' in 1994, ASEAN sought to develop a more significant set of strategies to be implemented at the regional and domestic levels through the Cooperation Plan on Transboundary Pollution in June 1995. The measures proposed in the declaration included increases to national capabilities in combating forest fires, the transfer of technology and knowledge sharing, and the construction of a regional mechanism to coordinate cooperation on fire fighting.[87] As noted in the case of counterterrorist cooperation, while the logic behind the agreement was sound there was no mechanism to enforce implementation. Thus, the 'haze' highlighted the problem of implementation within ASEAN as well as the limited extent to which ASEAN could positively influence its members and the security architecture of Southeast Asia more generally.

At the time of the 'haze', ASEAN's principle of non-interference prohibited the Association from commenting on internal affairs. This was particularly problematic given that the fires in Indonesia had largely been caused by corrupt internal practices. While Indonesia had laws to regulate and punish the use of fire for the purpose of land clearing, many of the business leaders who contravened these laws also held strong connections with Suharto's New Order regime. The combination of corruption and a lack of capacity (internal consolidation) rendered it either impossible or inadvisable for the relevant law enforcement agencies to combat the activities of illegal loggers.[88] The manifest inability of the Indonesian government to manage the issue was further illustrated by the continuation of extensive timber concessions and the Indonesian government's active role in encouraging the conversion of previously forested areas into palm oil plantations – a process that is most cheaply achieved by burning.[89] Equally significant, and indelibly interdependent with the considerations above, was the lack of will on the part of the Indonesian leadership to address the issue. As summarized by C.P.F. Luhulima, a Senior Fellow of the Centre for Security and International Studies in Jakarta, '[t]he problem with the haze is that it is always going northwards, never southwards, so Jakarta is never under a haze problem, that is why the interest is not big here'.[90]

Nevertheless, during the early stages of the crisis, the ASEAN members continued to uphold the ASEAN Way by avoiding public criticism. Early solidarity on the issue was such that the Malaysian government even suppressed the media's coverage of the issue.[91] The diplomacy that followed led to the adoption of a further agreement in December 1997 – The Regional Haze Action Plan. As with the ASEAN plan in 1995, the new agreement sought to implement preventative measures and regional monitoring mechanisms and to enhance fire-fighting capability. However, in the absence of mechanisms to enforce implementation, the plan provided little by way of tangible benefits. Despite early displays of solidarity, Singapore, followed by Malaysia, eventually broke ranks due to the mounting costs of the financial crisis and perceptions of Indonesia's lack of will to address the issue. Consequently, Singapore attempted to publicly pressure the Indonesian government into further action by uploading satellite imagery of the fires on the Internet.[92] Singapore's actions represented a clear contravention of ASEAN's modalities where the principle of non-interference prohibits implied and/or overt acts of public criticism.[93] Similar incidents followed and they are discussed in the context of the East Asian financial crisis below.

Since the 'haze' crisis, regular incidents of transboundary pollution continued in the region, including episodes in 2000, 2002, 2004, 2005 and 2006–07. ASEAN has continued to work on further initiatives designed to increase regional cooperation as well as the capacity of individual members. While there was talk in 2007 regarding an endorsement by the ASEAN ministers of a 'draft agreement on forest fire handling',[94] the most substantial agreement was widely held to be the ASEAN Agreement on Transboundary Haze, which was endorsed in June 2002. Once again, the agreement repeated the preventative measures contained in the declarations of 1995 and 1997 and called for the establishment of an ASEAN Coordinating Centre for Transboundary Haze Pollution Control.[95] While the agreement was hailed by the United Nations Environmental Program (UNEP) as 'a potential model for tackling transboundary issues worldwide', at the time of writing Indonesia (the target of the agreement) had not yet ratified the instrument into domestic law.[96] Thus, as a consequence of the continued failure to place regional interests above national interests, the 'haze' returned in 2010.[97]

The economic crisis of 1997–98

Economic development has always represented a central pillar of ASEAN regionalism as its relationship with domestic stability and regime security for each of the ASEAN members has provided a common basis for mutual identification and interest harmonization. Unsurprisingly, therefore, the period when ASEAN was generally acknowledged to be the most cohesive and effective coincided not just with ASEAN diplomacy in connection with the Cambodian crisis, but also with the unprecedented phase of economic growth between the 1980s and 1990s. During this period, the 'tiger economies' of Malaysia, Thailand and Singapore consistently achieved more than 10 per cent per annum increases in gross domestic product (GDP). This period of sustained high economic growth was, in part, a consequence of the adoption of export-oriented industrialization (EOI) so as to replicate the performance of the Japanese economy during the 1960s and 1970s. However, ASEAN had its own unique set of challenges in the economic sphere; as noted in the previous chapter, the gap between the wealthiest and poorest ASEAN economies widened as a consequence of membership expansion. Nevertheless, by 1993 the World Bank had singled out the Asian Tigers as models for long-term economic development and published a book entitled *The East Asian Economic Miracle.*[98] At the peak of Asian growth, some had anointed the next millennium as the 'Pacific Century'.[99]

However, the combined effect of the 'haze' and the economic crisis meant that by 'the end of 1998, this picture of ASEAN was hardly recognizable'.[100]

The economic crisis commenced with Thailand's devaluation of its currency (baht) in May 1997. Due to a fall in exports, as well as the borrowing of massive amounts of foreign currency to finance property development in Thailand, the size of Thailand's current account deficit ballooned and many investors (including Wall Street) assessed the Thai currency to be overvalued. Consequently, speculators attacked the Thai baht immediately after the government floated it. While not an ASEAN initiative, the ASEAN central banks initially tried to defend the baht with funds provided by the Bank of Thailand. However, it was not long before 'all evidence of practical solidarity disappeared'.[101] The speculators then moved on to other ASEAN states whose similar characteristics (including shared trade deficits) indicated their vulnerability to speculative attacks.[102] The crisis spread quickly and within a few months practically all the 'liberalized' economies within the region (the original ASEAN members except Singapore) had been ravaged by the effects of the crisis.[103]

The advent of the economic crisis has been explained, with varying degrees of emphasis, through a combination of domestic, regional and global factors. However, considerable debate remains over which of these spheres represented the primary cause. From the perspective of the International Monetary Fund (and the 'Washington establishment'), the crisis was a result of structural deficiencies such as weak corporate governance, poor standards of disclosure, lack of transparency, corruption and crony capitalism.[104] An alternative perspective holds that the economic fundamentals behind the affected Asian states were sound, despite the various trade difficulties experienced at the time. Therefore, and within this perspective, the real cause of the financial crisis was 'investor panic' which had itself been a consequence of failed banking regulation systems regionally and globally.[105] However, while some scholars claim that the weight of the evidence 'most strongly supports' the latter scenario, others suggest that the various structural inadequacies and institutional weaknesses underlined by the International Monetary Fund (IMF) did at least play some role during the financial crisis.[106] Moreover, it is also important to acknowledge the possibility suggested by Smith and Jones that a regional tendency to blame the crisis on cultural insensitivities and exogenous actors – including the IMF, the US and related 'Jewish conspiracies' – may also have 'served the interests of regional governments [and] ... thus enabled the largely unaccountable East Asian political class to evade blame for their own culpability in causing the meltdown'.[107]

Regardless of the cause of the crisis, one certainty is that it had immediate economic and political consequences. The devastating effects were such that ASEAN lacked the institutional mechanisms and capacity necessary to provide tangible assistance for the purpose of either the recovery of its member economies or the prevention of political instability. Thus, within twelve months, the currencies in the most effected economies had depreciated from between 39 per cent (e.g. the Malaysian ringgit) to as much as 84 per cent (e.g. the Indonesian rupiah).[108] Furthermore, at the peak of the crisis, the World Bank estimated that

Indonesia, Malaysia, the Philippines, South Korea and Thailand had lost $115 billion in foreign direct investment (FDI) while others have outlined how the equivalent of 18 per cent of GDP vanished from Southeast Asia and Korea in just seven months.[109] Further, Indonesia's per capita GDP (PPP) in 2007 (US$3,600) still remained lower than before the impact of the economic crisis in 1997 (GDP with PPP US$4,600). The economic crisis also bankrupted reserves and weakened the financial and property markets, reduced consumption and manufacturing, and generated high levels of inflation, unemployment, labour migration and political unrest.

The political unrest that followed soon led to regime contestation in Thailand, Malaysia and Indonesia. In the case of Thailand, Prime Minister Chavalit Yongchaiyudh was forced to resign, in part, for failing to adequately respond to the downward spiral of his country's economy and a perceived inability to properly negotiate with the IMF. In Malaysia, the strain of the economic crisis led to frictions between the policy prescriptions of the Deputy Prime Minister Anwar Ibrahim and those of Prime Minister Mahathir and culminated in a full-scale political crisis. Mahathir interpreted Anwar's calls for an end to 'crony capitalism' as a direct attack on his powerbase and he responded by sacking Anwar from cabinet amid charges of 'abuse of office, corruption and sexual misconduct'.[110] Nevertheless, in terms of regime contestation, the most devastating consequences of the economic crisis took place in Indonesia. Aside from the earlier mentioned decline in the value of the rupiah, some estimated that the average standard of living had been reversed by as much as three decades and that the rate of real unemployment had reached as high as 20 to 30 per cent.[111]

The thirty year rule of President Suharto's New Order regime had been grounded in performance legitimacy.[112] The economic severity of the crisis in Indonesia soon led to anti-Chinese rioting – exacerbated by political scapegoating[113] – culminating in massive student protests against the regime. Suharto was subsequently forced to resign in May 1998. A year later, Major General Agus Wirahadikusumah wrote that the fall of the New Order regime would also be interpreted as the end of the Indonesian armed forces sense of 'invulnerability'.[114] However, the fall of the regime also represented a new era as the new government adopted a series of reforms (collectively known as *reformasi*) thus marking a turning point towards the implementation and consolidation of democracy. As will be discussed in the next chapter, Indonesia's newfound democratic system of governance has resulted in a very different approach to foreign relations including a fresh interpretation of the future of regional integration and the ASEAN Way.

A further consequence of the crisis was the degeneration of relations between the ASEAN members together with an associated decline in the salience of the ASEAN Way. For example, the arrest of Anwar Ibrahim soon resulted in 'public criticism' by Thai officials along with the leaders of the Philippines (Estrada) and Indonesia (Habibie).[115] The extent of the contravention by these leaders is aptly summarized by Collins:

> Estrada made a series of public comments about Malaysia's political and judicial procedures, and he raised the prospect of boycotting the APEC summit that was held in Kuala Lumpur. Habibie also refused to rule out boycotting the summit and only agreed to attend after Anwar was released from detention. Both presidents met Anwar's daughter Nurual Izzah, who led protests against Mahathir, and stated their support for Anwar, with Estrada exhorting her to tell her father 'not to waver, because he is fighting for a cause, the cause of the Malaysian people'. Such actions were clearly at odds with the principle of non-interference. Not only were ASEAN members criticizing another member over its handling of an internal problem, but they were also giving tacit support to the opposition.[116]

While a 'greatly angered Mahathir' initially protested against 'unwarranted interference[s] in Malaysia's internal affairs', the Malaysian government soon resorted to several more aggressive measures. In the case of Indonesia, Malaysia questioned the legitimacy of the President Habibie's leadership while, in the case of the Philippines, security exercises were cancelled and there were even suggestions of possible support for insurgency movements in Mindanao.[117] Malaysia also stated that it would consider stopping permits for Indonesian and Filipino workers while warning the Thai Foreign Ministry that any critical comments within the Thai press could also negatively affect their bilateral relations.[118] At the time, Surin Pitsuwan, Thailand's Foreign Minister, responded by stating that the Malaysian government should not regard the countries making 'constructive remarks' on the nation's political situation as 'enemies' because such 'criticism and comments [are] … being made out of our friendship [and] … will help the Southeast Asian region as a whole'.[119]

The economic crisis had also contributed to a decline in other aspects of regional relations leaving the impression that the 'only shared regional value' was recourse to a Darwinian notion of survival of the fittest.[120] For example, in the wake of the crisis, a number of public insults were exchanged between Singapore, Malaysia and Indonesia that carried racist undertones while Malaysia and Singapore also resumed their quarrel over longstanding territorial disputes along with other issues related to the economic crisis. Furthermore, Malaysia forced the closure of a facility in Singapore trading shares with Malaysia (the Central Limit Order Book), knowing that the subsequent panic selling would primarily affect the Singaporean stakeholders – who owned 90 per cent of the shares.[121] Singapore, for its part, allegedly protested against Habibie's new leadership by withholding US$5 billion in loans to Indonesia. Meanwhile, tensions over the Spratly islands re-emerged between Malaysia and the Philippines (Malaysia having built further structures on its reefs) and Thailand's relations with Myanmar also worsened over 'border disputes, refugees and the drug trade'.[122] The economic crisis also impacted on other aspects of the region's comprehensive security. For example, most of the ASEAN states were forced to cut their security and defence budgets, suspend arms procurement programmes, and reduce allocation for defence research and development. The constrained budgets of the Asian states also affected the amount of money available to combat transnational crime including 'drug interdiction, opium poppy replacement crops, and cooperative regional responses'.[123] Finally, the social impact of the economic crisis was also likely to have enlarged the 'possible pool of recruits to crime'.[124]

Economic vulnerability: driving economic cooperation and institutionalization?

During the 1997 financial crisis, the ASEAN heads of government met at the Second *Informal* ASEAN Summit held at Kuala Lumpur in December 1997. A key result of the meeting was agreement over the ASEAN Vision 2020 which had been proposed a year earlier at the First Informal Leaders' Summit. In response to the divisions generated by the financial crisis, the ASEAN leaders sought to display a more united front by pledging 'closer *economic integration*' and the establishment of an ASEAN community 'bound by a common *regional identity*' via a '*concert* of Southeast Asian nations'.[125] At the empirical level, the financial crisis also helped to 'galvanize regional thinking' on some issues.[126] Consequently, the ASEAN members adopted the *Hanoi Plan of Action* and the *Statement on Bold Measures* at the sixth ASEAN Summit in December 1998. The declared purpose of the 'Hanoi Summit' was to commit members to a 'higher plane of regional cooperation in order to strengthen ASEAN's effectiveness in dealing with the challenges of growing interdependence within ASEAN and of its integration into the global economy'.[127] The associated *Statement on Bold Measures* aimed to increase the liberalization of trade in services, accelerate the implementation of the ASEAN Free Trade Area (AFTA) for the ASEAN-6 from 2003 to 2002 and also sought, via the implementation of a framework agreement on an ASEAN Investment Area (AIA), to develop special incentives and privileges for foreign direct investment (FDI).[128] The need to address the issue of FDI reflected a growing concern regarding the flow of FDI to China at the expense of the region.

Over time, there also emerged a 'distinctively intergovernmental structure' involving a complex array of meetings and summits for the purpose of formulating collective policies in response to regional problems.[129] In order to facilitate these developments, and to assist in the formulation of policy (particularly on the economic front), the Secretariat needed to be strengthened. Some of the measures included the addition of a second Deputy Secretary-General (DSG), a staff increase from sixty-four to ninety-nine, and an enlarged mandate for the Secretary-General. However, until the drafting the ASEAN Charter (Chapter 7), the ASEAN leaders refrained from any discussion of providing the Secretariat with some form of supranational capacity. Furthermore, the Secretariat remained underfunded, understaffed and incapable of handling its increased responsibilities.[130]

Despite the above achievements, together with the rhetoric of the Vision 2020, it is important to note that the financial crisis did not *immediately* result in the coordination of the region's economic policies through ASEAN. The CLMV countries, for their part, had been unimpressed by the level of disunity in the region. Further, they interpreted the events surrounding the economic crisis as a warning about the heightened vulnerability and sensitivity associated with both trade liberalization and the relaxation of political controls. These concerns were reinforced by perceptions of Indonesia's vulnerability to IMF demands, which were, in turn, interpreted by some pockets of elite as having contributed to the downfall of Suharto's New Order regime. Consequently, the CLMV members initially slowed the pace of reform in both the economic and political spheres.[131] Thus, one Ministry of Defence official from Singapore reflected on these developments by explaining that 'the new ASEAN countries, particularly Laos and Cambodia and perhaps Myanmar, [were] a little bit like rabbits caught in the headlights of globalization'.[132]

Disunity also emerged between the economic policies of the original ASEAN members. Singapore, for example, accelerated the pace of trade liberalization and economic reform while Malaysia acted against the advice of the IMF by imposing currency control mechanisms. Further, the original ASEAN members became more focused on their internal security dilemmas with the consequence that they provided little by way of regional assistance to the newer and poorer CLMV members for the purpose of capacity building and economic development. Such assistance had been expected by these countries and, moreover, was necessary in order to reduce the development gap so that the new members would have the *capacity* to keep pace with future commitments for regional economic cooperation and integration.[133] Further, while the economic crisis exposed the CLMV countries to substantial international pressures for liberal market reform, some scholars have argued that the extent of pressure fell short of ensuring such reforms would be inevitable.[134] As will be seen, and within a few years of the crisis, the behaviour of the Singaporean government indicated that its political elite had come to a similar assessment. From the Singaporean perspective, continued economic reforms, including trade liberalization, represented the only viable response to the internationally vulnerable economies of Southeast Asia. For the Singaporean elite, the advent of the financial crisis only reaffirmed this view.

Singapore's economic perspective can partly be explained by the fact that it has the strongest capacity in terms of its economic, political and military institutions. The country's economic bureaucracy is highly professional and it has long been considered one of the most liberalized economies in the world.[135] Consequently, Singapore led regional calls for economic unity during the months and years that followed the financial crisis and Singapore's then Prime Minister, Goh Chok Tong, pushed for the creation of a new East Asia free trade zone. His rationale was that this would boost trade between the Asian countries, thereby providing an additional tool to facilitate the region's recovery from the financial crisis and, in the longer term, provide a counterweight to the potential impact of free trade zones in Europe and North America.[136] In 1998, with the financial crisis having not yet passed, Singapore also pushed to accelerate the pace of trade liberalization under AFTA but, by this time, two of the original ASEAN members – Indonesia and the Philippines – were also cautious about the pace of regional integration and they subsequently contested the Singaporean proposal.[137] Thus, by the close of 1998, Singapore found that its belief in the value of monetary liberalization as a means to respond to the challenges of globalization had garnered little support from its ASEAN counterparts.

In the absence of regional support, Singapore responded by seeking to secure its own economic interests outside the ASEAN framework on a unilateral basis.[138] Subsequently, reports of a 'surprise plan to sign a free trade agreement (FTA) with New Zealand' emerged a year later and Singapore was asked by some of its ASEAN counterparts to explain why it was acting contrary to the 'collective interests' of ASEAN.[139] This FTA was the first of many; by 2010 Singapore had entered into at least eighteen bilateral and trilateral FTAs with actors ranging from the United States to the Hashemite Kingdom of Jordon.[140] Further verification of the motives behind Singapore's actions was provided by its Trade and Industry Minister, who acknowledged that Singapore's pursuit of bilateral FTAs had, 'to some extent', been influenced by its own disappointment with the pace of regional trade liberalization as well as global developments.[141] While several ASEAN members opposed Singapore's pursuit of bilateral FTAs, Malaysia was the most vocal in its criticism of Singapore, with several statements by senior Malaysian officials and dozens of disapproving articles in the Malaysian press.[142] Goh Chok Tong responded to this criticism by arguing that 'those who can run faster should run faster. They should not be restrained by those who don't want to run at all'.[143] Malaysia continued its criticism unabated and Singapore responded by accusing Malaysia of considering a free trade agreement with Japan; one which Malaysia's Prime Minister said he knew nothing about.[144]

Some ASEAN elite also asserted that Singapore's actions could undermine ASEAN-based multilateral negotiations with trading partners such as China, Japan and Australia.[145] Nonetheless, the limitations to ASEAN solidarity in the economic sphere soon became evident when, only a few months later, Thailand announced that it would be pursuing bilateral FTAs with the Czech Republic, Croatia and South Korea. In justifying Thailand's actions, Boontipa Simaskul, Director-General of the Department of Business Economics, said that such agreements were necessary not only because they help to increase export volume and market share but also because of the failure of the WTO 'Seattle talks, APEC's slow pace on trade liberalization and the increasing number of countries forming such pacts'.[146] In May 2002 the Philippines followed both Thailand and Singapore's example when its President, Gloria Arroyo, announced her intention to pursue a bilateral FTA with Japan. The final irony occurred five months later when Malaysia, previously Singapore's biggest critic on the issue, announced that it was now ready to pursue bilateral FTAs with its trading partners including, potentially, China, the United States and Japan (which it had previously denied).[147]

The economic unilateralism that has emerged in Southeast Asia may have provided nett benefits for the individual ASEAN members; however, the overlapping 'noodle bowl' of bilateral FTAs is not advantageous overall as it will facilitate 'trade diversion' along with a reduction in the efficiency of trade through raised administrative costs and the absorption of additional resources.[148] Further, as suggested by Christopher Dent, the manner and form by which these ASEAN states have pursued bilateral trade arrangements has been 'more likely to bring division rather than inclusion to regional community building endeavours in Southeast Asia over the long run'.[149] Thus, evidence of intra-regional competition and the continued pursuit of relative gains can be seen in the rhetoric of the region's leaders. For example, in the context of negotiations for a Thai–US FTA, Thaksin Shinawatra argued that 'we will be at a huge disadvantage to *others* if we lose our access to the US market, as other countries will pursue their own deals. We need to move now, before we have no more room to move'.[150]

Despite the continued pursuit of self-interest and relative gains, ASEAN has continued to progress with the implementation of AFTA. In 1998 the target tariff level of 0–5 per cent for the ASEAN six was accelerated to 2002 while the new members were granted longer implementation phases: 2006 for Vietnam, 2008 for Myanmar and Laos, and 2010 for Cambodia.[151] Further, ASEAN set a target date for the ASEAN-6 to remove all tariffs for products in the Common Effective Preferential Tariff (CEPT) inclusion lists and by the time ASEAN reached this date 99 per cent of all goods had reached this target.[152] However, since AFTA's inception, the share of intra-ASEAN exports as a percentage of total ASEAN exports has increased by only 3.6 per cent to around 25 per cent.[153] Further, the rate of usage of the AFTA tariff preferences remains extremely low – an estimated 5 per cent.[154] Here, the most significant problem is not so much the remaining tariffs (averaging 0.9 per cent) but that AFTA has not added much to the trade liberalization already undertaken by the ASEAN members on a unilateral basis.[155] Aside from a general need to create intra-ASEAN trade advantages beyond tariffs, Hadi Soesastro specifically argues that intra-ASEAN trade has, until recently, been impeded by a lack of enforcement mechanisms, the cost and ambiguity of the Rules of Origin (ROO), excise duties, customs procedures and discriminatory 'quality control measures'.[156] In the case of the latter, a senior Malaysian Foreign Ministry official stated in an interview:

> Let me give you some examples to illustrate how things are not so fine in ASEAN … I have heard of Malaysian goods being stopped at the border, they look at the old customs document and say this thing doesn't fall into that category.… So Thailand is a particular problem, and Thailand always gives these obscure reasons [why goods cannot enter] and so we want to have some way to resolve these problems.[157]

A further challenge was highlighted in Chapter 3 in the context of the GDP of each ASEAN member together with the economic divides associated with those figures. While Table 3.1 indicated that Vietnam has started to catch up with the original members of ASEAN, Cambodia, Laos and Myanmar remain far behind. At the socio-economic level, the gap between the wealthier and poorer ASEAN members is also particularly stark. For example, the 'UNDP's *Human Development Report* found that while less than 2 per cent of the population in Malaysia and Thailand live in poverty, 'the corresponding figures for Cambodia and Laos were 34 percent and 27 percent respectively.'[158] Consequently, the region has remained highly dependent on foreign aid from institutions such as the World Bank and the IMF. This dependency has been exacerbated by the level of foreign debt. By 2006, some of the ASEAN members also continued to maintain high levels of foreign debt and these countries included the Philippines, which owed US$54.1 billion, Malaysia US$57.8 billion, Thailand US$57.8 billion and Indonesia US$130.4 billion.[159] By 31 December 2008, and in the midst of the global financial crisis, the level of debt in these countries had increased, with the Philippines owing US$66.3 billion, Malaysia US$75.3 billion, Thailand US$65.1 billion and Indonesia US$155.1 billion.[160] Such debts have also rendered the ASEAN members more vulnerable to exogenous influence and interference. Given this, together with the more general influence of international financial institutions, regional 'autonomy is now constrained and policy preferences shaped by a range of external factors'.[161]

Despite the challenges to regional cooperation – as generated by continued domestic constraints (capacity) and international competition (globalization) *inter alia* – Figure 4.5 indicates that the majority of the participants from the 'elite' survey now believe that economic liberalization will benefit their country.

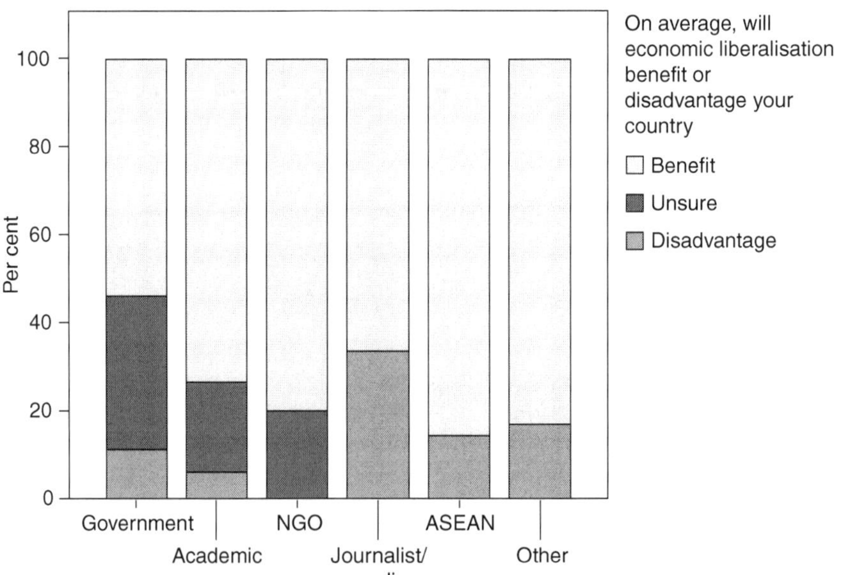

Figure 4.5 Perceptions of economic liberalization (government) (source: compiled by author).

As later chapters will verify, there were a number of reasons why the region's elite (and their leaders) also came to realize that it was increasingly necessary to forge a deeper accord between the ASEAN nations in order to facilitate greater cooperation and institutionalization – particularly on the economic front. First, the adverse effects of the economic crisis had been compounded by a number of other transnational security challenges including the 'haze' episode that was discussed in the previous section. Second, the heightened vulnerability of each member to these security challenges also contributed to a general consensus that economic cooperation and integration would provide the wealth and associated capacity necessary to 'enhance the region's security'. Third, the downfall of Suharto's New Order regime and the perception that the IMF contributed to such a downfall reinvigorated the need to deepen both 'national' and 'regional' resilience. Such resilience had been tested on several fronts, including domestic pressures concerning regime legitimacy and the multifaceted effects of globalization (e.g. the aforementioned growth of foreign debt). Finally, in order to reduce the region's development gap and simultaneously enhance regional stability, the ASEAN members needed to recover the high levels of FDI they had previously benefited from. The older ASEAN members, in particular, realized that this would require the projection of 'best managerial practice and ... the projection of a norm of political accountability into the regional order'.[162]

During the course of the last ten years, these imperatives have contributed to further momentum in terms of economic cooperation and integration. As further examined in Chapter 7, examples include the ASEAN Plus Three arrangement (APT), the ASEAN Swap Arrangement, the ASEAN Surveillance Process (ASP), the ASEAN Economic Community (AEC) and its associated plans of action and blueprint. While the continued operation of the principle of non-interference has been attributed as a reason why some of these initiatives were dismissed as either 'too complicated' or have required a 'level of coordination and cohesion that ASEAN had deliberately avoided in the past',[163] AFTA and other economic endeavours represent a normative development in as far as they require coordinated action through cooperative enterprises which, in turn, requires a degree of transparency and dialogue vis-à-vis the domestic policies of the ASEAN member-states.[164] Further, the eventual consensus that emerged regarding the utility (or even necessity) of greater regional economic cooperation and integration continues to be driven by the pursuit of performance legitimacy and a perception that resilience to global economic forces can only be achieved through collective responses. In this context, the notions of national and regional resilience continue to provide some explanatory value in regional affairs.

Conclusions

The political, security and economic issues reviewed in this chapter provide some significant caveats concerning the current boundaries of any regionalist project in Southeast Asia. Importantly, the onset of armed conflict vis-à-vis the

Preah Vihear Temple reveals low levels of both socio-cultural and political-security integration whilst also impinging on the threshold test to institutionalized regionalism: a security community. While Southeast Asia can continue to *technically* claim that there has not been any war between the members of ASEAN since the Association's inception, armed skirmishes in connection with the Preah Vihear Temple have demonstrated the danger of securitized borders where there is a close proximity between opposing armed forces. Consequently, as the next chapter notes, the highly securitized border between Thailand and Myanmar has also resulted in armed skirmishes through to the present decade. Meanwhile, the Sulawesi Sea incident continues to have the potential to follow a similar pattern. The risk of an escalation of conflict between proximate militaries is further exacerbated by the fact that most of the armed forces in the region remain under-professionalized. Adverse historical memories, nationalism and international scape-goating – as a political tool in response to weak political legitimacy – add to this complex web of potential conflict initiators.

In the case of the economic crisis and the 'haze', the initial rivalry and disunity that ensued detracted from ASEAN's credibility together with the level of mutual identification and reciprocity to be expected at high complex integration. Here, the 'haze' provided an example of how cooperation between the ASEAN states regarding transnational issues and problems is primarily limited to combating problems that 'equally' affect the states involved. In this instance – and given that the 'haze' in Indonesia always travels north to Singapore, Malaysia and Thailand – Jakarta's response was primarily limited to rhetorical declarations of intent. Moreover, the admission of Myanmar, Laos and Cambodia as members of ASEAN, at this critical juncture in time, simultaneously increased the material and normative divides between the ASEAN members. Given these developments, Alan Collins argues that the economic crisis and regional 'haze' reveals that ASEAN's modus vivendi is limited to 'a loose arrangement of states that have agreed not to make the difficult task of nation-building harder by criticizing one another'.[165] However, the reality is that even this limited benchmark does not stand when the national interests of the ASEAN member states have been significantly challenged. Public criticisms regarding human rights (e.g. the issue of the arrest of Anwar Ibrahim), Indonesia's failure to respond to the 'haze', and actions by Malaysia and Thailand over the Southern Thailand insurgency not only provide additional examples of when the ASEAN Way has been contravened, but also indicate that in the political and security sphere the ASEAN states have been unwilling to sacrifice national interests for the collective good of the region and, moreover, continue to interact on a competitive basis through the pursuit of relative gains.

Despite the caveats above, during the years that followed the financial crisis, ASEAN partially redeemed itself in the context of economic cooperation and integration. For example, ASEAN has progressed with the implementation of AFTA and launched other initiatives such as the AIA in an attempt to regain some of the FDI that it had lost to China. In order to support these developments, the ASEAN members also strengthened the ASEAN Secretariat. While these developments have contributed to the institutionalization of ASEAN, the Association remained intergovernmental in nature as the sovereignty of individual members was not significantly impeded – at least not beyond the economic sphere. Here, the willingness of the Southeast Asian nations to agree to economic cooperation, integration and institutionalization can be partly explained by the fact that these actions do not detract from regime security. Instead, the prospect of accelerated economic development provides the more authoritarian members with 'performance legitimacy' and thereby helps to protect these regimes from internal pressures for democratic reform. Successful cooperation in the economic sphere has also been driven by a related desire to build greater regional resilience. In this context, vulnerability to currency speculators during the financial crisis did help to galvanize regional thinking, as have other factors such as a desire to reduce dependence on extra-regional aid and finance. Nonetheless, it is also important to recognize that there have been limitations to economic unity (e.g. the pursuit of FTAs on a bilateral basis) as well as the empirical outcomes of such cooperative endeavours (e.g. the limited increase to intra-regional trade).

As noted at the outset, it has not been possible for this chapter, or indeed the study, to cover the vast array of the political and economic challenges to regional cohesion; neither has it been possible to cover the broad spectrum of ASEAN's declarations and agreements in response to these challenges. Nonetheless, it is apparent that the majority of declarations covered by the analysis have been high in ambition but low in implementation. While the chapter has already noted how breaches of non-interference and the ASEAN Way have frequently occurred in relation to bilateral disputes and conflicts of interest, when there has been ASEAN-wide unity on a given issue then any subsequent cooperation has always been guided by a strict adherence to the ASEAN Way – at least through to the turn of the millennium. Thus, the chapter noted that the implementation of ASEAN agreements remains a problem and the Association may risk maintaining little more than a 'declaratory' reputation should it continue to adhere to the principles of non-interference and consensus-based decision-making. Given these considerations, together with the inability of the ASEAN states to unilaterally guard against the pressures of a more globalized world, a growing proportion of the region's political elite have viewed it necessary to empower ASEAN with an increased capacity to respond not only to economic challenges but to also provide effective responses to both traditional and non-traditional security challenges. As the next chapter will examine, such challenges to ASEAN's modus operandi have also been generated by the emergence of new regional values as a consequence of democratic transitions in some ASEAN members.

5 Political transitions, changing values and visions for the future

The study has thus far investigated several issues including the major political, security and economic factors that have variously driven and/or challenged cooperation, institutionalization and complex integration in Southeast Asia. This chapter shifts the focus of attention to the issue of democratization and an associated pursuit of normative and institutional change in ASEAN, the most significant outcome of which was the launch of the Association's vision to establish a security community by 2015. The chapter analyses these developments through three sections. The first section examines the case study of Thailand; it evaluates how democratization has affected Thailand's national interests together with the values and norms that it has espoused in ASEAN. Here, one of the most significant outcomes of democratization was the government's attempt to reform the ASEAN Way through its proposal for 'flexible engagement'. The next section examines the impact of further democratic transitions in other countries including the Philippines and Indonesia. The analysis indicates that democratization has contributed to more innovative responses to security challenges and has enabled greater activism by political elite vis-à-vis human security challenges in other ASEAN members. Democratization has also contributed to a proliferation of NGOs, a greater role for civil society, and the emergence of Track 3 dialogue such as the ASEAN People's Assembly. Further, the section demonstrates how shifts towards or away from democratic systems of governance affect foreign policies and the values they espouse, including a willingness for other countries to play an active role in previously sensitive issues such as Aceh. While these developments have further undermined the ASEAN Way, the final section reveals how democratization within Indonesia, together with an emerging perception of the inadequacy of ASEAN, contributed to a renewed effort to reform ASEAN's norms and institutions.

Thailand: domestic change and regional values

During ASEAN's first three decades, the Association was perceived by some to be little more than a club of dictators; a characterization originally coined in 1997 by Thailand's former Deputy Foreign Minister Sukhumbhand Paribatra.[1] However, the reality was that the so-called 'third wave' of democracy had started to sweep through Southeast Asia ten years earlier. This democratic wave commenced with the 1986 'people power movement' in the Philippines, the transition towards a more consolidated form of democracy by Thailand from 1992, and finally the adoption of *reformasi* (democratic reform process) by Indonesia from 1998. Interestingly, the level of democracy in Malaysia, particularly in respect to civil liberties, increased during the period of Abdullah Badawi's rule and, arguably, the UN peacekeeping mission succeeded in establishing a degree of democracy in Cambodia. However, until this time, and with the exception of Thailand, 'strongmen' have historically ruled the original ASEAN governments:[2] Ferdinand Marcos in the Philippines, Lee Kuan Yew in Singapore, Mahathir bin Mohamad in Malaysia and Sukarno followed by Suharto in Indonesia. Further, political authority had also been closely linked to the military in the Philippines, Indonesia and, notably, Thailand.[3]

In the case of Thailand, the military continued to play a significant role in both domestic and foreign affairs through to the 1990s. In 1988, and while under the continued influence of the Thai military, a policy of 'constructive engagement' with Myanmar emerged; a policy that was refined and officially articulated in 1991.[4] According to Leszek Buszynski, constructive engagement had two purposes. As a political device, 'it was a means of ensuring Thailand's security as well as economic interests'. However, as a diplomatic device 'it was designed to deflect international attention from Thailand's cooperative policy in relation to SLORC' (Myanmar's State Law and Order Restoration Council) with the justification that there would be a subsequent improvement to the behaviour of the regime.[5] In the case of the former, key members of the Thai military, including General Chavalit, the commander-in-chief of the Thai armed forces, had established personal economic relations with the Burmese military, including logging concessions.[6] In the case of the second purpose, the political rhetoric of the time argued that the policy would have a positive effect on Myanmar 'through dialogue, influence, and persuasion rather than the policies of isolation and sanctions pursued by most of the international community'.[7] Subsequently, in 1994 ASEAN adopted Thailand's policy with Myanmar's possible membership in mind. In order to achieve this goal, Thailand's new Foreign Minister, Prasong Soonsiri, then invited the Foreign Minister of Myanmar, U Ohn Gyaw, to attend the ASEAN summit meeting in Bangkok as an 'observer'. As a goodwill gesture, the junta released Aung San Suu Kyi from six years of house arrest shortly before an ASEAN meeting in Brunei; this gesture was seen by some elites to validate ASEAN's constructive engagement policy. By 1996, Myanmar had become an official observer in ASEAN and a member of the ARF. Despite the protests of the European Union and the United States, the country was admitted as a full member in July 1997.

Meanwhile, Thailand became increasingly democratic following the election of Chuan Leekpai's Thai Democratic Party. During the time of his government, NGOs, the Thai middle class and business related interest groups became increasingly influential in connection with both domestic and foreign affairs.[8] Here the economic crisis is also relevant. Not only did the crisis lead to the resignation of Prime Minister Chavalit, but it also contributed to a new round of constitution writing in order to deepen the level of democracy and good governance in the country.[9] Further, the globalized nature of Thailand's economy meant that economic growth was dependent on the confidence of foreign capital investors. Thus, a subsequent perception that capital markets favoured democratic and stable regimes changed the 'political calculus' and 'impinged on local politics in a way that advantaged those who already advocated greater democratization'.[10] In the years that followed, Thailand further consolidated its democracy and it was during Chuan's second term in office (1997–2000) that the military largely withdrew from politics until a military coup in 2006. Meanwhile, through the appointment of Surin Pitsuwan as Thailand's Foreign Minister, Chuan Leekpai helped to build a professional and highly capable civilian controlled foreign ministry that quickly asserted itself as the lead actor in Thailand's foreign affairs.[11] This decline in the military's influence has, in turn, affected Thailand's foreign policy regarding Myanmar.

By the late 1990s, Thailand had become internationally recognized as having 'an accomplished record in promoting political stability, civil liberties and human rights through the process of democratization'.[12] According to Acharya, because Prime Minister Chuan valued this image he interpreted 'constructive engagement' to be irreconcilable with both his 'back to barracks' policy and Thailand's values and identity – including his promotion of Thailand's democratic credentials to the world.[13] Thus, following a proposal by Malaysia's then Deputy Prime Minister, Anwar Ibrahim, to allow for 'constructive interventions' in each other's internal affairs, Thailand's Foreign Minister, Surin Pitsuwan, launched his own initiative for regional change – flexible engagement. Surin argued that an effective response to the challenges of globalization would require the more advanced ASEAN members to more closely coordinate policies concerning trade, finance, investment and macroeconomic issues. He further argued that ASEAN's standing and voice had been impaired by a lack of transparency, the structures of the governments in power, and the issue of democracy and associated human rights problems.[14] At the 1998 Asia-Pacific Roundtable (APR) in Kuala Lumpur, a Track II dialogue run by ISIS Malaysia, Surin Pitsuwan stated the following:

> ASEAN members perhaps no longer can afford to adopt a noncommittal stand and avoid passing judgment on events in member countries. Respect for the principle of non-interference is one reason why the grouping had come this far; however, if domestic events in one member's territory impact adversely on another member's internal affairs, not to mention regional peace and prosperity, much can be said in favour of ASEAN members playing a more proactive role. Therefore, ASEAN countries have an overriding interest in the internal affairs of [their] fellow members and may, on occasion, find it necessary to recommend a certain course of action on specific issues that affect us all, directly or indirectly.... We may need to make intra-ASEAN relations more ... 'constructive' than before.[15]

Within two weeks, Surin attended a special address at Thammasat University in Bangkok. Here, the Foreign Minister specifically focused on political reform and the advancement of democracy and human rights but did not elaborate on how 'flexible engagement' could be implemented as a component of ASEAN's modus operandi. He stated that 'we should remember that each country is the product of different circumstances, opportunities and constraints. It is a process that each country should work out for itself, in its own way, at its own pace, in its own time'. He said that while he hoped Southeast Asia could retain its dynamism, ASEAN had no choice but to move in the direction of greater openness. More specifically, he stated that 'while reform is, by and large, a domestic process, delays or setbacks in one country can affect the region's recovery, as a whole, especially if that country has extensive trade and investment ties with others in the region'.[16]

Such statements led other ASEAN members to request further clarification, resulting in the circulation of Thailand's Non-Paper on Flexible Engagement (1998). As Haacke points out, the paper sought to justify the Thai proposal by arguing that there was 'a shared moral responsibility in realizing ASEAN's vision for "a concert of Southeast Asian Nations, outward looking, living in peace, stability and prosperity, bonded together in partnership in dynamic development, in a community of caring societies" – as adopted in the ASEAN Vision 2020'.[17] Thailand's Non-Paper further argued:

> [T]he dividing line between domestic affairs on the one hand and external or transnational issues on the other is less clear. Many 'domestic' affairs have obvious external or trans-national dimensions, adversely affecting neighbours, the region and the region's relations with others. In such cases, the affected countries should be able to express their opinion and concerns in [an] open, frank and constructive manner.[18]

Again, the Thai proposal for flexible engagement was 'also illustrative of an earnest [and continued] struggle for international recognition of Thailand's democratic credentials'.[19] As predicted by SIT, such was the extent of the esteem generated by a perception of membership in an international democratic society that, in 1997, Prime Minister Chuan gave a speech to his parliament that provided 'an almost Wilsonian vision of foreign policy by announcing Thailand's participation "on the international stage in the protection and promotion of democratic values and human rights".'[20]

The Chuan government's concern about the ASEAN principle of non-interference was reinforced by its failure in Myanmar. While certain Thai generals continued to benefit from corrupt trading with the Myanmar government and its military elite (the *Tatmadaw*), those not privy to such personal gain maintained historical memories of a Burmese attack on its Kingdom in the seventeenth century. More recently, the *Tatmadaw* had infiltrated Thai territory in the pursuit of insurgent groups, resulting in armed skirmishes along the border.[21] Finally, Thailand had been deeply affected by political instability inside

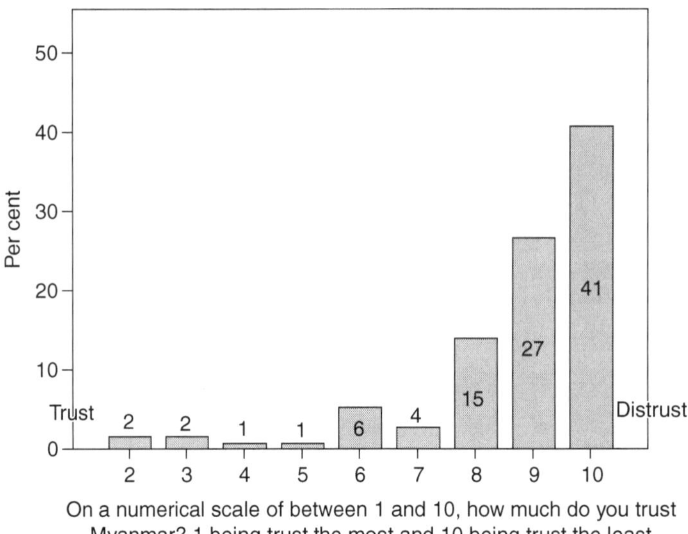

Figure 5.1 Thai perceptions of trust: Myanmar (source: author).

Myanmar as there has been an associated rise in transnational crime including human trafficking and the production of methamphetamines. For example, in 2002 official sources in Thailand reported that about 7.3 million Thais, or 11.5 per cent of the country's sixty-three million people, were either drug users or addicts; almost three million of these were 'students and other young people'.[22] The negative consequences of these developments have not only contributed to one of the most securitized borders in Southeast Asia, but are also reflected by the perceptions of the Thai survey respondents (communal sample) in Figure 5.1. When asked to view a list of Southeast Asian countries and rate them on a numerical scale between the country they trust the most (1) and the country they trust the least (10), 84 per cent of the eighty-one Thai respondents ranked Myanmar between 8 and 10 (trust the least).

Despite Thailand's concerns and subsequent lobbying, Thailand's proposal for 'flexible engagement' was, in the end, 'bitterly opposed by Myanmar' and rejected by all the other ASEAN members except the Philippines – the only other democratic nation at the time.[23] In addition to Myanmar, the remaining CLMV countries also strongly opposed the initiative as they had joined ASEAN under the assumption that the rules of interaction between the ASEAN members would not be changed and that membership in ASEAN would therefore remain a source of regime legitimacy rather than a force for domestic change.[24] While Indonesia's longest serving Foreign Minister, Ali Alatas, had until that time been a staunch supporter of 'non-interference', at the Thirty-first ASEAN Ministerial Meeting in July 1998 he initiated some face-saving diplomacy that led to what was eventually coined 'enhanced interaction'.[25] As a compromise, enhanced interaction carried different implications. Flexible engagement was intended to represent an official sanctioning of interference in other members' internal affairs but enhanced interaction would supposedly 'allow the ASEAN states to interact with one another constructively while preserving the non-interference principle'.[26] Interestingly, the term enhanced interaction has never appeared in any of the official documents of ASEAN. However, as will be seen in the next chapter, ASEAN's unofficial acceptance of enhanced interaction eventually contributed to a 'phased adjustment of the principle' towards flexible engagement.[27]

Despite the limitations of enhanced interaction, there were (and continue to be) significant economic, political and security factors explaining why, over time, ASEAN could not avoid an application of the principle in practice. In part this is because of the organization's political and economic ties to the West, connections that have been strengthened through ASEAN's formation of the ASEAN Regional Forum (ARF) and the Asia–Europe Meeting (ASEM). In the case of the ARF, its continued viability is important to ASEAN due to it being the principle multilateral security forum in the Asia-Pacific. As noted in the previous chapter, this provides ASEAN with a sounding board where it can attempt to influence the foreign policies of a number of the world's major powers including the US, the EU, Russia, China and Japan. By contrast, ASEM is primarily important as a potential gateway to the vast import and export markets in Europe. Nearly 60 per cent of the world's population lives in the ASEM countries and the group also accounts for more than half of world GDP and 60 per cent of global trade.[28]

While the agenda of ASEM was initially dominated by trade issues, the Seoul Summit expanded cooperation to engage with the regional concept of comprehensive security in response to such problems as environmental degradation, human rights, transnational migration and crime, the trafficking of persons and international terrorism. With the exception of terrorism, all these issues are relevant in the context of Myanmar. The importance of ASEAN's international stature in these two organizations has exacerbated the vulnerability of the organization to pressure by the EU and the US vis-à-vis Myanmar. Equally important, the presence of a military dictatorship within ASEAN, not to mention the existence of several other authoritarian and semi-authoritarian states in the group, is a major stumbling block to interest harmonization and policy coordination between the members of both ASEM and the ARF. Finally, ASEAN's international stature has also been affected and the West responded with unmasked cynicism, with a number of the European governments declaring their intention to treat the whole of ASEAN according to its lowest common denominator – Myanmar.[29]

Despite Thailand's shift back towards a more authoritarian style of government following the election of Thaksin Shinawatra's *Thai Rak Thai* (Thais Love Thai) Party, its government continued to launch various initiatives for reform in Myanmar. One example was the 'Bangkok Process', launched at ASEM, which provided a five-step 'roadmap' for reconciliation and democratic reform in

Myanmar. While the SPDC eventually agreed to participate in the process, it seems such consent was provided with the prior knowledge that Khin Nyunt would announce a seven-step roadmap for democracy; thus, the 'Bangkok process' was doomed from the beginning.[30] Thailand also continued to press for Aung San Suu Kyi's release from house arrest and called for the establishment of meaningful dialogue between her, the junta and the ethnic minority groups.

Thailand's foreign policy did, however, start to retreat to a more conservative and restrained position in certain areas. For example, Thailand's Minister of Defence, General Chavalit (who had replaced Prime Minister Chuan in the role) responded to a new spate of border tensions between Thailand and Myanmar by stating that 'repeated incursions by Burmese and Red Wa soldiers on Thai soil were a very small matter and should not be taken seriously'.[31] Despite the lobbying of the Thai Senate Foreign Affairs Committee for a strong military response, the emergence of the Thaksin government meant that Thailand would no longer be willing to jeopardize its economic interests in Myanmar for the sake of its democratic credentials and associated values.[32] As pointed out by a disgruntled employee from the Thai Office of the National Security Council, the leadership style of Prime Minister Thaksin held certain authoritarian tendencies and – as the next section elaborates – such leadership resulted in a return to non-interference in the context of the Southern Thai insurgency.[33] Nonetheless, the Thai government, as a whole, largely continued the momentum towards a more open political economy which, in turn, continued to expose the country's foreign policies to greater extra-mural influence.

Despite developments at the state leadership level, a significant proportion of the Thai elite continue to value democracy, as indicated by extensive interviewing with members of the Thai government and academia. Further, such ideational tendencies were verified in the elite level survey where all twelve of the

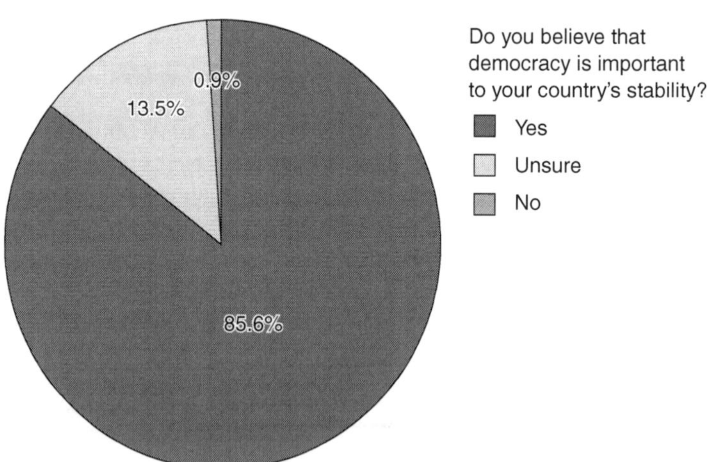

Figure 5.2 Thai grassroots perceptions of democracy (source: author).

elite respondents from Thailand (government and academic) maintained that democracy was both 'important to them personally' and also important to their 'country's stability'. Further, Figure 5.2 demonstrates a zeitgeist effect as far the values of Thai society are concerned. Here, 85.6 per cent of the Thai respondents in the 'communal level survey' indicated that democracy was 'important' to their 'country's stability'. These statistics tie in with Jorn Dosch's observation that there was very little controversy concerning Thailand's decision to send 420 soldiers to Iraq; in line with Chuan Leekpai's Wilsonian vision of foreign policy, the Thai public seemingly accepted the commitment as a part of its international duty 'in the promotion and protection of democratic values and human rights'.[34] At the elite level, however, the extent to which Thailand would return to an authoritarian model of government was constrained by another variable. Here, the relatively democratic ASEAN members (including Thailand) have 'opened international relations and foreign policy making to a larger number of actors compared with authoritarian regimes'.[35] This broadening of foreign policy inputs could potentially have a lasting impact on foreign policy formulation within Southeast Asia. The extent to which this has been the case forms part of the analysis in the remaining sections of the chapter.

Further democratic transitions, second tier activism and non-governmental networks

In terms of democracy, and prior to the economic crisis, Donald Emmerson assessed Southeast Asia to be the most recalcitrant region on earth; ten years after the crisis his assessment is relatively more positive as he argues that 'the region is not immune to change'.[36] Some support for this proposition is evident in the Freedom House Survey statistics in Table 5.1. Since the 1997–98 financial crisis, and through to 2010, civil liberties and political freedom have, on average, improved in six of the ten ASEAN countries. However, the democratic torch once held by the Philippines has since dimmed, with the country now being ranked as only 'partly free' (PF). Interestingly, both Singapore and Malaysia regressed for a number of years following the financial crisis while other countries, such as Brunei, Vietnam and Cambodia achieved marginal improvements in the level of civil liberties and political freedoms.[37] As indicated by the Freedom House data, the region's democratic torch has now passed to Indonesia. Following the financial crisis, Indonesia undertook a phenomenal political transition towards democracy. Prior to 1997, Indonesia had been ranked as 'not free' (NF) with an average score of 6; by 2006 it had reached the status of 'free' (F) with an average score of 2.5 and was the only Southeast Asian state to be listed as free in 2010.

Notwithstanding a degree of domestic instability, together with a temporary loss of a strong regionalist leader,[38] Indonesia's democratic transition did eventually lead to some major political achievements in the country.[39] One example concerns the resolution of a longstanding armed conflict between the Indonesian government and the Free Aceh Movement, or *Gerakan Aceh Merdeka* (GAM),

Table 5.1 Freedom House political freedom and civil liberties

Country	*1996*	*1998*	*2000*	*2002*	*2004*	*2006*	*2008*	*2010*
Indonesia	6.0 (NF)	5.0 (PF)	4.0 (PF)	3.5 (PF)	3.5 (PF)	**2.5 (F)**	**2.5 (F)**	**2.5 (F)**
Philippines	**2.5 (F)**	**2.5 (F)**	**2.5 (F)**	**2.5 (F)**	**2.5 (F)**	3.0 (PF)	3.5 (NF)	3.5 (PF)
Malaysia	4.5 (PF)	5.0 (PF)	5.0 (PF)	5.0 (PF)	5.0 (PF)	4.0 (PF)	4.0 (PF)	4.0 (PF)
Thailand	3.0 (PF)	**2.5 (F)**	**2.5 (F)**	**2.5 (F)**	**2.5 (F)**	3.0 (PF)	5.0 (PF)	4.5 (PF)
Singapore	4.5 (PF)	5.0 (PF)	5.0 (PF)	5.0 (PF)	5.0 (PF)	4.5 (PF)	4.5 (PF)	4.5 (PF)
Cambodia	6.0 (NF)	6.0 (NF)	6.0 (NF)	5.5 (NF)	5.5 (NF)	5.5 (NF)	5.5 (NF)	5.5 (NF)
Brunei	6.5 (NF)	6.0 (NF)	6.0 (NF)	6.0 (NF)	5.5 (NF)	5.5 (NF)	5.5 (NF)	5.5 (NF)
Vietnam	7.0 (NF)	7.0 (F)	7.0 (NF)	6.5 (NF)	6.5 (NF)	6.0 (NF)	6.0 (NF)	6.0 (NF)
Laos	6.5 (NF)	6.5 (NF)	6.5 (NF)	6.5 (NF)	6.5 (NF)	6.5 (NF)	6.5 (NF)	6.5 (NF)
Myanmar	7.0 (NF)	7.0 (NF)	7.0 (NF)	7.0 (NF)	7.0 (NF)	7.0 (NF)	7.0 (NF)	7.0 (NF)

Source: author, based on ‘combined average ratings’ located at www.freedomhouse.org.

through an August 2005 peace agreement. This peace process, the Helsinki Accord, led to regional autonomy for Aceh in July 2006. The final bill, formally known as the 'Law on the Governance of Aceh', was unanimously passed by the Indonesian parliament following extensive consultations and negotiations with GAM, Aceh's local government, the local legislature, human rights activists, Muslim religious leaders and academics. Aside from the government's willingness to negotiate, the process was also noteworthy due to the scale of the concessions granted including permission to create local political parties (such entities are not legally recognized elsewhere in the archipelago) together with permission for independent candidates to run in the subsequent elections.[40] Even more noteworthy, however, has been the role accorded to the international community in aiding and facilitating the peace. As implied by the name of the peace accord, the memorandum of understanding between the Indonesian government and GAM had been negotiated with the participation of the European Union in Helsinki.[41] It was through these negotiations that Indonesia agreed to the establishment of the Aceh Monitoring Mission led by the European Union. The agreement also successfully facilitated the decommissioning of GAM's arms together with accords for the granting of amnesty and the release of political prisoners.[42] President Yudhoyono's government has also had some success in negotiating 'demands for greater regional autonomy' vis-à-vis the West Papuan separatist movement 'without unduly compromising Jakarta's authority'.[43]

A further factor that contributed to the peace in Aceh was the December 2004 tsunami disaster. Aceh bore the brunt of the disaster, having lost more than 130,000 lives. The humanitarian crisis that followed generated international attention and added pressure for the Indonesian government to find a peaceful resolution. Significantly, the foreign educated President of Indonesia, Susilo Bambang Yudhoyono, resisted calls from nationalist leaders and religious clerics to keep the media and foreign aid operations out of Aceh.[44] Instead, President Yudhoyono permitted foreign militaries to enter Indonesian territory for the purpose of delivering humanitarian aid and undertaking reconstruction works. The fact that democratic Indonesia had become less possessive of its sovereignty paid dividends. The international community, buoyed by Indonesia's openness and willingness to embrace assistance (cf. Myanmar's response to Cyclone Nargis), subsequently provided billions of dollars in financial aid and loans.[45] While Acharya has suggested that democracies often deal 'responsibly and creatively with their neighbours', the democratic government of Indonesia has also revealed a heightened capacity to deal with the broader international community in such a fashion.[46]

The significance of granting permission to foreign military forces to enter Indonesian territory should not be underestimated. In part, the President had the necessary authority and political support to undertake these decisions because of a gradual withdrawal of the military from political affairs. As with Thailand, such a process was interdependent with both democratization and several more specific factors. As a retired General, President Yudhoyono himself had an esteemed background in the military and this provided his presidency with the legitimacy necessary to reinvigorate the *reformasi* process. Significantly, other reform minded officers had supported *reformasi* from the outset and these officers found a voice (agency) in the wake of Suharto's downfall. Consequently, the military gradually withdrew from politics and this withdrawal culminated in a constitutional amendment that terminated the seats that had been previously allocated to the military in parliament.[47] As with Thailand, the withdrawal of the military from political affairs coincided with the restructuring of *Deplu*, Indonesia's foreign ministry, so that it became independent from, rather than subordinate to, the Indonesian military (*Tentara Nasional Indonesia*, TNI). In the process, Deplu has evolved in a manner that reflects a 'multi-party environment where it must be neutral and learn to serve changing administrations'.[48] As with the earlier discussion of Thailand, the number of actors influencing Indonesia's foreign policy has increased, which has provided a positive influence on the quality of decision-making – a general phenomenon that has been noted for democracies across the globe.[49]

Democratization, and its impact on the values espoused by the Indonesian government, has also had implications for intra-regional relations. Within ASEAN, Indonesia has demonstrated a greater willingness to speak out on internal affairs, including the Myanmar issue as well as its support for Anwar Ibrahim's own pro-*reformasi* policies, support which greatly angered Mahathir at the time.[50] Meanwhile, when Singapore called on Indonesia to take stronger action against suspected terrorists, President Megawati replied that its democratic system didn't allow arbitrary arrests of the kind permitted by both Singapore and Malaysia's Internal Security Act (ISA).[51] In reflecting on these developments, together with the implications for the ASEAN Way, Indonesia's Director-General for ASEAN (Foreign Ministry), Adian Silalahi, stated that 'we still adhere to those principles' such as non-interference 'but I believe that on this issue we are more open now … Indonesia is more open, more flexible because of the democratization process'.[52] The open and flexible nature of the Indonesian government extends to Indonesia's recent economic performance. In contrast to the *negative* growth rates of –3.6 per cent in Malaysia and –3.3 per cent in Singapore for 2009, Indonesia's economy achieved a solid growth rate of 6.1 per cent in 2008 and 4 per cent in 2009.[53]

In the case of the Philippines, and prior to Indonesia's transition towards democracy, it had been the only supporter of Thailand's proposal for 'flexible engagement'. As with both Thailand and Indonesia, the manner by which democracy has been institutionalized within the Philippines has also increased the number of actors influencing the foreign policy process. For example, in an attempt to avoid the excesses of the Marcos era, the Philippine constitution provides its bicameral congress with substantial blocking powers vis-à-vis the nation's domestic and foreign policies. The constitution's safeguards also prohibit the president from declaring war in the absence of congressional support, and the ratification of treaties can only be done by the senate. Importantly, such democratic reforms also have the potential to generate greater trust due to heightened transparency regarding foreign and defence policies where, for example, the defence procurement and spending programmes of the Philippine government are now subject to significant legislative scrutiny.[54] Such transparency is also crucial in the economic realm as the economic crisis was 'partly blamed on elite centred regionalism' due to the claim that it prevented members from 'sharing vital economic information about their national economies as an early warning mechanism'.[55]

While the Philippines may have lost its status as being 'free' in terms of political and civil liberties, the Filipino government has historically played an active role regarding human rights issues in Southeast Asia and in Myanmar in particular.[56] For example, in November 2004 President Arroyo directly urged Myanmar's Prime Minister Soe Win to engage in political dialogue with the country's opposition leader, Aung San Suu Kyi. As with some other ASEAN nations, the broadening of the number of actors that contribute to foreign policy formulation in the Philippines has also provided more freedom for pockets of political elite to push for change in other ASEAN member-states, even if such activism conflicts with the formal position of the government's leaders. An early example of this occurred in December 2001 when sixteen congressional representatives from the Philippines crossed party lines to sign a 'manifesto of support' for the National League of Democracy.[57]

Similar developments have occurred in Thailand where numerous parliamentarians have developed strong personal interests in, and opposition to, Thailand's business relations with Myanmar. One of the most prominent politicians in this regard has been Kraisak Choonhavan, the Chairman of the Senate Committee on Foreign Affairs. In contrast to Thaksin Shinawatra's 'forward engagement' policy (which was reminiscent of constructive engagement where closer economic ties were encouraged), Senator Kraisak urged the Thai government to 'halt all forms of assistance to Burma and suspend bilateral cooperation until the new Burmese leadership makes a firm commitment to national reconciliation and democracy'.[58] While Jorn Dosch describes Kraisak's activism as a kind of 'parallel foreign policy', the subsequent frequency of similar 'foreign interventions' by parliamentarians in other ASEAN members means that the behaviour might be better characterized as *second tier activism*.

One of the most notable examples of second tier activism started in Malaysia. On 8 June 2004, Malaysian parliamentarians, from both sides of the House and from both Houses of Parliament, united to create the Malaysian Parliamentary Pro-Democracy Myanmar Caucus. This caucus was formed due to Myanmar's impending chairmanship of ASEAN and a subsequent realization that the 'region was about to encounter a major diplomatic crisis which would potentially have grave implications for the region's political and economic future'.[59] Thus, the caucus was designed to push Myanmar towards greater democracy, and to start this process it articulated a number of demands. First, the caucus requested the immediate release of all political detainees[60] and, second, it called upon 'the Myanmar government to respect ASEAN and international opinion and return to the mainstream of responsible international norms and behaviour'.[61] In a display of how far it was prepared to interfere in the domestic affairs of Myanmar, it then invited the National Coalition Government of the Union of Burma (an exiled opposition party) for talks.[62] Meanwhile, a public announcement from the Prime Minister's Department stated that Prime Minister Badawi had, in 'no uncertain terms', warned Khin Nyunt 'that something must come out of this' roadmap for democracy. Within two days, the group successfully called for other parliamentarians throughout ASEAN to join them.[63]

Second tier activism has also occurred on a coordinated basis between the ASEAN members. The Malaysian initiative led to the formation, in November 2004, of the ASEAN Inter-Parliamentary Myanmar Caucus (AIPMC), which includes parliamentarians from Malaysia, Thailand, the Philippines, Singapore, Indonesia and Cambodia. Despite the release of some political (and other) prisoners in compliance with one of the demands (whether intentionally or not), the Caucus issued a collective statement calling for the abdication of Myanmar's chairmanship of ASEAN and the suspension of its membership in ASEAN.[64] The AIPMC believed this position was necessary due to continued lack of progress over democratic reforms and political openness. However, the preparedness of some leaders to allow other ASEAN members to intervene in each other's internal affairs – whether at the leadership level or at the second tier – was not region-wide. In the same month, Prime Minister Thaksin threatened to walk out of the November 2004 Vientiane Summit should the ASEAN leaders make any reference to the Southern Thailand issue (Chapter 4). He justified his threat on the basis that this would amount to interference in Thailand's internal affairs. The timing of this statement eventually handicapped ASEAN's ability to censure Myanmar at the summit.[65]

The freedom for such second tier activism may also have had a push–pull effect at the level of ASEAN's leadership. A month earlier, the Black Friday (Depayin) incident occurred, where Aung San Suu Kyi and her supporters were violently attacked by agents of the government and there were an estimated seventy deaths. Aung San Suu Kyi was subsequently returned to house arrest 'out of concern for her safety', where she remained until her release in November 2010.[66] Reflecting the unsatisfactory nature of the SPDC's explanation for these events, the ASEAN Foreign Minister's statement explicitly addressed the incident and 'urged Myanmar to resume its efforts of national reconciliation and dialogue among all parties concerned' so as to lead to a 'peaceful transition to democracy'. An added sting was imparted with the assertion that ASEAN 'looked forward to the early lifting of restrictions placed on Aung San Suu Kyi and the NLD members'.[67] Notwithstanding the difficulty of obtaining consensus over the communiqué,[68] the statement was significant in as far as it refers specifically to political issues in the country.[69] Given mounting international pressure, some of which is analysed further in the next chapter, the declaration also signalled to the junta that there were limits to how far a state could hide behind the non-interference principle if the issue had direct and deleterious consequences for other ASEAN members.

Beyond these normative developments, political liberalization has also entailed a proliferation in non-governmental networks including NGOs, social movements and civil society. For example, since 1998 there has been a sevenfold increase in the number of NGOs operating in Indonesia.[70] Importantly, this proliferation has also been accompanied, to varying degrees, by greater engagement with the ASEAN governments as reflected by a report from an ASEAN Eminent Persons Group (EPG) in 2000. The report argued that 'the peoples of ASEAN must themselves ... take ownership ... of the ASEAN Vision 2020' where 'ASEAN matters should not only be the prerogative of governments, but also of businesses, the civil society, and ultimately the people'.[71] As far as the ASEAN nations are concerned, Bangkok remains a haven for NGO groups, as does the Philippines and Indonesia.[72] K.S. Balakrishnan also highlights the role of NGOs and civil society in the semi-democracy of Malaysia. While these non-governmental networks are relatively less inclined to directly oppose government policy, Balakrishnan argues that they have managed to constructively engage with the government in the formation of foreign policy, particularly in the realm of promoting humanitarian and Islamic causes, together with issues concerning the environment and development.[73] However, it is also important to note that at the ASEAN level such engagement has, until recently, been limited to think-tanks operating at the Track II level (such as the annual Asia-Pacific Roundtable in Kuala Lumpur) or to officially accredited NGOs.

In the context of Southeast Asia, regional think-tanks have a number of limitations. Such bodies generally maintain close links with their respective governments and they are also often dependent on financial funding and support from their respective government patrons.[74] In the case of NGOs, ASEAN has been granting official accreditation since 1979. However, the granting of this affiliation requires such NGOs to demonstrate objectives that enhance, strengthen and/or realize the aims of the Association. Further, only fifty-five NGOs had been granted accreditation by 2008 and they are required to invite their governments to attend meetings and provide an annual report to the ASEAN standing committee. Such requirements have limited the types of 'accredited' NGOs to professional bodies – such as the ASEAN Law Association and the ASEAN Federation of Accountants – rendering it an elite-driven enterprise.[75]

Further progress has occurred in other areas. The ASEAN–Institute for Security and International Studies (ISIS) network responded to the ASEAN Vision 2020 and the recommendations of 2000 EPG report by creating the ASEAN People's Assembly (APA) for the first time in November 2000 and this has provided closer networking between semi-official and non-official groups. While the Assembly has become an annual event, it initially lacked significant support from the CLMV countries and Singapore. For example, ASEAN–ISIS had intended to launch the APA in Singapore to coincide with the 2000 Summit but this became impossible due to 'political reasons'.[76] Meanwhile, Malaysia's often underestimated democratic credentials became evident when the Malaysian government, through its ASEAN–ISIS branch, organized the ASEAN Civil Society Conference (ACSC) in 2005 at the ASEAN Leaders' Summit in Kuala Lumpur. This marked a significant improvement in the engagement of non-governmental networks with ASEAN's political elite as this was the first time that civil society organizations were permitted to present their deliberations directly to the ASEAN heads of state.[77] The idea that such 'third-level' agency might have a direct impact on state and regional policies is akin to Acharya's definition of participatory regionalism or, in other words, provides an example of the type of bottom-up socio-cultural integration that was conceptualized in the first chapter. To this end, democratization has started to undermine the legitimacy of the former ASEAN model of elite-centred regionalism.[78]

Through the APA, NGOs were again permitted to present to the heads of state at the 12th ASEAN Summit in 2007 in Cebu (the Philippines). Despite Alan Collins' suggestion that that this development marks the establishment of an institutionalized form of ASEAN–NGO engagement, continued resistance to such engagement soon became evident when, in November 2007, the APA again had to be moved from Singapore to the Philippines because (in this instance) Singapore demanded that it vet all APA participants.[79] As a consequence of this – together with a more general reluctance by ASEAN 'to support their cause or involve them in its decision-making' – NGOs and civil societies (from Indonesia, Thailand, the Philippines, Cambodia and Malaysia) not only continued to push for more openness but have also become increasingly resentful of ASEAN.[80] However, the nature of their lobbying has contributed to perceptions that they hold an 'anti-governmental stance' and this has, in turn, detracted from the willingness of the political elite to engage with them.[81] Further, given the earlier comments in connection with the ASEAN–ISIS networks, there is a perception that ASEAN–ISIS – which determines the agenda of APA – has acted as a gatekeeper rather than a bridge for NGO access to the political elite. Consequently, the Solidarity for Asian People's Advocacy (SAPA), a third civil society conference dedicated to influencing ASEAN policy, was inaugurated in 2006. However, the existence of these three regional institutions may detract from their efforts by creating confusion and disunity between the NGOs and civil society members.[82] Such disunity may also be generated by the level of differentiation between the identities and interests of civil society groups. For example, while the empirical evidence in later chapters indicates greater regional awareness, there is little evidence of the emergence of a region-wide collective identity.

The normative developments above have also been influenced by extra-regional considerations and pressures. As noted previously, the ASEAN members have not only sought to secure access to markets through institutions such as ASEM, but ASEAN also values its role and international stature in institutions such as the ARF. These priorities and sensitivities have also rendered ASEAN more vulnerable to exogenous influence and pressure. An example of this occurred at the July 2004 ARF meeting where the United States pressured the Association over the Myanmar issue. Colin Powell, then US Secretary of State, ignored the official agenda for the meeting and for two days demanded that the junta release Aung San Suu Kyi.[83] At the same event, the European Union further pressured ASEAN by threatening to boycott the October ASEM summit unless the State Peace and Development Council was ejected or made political concessions before it was allowed to participate.[84] The more conservative actors in ASEAN held firm and the Association responded by rejecting these demands, with Thailand's foreign minister asserting that '[t]here should be no demands; there should be a good understanding'.[85] Nonetheless, Western pressure, together with genuine concern by political elites in some of the more democratic states over the human rights situation, did contribute towards what one Philippine official described as an 'intense debate' by ASEAN over the issue of a draft statement and whether or not to renew calls for the 'release of Aung San Suu Kyi' at the eleventh meeting of the ARF in July 2004.[86] Eventually, however, the consensus that emerged was in favour of a more moderate statement where 'the Ministers underlined the need for the involvement of all strata of Myanmar society in the ongoing national convention. The Ministers urged Myanmar to take every action that will add substance to the expression of its democratic aspiration.'[87] While Aung San Suu Kyi was not mentioned in the final document, references to 'Myanmar['s] society', the 'national convention' and 'democratic aspiration' continue to indicate that ASEAN is now more prepared to 'interfere' in the internal affairs its member-states.

Democratic outcomes: Indonesia's vision for the future

The previous sections have focused on how evolving political values and political systems in some of the ASEAN members have affected foreign policy formulation together with the nature and quality of interaction with other international actors. However, there has been a mixed correlation between democracy, stability and development as the comparatively authoritarian regimes of Singapore and Brunei continue to enjoy greater stability whilst simultaneously maintaining the highest levels of income in Southeast Asia on a per capita basis. In the case of Singapore, the gross national income per capita for 2009 (PPP) was $49,850 while for Brunei it was $50,920.[88] The success of these two economies – efficient management in the case of Singapore and oil wealth in the case of Brunei – has provided sufficient 'performance legitimacy' to keep the current regimes in power and, subsequently, has become a model for governance that other regimes have sought to replicate.[89] However, the authoritarian systems that continue to prevail in Southeast Asia have become increasingly incompatible with the emerging value systems of Indonesia and, at various times, Thailand and the Philippines.[90] Nonetheless, despite a mounting ideational divide in ASEAN, the destabilizing events that followed the end of the Cold War encouraged a stronger focus on domestic stability (national resilience) which, in turn, necessitated an accommodation of demands by some pockets of the ASEAN elite to undertake institutional adjustments to the ASEAN pact.

The financial crisis, followed by the collapse of President Suharto's New Order regime and Timor Leste's independence, *inter alia*, highlighted the interdependence between instability, regime weakness and foreign intervention. Moreover, these events also highlighted ASEAN's institutional incapacity to provide an effective response – particularly in relation to controversial security issues.[91] Thus, ASEAN did not have a role in the resolution of the Aceh dispute or the insurgencies in Southern Thailand and Mindanao. ASEAN has also been ineffective in resolving the historical and territorial conflicts that afflict the region – many of which were noted in Chapter 4. As Kwa Chong Guan summarized in interview, 'we [in ASEAN] do not resolve any conflicts, we merely sweep them under the carpet [so] … that in time we may have a very lumpy carpet'. Notwithstanding the fact that, as Kwa Chong Guan puts it, 'at least we [have] still got a carpet to stand on',[92] the ASEAN members have become increasingly aware of how the continuation of regional conflicts has detracted from the primary *raison d'être* behind ASEAN's existence: a modus vivendi based on the pursuit of domestic stability through economic development and regional cooperation. The utility of the institutional structures and traditional norms of ASEAN have also been challenged by the increased frequency of non-traditional security issues including the 2004 tsunami; disease (including SARS, bird flu and AIDS); and crime (e.g. illicit narcotics, money laundering, arms trafficking, and people trafficking and smuggling).[93] Here, globalization and the increasingly transnational nature of these challenges have necessitated more coordinated ASEAN-wide responses as a consequence of the belief that 'your security is my security'.[94]

While most of the ASEAN members appear to have accepted the need to coordinate their responses to regional problems, a significant divide between the authoritarian and democratic members remains over the manner and extent of cooperation and institutionalization necessary. At the level of the lowest common denominator – the authoritarian end of ASEAN's political spectrum – countries such as Myanmar continue to be most strongly motivated by a narrow pursuit of regime security where even the notion of sound economic management (performance legitimacy) can be sidelined as a secondary concern. Thus, while these governments have also evinced a willingness to commit to regional cooperation and institutionalization, such support has been on the proviso that these commitments do not translate into political interference. Given these caveats, and through to the Bali Concord II in 2003, the only significant political-security initiatives were the ASEAN Troika (1999) and the High Council (1976). However, while both of these schemes are designed to resolve the region's outstanding conflicts, neither have been utilized as they adhere to the traditional ASEAN Way by requiring a consensus from all the parties involved in a dispute and, even after such a consensus has been granted, their decisions carry no binding authority.[95]

In view of these problems, Indonesia's Director of Public Diplomacy in Deplu, Umar Hadi, reflected on the Bangkok Declaration 'as a solution to a given problem in a given time', but argues that today 'we need to reflect on whether this solution is still valid or is still workable for another set of problems'.[96] From his perspective, the answer is no; accordingly, the emerging comprehensive security environment in Southeast Asia has meant that cooperation and institutionalization can no longer be limited to the economic realm. In other words, the achievement of economic development, and the domestic stability that ensues, are mutually interdependent with political and security cooperation. Furthermore, it follows that such cooperation is unlikely to mature significantly before the transnational disputes of the region are resolved. Thus, 'a new political and security blueprint' was needed in order to equip ASEAN with an enhanced ability to respond to the challenges of the 'new world'.[97] As Umar Hadi adds:

> The point is that we look at ... economic cooperation [and it] is much more developed compared to other fields,... and when we reflect on ourselves, in Indonesia, what happened in 1998 with reformasi,... we did not develop our political life quite enough, so we didn't put our energy into political development as much as we put our energy into economic performance, so when [such] performance fails then you get chaos. So we put that into ASEAN: when you have very progressive cooperation in economics, in the economic sector, but you don't balance it with enough cooperation in the political and security field, then one day, you end up with a dysfunctional institution.... So in essence, we need to balance the two, cooperation in economics and the cooperation in political and security matters.[98]

As a consequence of these considerations, Indonesia's Deplu (Foreign Ministry) sought advice from Rizal Sukma, a scholar from CSIS in Jakarta, regarding the direction Indonesia should take during its chairmanship of ASEAN in 2003. In building on a Singaporean proposal for an economic community the previous year, Rizal Sukma suggested that the Indonesian government should 'reclaim its strategic centrality' by proposing the establishment of a security community. Informed by various scholarly works on the concept, Sukma drafted a concept paper, which he presented to the Indonesian Foreign Ministry on 20 March 2003.[99] Deplu then drafted what has been termed Indonesia's 'Non-Paper on ASEAN Security community' and circulated it along with various modified versions at several ASEAN meetings. These meetings included a Senior Officials Meeting (13–14 June 2003); the 36th ASEAN Ministerial Meeting Retreat in Phnom Penh (16 June 2003); a special SOM in Bogor, Indonesia (4–6 August 2003); and another SOM in Surabaya, Indonesia (26–28 August 2003).[100] During the course of these meetings the Philippines government wanted to include, by way of a complement, a socio-cultural pillar within the proposal.[101] Consequently, the negotiations that took place during these meetings culminated in an agreement at the 9th ASEAN Summit (Bali) in October 2003 to create an 'ASEAN Community'.

Indonesia had a number of more specific motives behind its proposal for an ASEAN Security community and the broader proposal for an ASEAN Community that followed. At one level, the proposal was ostensibly designed to resurrect ASEAN which, according to Rizal Sukma, 'had been floating without a sense of purpose' since the 1997 economic crisis.[102] As Amitav Acharya notes, the proposal was 'also motivated by Jakarta's desire, as it was assuming the chairmanship of the ASEAN Standing Committee (July 2003–July 2004), to reaffirm its leadership in ASEAN'.[103] Interestingly, the latter motive often represented the primary point of focus by interviewees from government and academia in other ASEAN states.[104] Given the earlier mentioned geo-strategic and political imperatives, the Indonesian architects of the proposal continued to be influenced by Indonesia's concept of regional resilience and the term subsequently appears in the Bali Concord II. A further motivation that had been raised by a Foreign Ministry official in Jakarta was that, at the domestic level, the Indonesian government wanted to institutionalize ASEAN in a manner that would protect Indonesia's newfound democracy, together with the governments in other ASEAN members, from illegitimate transitions of government, including military coups.[105]

The contentious nature of Indonesia's proposal was exhibited through the level of cynicism voiced by interlocutors from several ASEAN states as well as the ASEAN Secretariat. In the case of the latter, one senior official in the ASEAN Secretariat suggested that the proposal was so impractical that he wondered if its true purpose was to provide Indonesia with an excuse to walk away from ASEAN by demanding agreement over something that Jakarta knew the other member-states would reject.[106] Beyond the Secretariat, the most common perception of the Indonesian proposal was that it was motivated by a desire to regain Indonesia's image as the leader of ASEAN.[107] However, some more

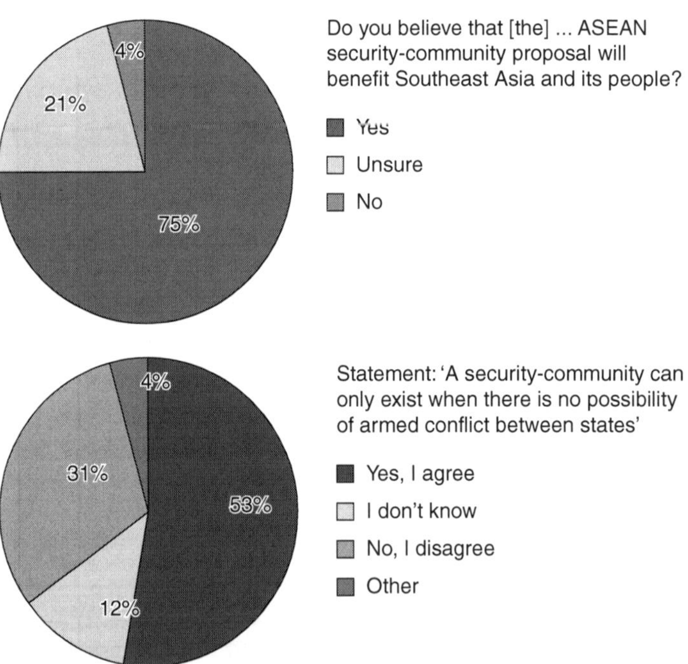

Figure 5.3 Elite level perceptions on the 'security community' (source: compiled by author from 'elite level survey').

cynically suggested that it had been induced by the United States for the purpose of its 'war on terror'.[108] Furthermore, Indonesian assurances that it had consulted extensively throughout the region were dismissed by several foreign ministry spokespeople in other countries who complained that the proposal had been rushed through and imposed in a very 'un-ASEAN like manner'. Despite the initial cynicism articulated through the various interviews above, a positive statistic to arise from the elite survey (Figure 5.3) was the fact that 75.9 per cent now believe (rhetorically at least) that the security community proposal will 'benefit Southeast Asia and its people'. Nonetheless, such optimism needs to be qualified by the survey responses from the government participants, where 42.1 per cent thought that a security community *could exist amidst the possibility of armed conflict.*

As noted in the introduction to the book, the Bali Concord II provides a structure for the ASEAN community based on the pillars of political and security cooperation, economic cooperation and socio-cultural cooperation. In the words of the Bali Concord II, these pillars 'are closely intertwined and mutually reinforcing for the purpose of ensuring durable peace, stability and shared prosperity in the region'. The scheduled date for implementation has since been accelerated to 2015.[109] The preamble to the Bali Concord II reaffirmed the principles of the Bangkok Declaration, ZOPFAN, the TAC, the ASEAN Concord and SEANWFZ. It also acknowledged the need to effectively and urgently address the challenge of 'translating ASEAN cultural diversities and different economic levels into equitable development opportunity and prosperity, in an environment of solidarity, regional resilience and harmony'. In the context of these considerations, but also reflecting the growing impatience of Singapore and Thailand over the pace of economic liberalization, the proposal for an ASEAN Economic Community (AEC) has the end goal of producing a 'single market and production base' within ASEAN.[110]

In the case of the ASEAN Socio-Cultural Community (ASCC), many of the goals are more pragmatic than might otherwise be inferred from the name. Reflective of a need to address some of the transnational comprehensive security issues that were mentioned in preceding paragraphs, the goals of the ASCC include an intention to 'intensify cooperation in the area of public health, including the prevention of diseases, such as HIV/AIDS and SARS'. The ASCC also aims to raise the 'standard of living of disadvantaged groups and the rural population' and seeks 'the active involvement of all sectors of society, in particular women, youth, and local communities'. The pillar also mentions the need to enhance the level of interaction between certain groups of elite (such as ASEAN scholars, artists and the media) for the purpose of (among other things) cultivating the 'people's awareness of ASEAN' and the creation of a 'regional identity'. As noted in the introduction to the book, the pursuit of increased interaction and the development of a 'regional identity' along with similar statements in related documents, such as 'the shaping and sharing of norms',[111] have clearly been informed by the academic literature on security communities and the constructivist school of thought more broadly.[112]

Meanwhile, the proposal to establish an ASEAN Security community (ASC) has been the subject of significant attention within the scholarly literature, with a mixture of critical and positive appraisals. Similar to some of ASEAN's former instruments and declarations, the ASC 'aims to bring ASEAN's political and security cooperation to a higher plane to ensure that countries in the region live at peace with one another and with the world at large in a *just*, *democratic* and *harmonious* environment'. As with the scholarly literature on a 'security community', the ASC states that the members 'shall rely exclusively on peaceful processes in the settlement of intra-regional differences and regard their security as fundamentally linked to one another and bound by geographic location, common vision and objectives'. The declaration maintains ASEAN's concept of 'comprehensive security' but, in order to avoid controversy, specifically states (somewhat inconsistently) that the concept is not representative of a desire to form a 'defence pact, military alliance or a joint foreign policy'. The proposal for an ASC was also significant for the fact that it declares a commitment to a 'democratic environment' and in specifically raising maritime issues (e.g. piracy and the South China Sea) argues because 'these concerns are *transboundary* in nature ... [they should] be addressed *regionally* in a holistic, integrated and comprehensive manner'.[113]

Indonesia's aspirations for ASEAN were most holistically articulated in its February 2004 *Draft Plan of Action for a Security community*. The plan of action contained seventy-five concrete steps to support its achievement along with concrete dates for implementation. The most significant proposals are listed in Table 5.2.[114] Despite Rizal Sukma's recommendation that Indonesia limits the focus of its proposal to the more feasible components that were eventually adopted in the final 'ASEAN Security community Plan of Action' and the subsequent 'Vientiane Plan of Action' (e.g. greater cooperation on transnational security issues), the Indonesian Foreign Ministry insisted on a regional peacekeeping force, a regional commission for human rights together with a related commitment to democratic governance and values. Faced with strong opposition from Myanmar and several of its ASEAN counterparts, it backed down and a compromise emerged where the proposals for a human rights and a peacekeeping force were removed. Furthermore, the language concerning some of the remaining initiatives and goals was watered down and a commitment to specific dates for implementation was also removed.[115] The ideals contained in Indonesia's Draft Plan of Action represented such a radical departure from the ASEAN Way that they were intolerable for the less democratic members of ASEAN. The Plan of Action, in its final format, was delivered at the ASEAN Leader's Summit in Vientiane in November 2004.

Within the Vientiane Action Program, the proposal for a security community was divided into five key components and these were expressed as (a) political development; (b) the shaping and sharing of norms; (c) conflict prevention; (d) conflict resolution; and (e) post-conflict peace-building.[116] The Vientiane Plan of Action and the ASC Plan of Action endorsed APA 'as a means to promote people-to-people contacts'.[117] Further, the security community pillar in the

Table 5.2 Select list from Indonesia's draft plan of action

Category	*Activities*	*Time line*
Political development	1 Developing a just, democratic and harmonious environment in ASEAN:	By 2017
	• anti-corruption campaign: strengthening legal infrastructure, capacity building, and concrete cooperation in asset recovery.	Continuously
	2 Promotion of human rights of ASEAN peoples:	By 2006
	• developing an ASEAN Charter of Rights and Obligations of Peoples;	By 2006
	• establishment of an ASEAN Regional Commission on Human Rights;	By 2006
	• protection of vulnerable groups, including the eradication of trafficking in persons especially women and children.	By 2006
	4 Resolution of outstanding land, sea, and air space boundary issues through delimitation and demarcation:	By 2010
	• identification of all boundary problems;	By 2005
	• resolution of bilateral/trilateral boundary delimitation and demarcation;	By 2010
	• development of borders regime to facilitate people's movement, border trade and border security.	From 2004
Conflict prevention	3 Enhancing cooperation on non-traditional security issues:	
	• enhancing the role of the ASEAN Ministerial Meeting on Transnational Crimes (AMMTC) as the main implementing body dealing with transnational crimes, including terrorism;	
	• ensuring border security with regard to traditional border crossing;	From 2005
	• strengthening ASEAN's capacity to prevent and control the spread of communicable diseases;	By 2005
	• establishing a regional framework to combat smuggling, illegal logging and illegal trade of natural resources.	By 2006
	• a drug-free ASEAN.	By 2015
Conflict resolution	2 Developing a regional peacekeeping arrangement:	
	• establishing an ASEAN Peacekeeping Force (standby arrangement) and its deployment mechanism.	By 2012.

Source: 'ASEAN Security-community Plan of Action' (draft as of 13 February 2004).

Vientiane Plan of Action managed to maintain various references to values such as 'human rights' and stated further that the 'ASEAN Member Countries [should] live at peace with one another and with the world at large in a just, democratic and harmonious environment'.[118] Nonetheless, the nature and contentions in the Vientiane Plan of Action can best be understood as a statement of intent rather than a structured (and/or legally binding) agreement with concrete commitments for implementation. Thus, the final structure remained inside the boundaries of the ASEAN Way as traditionally interpreted.

Despite the watering down of Indonesia's plan, statements of intent set expectations for results and so negotiations for agreement over the implementation of mechanisms for conflict resolution and post-conflict peace building continued. According to the Deputy Director-General of the 'ASEAN Department' in Lao Ministry of Foreign Affairs, implementation concerning the 'conflict resolution' and 'post conflict peace-building' remains difficult due to 'different political systems, cultures, religions, and the level of comfort or trust'.[119] Further, less than 30 per cent of agreements within ASEAN have been implemented and so the original ASEAN members (that is, Singapore, Indonesia, Malaysia, Thailand and the Philippines) have also pursued institutional reform that would improve this poor record of implementation.[120] In the context of these goals, together with other challenges within ASEAN's institutional framework, many of the political elite interviewed saw an opportunity for progress through negotiations for an ASEAN Charter with the intention of providing the Association with a legal identity and a more institutionalized and binding framework for operation.[121] Nonetheless, as the remaining chapters will validate, the number of issue areas for which institutional reform would be feasible was always going to be limited due to the continued diversity of interests between the ASEAN members.

Conclusions

The norms associated with the ASEAN Way have increasingly come under pressure since the 1990s. As Amitav Acharya notes, the early challenges that ASEAN faced – such as 'superpower rivalry' and 'inter-state rivalries and conflicts in Southeast Asia' – had previously legitimatized the norm of non-interference and, one could add, thereby constrained a deepening of complex integration.[122] However, most of the ASEAN states have accepted that contemporary security issues – such as crime, the environment and disease – cannot be adequately addressed in the absence of regionwide cooperation. Meanwhile, the relatively more democratic members have also pressed ASEAN to be more proactive in addressing the failure of some governments to provide adequate 'personal security' for their citizens. While all the ASEAN members endorsed the notion of 'personal security' as part of the concept of 'comprehensive security', the emphasis of the relatively more democratic members has evolved in a manner that is increasingly in line with modern notions of human security, including the protection of human rights. Here, the more globalized ASEAN members have also become more vulnerable and sensitive to international pressure and influence. Thus, adverse developments in the domestic affairs of each member state now have greater ramifications for ASEAN's international stature in addition to the region's security and economic stability.

The need for normative change was first recognized by the government of Thailand through its proposal for 'flexible engagement'. At the time, the Philippine government was the only supporter of the proposal. Their unity on the issue was not a coincidence as the two countries had recently undertaken a process of democratization. Consequently, the two countries had not only witnessed a withdrawal of the military from domestic and foreign affairs, but democratization also contributed a greater plurality of actors influencing foreign policy formulation. In the case of Thailand, and later Indonesia, this phenomenon eventually contributed to the emergence of foreign ministries that were more independent, proactive and innovative including, for example, Surin's proposal for flexible engagement. Here, it is important to note that Thailand's attempt at norm entrepreneurship in ASEAN was also motivated by the fact that domestic instability and poor governance in Myanmar had directly affected Thailand's traditional security (e.g. border incursions) as well as its non-traditional security (e.g. rising levels of drug addiction).

The chapter noted that the level of civil liberties and political freedoms have improved in six of the ten ASEAN nations during the course of last ten years. The spread of democracy has enabled a kind of second tier activism where individual politicians and other political elite have been given greater freedom to express their own opinions and to interfere in the internal affairs of other ASEAN members, including on issues of human rights abuse. One of the most notable examples of such second tier activism occurred with the formation of the ASEAN Inter-Parliamentary Myanmar Caucus (AIPMC). Not only did the AIPMC pressure the Myanmar government in relation to its poor human rights record, but it also called for Myanmar to be suspended from ASEAN membership. Importantly, the political advocacy of such second tier activists has not always coincided with the formal position of their governments. Again, this reflects the idea that democracy has also contributed to a broadening of the actors influencing policy formulation in ASEAN. In recent years there has been a proliferation in the number of domestic and regional NGOs and three region-wide civil society forums have been established – including APA. While the chapter noted continued resistance to their engagement by regional governments and political elite, particularly in the less democratic ASEAN members, their emergence does represent the beginning of a limited form of participatory regionalism and, moreover, increases the prospects for future socio-cultural integration beyond the 'elite level'.

One of the most significant developments in the chapter concerned the level of democratization that has emerged in Indonesia following the collapse of Suharto's New Order regime. Here, one important aspect of democratization has been the implementation of conflict resolution via peaceful means in Aceh. Significantly, the Indonesian government provided the European Union with a direct role in facilitating the peace and did not see this as an intervention in its internal affairs. The resolution of the Aceh conflict by the Indonesian government was also connected to the lessons learnt in the wake of the 2004 tsunami. The Indonesian government responded quickly to the crisis and welcomed foreign aid and foreign militaries in the recovery effort. The actions of the Indonesian government have provided it with an increased level of international stature and respect that has, in turn, led to greater foreign aid and FDI. Moreover, democratic Indonesia was one of the strongest economies in 2009 and this casts a further shadow on the Asian values argument. As with Thailand, the openness and flexibility of Indonesia's domestic and foreign policies have coincided with a more independent Foreign Ministry and the withdrawal of the military from politics.

Democracy in Indonesia has also contributed to a new regional outlook. For example, Indonesia has resisted pressures by its ASEAN colleagues to undertake measures that it deemed 'undemocratic', such as Singapore's call for Indonesia to take stronger action against suspected terrorists. As with Thailand and the Philippines, democratization has coincided with a more active engagement by Indonesia in the internal affairs of ASEAN members. Here, the Indonesian government has itself admitted that it now practices a policy in line with the Thai proposal for flexible engagement. However, through its proposal to establish a security community, Indonesia has now attempted to exercise a far higher level of norm entrepreneurship. Aside from representing a near complete abandonment of the ASEAN Way, the proposal sought to establish a level of cooperation, institutionalization and complex integration akin to the European Union. Problematically, however, such visions for the future challenged the foreign policies of the more authoritarian ASEAN members and the proposal subsequently met with considerable resistance. As noted, the emergence of an authoritarian–democratic divide also meant that the Thailand's proposal for 'flexible engagement' was never officially accepted by ASEAN. However, the next chapter will demonstrate that continued instability and poor governance in Myanmar eventually forced an 'in practice' application of the proposal. As Myanmar represents the 'lowest common denominator' in ASEAN's membership, the next chapter will also examine how Myanmar has affected regional norms, cohesion, cooperation and the Association's international stature. Based on these considerations, the chapter that follows includes an examination of the institutional outcomes of these proposals (e.g. the ASEAN Charter).

6 Myanmar in ASEAN

The key challenge to cohesion and the ASEAN Way?

In 2004, James Cotton observed that 'the road to a ... security community passes through Yangon'.[1] In agreement, this chapter focuses on the international relations of ASEAN and the manner by which Myanmar has challenged the cohesion and modus operandi of the Association since 2005. As will be seen, the long-term failure of ASEAN to either induce substantial change within Myanmar or to mitigate the transnational consequences of such instability, has further tested the operational boundaries of the non-interference principle and the associated ASEAN Way. In this regard, the first section examines the extent to which Myanmar's scheduled chairmanship not only provided robust evidence signifying the functional constraints of the ASEAN Way, but also revealed the institutional and ideational basis for disunity within ASEAN. The second section outlines how further events, including anti-government protests in September 2007, contributed to further regional and international pressure for ASEAN to be more active regarding the Myanmar issue. However, the section also outlines that that this pressure started to exceed what the other relatively authoritarian members were willing to agree to and, moreover, led to a situation of mutual disengagement between ASEAN and Myanmar where, at one point, there were even fears that Myanmar would walk away from ASEAN. The final section examines ASEAN's response to the devastating effects of Cyclone Nargis and reveals how the depoliticization of aid provided a new formula for meaningful cooperation between the ASEAN members that was not only agreeable to all the members but also enhanced the utility of the Association. Nonetheless, as far as ASEAN's regionalist project is concerned, the Myanmar crisis has further reinforced a loss of faith by some of the region's elite in ASEAN's current institutions. This, in turn, has exacerbated the divide between elements of the political elite who want to reform the Association and those who wish to retain the status quo. Given the fundamental nature of the principle of non-interference in the Association's operation, the continuation of these normative divisions will – over the mid to long term – also inhibit mutual identification between the ASEAN elite (i.e. elite level socio-cultural integration).

The ASEAN 'chairmanship crisis'

There is a Japanese proverb about a house being so unprepared that 'when the robber came, the residents first had to make the rope they needed to catch him with'.[2] It was not long before such an event emerged between the ASEAN members. On the basis of alphabetical rotation, Myanmar was due to take the helm in 2006, including the hosting of the ASEAN Summit, the ASEAN Ministerial Meeting (AMM), the ASEAN Post-Ministerial Conferences (PMCs) and the ASEAN Regional Forum. The extent of the forthcoming diplomatic crisis seemed to catch many unawares and a series of conflicting signals and statements emerged. Indicative of the continued desire to maintain good relations with ASEAN's western dialogue partners, a former Thai diplomat argued that 'if Myanmar has not changed by then [2006], it could prove very embarrassing for ASEAN, because its partners in the West would not attend the meeting'. The same diplomat articulated what he thought was the greatest threat of all: that 'it could even result in the break-up of ASEAN'.[3] In the context of these concerns, together with the human rights situation within Myanmar, the previous chapter highlighted the unprecedented role of activists and NGOs in calling for the disqualification of the country and that these calls had escalated to the older, more globalized and democratic members of ASEAN.[4] As will be seen, by 2006 the chairmanship issue had become one of the greatest obstacles to elite level solidarity in recent decades.

As far as the Association's traditional support for the SPDC was concerned, George Yeo, Singapore's Foreign Minister, commented that, in retrospect, 'subsequent developments in Myanmar undermined our position. ... Unless the Myanmar authorities handle the situation carefully, ASEAN's credibility and cohesion would be jeopardized'.[5] For example, despite the normative developments discussed in the previous chapter, ASEAN returned to upholding the non-interference principle at the 37th AMM (2004). However, ASEAN was subsequently criticized for sending the wrong message to the junta as the country's Prime Minister, Khin Nyunt, was removed from office just a few months later. For ASEAN, the ouster of Khin Nyunt came as a shock as the military executed it without any warning or consultation. Consequently, several ASEAN leaders publicly articulated their displeasure and the Foreign Minister of Malaysia, Syed Hamid Albar, argued that the event had hurt ASEAN's image because 'of the suddenness of the thing. All of us were caught by surprise that there is a change of leadership and the news that he has been arrested because of corruption and put under house arrest'.[6] Moreover, Myanmar's government, the State Peace and Development Council (SPDC), further embarrassed ASEAN by deciding to announce an extension of Aung San Suu Kyi's detention at the Vientiane Leaders' Summit in November despite having escaped censure in the final Leaders' Statement.[7]

Given these developments, the United States called on ASEAN to remove the SPDC from its scheduled Chair of the Association in 2006. In making this call, the US highlighted it had 'made clear that the situation in Burma has complicated our dealings with ASEAN'. The Malaysian government, in a return to a more conservative position, challenged this statement and suggested that the US should not issue threats to ASEAN in relation to Myanmar's human rights record. Five months later, in May 2005, and undeterred by previous objections to its interference, the US again reiterated its concern that Myanmar's chairmanship would threaten ASEAN–US relations.[8] For the first time since the ARF was launched, the United States' Secretary of State, Condoleezza Rice, did not attend the meeting. Given previous warnings by the US, her absence reflected US frustration that ASEAN had not yet blocked Myanmar from holding the chair in 2006.[9] US pressure continued to mount as it subsequently suggested a possible withdrawal of developmental assistance throughout the region should Myanmar chair the Association.[10] Thus, by the time of the 2005 ASEM summit, the future of the Association's relations with major western powers seemed to be at stake. Further, Myanmar had done little, if anything, to assist its ASEAN partners to reach a political compromise with either Europe or the United States. For some of the ASEAN members Myanmar's continued defiance, together with its impact on US relations, had become impossible to accept. Consequently, consensus between the ASEAN delegates shifted back in the direction of a position akin to the 36th AMM Communiqué (Chapter 5) with the demand (in combination with their European counterparts) that Myanmar undertake 'democratic dialogue' with all parties and re-engage with UN Special Envoy, Razali Ismail.[11]

Here, ASEAN's application of 'enhanced interaction' was significantly influenced by international pressure together with calculations of the potential economic and transnational security consequences of instability in Myanmar. Nonetheless, the provision of an effective response remained difficult because the continued political diversity of the grouping, together with human rights issues in several of the member-states, has meant that a number of other ASEAN members were hesitant to modify or abandon norms that have also protected them from intra-regional pressures for reform.[12] Thus, the public and private pressure mounted by ASEAN against Myanmar was significantly driven by the continued dependence of the region on its trade and security relations with the West. Because of this interdependence, ASEAN could not escape the need to at least attempt to maintain its international stature as a diplomatic community. Ernst Bower, a former US–ASEAN Business Council president and business consultant, summarized ASEAN's predicament with the statement that

> we are facing an unwelcome scenario in 2006 whereby ASEAN's global profile could be severely damaged by Myanmar's chairing of the grouping. Such damage would come at a time when it can be least afforded – when markets are bouncing back, foreign direct investment is returning to the region and intra-regional trade is growing nicely.[13]

In March 2005, and in the wake of a resolution unanimously approved by the Philippine Senate calling for ASEAN to bar Myanmar from the chairmanship, leading members of the Malaysian Parliamentary Pro-Democracy Myanmar

Caucus held a meeting with Prime Minister Badawi where they proposed a parliamentary motion to 'formally' demand the release of Aung San Suu Kyi and the speeding-up of democratic reform.[14] In the event that these demands were not met, Nazri Abdul Azizi stated that the 'members of parliament will make a [further] motion urging ASEAN to suspend Myanmar from taking the chair of ASEAN next year and until changes are carried out'.[15] The ASEAN Inter-Parliamentary Myanmar Caucus (AIPMC) proposed similar and additional motions for debate in the legislatures of Indonesia, Singapore and Thailand. However, indicative of the limitations of second tier activism, the parliamentary debate was blocked by Prime Minister Badawi a few days before its scheduled commencement.[16] One of the drafters of the motion, government lawmaker and parliamentarian Zaid Ibrahim, argued that the delay was a 'step backward' and suggested 'that there must have been pressure from the [Myanmar] regime'.[17] More likely, or in addition, the postponement and later cancellation was a consequence of 'unofficial signals' by the SPDC that it would voluntarily abdicate its seat as the Chair of ASEAN. In view of these factors, the pressure by Malaysia – when combined with that of the international community, and of the other ASEAN members, Singapore, Indonesia and the Philippines – may have borne fruit and produced temporary relief to the crisis.

A week after the statement by government lawmakers in Malaysia and amidst allegations of a further chemical weapons attack against minority insurgents,[18] Singapore's Prime Minister Lee Hsien Loong travelled to Yangon in an effort to find a diplomatic solution to the issue. While there, he stated that 'in an interdependent world, developments in one ASEAN country could impact on ASEAN as a whole'.[19] A few days later, Singapore's foreign ministry added that 'what happens in Myanmar affects ASEAN as a whole'.[20] Subsequently, Prime Minister Lee stated that the ASEAN ministers would discuss the chairmanship issue 'behind closed doors' during its Cebu (Philippines) retreat in April.[21] Meanwhile, there was a notable shift in the position of Indonesia – in line with the process of democratization noted in the previous chapter – where it suggested that it would be better for Myanmar to resolve its domestic preoccupations prior to assuming the chairmanship.[22] Nevertheless, at the retreat, the ASEAN foreign ministers soon became deadlocked over the issue after Myanmar's foreign minister, Nyan Win, criticized the US and the EU for their pressure over the chairmanship stating 'that is their attitude, not ours. We can decide ourselves because we are an independent country'.[23] In the end, ASEAN consensus remained unobtainable as some members – including Laos and Cambodia – advocated a strict adherence to the principle of non-interference, stating a concern that to take away the chairmanship would 'set a very bad precedent for ASEAN'.[24]

Meanwhile, the first 'official' visit by Soe Win, Myanmar's new Prime Minister, to his ASEAN counterparts occurred in April 2005 but was confined to the relatively less democratic belt of Indochina – Laos, Vietnam and Cambodia. The selection of 'who to meet with' was reflective of historical considerations and associated support for the principle of non-interference. Interestingly Laos, often viewed as the strongest remaining supporter of the regime in ASEAN (and certainly the most authoritarian), was also one of the first foreign nations to send dignitaries to visit Myanmar after Prime Minister Khin Nyunt was removed from office in October 2004. Nevertheless, by late April and at the sidelines of the Asian–African Summit, the first signs of a more conciliatory approach by the SPDC started to become evident. Here, Myanmar's Foreign Minister acknowledged the 'collective interests of the regional grouping and said that Myanmar does not want to be an obstacle in ASEAN'.[25] The Thai government was subsequently tasked with seeking a 'face-saving' solution with Myanmar that would include the SPDC's relinquishment of the ASEAN chairmanship. Consequently, Thailand's foreign minister, Kantathi Supamongkhon, announced that they had 'impressed upon Myanmar the concerns of the international community'.[26] Signals that the approach had been successful were soon evident as the SPDC later conveyed another conciliatory message, this time to Singapore, that they would 'take into account the interests of ASEAN as a whole' and that they would make an announcement concerning their final decision at the ASEAN Foreign Ministers Meeting in July.[27] M.C. Abad Jr., an ASEAN Secretariat spokesperson, confirmed the possibility of a face-saving solution when he stated that the 'issue of [the] future ASEAN chairmanship is high on the agenda of the Foreign Ministers [meeting and] … it is a matter that [the] ASEAN members take seriously'.[28]

Nonetheless, despite continued support from ASEAN's more conservative members, the SPDC eventually decided in favour of ASEAN's 'international interests' and at the AMM (July 2005) it announced that it would forgo the Chair of ASEAN. The face-saving reason provided by Lao Foreign Minister, Somsavat Lengsavat, was that Myanmar needed 'to focus on the national reconciliation process'.[29] The SPDC's relinquishment of the Chair came in the face of a host of benefits that the country could have expected through the chairmanship. These included additional funding for infrastructure, business opportunities and investment along with a potential (albeit limited) rhetorical boost to the government's credibility. While a diplomatic victory for ASEAN in some contexts, the question of Myanmar's chairmanship in ASEAN *after* 2006 has not been resolved. Thus, ASEAN's Secretary-General, Ong Keng Yong, stated that 'it was decided … Myanmar could come back anytime they like to resume the chair but that has created for us, as the Secretariat, an uncertainty'.[30] Further, as the AIPMC has argued, Myanmar's decision to decline the ASEAN Chair 'should not be seen as an excuse to ignore the urgent need for political reforms in Myanmar'. The AIPMC added that '[d]omestic instability in Myanmar will continue to afflict ASEAN long after this debate on Chairmanship is over'.[31]

The AIPMC's analysis that Myanmar would continue to affect ASEAN both regionally and internationally soon proved accurate. While the chairmanship issue forced ASEAN, as a whole, to be more open in its criticism of the SPDC, such developments did not result in any marked improvement to the political conditions within the country and, moreover, ASEAN's tougher stance did not succeed in shielding the Association from international pressure. As will be demonstrated, ASEAN's experiment in 'enhanced interaction' further isolated

ASEAN's relations with Myanmar and weakened any ascertainable 'collective identity' by raising tensions between the progressive and conservative members of the ASEAN elite. As had been feared by some regional policy makers, Myanmar increasingly turned towards other nations – such as China, India, Russia and North Korea – for diplomatic, military and economic support.[32] During the process of strengthening its bilateral relationships with extra-regional actors, the SPDC seemed to pay even less regard to the interests of ASEAN.[33] The manner by which ASEAN attempted to respond to this conundrum and the continued consequences for the Association's modus operandi form the subject of analysis below.

From critical disengagement to mutual disengagement

Despite Myanmar's abdication from chairing ASEAN in 2006, both the US and the EU indicated they expected more from Myanmar and ASEAN.[34] Given the institutional and diplomatic strains that ASEAN had confronted in its search for a resolution to the chairmanship issue, the ASEAN leaders likely felt that this pressure was not only unreasonable (and unrealistic) but was also affecting the cohesion of ASEAN. As Singapore's Prime Minister Lee Hsien Loong stated:

> Myanmar is a member of ASEAN. It's got certain internal problems … and we've discussed this with them. It's caused difficulties with our relations with our dialogue partners – the Europeans and the Americans – but within ASEAN, we have to manage these issues in a way which will be helpful, effective and constructive in the long term. Where we can cooperate, we move forward first. I think that is the way we have handled problems in ASEAN and it has worked for us. In the case of Myanmar, we have made our views known to Myanmar from the point of view of people who wish Myanmar well – that we hope they will be able to overcome their problems.[35]

Despite these sentiments, continued developments forced ASEAN to return to the Myanmar issue and, in the process, the ASEAN Way was undermined further. For example, in November 2005 the SPDC suddenly announced that it was moving its capital to Naypyitaw – in what was rumoured to be a reaction to its fear of invasion.[36] Myanmar's leadership did not even bother to inform ASEAN about the development; a development that also symbolized the SPDC's growing isolation from its own population, ASEAN, and the international community more broadly. As the Thai Prime Minister later complained, 'Burma never informs ASEAN neighbours' about developments in the country.[37] Further, the SPDC extended Aung San Suu Kyi's detention only a week before the eleventh ASEAN Summit in Kuala Lumpur (2005). In response, one of the ASEAN Foreign Ministers declared that the timing of the announcement was a 'slap in the face of ASEAN'.[38] However, the strongest implications for ASEAN's modus operandi, its engagement of Myanmar, and intra-mural relations more generally, occurred behind the scenes of the Kuala Lumpur Leaders' Summit.

Prior to Myanmar's abdication as Chair of ASEAN, the United States had raised the issue of Myanmar under 'other matters' at the UN Security Council on 24 June 2005. Then, in September 2005, Vaclav Havel and Bishop Desmond Tutu released a report contending that Myanmar fitted the criteria for intervention by the United Nations Security Council (UNSC).[39] Further, the AIPMC soon joined the call for greater involvement by the Security Council over the crisis of governance in Myanmar. On this occasion, the lack of solidarity that has been exacerbated by diverging strategic alignments within ASEAN was also evident as the Filipino government said it would support a possible US resolution if it came to a vote in the Security Council.[40] When Myanmar asked ASEAN to oppose the security resolution, Singapore's Foreign Minister, George Yeo, responded that 'ASEAN has lost the credibility and ability to defend Myanmar'.[41] The UNSC held its first ever briefing on Myanmar on 16 December with the US spearheading a drive for the UNSC to pass a resolution on the issue.

Meanwhile, the UN's Special Envoy to Myanmar and former Malaysian diplomat, Razali Ismail, had not been allowed to enter the country for twenty-two months and subsequently resigned because 'they do not want me back'.[42] While his resignation represented a setback for both ASEAN and the UN, it was specifically a disappointment for Malaysia given his distinguished career in the Malaysian Foreign Ministry and his former position as President of the United Nations General Assembly (UNGA). Meanwhile, ASEAN attempted to get the SPDC to agree to a fact-finding mission led by Malaysia's Foreign Minister. At the 2005 AMM, Malaysian Prime Minister Abdullah Badawi argued that 'so far we have stood by Myanmar on some of the regional meetings where there were objections to Myanmar's participation. How can we speak for Myanmar if we are not certain of what's happening in the country?'[43] Myanmar agreed to Foreign Minister Syed's visit in March 2006 but he returned early because he was not permitted to meet with Senior General Than Shwe or Aung San Suu Kyi. Despite initially reporting a degree of satisfaction that Myanmar was moving 'towards democracy', he later stated that the SPDC was treating both the National League for Democracy (NLD) and Aung San Suu Kyi as irrelevant to their proposed democratic transition. He also explained how 'there is a feeling that Myanmar is dragging us [ASEAN] down in terms of our credibility and image' and that they 'must be believable'. 'If [they] have a good story to tell, [they] must not be fearful of the things [they] have done. They must convince people and not only ASEAN that their plan is on track'.[44]

ASEAN sought to escape this diplomatic mess by highlighting the level of influence and subsequent responsibility that both China and India held in regard to Myanmar's political situation – both countries maintain strong military and economic connections. However, the Secretary-General's calls neglected the potential influence of Thailand. As mentioned, in 2009 Thailand accounted for 52.5 per cent of Myanmar's export revenue compared with 12 per cent for India and 9.2 per cent for China.[45] Nonetheless, ASEAN's diplomacy was unlikely to yield results due to the strategic importance of Myanmar for both countries together with the fact that neither China nor India are particularly vulnerable to international pressure vis-à-vis the Myanmar issue. Meanwhile, some of the ASEAN members felt that they had pushed the boundaries of 'enhanced interaction' to the limits of what the more conservative ASEAN members would be prepared to agree with. Moreover, ASEAN had personally discovered the limits of its intramural diplomacy with respect to Myanmar. As ASEAN's Secretary-General stated:

> ASEAN, you know, loves to look after everybody's ego and interests … so there is a very limited space for us to manoeuvre … the reason why Myanmar has done what it has done is because of its own national interests, but also maybe they feel ASEAN is not in a position to dictate terms for them.[46]

As a consequence of ASEAN pressure, a growing rift with Myanmar started to emerge and an early example occurred where Myanmar did not attend the inaugural Defence Ministers' Meeting in May 2006. Then, at a two day Ministerial Meeting of NAM (Kuala Lumpur), Myanmar's Foreign Minister, Nyan Win, refused to explain to his ASEAN colleagues the reasoning behind a further extension of Aung San Suu Kyi's detention, stating 'this is not an international issue … this is only a domestic issue'.[47] Further, despite a lack of cooperation with ASEAN's nominated envoy, the SPDC welcomed a visit by the UN's new Special Envoy, Ibrahim Gambari, who met with both Senior General Than Shwe and Aung San Suu Kyi.[48] Consequently, Syed Hamid lamented that Myanmar had not invited any ASEAN leader or foreign minister to visit its new capital but had instead accorded 'the honour' to a UN official.[49] Nevertheless, the UN's own limitations regarding the Myanmar problem quickly became apparent when the junta announced the earlier-mentioned extension of Aung San Suu Kyi's house arrest little more than a week after Ibrahim Gambari's visit. Thus, Singapore's Foreign Minister revealed a similar attitude when he concluded that 'we [ASEAN] will have to distance ourselves a bit if it is not possible for them to engage us in a way which we find necessary to defend them internationally'.[50]

A new approach arose at the AMM in July. Given ASEAN's inability to generate positive change in Myanmar, together with the diversity of political systems and values between the ASEAN members, the only collective decision feasible under a consensus-based decision-making system was what Lee Jones described as 'critical disengagement'. Jones defines critical disengagement as 'criticism of Burma's internal affairs in violation of non-interference, coupled with a resignation as to ASEAN's inability to influence Burma and a desire to transfer responsibility to the UN to "decouple" the SPDC's behaviour from ASEAN's standing'.[51] As Syed Hamid stated shortly before the July 2006 AMM:

> ASEAN has reached the stage where it is not possible to defend Myanmar if it does not cooperate with us or help itself by delivering tangible progress on economic and political reforms. An ASEAN 'hands-off' approach could potentially open the door to greater pressure and criticism of Myanmar.

> Individual ASEAN members may cooperate actively with other international players to exert more pressure on Myanmar. Myanmar has only itself to blame – its indifferent attitude to ASEAN has driven us to this point.... Unfortunately Myanmar appears to be deliberate in its disregard of our goodwill and concern.[52]

Further evidence indicating a shift towards critical disengagement occurred when Malaysia, as the ASEAN Chair, joined the Philippines in its support for the UNSC to debate the issue officially. Thailand also appealed for the UN to play a greater role in helping to resolve the situation in Myanmar.[53] Despite statements by various ASEAN members that they would not allow Myanmar to become isolated, ASEAN refused to defend Myanmar internationally when it was placed on the UNSC security agenda, leaving it to Cuba, as Chair of NAM, to protest against the development.[54] According to Lee Jones, the final obstacle to 'critical disengagement' was overcome when Prime Minister Thaksin (Thailand) was removed by a coup in September 2006. Thailand subsequently joined Singapore and the Philippines in breaking from an earlier NAM campaign against 'country specific-resolutions' in the UNGA to merely abstain with their vote. Meanwhile, Indonesia justified its vote against the resolution by reference to solidarity with the official position of NAM. However, Indonesia added that it shared the concerns stated in the document. Meanwhile, Malaysia also voted against the document for similar reasons.[55] However, the diversity of values and interests in Southeast Asia were again evident when Brunei, together with the Indochina states – Cambodia, Laos and Vietnam – also voted against the document.[56] Despite NAM's opposition, the UNGA passed the resolution on 18 January 2007.

Meanwhile, in December 2006, the US submitted a draft resolution to the Security Council. Indonesia, then a non-permanent member of the UNSC, stated that ASEAN would be unlikely to defend Myanmar should the Security Council pass the resolution.[57] However, at this level of international debate, even Indonesia struggled to decide on which course of action it should take as it later joined Malaysia in arguing that Myanmar is 'not a threat to regional peace and security'.[58] Unsurprisingly, the UNSC failed to adopt the draft resolution due to a double veto by China and Russia. Indonesia opted to abstain from the vote.[59] Nevertheless, regional unease about potential UNSC involvement led to a last-minute addition to the twelfth ASEAN Summit Chair's statement.[60] The communiqués amendment stated that ASEAN 'agreed on the need to preserve ASEAN's credibility as an effective regional organization by *demonstrating a capacity to manage important issues within the region*'. Syed Hamid subsequently stated that 'ASEAN, rather than the Security Council was in a better position to handle the Myanmar issue'.[61] Thus, to the extent that 'critical disengagement' may have emerged as an undeclared policy, it was to be inconsistently applied through to the time of the anti-regime protests in September 2007.

The elite-level divide over how to engage Myanmar continued through the remainder of 2006 and much of 2007. For example, the Philippines government declared that Myanmar would not be on the agenda during a series of preparatory meetings for the November 2007 ASEAN Summit in Singapore, and Singapore's Prime Minister declared that if the international community wants to continue to enhance its ties with ASEAN then it should not hold ASEAN hostage because of Myanmar. Here, Lee Hsien Loong continued to maintain that 'ASEAN had decided to leave Myanmar alone to sort out its own internal problems'.[62] Meanwhile, Malaysia's Foreign Minister called for ASEAN to 'put its act together' [sic], adding that 'if we start looking at our own national interest rather than the way ASEAN looks at things, then ASEAN is going to face problems'.[63] However, when the former UN Secretary-General Kofi Annan remarked that the situation in Myanmar fitted the 'responsibility to protect' doctrine,[64] the ASEAN Secretariat reasserted the traditional ASEAN Way and its Secretary-General declared that the policy of non-interference 'has helped because we provided peace and stability over the past forty years of ASEAN's existence'.[65]

The September 2007 protests and the evolution of mutual disengagement

As a partial consequence of *critical disengagement*, a number of events occurred between 2005 and 2006 that demonstrated the growing detachment of Myanmar from ASEAN and the international community more broadly. As discussed, Myanmar's capital was shifted to Naypyitaw and the UN Special Envoy to Myanmar quit his post having been refused entry for two years. Further, in April 2007 the SPDC restored diplomatic relations with North Korea.[66] The frequency and level of human rights abuses also reportedly increased during this period and the *Tatmadaw* launched large-scale anti-insurgent offensives in the Karen and Karenni states, displacing tens of thousands more villagers. Given these circumstances, US sanctions were extended and the International Committee for the Red Cross (ICRC) – which normally maintains political neutrality – publically accused the government of abusing the Myanmar people's rights; the junta responded by suspending five key field offices of the Red Cross. As noted, in December 2005, Aung San Suu Kyi's house arrest was extended and this was followed by a further extension of twelve months in May 2006. Given these developments, together with the events discussed in the previous section, by late 2006 the relationship between Myanmar and its remaining ASEAN counterparts had deteriorated to a point most accurately defined as 'mutual disengagement'.

Throughout 2007, Myanmar's isolation from ASEAN and the world continued to deepen and, in parallel, the level of discontent held by the people of Myanmar grew. As the size and frequency of anti-government protests rapidly increased – including an incident of 500 protestors on the 27 May anniversary of the 1990 elections – the government's usual intolerance for dissent soon resurfaced. The 'Anniversary protestors' were met by 'thugs' from the government's Union Solidarity and Development Association (USDA) and a further protest by the 88 Generation earlier that month also led to arrests by members of the same organization. Then, without warning, in August 2007, the junta increased the subsidized rate of petrol (gasoline) from US$1.18 to US$1.96 per gallon.[67] The decision proved to be a gross mistake in the context of Myanmar's regional and international relations. Largescale protests by concerned citizens including monks, nuns, students, members of the 88 Generation students and NLD supporters followed between 19 August and late September 2007. On 26 September the security forces cracked down and opened fire on a large demonstration in Yangon, and following further actions by the government (including raids of monasteries), the protests were largely halted.[68] In the end, the SPDC's violent response resulted in over 4,000 arrests and at least thirty-one deaths including that of a Japanese journalist.

The government's crackdown generated international outrage and increased pressure from key Western states, including the US and the EU, for ASEAN to take action. For example, the United States' Senate passed a resolution calling on ASEAN to expel, or at least suspend, Myanmar from membership in ASEAN.[69] Even Barry Desker, the Dean of the S. Rajaratnam School of International Studies, and an Ambassador for the Singaporean government, called for Myanmar's expulsion from ASEAN. Moreover, monks, exiled opposition groups and the United Nations Commissioner for Human Rights raised the possibility of applying the UN's 'Responsibility to Protect Doctrine' in order to force the SPDC to comply with internationals human rights norms. Meanwhile, the AIPMC and civil society organizations (CSOs) from the region – such as APA – also called on ASEAN to be more active in supporting democracy in Myanmar.[70] The crisis occurred just two months before the November Leader's Summit, when ASEAN was to present the final draft of its Charter. As will be discussed in the next chapter, the Charter was intended to advance ASEAN's regionalist project and address challenges like Myanmar by institutionalising and integrating ASEAN politically, economically and socially. However, the violent crackdown in Myanmar greatly undermined the legitimacy of the new Charter as not only had the Burmese dictatorship endorsed the document, but such endorsement did not lead to a resolution of the Myanmar deadlock despite the Charter's references to democracy and human rights.

The junta's crackdown forced the Association to respond a day later at the sidelines of a UNGA Plenary session. Singapore's George Yeo stated that:

> they were appalled to receive reports of automatic weapons being used … [and that] they [had] expressed their revulsion to Myanmar Foreign Minister Nyan Win over reports that the demonstrations in Myanmar are being suppressed by violent force and that there has been a number of fatalities.

Further, the Foreign Ministers had 'demanded that the Myanmar government immediately desist from the use of violence against demonstrators'.[71] While George Yeo made the statement in the capacity of the ASEAN Chair, the wording of the document had been previously circulated to the ASEAN Foreign Ministers and they had consented to the statement's release. As Jurgen Haacke contends, in practical terms the document represented a 'joint statement' as other

Foreign Ministers had contributed amendments and it was delivered in the presence of all the Foreign Ministers except Myanmar.[72] Further, aside from breaching the three primary principles of the ASEAN Way (sovereignty, non-interference and consensus),[73] the statement was important for providing a common position at the forthcoming meeting in the UNGA where a consensus resolution was reached that also 'strongly deplored the violent suppression of the peaceful demonstrations'.[74]

Meanwhile, Singapore's Minister of Foreign Affairs had earlier that day released a statement emphasizing the broader implications of the situation in Myanmar for the region as a whole, and he further suggested that the UN was 'the best hope for a peaceful resolution of the situation'.[75] Singapore's Prime Minister Lee Hsien Loong contacted the leaders of Malaysia, Indonesia, Thailand, Vietnam and the Philippines and, aside from gaining consensus on the aforementioned Chairman's Statement, he also obtained agreement on the importance of the proposed United Nations mission to Myanmar, which was to be undertaken by its special envoy Ibrahim Gambari.[76] With China's diplomatic support, Gambari was able to visit Myanmar on 2 October where he met with the SPDC's key leaders – including Senior General Than Shwe – as well as Aung San Suu Kyi. In a rare display of 'unanimity', a UNSC executive statement followed on 11 October urging the SPDC to exercise restraint and reaffirmed its support for the good offices of Ibrahim Gambari.[77] Meanwhile, most western states strengthened their sanctions regime against Myanmar but these measures were largely symbolic.[78] However, an important exception occurred when Air Bagan was forced to cancel all its flights to Singapore following a boycott of the company by Singapore's banks.[79] Given the close relationship that Singapore has historically maintained with Myanmar, such a decision represented an important development in regional relations.[80]

Singapore was, moreover, highly active in its international diplomacy with major powers including the US, Japan, India and China. While in New York for the UNGA meeting, Foreign Minister Yeo met with Christopher Hill, the US Assistant Secretary of State, where he conveyed a message similar to a previous press statement suggesting that the UN is 'the best shot we have and the key now is to build up the authority and the moral prestige of Ambassador Gambari'.[81] Yeo also undertook trips to China, India and Japan with a view to discuss 'how regional countries could support both a genuine process of peaceful reconciliation in Myanmar generally and Gambari's good offices role in particular'.[82] The AIPMC also held 'quiet' discussions with Chinese officials[83] and China, for its part, hosted a meeting with the US Deputy Assistant Secretary of State, Eric Johns, and three Myanmar ministers that reportedly discussed the issue of political transition and the potential release of Aung San Suu Kyi. Nonetheless, the Chinese government continued to emphasize an approach that would achieve 'stability, development and national reconcilement' but did not appear willing to jeopardize its economic and strategic interests in Myanmar.[84]

When the SPDC was in New York, the regime was unable to influence or prevent the earlier statement by the ASEAN Chair; however, 'the Burmese junta took its revenge' at the 2007 ASEAN Summit in Singapore.[85] In October, Singapore's ambassador to the UN informed the Security Council that it had invited Ibrahim Gambari to brief the leaders at the November EAS. His briefing described this as 'an important opportunity [for Gambari] to personally update and engage' the leaders from all sixteen EAS countries including China, India, Japan, South Korea, New Zealand and Australia together with all ten of the ASEAN members.[86] On 19 November, after Gambari had already departed on a flight for Singapore, the ASEAN leaders held an informal dinner to discuss the forthcoming agenda. Somewhat embarrassingly, a microphone was left on and significant segments of a 'heated' dialogue were clearly audible to the media in a room nearby.[87] Despite having previously agreed to Gambari's briefing, Myanmar objected to it at the dinner and Myanmar's Prime Minister subsequently threatened to scuttle the Charter before storming out of the meeting.[88] Myanmar's confidence to take this stance was likely strengthened by China's own opposition to the Gambari briefing. Further, while Indonesia, Thailand, Malaysia and the Philippines all suggested that this was no longer a matter that could be considered a domestic affair, Vietnam, Laos and Cambodia sided with Myanmar, arguing that 'one of our members is objecting'.[89] Some ASEAN members also objected on the grounds that Singapore had not adequately consulted with them before publically inviting Gambari to brief the EAS.[90]

The final outcome of the lengthy intra-ASEAN debate boiled down to just one point concerning what was then a unanimous consensus: from this moment on 'Myanmar was on its own' in its dealings with the UN and the international community.[91] After the meeting, Prime Minister Lee, flanked by all the ASEAN leaders except Myanmar, announced that while Gambari's group briefing was cancelled, individual leaders and Foreign Ministers would be welcome to meet with him privately. During his time in Singapore, Gambari was able to meet with senior officials from all the ASEAN countries except Vietnam, Laos and Cambodia.[92] The challenge for ASEAN and its Charter did not end with Myanmar; Gloria Arroyo departed from the November summit stating that unless the situation in Myanmar improves then her Senate might refuse to ratify the Charter. This risk was also identified as a possibility in Indonesia and Thailand.[93]

The SPDC then announced that it would be proceeding with the final stages of its roadmap for democracy and this caught many off guard.[94] The initial responses from ASEAN, together with regional analysts and the media, ranged from cautious support to outright skepticism; however, the decision to continue with the referendum immediately after a devastating cyclone did not help to placate the more critical end of the spectrum. Nonetheless, given the sum-total of regional relations vis-à-vis the Myanmar issue, Myanmar and ASEAN had effectively disengaged from each other. To the extent that some ASEAN members may have sought a modus vivendi akin to 'mutual disengagement', the fluctuating positions of both the US and the EU were likely to have encouraged (and rewarded) the idea that ASEAN could escape international pressure through a combination of regular criticism whilst simultaneously disengaging from meaningful attempts to encourage positive change in Myanmar.

As early as 2006, both the US and the EU had started to undertake a more conciliatory approach regarding ASEAN's position on Myanmar. For example, during a January 2006 visit to Malaysia US Assistant Secretary of State Christopher Hill announced that Condoleezza Rice would be attending the July ARF meeting.[95] As discussed earlier, her absence from the 2005 ARF meeting was widely interpreted as a protest against Myanmar's participation in the ARF, along with ASEAN's failure to force Myanmar to implement reform and improve its human rights record. Later that year, Condoleezza Rice personally commended ASEAN for undertaking an 'important evolution' in the pressure it applied against Myanmar.[96] She made the comment shortly after the aforementioned Foreign Ministers' Statement in July 2006. Rice also associated herself with the September 2007 ASEAN Chair's Statement with the implication that 'ASEAN had finally joined the side of Myanmar's long-term critics'.[97]

Meanwhile, the European Union indicated in April 2006 that it shared ASEAN's frustration over the deadlock in Myanmar and its Foreign Policy Chief stated that 'we think that together we have to see how we can get Myanmar to evolve in the direction that it is supposed to evolve in'.[98] Later, in the lead-up to a September 2007 ASEM meeting in Finland, the EU also confirmed that it would not allow its talks with ASEAN to be derailed by the Myanmar issue.[99] However, the relatively conciliatory tone by the EU and the US was inconsistently maintained. For example, negotiations regarding the first ASEAN–US Summit soon stalled over the issue of including Myanmar at the meeting.[100] Soon after, the EU Trade Chief warned that both ASEAN and the EU needed to be more proactive in their cooperation over the Myanmar issue so that Myanmar's poor human rights record would not hinder a possible trade pact between the two organizations. Nevertheless, he suggested that they 'needed to work through these problems … rather than to be held hostage by one country'.[101] Despite such reassurances, negotiations for a multilateral pact were halted in March 2009 and FTAs are now being sought on a bilateral basis in order to avoid an ASEAN–EU FTA conflicting with EU sanctions against Myanmar.[102] The US, however, did not allow the Myanmar issue to completely impede a trade arrangement with ASEAN. The pact was concluded in August 2006, but it was scaled down to a 'trade and investment facilitation arrangement' that does not require Senate approval. The US further maintained that the nature of the arrangement would not result in any increase to trade between the United States and Myanmar.[103]

From Nargis to the 2010 elections: restoring a limited consensus?

During the months that followed, ASEAN appeared to push the Myanmar issue to the sidelines of regional and international attention as far as was possible. However, ASEAN was forced to once again change its method of engagement on the evening of 2 May 2008 when Cyclone Nargis struck with devastating effect. The cyclonic winds that hit the Ayeyarwady delta exceeded 190 kilometres and the subsequent 3.5 metre high tidal surge wiped out entire villages.[104] Estimates of the eventual death toll ranged from 130,000 to 200,000 and the International Crisis Group further estimated that as many as 800,000 people might have been displaced by the cyclone.[105] The enormity of the destruction was demonstrated by images in the media – including CNN broadcasts – that graphically illustrated some of the children who perished during the storm.[106] Further, the ease with which many of the Ayeyarwady delta's homes and local structures could be blown down by the storm meant that many people had been seriously injured or killed as they were sandblasted by the winds whilst clinging to trees and other structures in an attempt to survive the cyclone.

The only institution in Myanmar with the capacity to respond to a natural disaster of this magnitude was the military (*Tatmadaw*). Amazingly, the SPDC did not immediately call upon the military to rescue any of the survivors of the cyclone or to assist with the country's recovery efforts.[107] While the government did declare a 'national emergency' in the five worst hit areas and subsequently activated its 'Natural Disaster Preparedness Central Committee' – which was chaired by the country's Prime Minister – it took several days before any aid arrived. Even then, much of the government's efforts were 'undermined by lack of communication, petty corruption and sheer incompetence'.[108] Despite continued chaos including the risk of widespread famine and disease,[109] Senior General Than Shwe declared the situation was 'returning to normal' just five days after the cyclone had struck. Then, while 'bloated bodies were [still] lying in the ditches and tens of thousands of victims were … waiting for assistance', Than Shwe declared that 'relief efforts had ended and the reconstruction phase had begun'.[110] Hunkered down in Naypyidaw, the SPDC leadership was seemingly incapable of grasping the extent of the crisis. On 5 May, the government also declared that the national referendum on its new Constitution would continue as planned on 10 May and that the scheduled vote would only be delayed by two weeks in the hardest high areas. The junta further argued that the 'referendum is only a few days away and the people are eagerly looking forward to voting'.[111]

The SPDC initially refused the delivery of international aid for the victims of the cyclone. Despite this, numerous reports outlined the highly proactive nature of the *Sangha* and NGOs inside Myanmar in their attempts to help in the recovery process. However, these groups, together with individuals indigenous to Myanmar, including doctors, were blocked in their efforts to help victims of the cyclone. Some monasteries were also prohibited from receiving aid and the government established roadblocks to further restrict relief workers from reaching the worst hit areas. By 14 May, reports were emerging that the SPDC had implemented a fine of $3,000, or five years' imprisonment, for any foreign nationals caught in the delta. Further, despite having lost everything, when limited government supplies eventually arrived, local government officers expected payment for non-food items such as emergency shelter tarpaulins. Numerous reports also suggested that local branches of government participated in the confiscation of aid or, in some cases, replaced the aid with inferior products, including rotten rice.[112] According to one informant, government employees placed UN labels on the bags containing the rotten and maggot-infested rice and informed the recipients that this how little the world thinks of them.[113]

The diversion of valuable resources in preparation for the referendum, the obstructionism of local efforts by NGOs and civil society, and the initial refusal of international aid by the SPDC, rejuvenated international outrage. At its pinnacle, the French Foreign Minister sought to invoke the UN's doctrine of the Responsibility to Protect (R2P). Had the principle been invoked then, at the very least, aid would have been dropped by air without the consent of the SPDC.[114] France's call was all the more notable given the support it received from other influential nations including the US, Canada, Australia and Germany. Thus, the EU Foreign Policy Chief, Javier Solana, also urged the UN to utilize 'all means necessary' to ensure the delivery of aid to those most in need.[115] However, the insurmountable challenge of securing UNSC authorization for such action, together with the logistical nightmare of facilitating the forced but effective delivery of aid, meant that it would never be a viable option. Nonetheless, various media outlets hopped on the 'intervention' wagon, with the *Australian* claiming 'It's time for an aid intervention', the *Time Magazine* suggesting that it's time to consider 'the more serious option' of 'invading Burma' while the *AsiaTimes Online* concluded that while an invasion was 'once a paranoid delusion' it was now a 'strong pre-emptive possibility'.[116]

The junta viewed the cyclone more as a 'security threat' than as a 'natural disaster', not only because of fears of invasion but also because granting permission for a massive relief effort would result in a large influx of foreign aid workers and media personnel. Thus, Singapore received reports that the Burmese military (*Tatmadaw*) had not been called in to help the victims of the cyclone because they had instead been ordered into 'defensive positions'.[117] While the West called on Thailand, India and China to unilaterally pressure the junta to allow foreign aid and emergency relief personnel into the country,[118] for weeks the SPDC continued to deny visa applications for foreign aid workers, and foreign aid agencies repeatedly warned that their aid was not getting to the victims most in need.[119] Given these threat perceptions, the SPDC was primarily concerned about its grip on power and the avoidance of 'alien cultural influences' that might translate into 'social instability'.[120] In the end, the only institution that was able to manage these concerns and thereby play a pivotal role in helping the victims of Nargis was ASEAN.

ASEAN released its first press statement on 5 May and, in order to assess the extent of the catastrophe, the Association dispatched its Emergency Rapid Assessment Team (ERAT) into Myanmar between 9 and 18 May.[121] The deployment of ERAT was enabled by previous agreements including the ASEAN Agreement on Disaster Management and Emergency Response that had been ratified by Myanmar and developed in the wake of the 2004 Asian tsunami. Meanwhile, on 8 May ASEAN's Secretary-General, Surin Pitsuwan, sought to raise resources for the disaster relief effort by initiating the ASEAN Cooperation Fund for Disaster Assistance. Further, on 12 May Surin organized a meeting between the ASEAN Secretariat, the World Bank and the UN's Office for the

Coordination of Humanitarian Affairs (OCHA) for the purpose of assessing potential support for a 'coalition of mercy' – a phrase that was later changed to 'Humanitarian Coalition for the Victims of Cyclone Nargis' – together with medium- and long-term measures that such a coalition would need to adopt.

ERAT reported to an emergency meeting of the ASEAN Foreign Ministers on 19 May where it had the difficult task of balancing praise – in order to overcome the SPDC's obstructionism – whilst maintaining a realistic picture of the challenge of assessment and the potential problems that lay ahead. Thus, the report claimed that the SPDC 'tried its level best to meet the demands of an adequate and organized response' but later stated that its assessment 'would have been more reflective of the realities on the ground had the team been permitted to conduct assessments in disaster-affected areas that ASEAN-ERAT selected'.[122] Given this problem, the continued recalcitrance of the junta, and the fact that ASEAN's international stature had again been challenged, heated discussions with Myanmar's Foreign Minister Nyan Win ensued. According to an official source from a Singapore embassy, the Indonesian Foreign Minister 'leaned across the table and asked the Foreign Minister of Myanmar what he thought ASEAN membership meant to Myanmar and what – at that time and in those circumstances – Myanmar's membership meant to ASEAN – in terms of ASEAN's internal coherence – international profile – and its membership's shared vision for the future'.[123]

In the end, ASEAN managed to force the SPDC to take a more cooperative position through a carrot and stick approach. The nature of the question by Indonesia's Foreign Minister revealed a level of frustration that questioned the utility of Myanmar's continued membership in ASEAN. Having explicitly outlined the potential stakes for Myanmar, the Foreign Ministers then explained to Nyan Win 'that the crisis offered Naypyidaw *a final opportunity* to allow the Association a role in facilitating the military's relations with the international community.'[124] ASEAN's narrow focus on humanitarian aid effectively depoliticized the Association's engagement with Myanmar and, aside from some potential long-term implications, this approach undoubtedly saved lives in the process. Thus, ASEAN subsequently obtained consent to establish the 'ASEAN Humanitarian Taskforce for the Victims of Cyclone Nargis' (which would provide an ASEAN-led coordinating mechanism for the effective distribution of aid) and consent to coordinate with the UN in holding an ASEAN–UN International Pledging Conference in Yangon on 25 May 2008. In order to maintain Myanmar's cooperation, George Yeo highlighted that the delivery of international aid 'through ASEAN … should not be politicized', but simultaneously warned that 'Myanmar should allow more international relief workers'.[125]

Despite the challenges of cooperating with the SPDC,[126] Surin Pitsuwan persisted and by the time the Pledging Conference had concluded he had transformed the initial 'Taskforce' into the Tripartite Core Group (TCG) consisting of three delegates each from Myanmar, ASEAN and the UN. The TCG was established to coordinate, facilitate and monitor the distribution of aid and Myanmar's Deputy Foreign Minister Kyaw Thu was the chair. The TCG then carried out a comprehensive joint assessment of recovery needs led by the

Post-Nargis Joint Assessment team (PONJA), consisting of experts from ASEAN, the UN, the International Organization for Migration, the World Bank and the Asian Development Bank. A total of 250 members of PONJA were dispatched by Kyaw Thu on 9 June, As part of the TCG, more than 250 aid workers and professionals were selected from the ASEAN countries but at a meeting immediately prior to their arrival in Myanmar Kyaw Thu reminded the PONJA experts that their assessments should not contain any political content.[127] Nonetheless, through the TCG structure, combined with ASEAN's mediatory role, the issue of visas had become far less problematic and by 18 August 1,035 visas had been issued and in the third week of August the last of the UN's flights from Bangkok's Don Muang airport took place.[128]

Beyond international aid, the usual circumstances surrounding the politics of Myanmar applied. For example, just one day after the International Pledging Conference, the SPDC announced that it would be extending Aung San Suu Kyi's detention for another year. Further, the human rights situation in the country continued to decline and by the close of 2008 the government had sentenced a further '200 political and labour activists, Internet bloggers, journalists, and Buddhist monks and nuns to lengthy jail terms'.[129] Meanwhile, ASEAN's success in re-establishing its utility for the SPDC correspondingly contributed to a reassessment of the utility of the UN. Here, increased pressure from the UN also contributed to Myanmar's re-engagement with ASEAN.[130] Further, Donald Emmerson argues that Surin Pitsuwan:

> [a]s an intermediary between angry donors and stubborn generals in Myanmar, … tried to save lives. But in doing so, he also helped save the junta's face, and to that extent his actions may have marginally prolonged its lease on life.[131]

Earlier he states that as ASEAN had effectively depoliticized intervention, this in turn is 'likely to undercut the ability of [the] … regional organization (ASEAN) to induce reform.'[132]

During the course of 2010, the Myanmar junta continued with its plans to hold the first nationwide elections in twenty years. Consequently, the SPDC implemented restrictive electoral laws in March 2010 including a prohibition against any individual participating in the election if they are currently serving 'a prison term as a result of a conviction in a court of Law'. As there was an estimated 2,250 political prisoners by September 2009, these laws effectively blocked a significant proportion of the potential opposition candidates from contesting the election.[133] Given this, and other developments, the election was strongly rigged in the military's favour and the main pro-military party, the Union Solidarity and Development Party (USDP), claimed that they won 80 per cent of the vote with the result that only a few democratic candidates won seats in either of the two parliaments.[134] Further, 25 per cent of the seats for both the new upper and lower houses are reserved for the military.[135] While Aung San Suu Kyi has since been released from house arrest, the question of whether the formation of the new parliament in 2011 will lead to any incremental steps toward greater civil liberties and political freedoms remains open. Nonetheless, Singapore Foreign Minister George Yeo reflected on developments in the country through to 2008 and subsequently assessed that ASEAN could only be given a 'C grade' for its handling of the Myanmar issue.[136]

Conclusions

Despite ASEAN's efforts, this chapter revealed the increasingly erratic and unpredictable behaviour of Myanmar's leadership. The junta shifted its capital to Naypyidaw, it failed to predict the civil dissent that arose out of its sudden announcement to significantly increase the price of fuel, and human rights abuses continued unabated. The Myanmar government did not attend ASEAN's inaugural Defence Ministers' Meeting, its leaders often accorded greater courtesy and cooperation to the UN than to ASEAN, and the SPDC maintained a practice of making embarrassing announcements at highly sensitive moments for ASEAN – such as announcing the continuation of Aung San Suu Kyi's detention just days prior to the ASEAN Summit in Kuala Lumpur. As reinforced through several other examples in this chapter, the importance Myanmar places on its membership in ASEAN is somewhat less than the remaining ASEAN states would likely hope for. Thus, the chapter demonstrates the rarity by which Myanmar has bowed to the collective interests of ASEAN, with such occurrences emerging only in the wake of substantial pressure at the intramural and extramural levels. The narrow and self-interested pursuit by the SPDC of its own regime interests, with little regard for ASEAN, reflects behaviour that is most adequately explained by the realist paradigm. At this low level of complex integration the political elite of Myanmar do not identify with ASEAN, or its ideal of a security community, and consequently the regime continues to conduct its relations without regard to logic of appropriateness – whether ASEAN or western defined.

The period covered by this chapter was also notable for the role of some of the original and relatively more democratic members of ASEAN. Here, the Foreign Ministers of both Singapore and Malaysia took the lead in criticizing Myanmar, seeking a regional consensus over how to respond to Myanmar, and in their international diplomacy vis-à-vis the UN and foreign powers. The fact that Singapore's banks refused to deal with Air Bagan may also have marked a turning point in Singapore's 'behind the scenes' relations with the junta. While Singapore's diplomacy was particularly successful in convincing both the EU and the US that the Association had done everything possible to pressure Myanmar, neither Singapore, nor ASEAN collectively, managed to achieve any tangible improvement to the crisis of governance in the country. ASEAN's success in satisfying some of the expectations by the international community was also a mixed blessing in other respects. When the Myanmar issue reached the UNSC's agenda, some of the ASEAN members appeared to be highly concerned that ASEAN would lose control over when exogenous actors could interfere in the region. Thus, Syed Hamid Albar declared that ASEAN, rather than the Security Council, was in a better position to handle the Myanmar issue. Former UN Secretary-General Kofi Annan's comments that Myanmar fitted the UN's Responsibility to Protect doctrine undoubtedly heightened such concerns. These developments, in addition to a democratic/authoritarian divide, further explain the continued shifts between ASEAN's engagement and disengagement from Myanmar.

Neither mutual disengagement nor critical disengagement represented the best possible foreign policy options for ASEAN. They were, however, the only feasible foreign policy options under a system of consensus-based decision-making. Given ASEAN's modus operandi together with the authoritarian blend of membership – e.g. Laos, Vietnam and Cambodia – it was in fact remarkable that ASEAN could find sufficient cohesion to formulate statements that included the words 'revulsion' and 'appalled' in their criticism of the SPDC – albeit through the Singapore Chair at the time. The development of mutual disengagement was all the more notable in that the region sought to pass responsibility to extra-mural actors such as China, India and the United Nations. Given the ideal of 'regional resilience', a goal that has existed since ASEAN's inception, these developments revealed a level of intra-mural frustration rarely witnessed in the Association's history. The apex of this frustration was reached when Myanmar asked ASEAN to defend it from UN action and Singapore's Foreign Minister responded that ASEAN had lost both the 'credibility and ability' to do so.

Notwithstanding the above achievements, the occurrence of collective response at a region-wide level was largely driven by international pressure. Throughout the chapter various ASEAN leaders, together with the Association's Secretary-General, sought to justify their criticism of Myanmar on the basis of how much the SPDC had affected ASEAN's international stature; however, the plight of Myanmar's people rarely appeared as the principle factor in such justifications. Further, ASEAN's position remained in a state of flux throughout the period and appeared to vary not only because of international pressure but also because of a tug-of-war between the more authoritarian and democratic members of ASEAN. While democracy may not be a prerequisite for a security community, the empirical evidence in this chapter, together with the previous chapter, suggests that the political institutions within each of the ASEAN members have considerably affected the way each member constructs its foreign policy. In view of the fact that Laos, Cambodia and Vietnam all continue to suffer from serious human rights challenges, then their leaderships undoubtedly remain concerned about how 'flexible engagement' might be applied to their own domestic affairs in the future. Given these considerations, the evolution of critical disengagement, followed by mutual disengagement, generated tangible tensions within the Association as some of the members were undoubtedly wondering when the same policy would be applied with respect to their own internal affairs. Cyclone Nargis and the depoliticization of engagement through the TCG mechanism have temporarily relieved these tensions. Nevertheless, at the institutional level of analysis, the Myanmar case study provides further caveats against the ability of ASEAN to continue to implement the type of reform that would be indicative of a higher level of complex integration. The next chapter verifies these limitations.

7 Regionalism anew?

Institutional outcomes and the limitations to change

The previous chapters have provided a broad sample of both the security challenges and normative limitations faced by ASEAN in the pursuit of its regionalist goals. The analysis has also provided some indication of how these challenges and limitations have been exacerbated by the diversity of political interests and values throughout the region. The extent of the security challenges and problematic relations in the region has, in turn, led some scholars to question various assertions that ASEAN represents some form of a security community. Given these constraints, the first section analyses the institutional outcomes that have occurred as a consequence of ASEAN's regionalist project. Having outlined these developments, the next section seeks further empirical explanations by utilizing a range of sources including the data from the 'elite' and 'communal' surveys. Based on an analysis of ASEAN's regionalist goals in previous chapters, and having provided an analysis of the degree of tangible progress to date in this chapter, the final section seeks further explanatory insights by continuing to analyse the survey data for the purpose of measuring the extent of interaction, knowledge and affinity between the societies of Southeast Asia.

Institutional outcomes: mixed performance in the economic, political and security spheres?

There is some debate about whether ASEAN's regionalist visions amount to a Deutschian type of a security community. However, the accomplishment of ASEAN's goals would in fact exceed the scholarly definitions of a security community. Thus, the beginning of this book noted that recent ASEAN declarations have provided a commitment to create an ASEAN Community involving greater 'integration' where the 'members shall rely exclusively on peaceful processes in the settlement of differences and disputes'. More specifically, in the course of 'achieving a more coherent and clearer path for cooperation', together with 'peace, stability, democracy and prosperity in the region', the ASEAN members have pledged to create a 'common regional identity', greater 'cohesiveness and harmony' (including a 'we-feeling'), the establishment of a 'rules-based community', regional 'stability', 'enhanced defence cooperation', the resolution of 'territorial' and 'maritime issues', greater cooperation in tackling 'transnational crime' (including 'ensuring a drug free ASEAN by 2015'), the 'strengthening of law enforcement cooperation', 'the prevention and control of infectious diseases', 'strengthening the rule of law and judiciary systems', 'enhancing good governance in public and private sectors', the 'strengthening of democratic institutions and popular participation', the 'promotion of human rights' and the establishment of 'a single market and production base'.[1] While ASEAN has acknowledged that the realization of these goals will require greater 'political and security cooperation', such developments would also evidence well-developed levels of trust, interest harmonization, foreign policy coordination and institutionalization.

Given the rationale behind the formation of ASEAN (Chapters 2 and 3), it is not surprising that some of the most significant progress has occurred in the economic sphere. For example, Chapter 4 outlined some of the immediate economic developments following the financial crisis and noted how perceptions of economic vulnerability – domestic and international – helped to galvanize common interests leading to greater economic cooperation. While the chapter discussed the Hanoi Summit, it is important to refer to it again as it led to several agreements and mechanisms for greater cooperation and institutionalization. Further, the Hanoi Summit also reflected concerns about increased competition from China and India, together with an associated desire to engage major powers in the broader Asia–Pacific to enhance trade and security. Thus, it was through the Hanoi Summit that ASEAN formalized annual meetings with China, South Korea and Japan by developing the ASEAN Plus Three (APT) arrangement.[2]

The first APT 'informal summit' occurred in 1997 and the summit has since been institutionalized as an annual event. Through this forum, the drive for greater East Asian integration (primarily economic) has led to several programmes that could facilitate greater economic resilience and stability, including the Chiang Mai Initiative. This initiative incorporated an expansion of the ASEAN Swap Arrangement, which had operated in a limited capacity since 1997.[3] The arrangement seeks to protect against 'currency speculators' (one of the 'causes' of the Asian financial crisis) by providing assistance with short-term liquidity problems through loans and/or credits from the currency reserves of the ASEAN central banks. Upon its creation, there was a total facility of US$100 million but the Chiang Mai Initiative initially expanded this to US$1 billion. By early 2007, the Chiang Mai Initiative had also led to the establishment of sixteen bilateral swap arrangements (BSAs) between ASEAN and the 'plus three' countries to the value of US$75 billion.[4] However, the long-term goal has been to multilateralize the arrangement and this vision came into reality through the finalization of the Chiang Mai Initiative Multilateralization (CMIM) in December 2009. The CMIM involves an enlarged US$120 billion swap arrangement and was a collective response of the APT countries to the global financial crisis.[5] The CMIM was activated in March 2010. While this is an APT effort, the expansion of the CMIM has also helped to boost ASEAN integration.[6]

'[I]ntraregional trade as a percentage of the region's total trade is perhaps the best measure of ASEAN's economic integration'.[7] Here, the most prominent initiative has been the ASEAN Free Trade Area (AFTA). However, Chapter 4 noted that it has not led to a significant increase in intra-regional trade and there is a very low use of AFTA's preferential tariff rates. Nonetheless, ASEAN has accepted that it needs to create trade advantages beyond mere tariff reduction and has embarked on a series of additional initiatives to support its goals. Such measures include product standardization, customs reform, harmonized trade nomenclatures, mutual recognition arrangements, the liberalization of trade in services, and the facilitation of more efficient transportation.[8] Further economic agreements in recent years include the ASEAN Surveillance Process, the E-ASEAN Framework Agreement, the ASEAN Development Fund, the Asian Bond Fund, the Asian Bond Market Initiative and the AFTA Plus agreements. However, for the purpose of economic integration and cooperation, one of the most significant developments was the proposal for an ASEAN Economic Community (AEC).

While the incorporation of the AEC in the Bali Concord II was noted in earlier chapters, the AEC was first proposed by Singapore in 2002.[9] As with the ASEAN Security community, the AEC seeks to consolidate four decades of agreements and statements of intent into a single and more unified vision. The key purpose of the AEC, as declared in the Bali Concord II, has been

> to create a stable, prosperous and highly competitive ASEAN economic region in which there is a free flow of goods, services, investment and a free flow of capital, equitable economic development and reduced poverty and socio-economic disparities in the year 2020 [now 2015].[10]

A detailed roadmap for the realization of these goals was provided by the ASEAN Economic Community Blueprint in 2007. For example, in the context of free flow of goods, the Economic Blueprint seeks to address issues of transparency, standards and technical barriers to trade. The Economic Blueprint also provides 'strategic schedules' and 'clear roadmaps' addressing the 'free flow' of services and investment and the 'freer' flow of capital.[11] The liberalization of the trade in services dates back to the 1995 'ASEAN Framework Agreement on Services'; however, the economic blueprint provides relatively more detailed and firmer commitments complete with specified dates for the implementation of individual components.[12]

Equally significant has been an agreement on a dispute settlement mechanism to resolve trade disputes. The process started with the ASEAN Protocol on the Dispute Settlement Mechanism (DSM) in 1996 and, as a consequence of a commitment by the Bali Concord II to implement the recommendations of a High Level Taskforce on ASEAN Economic Integration, the DSM was strengthened by the 2004 ASEAN Protocol on Enhanced Dispute Settlement Mechanism (EDSM). By resembling the WTO DSM in form and in practice, including a binding process of arbitration, the EDSM moves beyond the ASEAN Way and, in the economic sphere, represents a significant step towards a more institutionalized and legalistic Association.[13] However, as with the High Council, the

ASEAN members continue to evince a preference to utilize alternative DSMs. For example, in February 2008, the Philippines utilized the WTO DSM in a dispute over fiscal measures on cigarettes adopted by Thailand.[14]

Notwithstanding the limitations to the ASEAN EDSM, the mechanism was reinforced as a component of the ASEAN Charter's modus operandi. While the Charter is discussed later, at this juncture it is important to note that it provides for a more flexible decision-making system on economic matters. Further, the Charter creates a legal personality for ASEAN which not only enables other countries to direct Official Development Aid (ODA) through the ASEAN Secretariat,[15] but also has the potential to strengthen the capacity of ASEAN – through the ASEAN Coordinating Council comprised of Foreign Ministers – to negotiate FTAs with countries exogenous to Southeast Asia.[16] Interestingly, ASEAN has negotiated several FTAs and Comprehensive Economic Partnership (CEP) agreements since the ASEAN Charter, including the ASEAN–Australia–New Zealand FTA – the most comprehensive accord ever concluded by ASEAN.[17] Nonetheless, a broad East Asian FTA will ultimately be necessary to mitigate the ever-growing noodle bowl of smaller FTAs that generate economic inefficiencies through different tariffs, rules of origin and standards.[18]

As with AFTA, the CMIM and the ASP, the realization of ASEAN's remaining economic goals has not been, nor is likely to be, problem-free. For example, John Ravenhill notes that the '*qualifier* in the commitment to a "freer flow of capital" [in both the AEC and Economic Blueprint] immediately suggested a hedging that critics saw as all-too-characteristic of ASEAN's history of "flexible" commitments to economic integration'.[19] Meanwhile, even in the economic sphere, the extent of solidarity between the ASEAN members remains questionable. For example, in November 2006 investment flows started to put upward pressure on the Thai baht and the Thai Central Bank imposed capital flows without consulting its ASEAN partners. Various stock markets in the region subsequently plunged as investors lost confidence. The Thai Finance Minister defended his country's actions by stating that in a 'small nation like ourselves, if we don't protect ourselves, who else will protect us?'[20] This behaviour is reminiscent of the behaviour that followed the 1997 Asian financial crisis. Meanwhile, the implementation of the Economic Blueprint may be delayed as a consequence of the 2008–10 global financial crisis because it has led to intense domestic pressure to stop economic reforms and, particularly, trade liberalization[21] – a scenario that also followed the 1997 Asian financial crisis. Thus, in November 2010, ASEAN Secretary-General Surin Pitsuwan warned that ASEAN's goal for a single market by 2015 was already in peril.[22]

However, ASEAN continues to follow a pattern where consensus has been relatively easier and more frequently attained in the economic sphere. For example, the Economic Blueprint, at forty-eight pages, contains far more detail and many more commitments than the ASEAN Political Security Commitment (sixteen pages) and the ASEAN Socio-Cultural Community Blueprint (thirty pages including an extensive 'glossary' at the end). Further, the ASEAN members were able to agree to the Economic Blueprint at the same time as the

ASEAN Charter – nearly two years ahead of the other two blueprints. ASEAN has also initiated a process for regular reports on progress and the first of these was released in 2010. While the language remains circumspect and discreet, it does, however, provide a higher level of transparency than had previously been the case. Meanwhile, the ASEAN members have selected Singapore as the location for East Asia's first economic and financial surveillance office and the CMIM will be managed through this office.[23] Importantly, distinctly new patterns of governance are starting to emerge in the areas of trade and finance.[24] As Helen Nesadurai notes, recent developments reveal 'that member governments do sometimes choose to deviate from ASEAN's sovereignty-centric norms and practices, but only when they recognise that failure to cooperate could undermine the prospects for economic growth'.[25]

At the extra-regional level, there have been further institutional developments that also cross into the political and security spheres. For example, at the APT Summit in 1998, South Korea proposed the idea of an 'East Asian Community' and a similar idea was suggested by Japanese Prime Minister Junichiro Koizumi in January 2002. Under the leadership of Japanese Prime Minister Hatoyama, the idea was again reiterated in 2009.[26] Nonetheless, ASEAN advanced the concept through the establishment of an East Asian Vision group and its report *Towards an East Asian Community*. The final report of the East Asia Study Group in 2002 led to a number of recommendations, including the formation of an East Asian FTA and the East Asia Summit.[27] However, in the context of the East Asia FTA, a Japanese proposal at the August 2006 Economic Ministers Meeting to commence negotiations in 2008 for a sixteen-nation FTA (including Australia, India and New Zealand) was unenthusiastically received by the ASEAN leaders.[28]

Meanwhile, the first East Asia Summit (EAS) was held in December 2005 and it is designed to facilitate strategic dialogue and cooperation on key challenges facing the East Asian region. The sixteen members include all the ASEAN states as well as India, Australia, New Zealand, Japan, South Korea and China. Some of the major topics it has addressed include terrorism, maritime security, energy security, pandemic diseases and climate change.[29] The second East Asia Summit was held in the Philippines and it identified five 'priority areas' for cooperation: finance, energy, education, avian flu prevention and disaster management.[30] Reminiscent of Mahathir's proposal for an EAEG, the issue of how inclusionary membership should be has been a point of contention between the ASEAN members. However, following an Australian proposal to create an 'Asia Pacific Community', together with continued lobbying by Japan in regards to its proposal for an East Asia Community, ASEAN vigorously guarded its historical leadership in the institutions of the broader Asia-Pacific by proposing, in 2010, an expansion of the EAS to include Russia and the US. While the EAS has already provided a valuable forum for dialogue, the EAS duplicates the activities of other institutions – such as the ARF, APT and APEC – and, as a Leaders' Summit, may also weaken their relevance.

Given ASEAN's aspirations in the political and security sphere, together with the motives behind them, numerous interviewees from government and academia saw an opportunity for greater political and security cooperation and institutionalization through the ASEAN Charter; a charter that was intended to provide the Association with a legal identity and a more institutionalized and binding framework for operation.[31] In reality, however, the issue areas for which institutional reform would be feasible were always going to be limited due to the nature and diversity of the ASEAN member-states. Nonetheless, the early thrust of negotiations for the ASEAN Charter was refreshingly bold and progressive. The most significant development during negotiations for the ASEAN Charter occurred when the ASEAN-commissioned Eminent Persons Group (EPG) released a detailed set of recommendations in December 2006. Despite the involvement of representatives from all the ASEAN countries in authoring the report, it acknowledged the need to calibrate ASEAN's principle of 'non-intervention' and called for the institutionalization of further 'dispute settlement mechanisms' – including compliance monitoring and enforcement mechanisms. Interdependent with a 'recalibration of non-interference' was the recommendation that democratic values, good governance, the rule of law and respect for human rights and fundamental freedoms (among others) be constituted as a fundamental component of ASEAN's 'principles and objectives'.[32]

Another key recommendation of the EPG report was that the Association should be vested with the power to suspend the 'rights and privileges of membership' in order to redress serious breaches of ASEAN agreements, objectives and major principles – e.g. human rights violations.[33] However, the report did not go so far as to recommend a set of rules that would permit the termination of membership. In relation to ASEAN's traditional mode of decision-making, the EPG report suggested that 'consensus should be preserved as the guiding principle', but argued that consensus 'should aid, but not impede, ASEAN's cohesion and effectiveness'. More significantly, the report recommended the creation of 'rules of procedure' that would provide the ASEAN Summit (renamed the ASEAN Council) with the power to vote where consensus could not be achieved. At the very least, the report recommended that there should be a flexible application of the 'ASEAN minus X' or the '2 plus X' formula, should other ASEAN members be unable or unwilling to enter an agreement.[34] Should this mechanism be utilized, the other members would presumably be able to join later. Importantly, the EPG report reflected that 'ASEAN's problem is not one of lack of vision, ideas or action-plans. The problem is one of ensuring compliance and effective implementation'.[35]

The EPG report was followed by an announcement at the July 2007 ASEAN Foreign Ministers Meeting that the ministers had agreed to establish a Human Rights Body.[36] In revamping one of the original proposals from Indonesia's Draft Plan of Action for a Security community (Chapter 5), the ASEAN Foreign Ministers announced that they had overcome various objections by Myanmar – together with Cambodia, Laos and Vietnam – regarding the proposal and whether it should be included as a component of the Charter.[37] However, indicative of trouble on the horizon, Singapore's Foreign Minister George Yeo informed the press that the ASEAN leaders hoped to finalize the 'specifics' for the Human Rights Body in time for the November 2007 Summit in Singapore.[38] As will be seen, the Association's failure to modify its decision-making process (as recommended by the EPG Report) significantly impeded how much the Charter would reform ASEAN.

The ASEAN leaders finalized their agreement on the Charter at the Singapore Summit on 20 November 2007 and it entered into force on 15 December 2008. The ASEAN Secretariat views the Charter as serving 'a firm foundation in achieving the ASEAN Community by providing legal status and [an] institutional framework for ASEAN'.[39] Such an institutional framework has been strengthened, *inter alia*, by the provision of an enhanced role for the ASEAN Secretary-General, the appointment of two new Deputy Secretary-Generals, a broadening of the functions and responsibilities of the ASEAN Foreign Ministers, the appointment of permanent representatives to ASEAN from each member-state, and the increased frequency of ASEAN meetings including the Leaders' Summit.[40] Importantly, the ASEAN Charter implemented a key recommendation of the EPG in the economic sphere by adopting the ASEAN-X formula where an economic agreement in ASEAN can proceed in the absence of all the members – but only when there is a consensus to do so.[41] Nonetheless, the actual contribution of the Charter to the political, economic and socio-cultural future of the region remains a point of contention between regional analysts. Similar to previous instruments and communiqués by ASEAN, the preamble to the ASEAN Charter reiterated a respect for the fundamental importance of principles such as sovereignty, equality, territorial integrity, consensus and non-interference.[42] Consequently, the Charter did not provide any binding commitments regarding conflict resolution and only some general references to the possibility of a dispute settlement mechanisms concerning interpretations of 'specific ASEAN instruments' (Article 24.1).

From the perspective of Singapore's Ambassador Barry Desker, the Charter was 'a disappointment because it codifies existing norms and maintains its historical identity as an inter-governmental organization'.[43] With only 30 per cent of agreements being implemented during the previous forty years, such analysts argue that that the problem of compliance will remain due to ASEAN's failure to change its modus operandi.[44] ASEAN's poor record of accomplishment continues to be attributed to the principle of non-interference and the practice of consensus-based decision-making which provides each member with an implicit right of veto. However, the ASEAN members seem to continue to confuse 'an aversion to supranationalism with an unwillingness to accept binding commitments voluntarily entered into'.[45] Accordingly, the continuation of the ASEAN Way has not only consolidated an institutional aversion to supranationalism (i.e. pooled sovereignty), but also means that the Association's effectiveness remains constrained by its lowest common denominator – Myanmar. Disappointment in the Charter was undoubtedly heightened by the fact that the most significant EPG recommendations concerning the political and security spheres were not incorporated in the final draft.

ASEAN was also unable to finalize the terms of reference for its proposed Human Rights Commission in time for the Charter. In the end, the final Charter delivered just two clauses and five lines on the issue. After stating that the body would conform to the purposes and principles of the Charter (including non-interference and consensus), the second clause adds that the 'ASEAN human rights body shall operate in accordance with the terms of reference to be determined by the ASEAN Foreign Ministers Meeting'.[46] Two years later, when a 'consensus' finally emerged, the terms of reference were announced at the October 2009 ASEAN Summit in Thailand but, unsurprisingly, the newly formed ASEAN Intergovernmental Commission on Human Rights (AICHR) has been interpreted by some analysts as largely 'toothless'.[47] In line with the ASEAN Way, the Commission does not have a rules-based element and does not have the power to investigate human rights concerns within countries. To the contrary, its purpose has been said to 'promote' rather than 'protect' human rights. Thus, given the divide in political values and a subsequent contradiction between the Charter's commitments to human rights and non-interference, there is little reason to believe that most ASEAN members will respect such human rights commitments or any associated references to democracy.[48] Therefore, unsurprisingly, neither the APA nor SAPA were named in the final Charter and this provided an indication that, despite some of the positive developments outlined in Chapter 5, 'CSO aspirations for having an input on policy are not likely to be met'.[49]

Elite level dynamics: further explanatory factors

While the ASEAN Charter may represent a 'work in progress',[50] it does not provide an adequate platform through which ASEAN will be able to realize the broad array of its political and security aspirations; nor has ASEAN made significant progress towards moving 'political and security cooperation' to the 'higher plane' that is necessary, as acknowledged by ASEAN, for the Association to realize its regionalist goals. Chapters 2 through to 6 have identified a broad array of historical and contemporary considerations that provide some explanation about why the ASEAN members continue to act in the absence of a 'sense of community' and thereby struggle with both cooperative endeavours and the level of supranational institutionalism necessary to support this cooperation. Some of these interdependent factors include historical animosities, the continuation of long-standing disputes, regional competition in the security and economic spheres, different strategic interests and alignments, and differing levels of capacity and economic development. In line with the theoretical framework in Chapter 1, these factors also have associated consequences for regional levels of trust and threat perceptions, as well as common interests and values. Consequently, the analysis in this section utilizes additional research, including the survey and interview data, to provide further explanatory insights concerning the challenges to ASEAN's regionalist project.

Amity and enmity in regional perceptions

As noted, perceptions concerning norms, values, strategic orientations, security cooperation and supranational institutionalization reflect the degree to which different states or communities identity with each other. Further, the theoretical framework in Chapter 1 outlined how the level of complex integration, as necessitated by ASEAN's goals, would be demonstrated by a significant level of trust and the relinquishment of the use of force to resolve differences. As has also been noted, the existence of 'dependable expectations of peaceful change' is the defining element of ASEAN's security community and thereby the putative end goal (and end result) of the evolutionary process of complex integration. Given these considerations, both the communal level survey and the elite level survey sought to examine perceptions concerning the risk of conflict and associated levels of trust throughout the region. Here, the perceptions displayed in the 'elite sample', concerning the risk of conflict, were mediocre at best. When asked whether there were any circumstances where one could envisage armed conflict between two or more ASEAN states, half of the respondents indicated 'no', but 22.3 per cent said 'yes' and a further 26.7 per cent were 'unsure'. Figure 7.1 outlines the responses at the individual country level. Interestingly, perceptions of the highest risk of conflict came from the elite respondents in Cambodia (29 per cent), Thailand (42 per cent) and Singapore (47 per cent).

The elite survey also examined the interdependent issue of trust and a similarly disconcerting set of perceptions arose. When asked to provide a 'yes' or 'no' answer concerning whether they could trust other countries in Southeast Asia to be good neighbours, 59.8 per cent responded 'no'. Here, the data from the communal level survey is also interesting to note, as a significantly larger

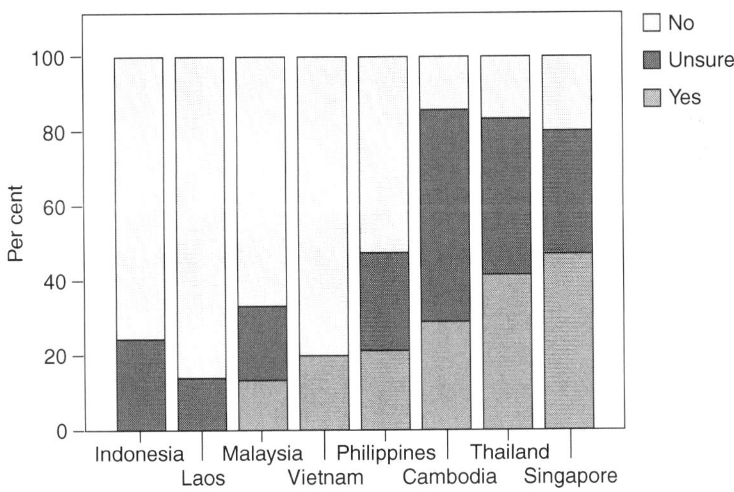

Figure 7.1 Elite perceptions concerning the risk of conflict (source: author).

sample was feasible (819 respondents) and their responses also corresponded with the elite sample – thereby providing a degree of validation for the statistics. On the issue of trust, the communal respondents were also asked whether they believed they 'can trust all the countries in Southeast Asia to be good neighbours' and they were provided three options. While 37.5 per cent responded 'yes', 36.1 per cent were 'unsure' and 26.4 per cent answered 'no' to the question. In other words, 62.5 per cent of the communal sample fell short of believing that they could trust their Southeast Asian neighbours to be good neighbours. As per Figure 7.2, the three most distrusting countries were Myanmar, Singapore and Indonesia.

The survey responses concerning the risk of conflict and distrust are empirically validated by regional trends in military expenditure and the nature of certain military acquisitions. As illustrated in Table 7.1, sustained increases in the level of military expenditure have been particularly prevalent in Myanmar, Thailand and Singapore; interestingly, it was the Singaporean respondents who maintained the highest levels of distrust and threat perceptions. While a proportion of the defence expenditure in Southeast Asia has been motivated by continued domestic instability and local insurgencies, not all of these increases can be attributed to such domestic intentions.[51] For example, Singapore's total defence strategy embraces a policy of 'forward defence' where, in the event of war, Singapore would aim to secure the water supply in the Malaysian state of Johor and seek to disable the Malaysian armed forces in 'a brutal and fearless pre-emptive strike'.[52] Interestingly, since 1998 (and the end of the Asian

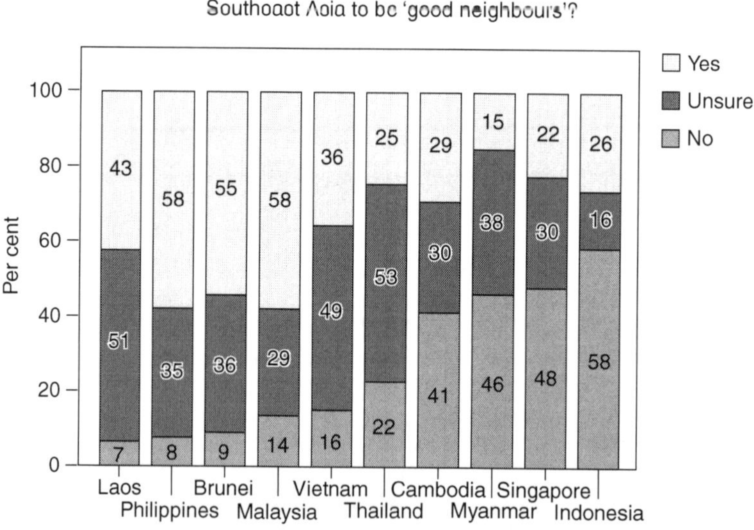

Figure 7.2 Trust throughout Southeast Asia (source: author).

Table 7.1 Defence expenditure (US$ millions)[54]

Year	*2000*	*2001*	*2002*	*2003*	*2004*	*2005*	*2006*	*2007*	*2008*	*2009*
Singapore	4,800	4,400	4,600	4,700	5,102	5,570	6,400	6,321	7,660	8,230
Indonesia	1,500	878	6,600	6,400	7,730	2,470	2,590	10,300	3,400	3,500
Malaysia	2,800	3,300	3,400	2,400	2,742	2,470	3,080	3,206	4,180	4,030
Myanmar	2,100	1,100	3,000	6,260	5,265	6,230	6,230	6,920	7,540	8,160
Philippines	1,500	1,100	1,600	783	825	837	909	909	1,420	1,160
Thailand	2,500	1,900	1,800	1,930	1,954	2,020	2,130	2,275	4,290	5,130
Vietnam	950	2,400	2,400	2,900	2,781	3,150	3,430	3,439	2,900	2,800

financial crisis), all Singaporean housing developers have been required to build bomb shelters in every new house – not exactly the kind of behaviour to be expected amidst a friendly 'ASEAN community' that enjoys dependable expectations of peaceful change.[53]

Naturally, traditional security threats are not the only issues generating distrust and animosity within the region. For the purpose of understanding some of the causal elements to the survey perceptions of trust and the 'risk of conflict', a qualitative analysis of the interview material is also insightful. In the context of Thailand, for example, various interlocutors raised a number of issues that have contributed to regional animosity, including problems with border demarcation, the burning of the Thai embassy in Cambodia,[55] the history of Thailand's removal of the 'Emerald Buddha' from Laos,[56] Thai customs procedures and unrealistic quality control restrictions against Cambodian goods.[57] In the case of Singapore, by way of another example, some of the complaints regarded continued problems over the construction of a new bridge between Malaysia and Singapore,[58] Singaporean land reclamation projects, allegations that Singapore is protecting economic criminals from Indonesia,[59] and allegations that it is complicit in smuggling and sea piracy through the re-registration of stolen ships.[60] More broadly, in relation to immigrant workers, for example, elites in the Philippines complained about the treatment of Filipino workers in Singapore[61] while Indonesians complained about the treatment and deportation of their workers from Malaysia.[62]

Aside from the continued influence of history on regional perceptions, a common complaint was the frequency of recourse to self-interested behaviour at the expense of the collective interests of the region.[63] For example, during an interview, a senior Foreign Affairs spokesperson in Cambodia complained that

> one thing that really upsets us is that whenever there is any disagreement, whenever there is a difference of opinion, then Thailand marches its troops and tanks right up to our border and then points them at us. What kind of neighbour does that?[64]

These comments were made in the context of continued territorial disputes with Thailand and were also likely influenced by the alleged propensity of Thai troops to shoot Cambodians illegally crossing the border into Thailand for work.[65] A further factor that may also explain the level of mistrust in the region is a tendency of political elites (from most ASEAN states) to pander to their domestic constituencies at the expense of regional relations; the most recent example of this type of behaviour occurred in the context of armed violence over the Preah Vihear Temple. In regard to such tactics, there needs to be greater emphasis on long-term collective gain (cooperation) rather competitive behaviour through the short-term pursuit of self-interest. However, in the absence of adequate collective identification (i.e. socio-cultural integration), segments of the political elite will continue to benefit from salient and competitive (adverse) comparisons with 'other' ASEAN states. A government officer from Cambodia summarized the challenges facing ASEAN in the following manner:

> From my point of view it is very hard to build this security community because there is a lack of trust between ASEAN members and also a distinct lack of military transparency. Some members increase expenditure on their military every year even though there is no apparent threat but once you increase expenditure then weaker states feel a distinct threat from these expanding states. Some ASEAN countries want a blue sea navy. This is the case with both Indonesia and Thailand. Can we be a security community if we don't feel that ASEAN is secure? In this region the countries put first their own national interests and regional interests are a distant second place.[66]

Anecdotal evidence of the kind of problematic thinking and perceptions raised by the Cambodian interviewee was evident in most of the ASEAN countries including Singapore and Indonesia. For example, during an interview with a senior defence official from Singapore, one of his opening statements was that 'ASEAN today is not a happy band of brothers'.[67] Equally troubling for ASEAN's goals were the comments of a retired Admiral from Indonesia; his perspective reflected the kind of attitude to be expected from low-complex integration (i.e. where the realist model of behaviour prevails) as he stated that a 'security community means different things to different people; to increase your security is to decrease my security'.[68]

Political values, strategic allignments and economic interests

The continuation of various sources of distrust – as evidenced above and by various examples in earlier chapters – is particularly problematic for ASEAN's pursuit of greater regionalism as the ASEAN members will be less likely to agree to cooperative endeavours in the absence of trust.[69] However, as indicated by the conceptual framework in Chapter 1, the level of regional distrust and enmity is also interdependent with the level of state weakness that continues to plague several of the ASEAN members.[70] As Jane's Stability Indicators in Figure 7.3 illustrate, Singapore is currently the only 'strong state' in Southeast Asia with a score of eighty-seven out of 100. However, between the remaining states in Southeast Asia there is also a considerable diversity in the level of state weakness with Myanmar receiving an overall ranking of just '49' while Brunei and Malaysia each obtained a score of '68'. The plight of some countries was even worse in some sectors. In terms of economic stability, for example, Cambodia only scored forty-two while Myanmar scored a dismal thirty-two. Further, Thailand only received a rating of forty-one for political stability.

Importantly, state weakness also affects the structure of the regional order and, therefore, the form of regionalism that will be more likely to be viable.[71] At one level, it influences the capacity of a state to enter into cooperative endeavours and/or to divert resources towards the institutions of ASEAN. Such states are typically more introverted as the focus of security moves towards 'intra-state, centrifugal challenges – secessionists, terrorists, militias and others.'[72] At another

		Brunei	Cambodia	Indonesia	Laos	Malaysia	Myanmar	Philippines	Singapore	Thailand	Vietnam
Political factors	Clarity of system of governance	7	6	7	6	5	6	6	7	2	7
	State adherence to system of governance	6	5	6	5	6	4	6	8	4	7
	Public acceptance of organs of state	7	6	6	8	5	5	6	8	3	7
	Strength of state institutions	6	4	7	4	6	3	5	7	5	6
	Presence of non-military interests in the status quo	7	5	5	4	7	4	4	7	4	5
	Support of military for the state	8	5	8	7	6	9	6	8	4	7
Political stability		76	57	72	59	69	57	61	83	41	72
Social factors	Social cohesion	7	7	5	7	5	4	5	8	6	6
	Crime	7	4	5	5	7	6	4	8	6	4
	Health	6	4	4	4	6	3	4	8	6	4
	Demographic stability	6	5	5	6	5	6	5	8	6	5
Social stability		72	56	53	61	64	53	50	89	67	53
Economic factors	Employment and labour	6	4	6	4	6	3	6	8	5	6
	Economic policy	8	4	6	4	5	3	6	8	4	7
	Robustness of economy	6	3	5	4	6	3	7	8	4	7
	Infrastructure	6	4	4	4	6	2	5	8	5	6
	Resource reliance	5	4	4	4	6	3	4	6	5	4
Economic stability		64	42	56	44	64	31	62	84	51	67
Military and security factors	State control of security forces	7	6	7	6	6	8	6	8	5	7
	Professionalism of security forces	5	4	4	4	5	3	4	8	4	5
	Efficacy of security forces	6	5	7	5	6	6	5	8	5	5
	Challenge from NSAGS and crime groups	7	5	4	6	5	5	4	6	4	7
	Weapons proliferation	7	5	5	5	7	5	5	8	5	7
Military and security stability		71	56	60	58	64	60	53	89	51	69
External factors	Involvement with multilateral institutions	5	4	7	4	7	1	7	8	7	6
	Regional relations	6	4	7	4	8	0	7	8	5	7
	Threat of foreign military intervention	4	4	8	4	7	6	7	8	7	6
	International reputation	4	5	7	5	7	2	6	8	7	5
External stability		53	47	81	47	81	42	75	89	72	64
Country stability		68	52	64	54	68	49	60	87	55	66

Figure 7.3 Jane's intelligence stability indicators (December 2010) (source: based on indicators located at www.janes.com).

Note: Jane's outlines the methodology behind the rankings in the following manner: 'Country Stability Ratings provide a quantitative assessment of the stability environment of a country or autonomous territory. All sovereign countries, non-contiguous autonomous territories and de facto independent entities are included in the assessments. To gauge stability, 24 factors (that rely on various objective sub-factors) are rated. The 24 factors are classified within five distinct groupings, namely political, social, economic, external and military and security. The Country Stability team assesses the stability of each factor as between zero and nine. The various factors are then weighted according to the importance to the particular country's stability. Stability in each of these groupings is provided, with zero being entirely unstable and 100 stable. The weighted factors are also used to produce an overall territory stability rating, from zero (unstable) to 100 (stable). Finally, the team then assesses global stability levels, so that weighting and ratings are standardized across all regions.'

level, the degree of state capacity also has an influence on the political interests of the state. For example, weak states are more likely to resort to the promotion of internal conflict in the hope of 'riding an ethnic or political wave to political and economic gain', engagement in divide-and-rule tactics or 'siding explicitly or implicitly with one group against another'.[73] Further, the example of Thailand's militant behaviour concerning the Preah Vihear Temple (Chapter 4) reinforces the arguments of some scholars who suggest that because many weak states lack legitimacy, and are in the early process of nation-building (i.e. nationally incongruent, see Chapter 1), there is a greater likelihood that neighbourhood relations will be sacrificed for self-interest and regime survival.[74] Further, had there been 'greater state coherence' then it would have been 'more difficult for pan-nationalist ideologies to penetrate the state and to challenge pragmatic policies'.[75] Importantly, trust is also difficult to sustain where the prospect of regime change in weak states has far greater implications for foreign policy formulation – e.g. Singapore's defence expenditure could be partly explained by the longer term risk of a radical Islamic government coming to power in either Malaysia or Indonesia.[76]

Problematically, however, Chapter 1 noted that state strength is necessary to sustain an efficient and consolidated democracy.[77] Meanwhile, Chapter 5 also noted the relevance of political systems and the chapter provides evidence concerning the impact of democratic values on government policies. Although Deutsch has argued that a commonality of main values is more important than specific democratic values,[78] the analysis has not been able to ascertain an alternative basis for the delineation of common regional values other than some limited mutual identification in response to significant exogenous threats (e.g. during the Cold War). Meanwhile, the limited nature of the institutional outcomes in the political sphere indicates that the consolidation of common interests has not been wide enough or deep enough to move the association beyond that of a 'mutual sovereignty reinforcement coalition'.[79] The European Union, by contrast, demonstrates that common values represent a higher-order variable in that they typically coincide with a deeper and broader convergence of interests. In the case of the EU, its member-states have a common identity that is not only based on a shared culture, religion and historical experience, but also shared democratic values.[80] Further, Mohammad Ayoob has noted how authoritarian states typically 'obsess about sovereignty'.[81] Thus, in contrast to the arguments of Deutsch, Chapter 1 noted that it would be difficult for countries to enjoy a shared value system in the absence of common political values – e.g. contrast the behaviour of Indonesia with Myanmar in Chapters 5 and 6.

The diversity of political values, together with the associated implications for political interests and policy formulation, was also evident in the survey data. As previously stated, the proposal for a security community, together with the ASEAN charter that followed, reflected the desire by some of ASEAN's elite for institutional and normative change. However, the continuation of diverse political values has meant that regional elites remain divided over the continued utility of non-interference and consensus-based decision-making. For example, the elite survey asked if the principle of non-interference is as important now as it was a decade ago. As Figure 7.4 illustrates, 46.7 per cent responded 'yes' while 39.1 per cent and 'no' and 14.1 per cent were 'unsure'. However, 54.8 per cent of the 'elite sample' envisioned circumstances 'where some ASEAN member-states could be justified in diplomatically intervening in the internal affairs of another member-state or states'. While these figures provide a positive indication that normative change is already underway, and further inform the content of recent ASEAN declarations, the extent of change has not yet been broad enough to result in the level of institutional progress necessary to realize the aspirations of the more democratic ASEAN members.

Meanwhile, some insight on the thinking of the authoritarian side of the divide was provided by the former Director of the Cambodian Institute of Cooperation and Peace, Dr Chap Sotharith, who argues that

> there is a dilemma between democracy and authoritarianism. For example, there is a strong authoritarian element in both Malaysia and Singapore but it is because of this that the two countries are so stable. ... The Centre for Human Rights has been preaching democracy, freedom of speech and the empowerment of the people. But again, how do you empower farmers? How do they know what is in the interests of the country and its people?[82]

Nonetheless, Figure 7.5 indicates that such perceptions are not in line with the values of ASEAN's citizens at the grassroots level. Here, an overwhelming majority of the respondents from the communal level survey stated that democracy was personally important to them. The only notable exception occurred within the Brunei sample but this can be partly understood through the notion of

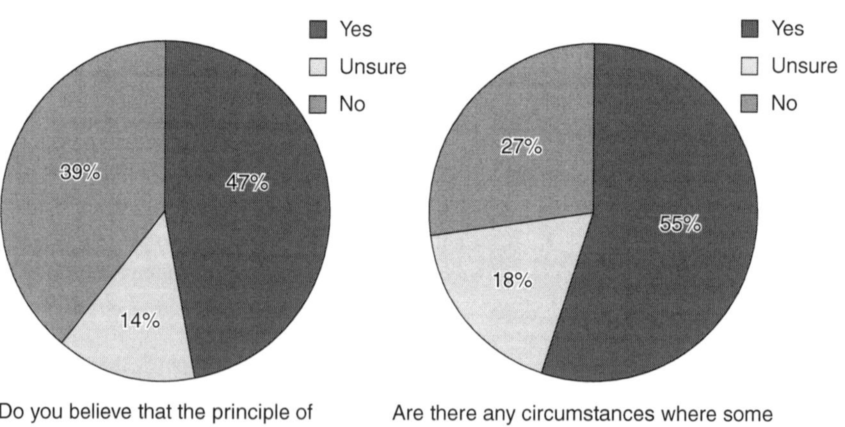

Figure 7.4 Non-interference and 'diplomatic interventions' (source: author).

'performance legitimacy' and the fact that the country's oil and gas wealth has meant that Brunei's GDP per capita (PPP) has now grown to US$50,100 (2009) rendering it one of the wealthiest nations in Southeast Asia. Given the indications of perception in the communal level survey, Southeast Asia's more authoritarian regimes are not constrained to the *status quo* because of some kind of Asian value set. Rather, the recent record in Indonesia indicates that when a political system becomes more democratic, its constituents are more than capable of adapting to a new system of governance. Therefore, as has occurred in Indonesia, should the political systems of other members change (e.g. Myanmar) then such change, when supported by democratic values at the grassroots level, has the potential to contribute to a rapid recalibration of foreign policy in a manner that is more supportive of regionalism.

Meanwhile, Donald Emmerson suggests that the divide in political values may in fact represent the greatest challenge to the emergence of a collective identity and, therefore, any substantive sense of community between the ASEAN elite.[83] While various components in this chapter and in previous chapters lend support to Emmerson's claim, a return to a qualitative analysis of elite perceptions also reveals the potential difficulty of cooperation and institutionalization in the political and security sphere and provides some insight concerning the contradictory norms and values within the ASEAN Charter and other recent statement of intent. Thus, one officer from the ASEAN Secretariat explained that there have been two interpretations of the meaning of democracy.[84] This is illustrated

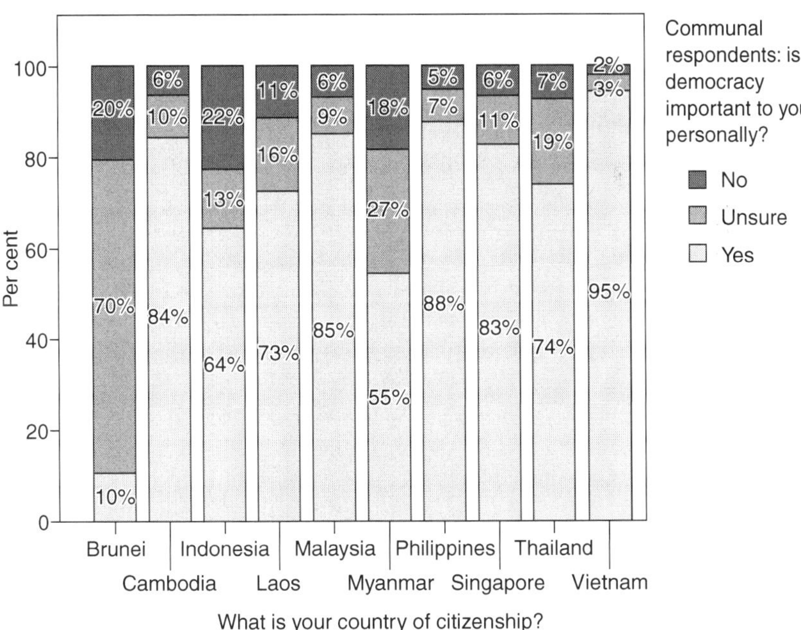

Figure 7.5 Beyond the elite: perceptions of democracy (source: author).

in the account of a senior scholar from the Diplomatic Academy of Vietnam (within Vietnam's Ministry of Foreign Affairs) who stated that 'the Bali Concord does not mean a common concept of democracy [domestically] ... it was [advocated] in relation to the political development of the region', or in other words, that ASEAN would institutionalize a democratic and consensus-based decision-making process for the regional governments on issues of mutual relevance and concern for the ASEAN members. From the Indochinese perspective, their agreement to democratic reforms in the Bali Concord II had nothing to do with domestic politics, as that is an internal matter protected by the principle of non-interference.[85]

In regard to a possible dichotomy regarding the interpretation of recent ASEAN agreements and the subsequent commitment that they require, it is informative to note the reflections of a scholar from the University of Brunei Darussalam. In a paper presented to the 2007 Asia-Pacific Roundtable Conference in Kuala Lumpur, Haja Sainah Haji Saim commented that 'as members of ASEAN, we need to know into what agreement our country has entered; in what sort of agreement our country has signed.... However, we are not transparent enough and not knowledgeable enough'.[86] Thus, Noel Morada states that

> there is a disparity in conceptions about the meaning of an ASEAN Security community, it means different things to different people and we even wonder if some of the newer states even fully understood what they were signing onto when they agreed to the ASEAN Security community.[87]

Nonetheless, the ASEAN proposal for a security community, the associated plans of actions, and the ASEAN Charter in its final form, all envision 'an ASEAN that is more intrusive than most of its members will tolerate'.[88] While Indonesia was pivotal in driving this outcome, and some other ASEAN members such as the Philippines may have provided some lesser contributions, it is difficult to avoid an assessment that some ASEAN members have consented not just because of different interpretations but also because these instruments have very little binding authority. Meanwhile, their agreement appeases some of the more powerful ASEAN members while also providing a degree of added legitimacy and regional esteem. Thus, through (a) the persistence of an intergovernmental model of ASEAN; (b) the lack of supranational institutionalization associated with it; and (c) an avoidance of any binding commitments, the repeated dichotomy between rhetoric and practice in Southeast Asia can be better understood.[89]

Beyond political values, a lack of regional collective identification and socio-cultural integration (a prerequisite for ASEAN's 'security community') was also reflected by a lack of common interests in the political sphere. While earlier components of the book have provided various examples of clashing regional interests, the survey data provides a further example regarding the region's strategic alignment. Here, the elite-level survey asked the respondents to rank, in order of importance, their 'country's three greatest strategic allies' and the results, as illustrated in Table 7.2, indicate a reasonably high level of divergence over the subject.[90] For example, the top three strategic partners for Singapore and Indonesia were all exogenous to the region. More specifically, two government respondents from Laos alternatively listed Cuba and Russia in their top three rankings. Other rudimentary insights could also be gained from the data. For example, Donald Weatherbee argues that the Philippines is a regional outlier[91] and the survey statistics support this contention as the Philippines was the least cited strategic ally (receiving only 1 per cent of the total number of responses) while other countries, such as China and Australia, received respective scores of 8 and 6 per cent. Coincidently, these survey responses coincide with the arguments of some regional specialists. For example, Tobias Nischalke had previously argued that the ASEAN members 'see relations with outsiders as more relevant to their security than relations with ASEAN' and thus, 'at the bottom line, security is guaranteed through outside alliances, not collective security with ASEAN partners'.[92]

The elite survey also asked whether the foreign policies of America, China and Japan had a positive role in Southeast Asia. In regard to the question on Chinese foreign policy, nearly 90 per cent of the Lao participants and more than 70 per cent of the Malaysian participants responded 'yes'. However, less than 30 per cent of the Singapore and Cambodian respondents answered 'yes' to the same question. In the context of US foreign policy, the entire elite sample was, on average, more critical but the nearly 70 per cent of the Filipino elites did believe that the foreign policy of the US had a positive role in Southeast Asia. This response reflects the longstanding alliance between the US and the Philippines; an alliance that has recently been reinforced in the context of the 'war on terror' (Chapter 4).

Similar questions in the communal survey are also relevant to the extent that the foreign policy preferences of state elites reflect, or are constrained by, the identity (including norms and values) of the broader society within that state. Aside from the framework in Chapter 1, such contentions also connect with Robert Putnam's game theory (and later reincarnations) that provide a nexus

Table 7.2 Strategic allies for individual countries by overall rank[92]

Country	*Rank 1 (%)*	*Rank 2 (%)*	*Rank 3 (%)*
Singapore	**United States (20)**	Indonesia (13)	**Australia (13)**
Malaysia	Indonesia (28)	Brunei (23)	Thailand (21)
Indonesia	**United States (21)**	Malaysia (14)	**Japan (14)**
The Philippines	Indonesia (20)	**United States (14)**	Singapore (14)
Thailand	Singapore (23)	Malaysia (19)	**United States (13)**
Cambodia	Malaysia (17)	Singapore (17)	**China (11)**
Myanmar*	Laos	Malaysia	Thailand
Laos	Vietnam (36)	**China (21)**	Cambodia (14)
Brunei*	Malaysia	Singapore	Indonesia
Vietnam	Laos (33)	**China (17)**	Singapore (17)

Source: author.

between domestic and international politics.[93] The communal survey did not specifically ask about 'foreign policy' but, rather, whether certain countries 'played a positive role in their region'. Here, there was a similar pattern of divergence regarding the role of Japan, China and the United States in the region. For example, while China fared well in Laos, Vietnam, Singapore, Indonesia and Malaysia, more negative perceptions were again evident in Cambodia where 47.1 per cent of respondents indicated that China does not 'play a positive role in the region'. Meanwhile, the communal sample corresponded with the elite sample concerning the role of the United States. The survey respondents in the sample were, as with the elite respondents, the most critical of the US role, and only 39.1 per cent indicated that America played a positive role in the region. Here, as with some of the percentages for other questions, the region's history may have had some influence as the most negative responses came from Laos, where 74.2 per cent were either 'unsure' or felt that America did not play a positive role.

As has been noted in previous chapters, common threat perceptions have, at times, led to interest harmonization and cooperation. For example, Chapter 4 noted relatively common threat perceptions concerning terrorism and, interestingly, the sharing of intelligence was commonly perceived by interviewees to be one of the more feasible areas of cooperation (at least bilaterally). However, when one looks beyond the narrowly defined fear of 'terrorist acts', the limitations to common threat perceptions are readily apparent. Within the communal level survey, there was a significant divergence in perceptions concerning which categories of transnational crime affected each country the most. Here, the respondents were asked to select the categories of transnational crime that had the greatest impact on their country. In the case of 'terrorism', for example, the highest response rates came from Indonesia (36.9 per cent) and the Philippines (39.3 per cent). Meanwhile, the category of 'people smuggling' received the highest percentages in Cambodia (31.8 per cent) and Vietnam (46 per cent). In the case of narcotics, by contrast, the highest responses came from Thailand (35.4 per cent), Malaysia (38.5 per cent), Laos (44.9 per cent) and Brunei (75 per cent).[94] Such divergent perceptions of threat lead to divergent priorities and when these trends are considered in the context of the larger picture of diversity – with many facets having been noted in previous chapters – then the challenge of substantial security and political cooperation and institutionalization becomes all the more apparent.

Meanwhile, perceptions of economic values and interests indicated by the elite level survey data also provide some further contextualization as to why cooperation in the economic sphere has been relatively better than the political and security sphere. For example, when asked the question, 'On average, will economic liberalization benefit or disadvantage your country?', 67.4 per cent believed that it would 'benefit' their country while only 10 per cent indicated that it would 'disadvantage' it, and the remaining 22.2 per cent selected that they were 'unsure'. Similarly, 77.8 per cent of elite level respondents believed that their own national economy was either compatible with the economic structures of all the ASEAN states or at least the ASEAN states that were already structurally defined as a 'market economy'. However, some caveats about economic regionalism were expressed within the elite survey sample. Thus, when the survey asked whether the formation of an 'economic community' (the economic pillar), through economic liberalization, would overcome the main problems the member-states would likely face as a consequence of economic liberalization, only 24.5 per cent answered 'yes' while 65.5 per cent of regional elites answered 'no' or were 'undecided'.

In terms of 'perceptual divergence' in the economic sphere, the statistics in Table 7.3 reflect the notion of a possible core and periphery in terms of an elite level economic identity. Here, the economic interests and values continue to be loosely divided on the basis of the original and newer ASEAN members. Thus, when the Thai, Singaporean, Malaysian, Indonesian and Filipino respondents were asked if they believed that their national economy was compatible with 'the economic structure of some or all of the other nine ASEAN states', between 80 and 100 per cent responded that it would be either easy to integrate with all the economies of the ASEAN members or that it would be easy to integrate with those countries that have a market economy (Q.A1 in Table 7.3). Similarly, 67 per cent of the original ASEAN members believed that economic liberalization would benefit their country (Q.A2). By contrast, between 67 per cent and 83 per cent of the respondents within Myanmar, Laos and Cambodia responded negatively to the question as to whether or not they perceived their country to be compatible with the economies of the remaining ASEAN countries. Further, in terms of an overall position assessed for each country (calculated on the basis of the sum-total of the positive/neutral/negative assessments for the three economic questions), Vietnam was the only example amidst the newer member-states to maintain a 'positive' ranking overall.

Nonetheless, as was also noted in Chapter 4, the pursuit of greater economic cooperation, integration and institutionalization has been relatively more palatable because ASEAN's political elite have come to realize that such collaboration provides performance legitimacy and, thereby, regime security. Meanwhile, for the more democratic members, economic cooperation and institutionalization is also seen as beneficial for similar reasons; however, the 'end of the means' is development and internal consolidation rather than narrower considerations of 'control' and/or 'power'.[95] Therefore, there is a lower likelihood of democratic values clashing with authoritarian values for the purpose of economic collaboration and the empirical record has, accordingly, demonstrated a relatively higher convergence of interests where policy coordination has been easier to achieve in the economic sphere. Further, this convergence of interests has been driven by a common sense of economic vulnerability (converging threat perceptions) in a more globalized world together with a region-wide consensus that a focus on economic development will be the key variable in facilitating domestic and regional stability. Importantly, the mere perception that economic integration is providing mutual benefits for all or most of the ASEAN members (regardless of the true causation) may provide adequate motivation for future economic

Table 7.3 Overall summary of economic perceptions

Country	*Q.A1: perceptions of compatibility (%)*	*Q.A2: consequences of liberalization (%)*	*Q.A4: the formation of an economic community (%)*	*Overall position on the economic pillar*
Malaysia	Positive (100)	Positive (73)	Positive (57)	Positive
Singapore	Positive (80)	Positive (87)	Neutral (64)	Positive
Indonesia	Positive (82)	Positive (60)	Neutral (40)	Positive
The Philippines	Positive (85)	Positive (39)	Neutral (47)	Positive
Thailand	Positive (83)	Positive (75)	Neutral (55)	Positive
Myanmar	Negative (67)	Positive (100)	Neutral (100)	Neutral
Vietnam	Positive (80)	Positive (100)	Neutral (60)	Positive
Laos	Negative (67)	Neutral (67)	Neutral (67)	Negative
Cambodia	Negative (83)	Positive (50)	Negative (60)	Negative

cooperation. In this regard, confidence in ASEAN (i.e. the esteem component of SIT, Chapter 1) will likely be strengthened by the fact that the ASEAN economies have performed very well in recent times. For example, through to 2007 the region had reached steady growth rates of above 6 per cent in terms of real GDP. Further, while the rate of growth (GDP) dropped to 1.1 per cent in 2009 (as a consequence of the global financial crisis), it reached an impressive estimate of 7.7 per cent growth in 2010.[96]

Communal level dynamics: opportunities and challenges

As ASEAN's declarations of intent have been primarily an elite project, with little involvement of CSOs, the book has focused on elite responses to security issues and elite level cooperation. Further, the analysis has sought additional insights and evidence through an examination of elite perceptions – e.g. the interview and survey data. During the process of this examination, the analysis has drawn on examples relevant to domestic, regional and extra-regional influences on complex integration and ASEAN's regionalist project. Where the analysis has considered communal perceptions, it has done so in the context of ascertaining possible influences on 'state interests' including potential issues of concern such as domestic sources of instability, animosity and distrust. Therefore, while some components of the analysis have touched on the socio-cultural pillar of complex integration and the 'ASEAN community' (e.g. elite level collective identification), this section explicitly addresses some of the trends concerning socio-cultural integration at the grassroots level. As indicated at the outset of this book, it was not possible for this analysis to provide more than a rudimentary perspective of the dynamics relevant to grassroots regionalization. However, such an analysis, as preliminary as it is, remains insightful as the region-wide data obtained for this study is the first of its kind and, importantly, the realization of more substantive forms of political, security, economic and socio-cultural regionalization will, at some point, need to involve, or will be complemented by, developments at the communal level.

As the theoretical framework in Chapter 1 noted, long-term bottom-up (communal-driven) processes may contribute to complex integration and the emergence of a security community. In this regard, the previous section has already noted very strong support for democracy at the grassroots level and suggested some possible implications for ASEAN regionalism in the event that any of the current authoritarian regimes should be replaced in the future. Grassroots level perceptions, interests and values are also important because of the potential for nationalistic backlashes against regionalist endeavours. Such backlashes may occur because of the many historical animosities, ethno-religious divisions, or the elite practices of scapegoating for domestic political gain that have been noted throughout this book. Grassroots perceptions are equally important for the more democratic states because domestic support for regionalist endeavours will, in turn, influence the likelihood that their government will also support regionalism in an attempt to gain greater support from their electorates.

Given these considerations, *inter alia*, other regional scholars have also emphasized the importance of grassroots perceptions and any associated sense of regional collective identification.[97] Importantly, Chapter 1 outlined how the constructivist literature in general has emphasized the role of socialization (transactionalism) in building a sense of trust and community in a way that can overcome potential challenges to regionalism at the grassroots level. Thus, one of the more interesting insights to stem from the communal survey data was the possibility that increased interaction does not necessarily contribute to a sense of collective identity and 'we-feeling' or patterns of reciprocity in regional relations. For example, while 98.4 per cent of the Singaporean respondents had (unsurprisingly) travelled overseas, 48 per cent of those respondents said they could not trust their neighbours to be good neighbours. Similarly, all of the Burmese respondents had travelled overseas (as they were sampled in Singapore) and 46 per cent of this group also indicated that they did not trust their neighbours. Further, the respondents from the two most distrusting countries (Indonesia and Singapore) also indicated some of highest frequencies of newspaper readership and the regularity with which they watched the news on TV was similarly high.

Meanwhile, Amitav Acharya once wrote that Southeast Asia's 'social and political identity ... [is] derived from the conscious promotion of the regional concept by its states, societies, and peoples'.[98] Further, Leonard Andaya, who Acharya cites, argues that 'Southeast Asia is no longer simply a term of convenience. Southeast Asians themselves now think regionally'.[99] While the conscious promotion of a Southeast Asian identity by ASEAN and its members may succeed in the longer term, these assessments are either premature or overly optimistic at the present

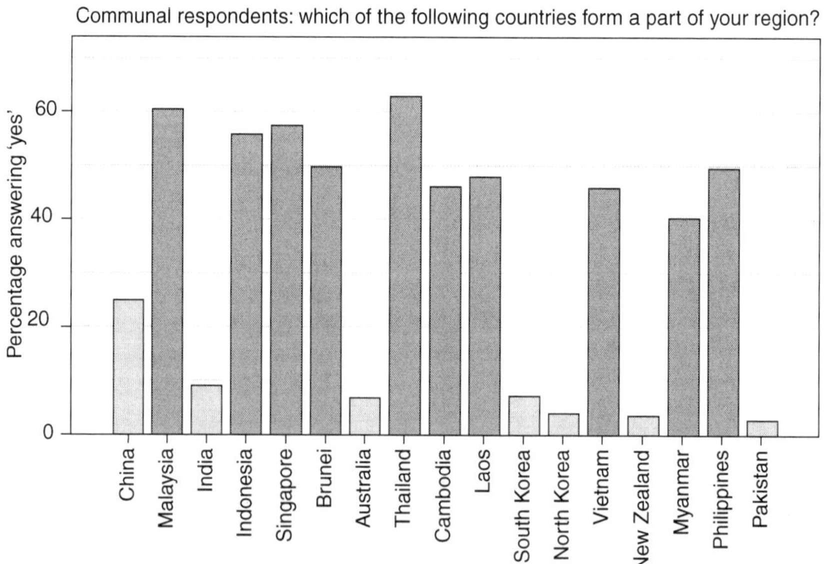

Figure 7.6 Communal perceptions of 'region' (source: author).

moment. Nonetheless, some of the most positive statistics to emerge from the communal survey data concerned perceptions of region and the levels of knowledge about ASEAN. For example, when asked 'Which of the following countries form a part of your region?', Figure 7.6 illustrates that the survey participants were relatively successful in being able to distinguish between the Southeast Asian countries and the countries outside the region. Furthermore, while Figure 7.7 illustrates that 38.37 per cent of respondents indicated that they didn't really know what ASEAN does and 8.29 per cent stated that they had never heard of the Association prior to participating in the survey, 52.05 per cent of respondents considered themselves to have either a 'very good' or 'reasonable' knowledge of ASEAN. Remarkably, 49.2 per cent of the respondents from rural areas in Southeast Asia also indicated that they either had a 'very good' or 'reasonable' knowledge of ASEAN.

More specifically, while no individual country had a significant frequency (or mode) of response for the option that 'they knew ASEAN well', the countries who felt they 'understood ASEAN reasonably well' (as calculated by 'mode') were Laos (41.9 per cent), Cambodia (42.5 per cent), the Philippines (52.3 per cent), Indonesia (52.3 per cent) and Vietnam (52.8 per cent). The countries with the highest frequency of responses for those who 'didn't feel that they really knew what ASEAN does' (but had at least heard of the Association) were Myanmar and, somewhat surprisingly, Thailand (35.4 per cent), Singapore (50.8 per cent), Malaysia (56.1 per cent) and Brunei (58.3 per cent). However, in contrast to the level of knowledge displayed in Vietnam (*inter alia*), a *Straits Times* 'straw poll' found that only 12.5 per cent of Singaporean teenagers 'knew what the acronym ASEAN stood for and could name the ten countries in the grouping'.[100] Nonetheless, while the earlier figures are relatively positive, ASEAN's plan to implement a greater level of education about the organization in the schools of Southeast Asia remains important for the purpose of strengthening the socio-cultural pillar of the ASEAN community.

Two primary observations arise out of this preliminary analysis of the degree of socio-cultural regionalization. The first is that the level of interaction within the region does not seem to have any significant positive correlation with the categories of 'trust', 'the knowledge of ASEAN', or 'perceptions of region'. The ambiguity of these figures suggests the need for further research through a larger and more representative sample on the role of various facets of regional interaction. In the

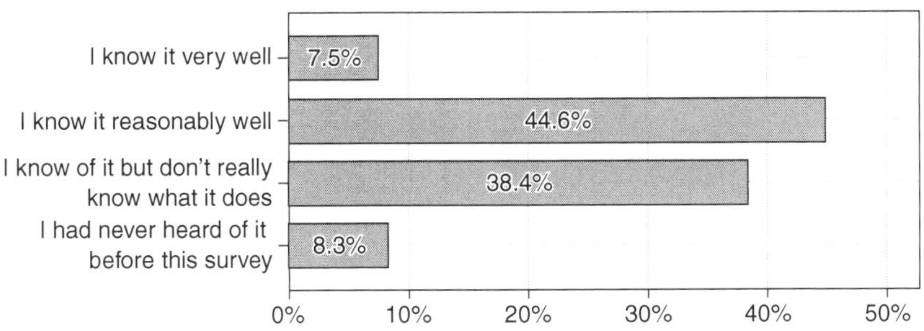

Figure 7.7 Communal level knowledge of 'ASEAN' (source: author).

meantime, some factors that may explain the data include the limited focus in local news services on events in the region,[101] the particular countries that respondents travel to (not just the frequency of travel), and the nature and quality of interaction (e.g. positive or negative). Thus, in the case of the latter, past practices where the political elite and/or the local media have drawn negative comparisons with neighbouring states and communities (e.g. the Preah Vihear Temple and Pendet Dance incidents in Chapter 5) have continued to negatively affect perceptions of neighbouring states. Moving beyond theories of transactionalism and socialization, the second set of observations is relatively more concrete in as far as the implications to the existence of a community and regionalization are concerned. For example, the participants in the survey indicated a surprisingly significant understanding of a 'Southeast Asian' region and the level of knowledge on ASEAN was also very good. However, the period of membership in ASEAN has not positively affected the ascertainable levels of affinity, kinship and trust extant within Southeast Asia. How these observations connect with the broader picture presented by the chapter are considered both below and in the concluding chapter.

Conclusions

While the first section outlined a number of limitations to the extent of cooperation and integration in the political-security sphere, the section also noted that economic integration remains the most likely area for success in the future. Not only will the Southeast Asian governments acquire greater 'performance legitimacy' (and thus regime security) by advancing the level of economic wealth, but economic cooperation and integration does not immediately entail the types of political reform that might necessitate democratic change and/or the relinquishment of power. Consequently, a relatively higher level of interest harmonization has occurred in the economic sphere. Meanwhile, given the authoritarian status of most of the ASEAN member governments, the principles of non-interference and consensus-based decision-making will likely remain in place for the foreseeable future. Simply put, before consensus and non-interference can officially be overruled, the modus operandi currently in place dictates that there must first emerge a 'consensus' regarding such change. Nonetheless, a significant proportion of the regional elite indicated that they no longer believed the principle of non-interference to be as important as it was a decade ago.

Due to democratization, the Philippines and Indonesia have been the most significant exemplifiers of normative change and political reform within ASEAN. However, the statistics from the survey data also revealed that elements of the elite in many of the remaining ASEAN countries have also been socialized towards accepting a more active involvement by the ASEAN states in each other's internal affairs – under 'appropriate circumstances'. However, such perceptions have not uniformly emerged in each country and in some members, such as Myanmar, these views would likely represent the opinion of a very small minority. Consequently, the chapter also noted that attempts to change ASEAN's values, modus operandi and level of institutionalization were challenged by the more authoritarian ASEAN members. In this regard, the ASEAN Charter provided an early but determinative insight concerning the current limitations to Southeast Asian regionalism. Nonetheless, and despite a clash of values within ASEAN, the Charter still 'envisions an ASEAN that is more intrusive than most of its members will tolerate' at the present time.[102] While Indonesia, the Philippines and a few other ASEAN members may have contributed to this outcome, it is difficult to avoid an assessment that several of the ASEAN members acceded to the Charter, together with many other "statements of intent", simply because these instruments have very little binding authority. Meanwhile, their agreement appeases some of the larger and more powerful members while also providing a degree of added legitimacy and greater regional and international esteem. This, more than anything, explains the current dichotomy between rhetoric and practice in Southeast Asia.

Beyond the normative perceptions of the region's elite, the chapter examined the level of potential socialization (transactionalism) taking place and also examined whether there was any correlation between the frequency of 'transactions' (e.g. travel and foreign friends) and the level of knowledge about ASEAN and the Southeast Asian region. The analysis revealed that while grassroots regionalization does appear to have contributed to relatively high levels of regional knowledge and awareness, it has not yet generated a significant collective identity (socio-cultural integration). Consequently, the most disconcerting indicators were those concerning a lack of trust at the grassroots level as the majority of people from the communal survey sample either did not trust, or were unsure whether they could trust, all the countries in Southeast Asia to be 'good neighbours'. Further, there appeared to be little correlation between trust and patterns of interaction (i.e. socialization). At such a low level of socio-cultural integration, misunderstandings and misperceptions regarding other states and communities are likely to be more prevalent.

Perceptions of trust are also relevant to testing the existence of a security community. Importantly, the lowest levels of trust were demonstrated within the elite survey sample where 56.8 per cent of respondents indicated that they could not trust all the Southeast Asian countries to be good neighbours. Further, half of the elite survey sample were either unsure or could envisage armed conflict; this result indicates that ASEAN struggles to satisfy the threshold test to a security community – dependable expectations of peaceful change. The absence of dependable expectations of peaceful change was also indicated by regional patterns of military expenditure along with the behaviour and policies of some member states. Further, in the context of socio-cultural integration, there has been a lack of collective identification due to divergent histories, religions, cultures, norms and values. Given these trends, together with the other considerations in the chapter, the mid-term prospects for significant political-security and socio-cultural integration remain very low. A final analysis concerning the manner by which the insights in this chapter link with the previous chapters, together with the prospects for the realization of ASEAN's regionalist project, is provided in the next chapter.

Conclusion

Retrospect and prospects

In order to assess ASEAN's regionalist project, the book has sought to delineate the character of ASEAN, and the level of complex integration associated with it, by way of an investigation of a broad spectrum of historical considerations and contemporary challenges. As a complement to this approach, extensive fieldwork has also been undertaken involving over 150 in-depth interviews and two separate survey designs with 919 participants. The exacting nature of the critique provided in this chapter (and in the body of the work) has been invited by the relatively high and ambitious benchmarks set by ASEAN in its declaration to forge an 'ASEAN community' (including a 'security community') by 2015. Consequently, the first section of this chapter provides a concluding analysis of the material covered in previous chapters in order to assess ASEAN's record of cooperation, the impact of different values, and the implications for supranational institutionalization. Given the continuation of a scholarly debate about the effectiveness of ASEAN, the second section also provides a concluding assessment concerning how ASEAN should be characterized and the associated level of complex integration. These considerations, moreover, also inform an analysis of the likely political-security, economic and socio-cultural trends in Southeast Asia, including the extent to which ASEAN might shape Southeast Asia's regional order in the future. Nonetheless, based on a medium-low level of complex integration in Southeast Asia, the chapter concludes that it will be several more decades before it will be possible for ASEAN's regionalist visions to be realized.

Cooperation, values and institutionalization

At the time of ASEAN's formation there was only a very low level of complex integration between the states and communities of Southeast Asia. Despite this, together with a related history of conflict and ethno-religious differences, a modus vivendi emerged between the political elite of five Southeast Asian countries and the major outcome was the formation of ASEAN in 1967. Such collaboration was necessitated by widespread volatility in the regional security order and an associated desire to avoid inter-state conflict so that each member could focus on greater domestic stability and the notion of national resilience (*ketahanan national*). For the ASEAN members, a primary goal of national resilience was regime security and this, in turn, required greater performance legitimacy through economic growth. However, the road to ASEAN's formation was highly tumultuous. With the exception of the Five Power Defence Arrangement (FPDA), several earlier attempts to create institutions for economic and/or security cooperation failed. Further, regional relations between the original ASEAN members had not fully reconciled by the time of ASEAN's formation. Thus, shortly thereafter, hostile relations between Singapore and Malaysia erupted while Malaysia and the Philippines suspended their diplomatic relations as a consequence of the Corregidor Affair (Chapter 3). Given these developments, together with the range of other historical components that were examined in earlier chapters, the formation of even a limited mechanism for dialogue reflected the enormous sense of vulnerability that was then felt by the ASEAN members.

Due to the continuation of intra-mural divides, ASEAN did not move beyond limited dialogue during its first decade. For example, ASEAN's formative instrument – the Bangkok declaration – was very circumspect in terms of the official goals it expressed and the institutional structures it established. Thus, while the Bangkok Declaration referred to the prospect of economic collaboration, it did not refer to cooperation or collaboration in relation to political and security issues. Further, the instrument only provided for an annual meeting of the foreign ministers and made no reference to meetings between the leaders. Consequently, the ASEAN leaders did not meet until a decade later. In the interim, the Association's only noteworthy achievement was the declaration for a Zone of Peace, Freedom and Neutrality (ZOPFAN) in 1971. However, while ZOPFAN sought to create a zone that was free from foreign interference, the declaration was primarily symbolic in nature as it did not provide any binding components or dates for implementation. Consequently, some of the ASEAN members (notably Thailand and the Philippines) continued their alliances with outside powers, and foreign bases were permitted to remain in the region (Chapter 2).

Over time, the ASEAN members came to realize that they would need to reach a higher level of collaboration – through the institutions of ASEAN – in order to advance national resilience. Further, the region's political elite also believed that such collaboration would build regional resilience so that internal sources of instability (e.g. the dangers of subversion) would be prevented from 'infecting neighbouring states'.[1] As reflected by the ZOPFAN agreement, it was also hoped that greater collaboration would lead to regional resilience from foreign interference. Consequently, the ASEAN leaders agreed to both the Treaty of Amity and Cooperation (TAC) and the first ASEAN Concord (Bali Concord) when they finally met at the 1976 Bali Summit. Collectively, the documents acknowledged the mutual interdependence of security and further consolidated the ASEAN Way (including non-interference and consensus-based decision-making) and this has, *in principle*, guided ASEAN's modus operandi through to the present day.

Despite the above normative developments, the ASEAN Concord contained a latent contradiction through provisions for the establishment of a High Council that would resolve regional disputes. Nonetheless, as any disputants must first consent to arbitration by the High Council, the good offices of the High Council have never been invoked. Aside from the ASEAN Way and conflict resolution, the ASEAN Concord was also symbolically important for expanding ASEAN's *raison d'être* to include political cooperation and this was complemented by some limited institutionalization via the establishment of the ASEAN Secretariat in Jakarta. Meanwhile, the TAC also sought to consolidate commitments regarding a respect for sovereignty and territorial integrity, the settlement of differences or disputes via peaceful means, and a renunciation of the threat or use of force. While these aspects of the treaty were partly a consequence of historical animosity between the ASEAN members, they also arose from a fear that the ASEAN members could be unwillingly drawn into armed conflict as a consequence of the Cold War.

By 1975, the Southeast Asian states of Laos, Cambodia and South Vietnam had all fallen to communism. Then, in 1978, Vietnam occupied Cambodia, thus rendering Thailand a frontline state in an armed conflict with military support from two extra-regional powers – China and the Soviet Union. The realization of ASEAN's fears led to one of the strongest periods of cohesion and cooperation in the Association's history. Further, the ASEAN members demonstrated a capacity to respond with a collective diplomatic voice (i.e. a diplomatic community) when they were adequately challenged by a common external threat. However, such moments of cohesion were generally short-lived as the persistence of competing interests (i.e. at low-complex integration) soon led individual members down alternative and conflicting paths in the foreign policies they advocated. Thus, in the case of the Cambodian crisis, once it became apparent that ASEAN's diplomacy was no longer likely to achieve a peaceful resolution on the issue, then one by one the ASEAN states started to breach the official position of the Association.

In retrospect, regional cooperation and displays of unity have most significantly been driven by common challenges and threats in the security and economic spheres – whether derived from intra-regional or extra-regional sources. For example, nuclear proliferation led to a convergence of interests regarding the formation of a Southeast Asia Nuclear Weapons Free Zone (SEANWFZ). Meanwhile, the end of the Cold War also renewed a desire for deeper cooperation and collaboration between the ASEAN members due to a renewed sense of vulnerability amidst a less predictable and increasingly globalized world. Consequently, the 1998 Hanoi Summit provided a commitment to achieve a 'higher plane of cooperation in order to strengthen ASEAN's effectiveness in dealing with the challenges of growing interdependence within ASEAN and of its integration into the global economy' (Chapter 4). Meanwhile, the earlier 1992 Singapore Summit specifically committed to greater economic *and* political cooperation. In line with this goal, the summit also committed to further institutionalize the ASEAN Secretariat (e.g. conferred ministerial status to the ASEAN

Secretary-General) and ASEAN membership was later enlarged to include all the Southeast Asian states at the time. For similar reasons, the Association also sought to extend its diplomatic voice beyond the region through the establishment of the ASEAN Regional Forum (ARF). However, due to a low level of political-security and elite-level socio-cultural integration, few of the initiatives in either ASEAN or the ARF led to tangible progress regarding multilateral cooperation on political and traditional security issues.

Notwithstanding the caveats above, common challenges have generated greater *functional cooperation* in a range of non-traditional security areas. For example, Chapter 4 noted how the region-wide threat of terrorism has generated improved cooperation regarding the sharing of intelligence. Further, a more detailed analysis of functional cooperation would reveal that there has been some progress in terms of responding to transnational crime (e.g. ASEANPOL), disease (e.g. HIV/AIDS, SARS and bird flu) and disaster management following the 2004 Asian tsunami (e.g. ERAT, Chapter 6). Meanwhile, trilateral cooperation has recently emerged in response to the problem of piracy in the Malacca Straits. However, extra-regional considerations also served to motivate this development as Japan and others had previously offered the assistance of their navy in patrolling the area – a precedent that the ASEAN states were keen to avoid. Nonetheless, beyond limited functional cooperation, the diversity of strategic interests and alignments continues to constrain the feasibility of significant cooperation and integration between the ASEAN members. Thus, some of the ASEAN members remain closely aligned with the US while others, such as Myanmar, have become more dependent on China. Further, state weakness, gaps in capacity, and associated divides in the level of economic development, have limited the number of issue areas with the potential for interest harmonization. Meanwhile, regional competition, continued conflict and associated distrust also represent further constraints to the level of cohesion, cooperation and complex integration that is feasible within ASEAN.

While a diversity of interests, continued competition, and animosity in ASEAN's intramural relations, will be the subject of focus in the next section, at this juncture it is important to acknowledge that ASEAN has maintained a relatively stronger record in terms of a degree of interest harmonization and policy coordination (cooperation) in the economic sphere and such outcomes are symbolic of a gradual transition to a higher level of economic integration. However, in as far as a convergence of interests is concerned, Chapter 4 noted how ASEAN unity quickly dissipated following the 1997–98 East Asian financial crisis. Nonetheless, during the course of the next few years a degree of cohesion returned and ASEAN reconsolidated its attempts to increase the level of economic cooperation and integration. The ASEAN members subsequently agreed to a broad array of additional economic agreements – such as the CMIM and the EDSM – culminating in proposals for an ASEAN Economic Community and its associated action plans and blueprint. Collectively, these agreements provide the ambitious goal of establishing ASEAN as a single market by 2015. Importantly, the ASEAN members were also willing to adopt a more flexible decision-making system in relation to economic agreements. Despite the number of economic agreements that ASEAN has reached – together with the extensive amount of detail provided in many of them – economic collaboration, cooperation and integration has been far from problem free. Because the ASEAN Way coincides with an aversion to legally binding agreements, many of the economic initiatives have either not been implemented or their implementation has been significantly delayed. Nonetheless, these issues have been even more problematic in the political and security spheres.

The challenges that ASEAN has faced in its attempts to achieve greater collaboration and cooperation can be further explained by reference to the region's norms and values. In the context of norms, the ASEAN Way was initially necessary because there was no alternative basis for collaboration given that, at the time of the Association's formation, the differences between the Southeast Asian states far outweighed the similarities. Despite this, a degree of commonality emerged between the ASEAN members concerning their anti-communist stances and authoritarian values. However, the combined effect of these norms and values included a traditional obsession about sovereignty and, therefore, a strong predilection for decentralized decision-making. Thus, while Ferguson acknowledges that 'it is clear then that the organization does not have strong mechanisms to enforce norms on its member governments, nor institutionalized means of conflict resolution', he nonetheless contends that 'the process-based nature of ASEAN, and its person-to-person dialogue, has allowed a slow evolution of a regional agenda where no consensus had existed previously'.[2]

Despite the above achievements, the evolution of a regional agenda – where any associated commitments can be feasibly implemented – has been challenged in recent decades due to the emergence of new political systems and values. While political liberalization in the original ASEAN members might arguably reflect the long-term processes of socialization through ASEAN, a more significant role can be attributed to a combination of grassroots (bottom-up) pressures and extra-regional influences – e.g. the effects of globalization and increased information and communications technology. Here, the limited impact of ASEAN regarding the intra-regional diffusion of new norms and values – together with any associated effects on the quality of governance – is a long-term consequence of an institutionalized avoidance of issues related to the internal affairs of the ASEAN members.[3] Consequently, the schism in the region's values continued to widen following the expansion of ASEAN's membership to cover all of Southeast Asia. For the purposes of this book, however, the growing diversity of political values and systems is primarily important for the extent to which it detracts from elite-level socio-cultural integration as political values now represent one of the most significant sources of division in regional relations.

The manner by which different political values and systems have started to strain regional relations and norms is aptly elucidated by the case study of Thailand. During the 1990s, Thailand embarked on a gradual process of democratization and its subsequent values and identity became increasingly incompatible with its former policy of 'constructive engagement' where it uncritically engaged with other ASEAN members for the purpose of economic gain. Such engagement had taken place regardless of any human rights abuses or other problems in neighbouring ASEAN governments. Thailand subsequently sought to replace 'constructive engagement' – including the principle of non-interference – with a policy of 'flexible engagement'. According to Thailand, flexible engagement would enable the ASEAN states to be more flexible in commenting on each other's internal affairs – especially when domestic issues had transnational consequences. However, this policy faced strong opposition from all the other countries except the Philippines – the only other democracy at the time.

As the political systems of some other ASEAN members have democratized (albeit to varying degrees), the number of actors contributing to government policy formulation has increased. These developments have enabled a greater role for NGOs and civil society as well as activism by individual parliamentarians that has, at times, conflicted with the official policies of their government. These developments, in turn, have contributed to an erosion of the non-interference principle along the lines originally proposed by Thailand. The gradual evolution of ASEAN towards a practice of 'flexible engagement' has been most notable regarding the Myanmar issue. Several developments in Myanmar also contributed to this outcome, including continued human rights abuses, the violent crackdown in 2007 against protestors, and the junta's response to Cyclone Nargis. Meanwhile, parliamentarians from several of the ASEAN countries formed the ASEAN Inter-Parliamentary Myanmar Caucus (AIPMC), which also lobbied ASEAN to suspend Myanmar's membership of the Association. Some of the region's political elite, such as Ambassador Barry Desker from Singapore, even called for Myanmar's expulsion from ASEAN. Such pressures, *inter alia*, led to the cancellation of Myanmar's scheduled chairmanship in ASEAN and some of the strongest ever statements about the internal affairs of one of ASEAN's own members. However, ASEAN's disillusionment with the country, together with its willingness to interfere in Myanmar's internal affairs, not only led to an estrangement between the Association and Myanmar (e.g. mutual disengagement, Chapter 6), but eventually generated further divisions with other relatively authoritarian members.

Given these challenges, recent regionalist endeavours by ASEAN – including the proposal for a security community – have been remarkable not just because of the level of supranational institutionalization and complex integration necessary to support ASEAN's regionalist commitments, but also because of extent to which the documents are (a) underpinned by new regional values and (b) explicitly declare a commitment to new regional values – e.g. democracy and a commitment to the protection of human rights. However, despite these commitments, in practice the ASEAN members remain divided over the extent of cooperation and institutionalization they are willing to endorse. Again, this divide is directly attributable to a low level of political-security and elite-level socio-cultural integration as reflected by the range of *political systems* and *values* in the region.

For example, Indonesia is currently the most democratic nation in the region and it has been the main driver of recent political and security commitments in ASEAN. As a democracy, its political values have also rendered it more willing to commit to substantive institutionalization – i.e. pooled sovereignty. Moreover, countries such as Indonesia and the Philippines have also been motivated by the actions of authoritarian governments (such as the SPDC) and how these actions have clashed with their own democratic and humanitarian values.

Meanwhile, a broader number of the ASEAN members have endorsed ASEAN's roadmap for greater regionalism because of the growing interdependence of transnational security challenges and a subsequent recognition that they cannot provide an adequate response in the absence of institutionalized mechanisms for regional cooperation. However, in this regard, the diversity of values and interests has meant that even the original ASEAN members (the ASEAN core) differ over how far such institutionalization should be developed. Consequently, while some of the more ambitious proposals to stem from the Bali Concord II have been abandoned – such as Indonesia's proposal for a regional peacekeeping force – ASEAN's record, in terms of the regionalist endeavours that were agreed to by all the ASEAN members, has not been particularly promising.

The fact that Myanmar, one of the most infamous dictatorships in the world, has been willing to endorse ASEAN's regionalist enterprises – such as the ASC, the Vientiane Plan of Action/Vientiane Action Program (VPA) and the ASEAN Charter – provides the strongest evidence of the limited extent to which ASEAN has managed to modify its values, norms, modes of cooperation, and any associated level of institutionalization. Aside from some initiatives and agreements with regard to the economic pillar, the ASEAN Charter is primarily significant for reinforcing a low level of political-security integration by retaining consensus based decision-making and the principle of non-interference in the domestic affairs of other states. Accordingly, the Charter did not provide any binding commitments in the realm of political and security cooperation and it also failed to garner any meaningful agreement over the protection of human rights. Here, the palpable gap between aspirations and outcomes further symbolizes the growing divide between the democratic and authoritarian regimes of Southeast Asia more generally. Given these considerations, ASEAN has now reached a point where its norms are more burden than benefit. Consequently, further progress regarding the level of complex integration in ASEAN will be significantly impeded unless ASEAN's modus operandi is changed to allow greater involvement in each other's internal affairs, which, in turn, will coincide with supranational institutionalization at high complex integration.

Due to the continuation of consensus-based decision-making, ASEAN's record has not significantly improved since the implementation of the Charter. For example, two years after the Charter, the ASEAN Intergovernmental Commission on Human Rights was established. However, in line with what has now become an almost habitual gap between ASEAN's aspirations and practices, not only does the Commission have no binding authority but it does not even have the power to investigate human rights issues within countries. As noted in the previous chapter, ASEAN has not yet been able to implement a dispute settlement mechanism covering political and security issues. For example, the earlier mentioned ASEAN High Council, as a potential mechanism for conflict resolution, has never been activated because all parties to a dispute must first agree to its use and, moreover, its decisions do not have any binding authority. Meanwhile, the pace of cooperation and institutionalization remains inadequate for the purpose of realizing ASEAN's proposal for a security community by 2015. Most importantly, the failure of the Charter and other instruments to vest the ASEAN Secretariat with a significant degree of supranational institutionalization (in terms of both 'scope' and 'depth') means that even when consensus is reached on a given issue, weak enforcement mechanisms will continue to contribute to a lack of implementation.

Characterizing ASEAN and future directions

In 1984, Donald K. Emmerson wrote,

> what's in a name? That which we call a rose by any other name would smell as sweet. Some names like 'rose', acknowledge what exists. Others, like 'unicorn', create what otherwise would not exist. In between lie names that simultaneously describe and invent reality. 'Southeast Asia' is one of these.[4]

Not only does this analogy aptly encapsulate the contested nature of 'Southeast Asia' as a region, but it also applies to the character of ASEAN. While ASEAN has been stamped with many different labels ranging from an 'imitation community' to a 'security community', the latter has been the most controversial. In 1998, Amitav Acharya wrote that the 'ASEAN experience somewhat blurs the distinction between a nascent, ascendant, and mature security community. Several characteristics of a mature security community are present in Southeast Asia'.[5] Acharya is somewhat more circumspect in a later book when he argues that 'ASEAN fits the concept of a "nascent security community", although its progress towards the ascendant or mature level looked more promising in the early 1990s than in the later part of the decade'.[6] Yuen Foong Khong also supports the contentions of Acharya by suggesting that the only remaining question 'is whether enough of the ASEAN spirit can be retained to nurture the nascent pluralistic security community that has been so helpful in providing a modicum of order of the ASEAN states'.[7]

Given the analysis in this book, the positive appraisals of Acharya and Khong are questionable. Nonetheless, ASEAN has made many important contributions to Southeast Asia's regional order. As has already been noted, a relatively higher convergence of interests in the economic sphere has emerged and ASEAN has subsequently achieved a degree of economic cooperation above and beyond the political-security sphere. Consequently, economic integration has advanced beyond a medium-low level (but not yet a medium-high level) and such a prognosis is supported by developments such as the implementation of AFTA, the CMIM and the EDSM. Meanwhile, the fact that the ASEAN members continue to devote considerable amounts of energy and resources to the institutions of ASEAN is demonstrative of each member's assessment concerning the continued importance of the Association. However, as noted by former Secretary-General Rodolfo Severino, the funding of the ASEAN Secretariat remains less than what is needed and the subsequent failure of the ASEAN Charter to address this issue was disappointing.[8] Finally, the occurrence of several hundred ASEAN meetings every year has inevitably helped to build regional transparency, mutual understanding and relatively more peaceful relations.

Notwithstanding the above achievements, several problems emerge given a dichotomy between the behaviour expected at low political-security integration and the benchmarks set by ASEAN including its goal to forge a security community. For example, despite Yukiko Nishikawa's contention that 'various claims regarding the "Asian" and the "ASEAN Way" of security management seem to have gained acceptance among Asian leaders',[9] the salience of ASEAN's norms has, in practice, been highly transient. For example, the book has identified numerous occasions where the principle of non-interference has been breached and examples include Singapore's response to the 'haze', various accusations over the Southern Thailand insurgency, and ASEAN's response to its Myanmar crisis. Consequently, Nicholas Khoo provides an opposing view where he states: 'after all, one could argue that the prevalence of a contrary norm, namely interference in other states' affairs, appears to be a regularized pattern of behaviour in Southeast Asia'.[10] Nevertheless, the extent to which the political elites have 'rhetorically' accepted ASEAN's guiding principles more accurately reflects an inability to agree on alternatives that are more effective rather than a genuine preference to maintain the *status quo*. While ASEAN's interferences regarding the Myanmar issue may reflect the growing weight of more progressive forces in ASEAN, regional differences concerning political values also detract from the depth and breadth of collective identification and render ASEAN's regionalist goals less feasible.

A relatively low level of political-security integration is further evident due to the continued pursuit of short-term interests and relative gains that often conflict with the collective interests of ASEAN. The pursuit by Singapore, Thailand, and Malaysia of bilateral free trade arrangements is a case in point. A lack of collective identification and integration was also visible in the case of the South China Sea dispute, where a common position has not been maintained. In terms of elite level socio-cultural integration, the level of collective identification is partly constrained by the nature of the region's exogenous relations. As argued in Chapter 7, the extent to which security is generated by extra-mural alliances and relations renders the strategic importance of other ASEAN members relatively less important. Here, the differences between the ASEAN members' respective security alliances exemplified the level of divergence between both the strategic interests and worldviews of the Southeast Asian states. In relation to the intricate 'spider web' of bilateral alliances, countries such as the Philippines are strongly aligned with the United States while others, such as Myanmar, are highly dependent on China. Thus, the problem is that 'in ASEAN's case it is clear that intra-ASEAN security relations are subordinate to those with outside powers' and, consequently, the contention that there is only a low level of political-security integration is further substantiated.[11]

As noted, continued distrust has also been a major issue in ASEAN. Cooperation and cohesion, as constituents of a community, cannot reach any significant level in the absence of trust between the members. On the issue of trust, the respondents from both the elite and communal samples indicated relatively low levels of trust. The level of distrust in the region, together with the associated perceptions of threat, coincided with the nature of some ASEAN members' military expenditure and defence procurements together with their foreign and defence policies. Equally important was the fact that the most distrusting categories of respondents (at both the elite and communal levels) were from Indonesia and Singapore – two of the original ASEAN members. Thus, both the frequency and quality of interaction between the communities of Southeast Asia has not been sufficient to generate an adequate level of trust for the purpose of advancing integration in the political-security and socio-cultural spheres.

A lack of distrust within Southeast Asia has also been compounded by the continuation of numerous territorial disputes. Here, the most problematic of these disputes have either involved or come close to involving actual armed conflict in recent years. For example, at the time of writing, armed skirmishes had occurred between Thailand and Cambodia over the Preah Vihear Temple as recently as February 2011. Other land-based disputes should not be discounted either. For example, the highly militarized border between Thailand and Myanmar contributed to a low-level skirmish in March 2002 (when the Thai military fired shells at Myanmar's *Tatmadaw*), and as recently as July 2006 the *Tatmadaw* also attacked a Thai military helicopter. Meanwhile, in the context of the South China Sea, armed skirmishes have occurred between the Philippines and Vietnam as recently as 1999 and the rapidity with which Malaysia and Indonesia resorted to gunboat diplomacy in 2005, over a territorial dispute in the Sulawesi/Celebes Sea, is also problematic for the purpose of progressing beyond a low level of political-security integration.

Meanwhile, the competitive pursuit of relative gains (e.g. over territorial disputes), together with the nature of the ASEAN Way, has also helped to reinforce a low level of political-security integration. Consequently, these dynamics have rendered unsuccessful any attempts to institutionalize conflict resolution mechanisms. Here, the two most notable examples concern the earlier-mentioned High Council and various plans of action and negotiations leading to the ASEAN Charter.[12] Further, the relatively high level of concern raised by respondents from some countries (such as Indonesia and Singapore) over the risk of armed conflict renders recent patterns of military expenditure intelligible. As revealed in earlier chapters, 'the persisting tendency among ASEAN members to engage in contingency-planning and war-oriented resource mobilization against each other suggests important limits to community-building…' in Southeast Asia.[13]

Given these considerations, regional 'expectations of peaceful change' fall well short of being dependable and, moreover, such behavioural patterns also conflict with the behaviour to be expected in an integrative peace (i.e. medium-high complex integration) or a stable peace (i.e. a 'security community' at high complex integration).

ASEAN is not currently a security community in any form. To claim otherwise would not only detract from the meaning of ASEAN's own statements of intent, but would also undermine the utility of the concept of a security community. While a security community necessitates high complex integration (Chapter 1), as illustrated in Figure 1.1, there is very little integration between the ASEAN states in the political-security sphere. Consequently, the risk of war is not only perceived as possible by a disconcerting percentage of elite in some countries, but the military policies of various states demonstrate that it remains an active contingency in parts of the region. While the level of socio-cultural integration at the grassroots level also remains low, a degree of cohesion and collective identification between the political elite of Southeast Asia – e.g. functional cooperation in relation to non-traditional security issues – symbolizes progress to a medium-low level of socio-cultural integration when the analysis is limited to the political elite of the region.[14] Further, a degree of elite level collective identification is also substantiated by the fact that the initiatives associated with 'ASEAN regionalism' have primarily been *elite* projects. Meanwhile, as noted earlier, a relatively significant amount of progress has occurred in the economic sphere of integration. However, even here problems remain and the interstate relations of Southeast Asia primarily conform to the model of commercial liberalism outlined in Chapter 1 (Figure 1.3). Accordingly, economic integration has not significantly advanced beyond a medium-low level.

Given the considerations above, ASEAN is best characterized as representing a *limited* economic and security regime because the ASEAN states are, on balance, currently bound by only a medium-low level of complex integration.[15] While the rhetoric of the ASEAN satisfies the definition of a regime in the full sense of the term (i.e. medium-high integration), the inconsistency by which the ASEAN states adhere to their self-declared principles, norms and rules means that, in practice, they have not moved beyond the characteristics of a limited regime. Meanwhile, ASEAN maintains some utility as a diplomatic community but its capacity to exercise a collective voice internationally has generally been limited to rare instances where security issues have commonly affected all the ASEAN members. Therefore, ASEAN's occasional utility as a diplomatic community does not symbolise a deepening of complex integration because any associated *convergence of interests* in the political-security sphere has only been transient and issue specific. Further, while the level of complex integration may be on the verge of a medium-low level, a transition to a medium-high level of integration (i.e. the model of institutional liberalism in Figure 1.3) represents a significant step, and, should ASEAN successfully evolve in this direction, the process will like take place over a number of decades rather than years. Finally, a high level of complex integration, symbolized by a security community, is even further away.

Based on the above dynamics, the ASEAN elite will be likely to continue with a practice of reimagining the meaning of their commitments as the scheduled dates for the implementation of the ASEAN Community (and associated commitments for regionalism) move closer. Such practices date back to the beginning of ASEAN's foundation and include the retrospective appointment of Indonesia as its official interlocutor in the handling of the 1970s Cambodian crisis in order to mask a breach in solidarity (Chapter 3). More recently, a senior official joked that the Association will simply reinvent its commitment to establish a 'drug free ASEAN by 2015' by arguing that it was only referring to the production of opium (largely eradicated through United Nations Office of Drugs and Crime (UNODC) assistance *inter alia*) rather than the much more problematic issue of methamphetamine production and consumption in the region. In the meantime, economic cooperation and integration will likely remain the most successful pillar of the 'ASEAN community'. However, more significant progress in this sphere remains contingent on the capacity of individual ASEAN members to adopt the domestic reforms necessitated by future economic commitments. While the relatively developed ASEAN economies may be able to side-step this 'capacity' problem through the adoption of a more flexible decision-making process,[16] future progress will also be dependent on the economic entrepreneurship of the ASEAN leaders, including an ability to formulate ASEAN agreements with more significant trade benefits than those provided through other sources such as the WTO or IMF.

For the purpose of future advances in political-security integration, several of the ASEAN members will also need to make further progress in terms of internal consolidation. While some of the newer ASEAN members have maintained solid economic performance (e.g. Vietnam), Myanmar's economic system and associated government services are on the brink of collapse (e.g. the health and education sectors). Meanwhile, continued political and security sector reforms will also need to be complemented by the consolidation of nation-building policies that can successfully resolve disputes grounded in ethnic and/or religious rivalries (e.g. insurgencies) and other sources of domestic instability. Here, ASEAN can develop a significant role in terms of facilitation and reinforcement. For example, the development of the Tripartite Core Group (TCG) mechanism, in response to Cyclone Nargis (Chapter 6), demonstrated how ASEAN can play a significant role in the coordination of international aid following a natural disaster. Such a role could be developed further in relation to the longer-term coordination of international aid for capacity-building projects. The legal personality generated by the ASEAN Charter may assist in this regard. Should ASEAN maintain a constructive dialogue in relation to human rights issues and other political issues in member states, then this diplomatic pressure may generate incremental improvements regarding individual issues and, in the longer term, may assist in the socialization of new norms and values. Here, the continued development of government exchange programmes, professionalization programmes and human rights training courses may also provide long-term benefits.

At the grassroots level, ASEAN can also assist in the advancement of socio-cultural integration by continuing with its programmes for curriculum reform, student exchanges and scholarships. While a long-term process, the professionalization of the education sectors in the weaker ASEAN members will help to reduce teaching practices that contribute to distrust (e.g. through negative and salient intercommunity comparisons) whilst also building a greater sense of mutual identification. In terms of 'higher education', the continuation and expansion of the number of exchange programmes and scholarships[17] will also help to build greater trust and collective identification while also contributing to regional knowledge, technical skills and economic development of the poorer members of ASEAN. Meanwhile, globalization, interdependence and complex integration will expose various communities in Southeast Asia to new ideas, norms and values. For example, the survey data concerning grassroots perceptions of democracy represents a potential indicator concerning how this process is already under way. In the interim, the power of the new military backed government in Myanmar to control the flow of information continues to be weakened by a proliferation of communications and information technology. Such processes have the potential to lead to added grassroots (bottom-up) pressures to adopt political reforms and, eventually, may also lead to further regime change.

Despite the potential for certain bottom-up processes to contribute to regionalization (i.e. complex integration), any tangible outcomes in this regard will require several decades in order to take shape. Nonetheless, one possible exception involves sudden and unexpected regime change – such as occurred when Suharto's New Order regime collapsed in Indonesia. In the case of Indonesia, however, the immediate consequences of Suharto's downfall were negative in relation to Southeast Asian regionalism as (a) there was a decrease in the level of comprehensive security (e.g. rising transnational crime) and (b) ASEAN was perceived to have lost its 'natural leader'. Nonetheless, once Indonesia consolidated its new democratic system, it re-emerged a few years later as a leader in terms of normative and institutional reforms in ASEAN. Should similar events occur in Myanmar there is the possibility that the country might more significantly contribute to, or be less resistant to, ASEAN regionalism in the future. However, given the current strength of the military, such an outcome remains a distant prospect.

In the interim, while the principle of non-interference has been weakened (e.g. with respect to Myanmar), the principle of consensus-based decision-making in the political-security sphere will continue out of necessity. This is because a continued emphasis on Indonesia's notion of 'unity in diversity' will remain necessary in order to ensure the survival of the Association until all (or at least a significant number) of the ASEAN members have internally consolidated and democratized. Problematically, even amongst the ASEAN core (the original ASEAN members), there has not yet been an adequate convergence of interests. Therefore, even if the ASEAN model of consensus-based decision-making were to be modified along the lines of an 'ASEAN-X' or '2 plus X' formula then ASEAN would still be constrained in terms of its progress with political-security integration. Nonetheless, the adoption of a new decision-making method, along the lines of a two-tier system, would at least enable greater progress than is currently the case.

In summary, the difficulties that ASEAN currently faces in carrying out its regionalist project are indelibly interdependent with a growing divide between the democratic and authoritarian regimes of Southeast Asia. Until the ASEAN members' political systems and values converge to become more compatible then significant *interest harmonization* and *policy coordination* will also be difficult to achieve. However, many of the ASEAN members must first continue with the process of internal consolidation in order to acquire the levels of stability and capacity that are necessary for such ideational convergence. These factors, combined with a general lack of trust, explain not just the difficulty of political and security integration but also the difficulty of implementing more specific multilateral security arrangements and mechanisms for preventative diplomacy, conflict resolution and post-conflict peace-building. In the meantime, and despite some of the challenges that were raised, cooperation and integration based on the economic pillar (i.e. the 'ASEAN Economic Community') is likely to remain the most feasible. It is here, together with functional cooperation in some of the less sensitive security issues (e.g. transnational crime), that there is some evidence of a transition towards a degree of mutual identification and integration in line with constructivist processes articulated in Chapter 1. Over time, an associated rise in the level of interdependence and interaction between the elites and people of Southeast Asia may produce positive spill-over effects facilitating continued increases in the level of trust and an ascertainable sense of a collective identity. Nonetheless, decades, rather than several years, will be necessary in order for the ASEAN states to develop the *capacity* and *intention* to truly consolidate along the lines of the 'ASEAN community' envisioned in the Bali Concord II.

Notes

Introduction

1 Bjorn Hettne, 'Globalisation and the New Regionalism', in *Globalism and New Regionalism*, ed. Bjorn Hettne, Andras Inotai, and Sunkel Osvaldo (New York: St Martin's Press, 1999), p. xxi.
2 Mary Farrell, 'The Global Politics of Regionalism: An Introduction', in *Global Politics of Regionalism*, ed. Mary Farrell, Bjorn Hettne and Luk Van Langenhove (London: Pluto Press, 2005), p. 8.
3 Louise Fawcett, 'Regionalism from an Historical Perspective', in *Global Politics of Regionalism: Theory and Practice*, ed. Mary Farrell, Bjorn Hettne and Luk Van Langenhove (London: Pluto Press, 2005), p. 25.
4 Karl Wolfgang Deutsch, Sidney A. Burrell and Robert A. Kann, *Political Community and the North Atlantic Area: International Organisation in the Light of Historical Experience* (New York: Greenwood Press, 1957).
5 Robert Jackson and Georg Sorensen, *Introduction to International Relations: Theories and Approaches* (New York: Oxford, 2003), p. 49.
6 Laurie Nathan, 'Domestic Instability and Security Communities', *European Journal of International Relations* 12, no. 2 (2006): p. 276, Amitav Acharya, *Constructing a Security community in Southeast Asia: ASEAN and the Problem of Regional Order* (London: Routledge, 2001), p. 201.
7 Deutsch *et al.*, *Political Community and the North Atlantic Area: International Organisation in the Light of Historical Experience*, p. 5.
8 Emanuel Adler and Michael Barnett, 'Security Communities in Theoretical Perspective', in *Security Communities*, ed. Emanuel Adler and Michael Barnett (Cambridge: Cambridge University Press, 1998), p. 3.
9 Deutsch *et al.*, *Political Community and the North Atlantic Area: International Organisation in the Light of Historical Experience*, p. 5.
10 'Declaration of ASEAN Concord II (Bali Concord II)', ASEAN Secretariat, 2003, www.aseansec.org/15159.htm.
11 Ibid.
12 David Martin Jones and Michael L.R. Smith, 'Making Process, Not Progress', *International Security* 32, no. 1 (2007): p. 158.
13 'Cebu Declaration on the Acceleration of the Establishment of an ASEAN Community by 2015', ASEAN Secretariat, 2007, www.aseansec.org/19260.htm.
14 Rizal Sukma, for example, stated in interview that he was influenced by the works of Michael Leifer and Amitav Achara when he helped formulate Indonesia's draft proposal for a security community. Interview with Rizal Sukma, Executive Director, *CSIS* (Jakarta), 21 April 2006.
15 For example, see Nicholas Khoo, 'Deconstructing the ASEAN Security community: A Review Essay', *International Relations of the Asia-Pacific* 4 (2004): pp. 35–46. See

also David M. Jones and Michael Smith, *ASEAN and East Asian International Relations: Regional Delusion* (Northhampton, MA: Edward Elgar, 2006).

16 Donald K Emmerson, 'Security and Community in Southeast Asia: Will the Real ASEAN Please Stand Up?', *Southeast Asia Forum* (2005): p. 5.

17 Martin Griffiths, Terry O'Callaghan and Steven C. Roach, *International Relations*, 2nd edn (New York: Routledge, 2008), p. 280.

18 Joshua S. Goldstein and Jon C. Pevehouse, *International Relations: Brief Fifth Edition* (New York: Longman, 2010), p. 229.

19 Barry Buzan and Ole Waever, *Regions and Powers: The Structure of International Security* (Cambridge: Cambridge University Press, 2003), p. 476.

20 Robert E. Kelly, 'Security Theory in the "New Regionalism"', *International Studies Review* 9, no. 2 (2007): pp. 197–213. See also: Fawcett, 'Regionalism from an Historical Perspective', p. 24.

21 For example, contrast the earlier cited works by Amitav Acharya with David Martin Jones and Michael Smith: Jones and Smith, *ASEAN and East Asian International Relations: Regional Delusion.*

22 While a short synopsis of the methodology is provided here, a detailed outline of the methodology is provided in the original PhD dissertation. See, Christopher Roberts, 'ASEAN's Security community Project: Challenges and Opportunities in the Pursuit of Comprehensive Integration' (PhD, Academy Library UNSW@ADFA: 2008).

23 In one email the sender was identified as (tan_yong_piu@nea.gov.sg) and read: 'Dear user iscroberts@ntu.edu.sg, We have received reports that your account was used to send a large amount of spam during this week. Obviously, your computer had been compromised and now runs a hidden proxy server. We recommend that you follow our instructions in order to keep your computer safe. Have a nice day, ntu.edu.sg technical support team'. Interestingly, the attachment that contained the 'instructions' I was to follow had been removed by the NTU computer system as it was deemed a 'security risk'. In another email identified as coming from '2462@gems2.gov.sg' the statement read: 'You have downloaded these illegal cracks?' Again, the attachment was removed from the NTU server as a 'security threat'. The heading of yet another email read 'Delivery reports about your e-mail' and was listed as having come from 'zahrah@nie.edu.sg' (an institute which I have never contacted nor had any affiliation with); however, the content of the message was garbled and the attachment was again deleted by the NTU server because it was a 'security risk'. Other emails of a similar genre were also received between January and July 2006 when my research focused on survey and interview work with the ministries of defence and foreign affairs in Singapore. Interestingly, no further emails of a similar nature were received since departing Singapore in July 2006.

24 However, small rural samples were utilised as a 'control' in the Philippines and Thailand.

25 Phillips W. Shively, *The Craft of Political Research* (New Jersey: Pearson Prentice Hall, 2005), pp. 100–101.

1 Security, cooperation and identity in international relations

1 'Declaration of ASEAN Concord II (Bali Concord II)', ASEAN Secretariat, 2003, www.aseansec.org/15159.htm.

2 Mary Farrell, 'The Global Politics of Regionalism: An Introduction', in *Global Politics of Regionalism*, ed. Mary Farrell, Bjorn Hettne and Luk Van Langenhove (London: Pluto Press, 2005), p. 8.

3 Raimo Vayrynen, 'Regionalism: Old and New', *International Studies Review* 5 (2003): p. 39.

4 William Wallace, ed., *The Dynamics of European Integration* (London: Pinter, 1990), p. 9.

5 Shaun Breslin, 'Theorising East Asian Regionalism(s): New Regionalism and Asia's Future(S)', in *Advancing East Asian Regionalism*, ed. Melissa G. Curley and Nicholas Thomas (Oxon: Routledge, 2007), p. 29.
6 Farrell, 'The Global Politics of Regionalism: An Introduction', p. 8.
7 Bahar Rumelili, *Constructing Regional Community and Order in Europe and Southeast Asia* (New York: Palgrave MacMillan, 2007), p. 2.
8 Ibid., p. 2.
9 John Baylis, Steve Smith and Patricia Owens, *The Globalization of World Politics: An Introduction to International Relations* (Oxford: Oxford University Press, 2008), p. 578.
10 Rasma Karklins, 'The Concept of Collective Identity' (paper presented at the Directorate of Communication and Research, Strasbourg, 17–18 April 2001), p. 1.
11 Alexander Wendt, *Social Theory of International Politics* (Cambridge: Cambridge University Press, 1999), p. 17.
12 Joel Charon, *The Meaning of Sociology: A Reader* (Englewood, CA: Prentice Hall, 1987), pp. 63–69.
13 Vayrynen, 'Regionalism: Old and New', pp. 37, 39.
14 Robert E. Kelly, 'Security Theory in the "New Regionalism"', *International Studies Review* 9, no. 2 (2007): p. 205.
15 Ibid., p. 205.
16 Patrick Morgan, 'Regional Security Complexes and Regional Orders', in *Regional Orders: Building Security in the New World*, ed. David A. Lake and Patrick M. Morgan (Pennsylvania: Pennsylvania State University Press, 1997), p. 26.
17 Richard Ned Lebow, 'Reason, Emotion and Cooperation', *International Politics* 42, no. 3 (2005): p. 303.
18 Muthiah Alagappa, 'Constructing Security Order in Asia: Conception and Issues', in *Asian Security Order: Instrumental and Normative Features*, ed. Muthiah Alagappa (Stanford, California: Stanford University Press, 2003), p. 39.
19 Barry Buzan and Ole Waever, *Regions and Powers: The Structure of International Security* (Cambridge: Cambridge University Press, 2003), pp. 53–54.
20 Alex Warleigh-Lack, 'Towards a Conceptual Framework for Regionalization: Bridging "New Regionalism" and "Integration Theory"', *Review of International Political Economy* 15, no. 5 (2006): p. 751.
21 This model is adopted from an earlier model of 'comprehensive integration' developed and published by the author in: Christopher Roberts, 'The ASEAN Security community Project: The Prospects for Comprehensive Integration in Southeast Asia', *The Indonesian Quarterly* 34, no. 3 (2006): p. 278.
22 For example, see: Louise Fawcett, 'Regionalism from an Historical Perspective', in *Global Politics of Regionalism: Theory and Practice*, ed. Mary Farrell, Bjorn Hettne, and Luk Van Langenhove (London: Pluto Press, 2005), p. 24.
23 Karl W. Deutsch, *The Analysis of International Relations*, 2nd edn (New Jersey: Prentice Hall, Inc., 1981), p. 198.
24 Martin Griffiths, Terry O'Callaghan and Steven C. Roach, *International Relations*, 2nd edn (New York: Routledge, 2008), p. 155.
25 Wendt, *Social Theory of International Politics*, pp. 259–263.
26 Ibid., p. 310.
27 Steven L. Lamy, 'Contemporary Mainstream Approaches: Neo-Realism and Neo-Liberalism', in *The Globalization of World Politics*, ed. John Baylis, Steve Smith, and Patricia Owens (Oxford: Oxford University Press, 2008), p. 131.
28 In summary, the states of the grouping may constitute a limited economic and security regime at a medium-low level of complex integration. A regime is defined as 'sets of implicit or explicit principles, norms, rules, and decision-making procedures around which actors' expectations converge in a given area of international

relations'. Ralf Emmers, *Cooperative Security and the Balance of Power in ASEAN and the ARF* (London and New York: RoutledgeCurzon, 2003), p. 2.

29 Alagappa, 'Constructing Security Order in Asia: Conception and Issues', p. 82.

30 While this term, as introduced here, has its origins in sociological liberalism (Deutsch), it also embraces the central tenets of liberal institutionalism, albeit with the blend of ideational considerations that is intrinsic in constructivism. This is in line with the shift in theoretical thinking that has been called for in Lamy, 'Contemporary Mainstream Approaches: Neo-Realism and Neo-Liberalism', pp. 135–138.

31 Kelly, 'Security Theory in the "New Regionalism"', pp. 197–213.

32 *Your Guide to the Lisbon Treaty* (Brussels: European Commission, 2009), p. 5.

33 An integrative peace is a tier of integration just below a security community. In an integrative peace the 'actors maintain a predominantly cooperative and positive relationship'. Rikard Bengtsson, 'The Cognitive Dimension of Stable Peace', in *Stable Peace among Nations*, ed. Arie M. Kacowicz, Yaacov Bar-Simon-Tov, Ole Elgstrom, and Alexander Jerneck (Maryland: Rowman and Littlefield, 2000), p. 94.

34 Lamy, 'Contemporary Mainstream Approaches: Neo-Realism and Neo-Liberalism', p. 132.

35 Bengtsson, 'The Cognitive Dimension of Stable Peace', p. 94.

36 Arie Kacowicz, 'Regionalization, Globalization, and Nationalism: Convergent, Divergent or Overlapping?', *Alternative: Social Transformation and Humane Governance* 24 (1999): p. 543.

37 Peter J. Katzenstein and Rudra Sil, 'Rethinking Asian Security: A Case for Analytical Eclecticism', in *Rethinking Security in East Asia: Identity, Power, and Efficiency*, ed. J.J. Suh, Peter J. Katzenstein, and Allen Carlson (Palo Alto: Stanford University Press, 2004), p. 2. In relation to the theoretical relevance of domestic security see Laurie Nathan, 'Domestic Instability and Security Communities', *European Journal of International Relations* 12, no. 2 (2006): p. 293.

38 'Concepts of Comprehensive Security and Cooperative Security', *CSCAP Newsletter*, no. 6 (1997): p. 1.

39 Raimo Vayrynen, 'Stable Peace through Security Communities', in *Stable Peace among Nations*, ed. Yaacov Bar-Siman-Tov, Ole Elgstron, Alexander Jerneck and Arie M. Kacowicz (Oxford: Rowman & Littlefield, 2000), p. 112.

40 Emanuel Adler and Michael Barnett, 'A Framework for the Study of Security Communities', in *Security Communities*, ed. Emanuel Adler and Michael Barnett (Cambridge: Cambridge University Press, 1998), p. 35.

41 Amitav Acharya, *Constructing a Security community in Southeast Asia: ASEAN and the Problem of Regional Order*, 2nd edn (London: Routledge, 2009), p. 19.

42 Kacowicz, 'Regionalization, Globalization, and Nationalism: Convergent, Divergent or Overlapping?', p. 12, Nathan, 'Domestic Instability and Security Communities', p. 276.

43 Alex J. Bellamy, *Security Communities and Their Neighbours: Regional Fortresses or Global Integrators?* (Basingstoke: Palgrave Macmillan, 2004), p. 6.

44 Jewellord T. Nem Singh, 'Process of Institutionalisation and Democratisation in ASEAN: Features, Challenges and Prospects of Regionalism in Southeast Asia', *UNISCI Discussion Papers*, no. No. 16 (2008): pp. 161–162.

45 Robert Jackson and Georg Sorensen, *Introduction to International Relations: Theories and Approaches* (New York: Oxford, 2003), p. 117. Keohane further argues that institutions can take one of three forms: formal intergovernmental organisations, international regimes and conventions. He broadly defines institutions as 'persistant and connected sets of rules (formal and informal) that prescribe behavioral roles, constrain activity, and shape expectations.' Robert Keohane, 'Neoliberal Institutionalism: A Perspective on World Politics', in *International Institutions and State Power: Essays in International Relations Theory*, ed. Robert Keohane (Boulder, CO: Westview Press, 1989), p. 3.

46 Joseph S. Nye Jr., *Understanding International Conflicts* (New York: Harper Collins, 1993), p. 39.
47 Fawcett, 'Regionalism from an Historical Perspective', p. 21.
48 Adapted from Keohane, 'Neoliberal Institutionalism: A Perspective on World Politics', p. 4.
49 Kacowicz, 'Regionalization, Globalization, and Nationalism: Convergent, Divergent or Overlapping?', pp. 12–13.
50 Deutsch, *The Analysis of International Relations*, pp. 239–240.
51 Bellamy, *Security Communities and Their Neighbours: Regional Fortresses or Global Integrators?*, p. 10.
52 Adler and Barnett, 'A Framework for the Study of Security Communities', p. 30.
53 Zhiqun Zhu, 'Prospect for Integration in Pacific-Asia', *Asian Profile* 28, no. 6 (2000): p. 510.
54 In regard to the fallacy of distinquishing between pluralistic and amalgamated security communities, see Christopher Roberts, *ASEAN's Myanmar Crisis: Challenges to the Pursuit of a Security community* (Singapore: ISEAS, 2010), pp. 3–4.
55 Bellamy, *Security Communities and Their Neighbours: Regional Fortresses or Global Integrators?*, p. 38. See also Andrew Hurrell, 'Norms and Ethics in International Relations', in *Handbook of International Relations*, ed. Walter Carlsnaes, Thomas Risse and Beth Simmons (London: Sage, 2005), pp. 141–142.
56 Lebow, 'Reason, Emotion and Cooperation', p. 294.
57 Peter J. Katzenstein, *The Culture of National Security: Norms and Identity in World Politics* (New York: Columbia University Press, 1996), p. 23.
58 Leszek Buszynski, *Asia Pacific Security – Values and Identity* (New York: Routledge, 2004), p. 17.
59 Ibid.
60 Alexander Wendt, 'Anarchy is What States Make of It: The Social Construction of Power Politics', *International Organization* 46, no. 2 (1992): p. 398. See also Lebow, 'Reason, Emotion and Cooperation', p. 284.
61 Trine Flockhart, '"Complex Socialisation": A Framework for the Study of State Socialization', *European Journal of International Relations* 12, no. 1 (2006): p. 94. Throughout this study references to the 'state' equate to references to the government and agents in power.
62 Quoted in Colin Wight, 'State Agency: Social Action without Human Activity', *Review of International Studies* 30, no. 2 (2004): pp. 275–276.
63 Amitav Acharya, *Constructing a Security community in Southeast Asia: ASEAN and the Problem of Regional Order* (London: Routledge, 2001), p. 32.
64 Wendt, *Social Theory of International Politics*, p. 170.
65 Acharya, *Constructing a Security community in Southeast Asia: ASEAN and the Problem of Regional Order*, pp. 24–25.
66 Michael Barnett, 'Social Constructivism', in *The Globalisation of World Politics: An Introduction to International Relations*, ed. John Baylis and Steve Smith (Oxford: Oxford University Press, 2006), pp. 252–255.
67 Flockhart, '"Complex Socialisation": A Framework for the Study of State Socialization', p. 96.
68 Barnett, 'Social Constructivism', p. 255.
69 Flockhart, '"Complex Socialisation": A Framework for the Study of State Socialization', p. 152.
70 Kate O'Neill, Jorg Balsiger and Stacy D. VanDeveer, 'Actors, Norms, and Impact: Recent International Cooperation Theory and the Influence of the Agent-Structure Debate', *Annual Review of Political Science* 7 (2004): p. 160.
71 Charles W. Jr. Kegley and Gregory A. Raymond, *When Trust Breaks Down: Alliance Norms and World Politics* (Columbia: University of South Carolina Press, 1990), p. 248.

72 Vayrynen, 'Stable Peace through Security Communities', p. 109.

73 Quoted in Christopher Hemmer and Peter J. Katzenstein, 'Why is There No Nato in Asia? Collective Identity, Regionalism, and the Origins of Multilateralism', *International Organization* 56, no. 3 (2002): p. 586.

74 Alagappa, 'Constructing Security Order in Asia: Conception and Issues', p. 79.

75 Peter Hays Gries, 'Social Psychology and the Identity-Conflict Debate: Is a "China Threat" Inevitable?', *European Journal of International Relations* 11, no. 2 (2005): p. 233.

76 Bellamy, *Security Communities and Their Neighbours: Regional Fortresses or Global Integrators?*, p. 43.

77 John Turner, *Rediscovering the Social Group* (Oxford: Basil Blackwell, 1987), p. 1.

78 Christopher Hemmer and Peter J. Katzenstein, 'Why is There No Nato in Asia? Collective Identity, Regionalism, and the Origins of Multilateralism', in *Critical Concepts in Political Science*, ed. Matthew Evangelista (Milton Park: Routledge, 2005), p. 114.

79 Flockhart, '"Complex Socialisation": A Framework for the Study of State Socialization', p. 94.

80 Gries, 'Social Psychology and the Identity-Conflict Debate: Is a "China Threat" Inevitable?', p. 241.

81 Jennifer Crocker and Riia Luhtanen, 'Collective Self-Esteem and Ingroup Bias', *Journal of Personality and Social Psychology* 58, no. 1 (1990): pp. 62–63.

82 Flockhart, '"Complex Socialisation": A Framework for the Study of State Socialization', p. 95.

83 Gries, 'Social Psychology and the Identity-Conflict Debate: Is a "China Threat" Inevitable?', p. 237.

84 Benjamin Miller, 'Between the Revisionist and the Frontier State: Regional Variations in the State War-Propensity', *Review of International Studies* 35, S1 (2009): p. 85.

85 Ibid.

86 Ibid.

87 In this correspondence Amitav Acharya states that he is not sure whether the 'security approach will hold for piracy. It's more about avoiding war than developing specific forms of security cooperation'. Amitav Acharya, email, 21 September 2001.

88 Ole Weaver argues that in the EU 'the state model still dominates and national identities differ; as a result, the West European security community is not yet full-fledged'. Quoted in Vayrynen, 'Stable Peace through Security Communities', p. 116.

89 Edward D. Mansfield and Brian M. Pollins, 'The Study of Interdependence and Conflict: Recent Advances, Open Questions, and Directions for Future Research', *Journal of Conflict Resolution* 45, no. 6 (2001): pp. 834–835.

90 Amitav Acharya, 'Multilateralism: Is There an Asia-Pacific Way?', The National Bureau of Asian Research, 1997, www.nbr.org/publications/analysis/vol. 8no2/v8n2.pdf.

91 Donald E. Weatherbee, *International Relations in Southeast Asia: The Struggle for Autonomy* (Lanham, MD: Rowman & Littlefield Publishers, 2009), p. 11.

92 Deutsch *et al.*, *Political Community and the North Atlantic Area: International Organisation in the Light of Historical Experience*, pp. 156–157.

93 Ganesan also argues that 'powerful perceptions of threat' externally 'have made ASEAN cohere better'. N. Ganesan, 'ASEAN: A Community Stalled?', in *The Asia-Pacific: A Region in Transition*, ed. Jim Rolfe (Hawaii: Asia-Pacific Center for Security Studies, 2004), p. 129.

94 Kelly, 'Security Theory in the "New Regionalism"', pp. 213–216.

95 Ralf Emmers, *Cooperative Security and the Balance of Power in ASEAN and the ARF* (London and New York: RoutledgeCurzon, 2003), p. 42.

96 Vayrynen, 'Stable Peace through Security Communities', p. 119. See also Ronald L. Jepperson, Alexander Wendt, and Peter J. Katzenstein, 'Norms, Identity and Culture in National Security', in *The Cutlure of National Security: Norms and Identity in World Politics*, ed. Peter J. Katzenstein (New York: Columbia University Press, 1996), pp. 60–63.

97 Richard W. Mansbach and Kristen L. Rafferty, *Introduction to Global Politics* (New York: Routledge, 2008), pp. 257–258.

98 Farrell, 'The Global Politics of Regionalism: An Introduction', p. 2.

99 Kacowicz, 'Regionalization, Globalization, and Nationalism: Convergent, Divergent or Overlapping?', p. 538.

100 John McFarlane, *Transnational Crime and Illegal Immigration in the Asia-Pacific Region: Background, Prospects and Countermeasures* (Canberra: Strategic and Defence Studies Centre, 1999), p. 1.

101 Quoted in Lamy, 'Contemporary Mainstream Approaches: Neo-Realism and Neo-Liberalism', p. 132.

102 Acharya, *Constructing a Security community in Southeast Asia: ASEAN and the Problem of Regional Order*, p. 32.

103 Fawcett, 'Regionalism from an Historical Perspective', p. 34.

104 Philip Alan Reynolds, *An Introduction to International Relations* (London: Longman, 1980), p. 49.

105 Karin von Hippel, 'Democracy by Force: A Renewed Commitment to Nation Building', *The Washington Quarterly* (2000): p. 96.

106 Nikki Slocum and Luk Van Langenhove, 'Identity and Regional Integration', in *Global Politics of Regionalism: Theory and Practice*, ed. Mary Farrell, Bjorn Hettne, and Luk Van Langenhove (London: Pluto Press, 2005), p. 138.

107 Kacowicz adds, '[it] is a geographically bounded legal entity under a single and recognized government, the population of which psychologically considers itself to be related, through historical, linguistic, racial, or other links'. Kacowicz, 'Regionalization, Globalization, and Nationalism: Convergent, Divergent or Overlapping?', p. 532.

108 Christopher Roberts, 'ASEAN Institutionalisation: The Function of Political Values and State Capacity', *RSIS Working Paper*, no. 217 (2010): p. 9. While broader, the term PSSR has been adopted from the notion of security sector reform. For an example, see Mark Beeson and Alex J. Bellamy, *Securing Southeast Asia: The Politics of Security Sector Reform* (Abingdon: Routledge, 2008).

109 Michael Brzoska, 'The Concept of Security Sector Reform', in *Security Sector Reform*, ed. Connie Wall (Bonn: Bonn International Center for Conversion, 2000), p. 6.

110 Alagappa, 'Introduction: Predictability and Stability Despite Changes', p. 21.

111 Kelly, 'Security Theory in the "New Regionalism"', p. 216.

112 Beeson and Bellamy, *Securing Southeast Asia: The Politics of Security Sector Reform*, p. 14.

113 Martin Griffiths and Terry O'Callaghan, *International Relations: The Key Concepts* (New York: Routledge, 2003), pp. 207–208.

114 Karl Wolfgang Deutsch, Sidney A. Burrell and Robert A. Kann, *Political Community and the North Atlantic Area: International Organisation in the Light of Historical Experience* (New York: Greenwood Press, 1957), pp. 123–125.

115 Zhu, 'Prospect for Integration in Pacific-Asia', p. 517.

116 John W. Patty and Roberto A. Weber, 'Agreeing to Fight: An Explanation of the Democratic Peace', *Politics, Philosophy & Economics* 5, no. 3 (2006): p. 36.

117 John R. O'Neal and Bruce M. Russett, 'The Classic Liberals Were Right: Democracy, Interdependence, and Conflict, 1950–1985', *International Studies Quarterly* 41 (1997): pp. 267–268.

118 See, for example, Singh, 'Process of Institutionalisation and Democratisation in ASEAN: Features, Challenges and Prospects of Regionalism in Southeast Asia', pp. 143–145.

119 Amitav Acharya, 'Democratisation and the Prospects for Participatory Regionalism in Southeast Asia', *Third Word Quarterly* 24, no. 2 (2003): pp. 377–78, Singh, 'Process of Institutionalisation and Democratisation in ASEAN: Features, Challenges and Prospects of Regionalism in Southeast Asia', pp. 143–145.
120 Farrell, 'The Global Politics of Regionalism: An Introduction', p. 4.
121 Ibid. Such contentions have been reinforced by game theory. For example, see Robert Putnam, 'Diplomacy and Domestic Politics: The Logic of Two Level Games', *International Organization* 42, no. 3 (1988): pp. 427–460.
122 Benjamin Miller, 'When and How Regions Become Peaceful: Potential Theoretical Pathways to Peace', *International Studies Review* 7 (2005): p. 251.
123 Kai He, 'Indonesia's Foreign Policy after Soeharto: International Pressure, Democratization, and Policy Change', *International Relations of the Asia-Pacific* 8, no. 1 (2008): p. 48.
124 The PITF studies are located at http://globalpolicy.gmu.edu/pitf. See for example Jack A. Goldstone, Robert H. Bates, Ted Robert Gurr, Michael Lustik, Monty G. Marshall, Jay Ulfelder and Mark Woodward, 'A Global Forecasting Model of Political Instability', in *Annual Meeting of the American Political Science Association* (Washington, DC: Political Instablity Task Force, 2005), pp. 28–29.
125 Michelle Benson and Jacek Kugler, 'Power Parity, Democracy, and the Severity of Internal Violence', *The Journal of Conflict Resolution* 43, no. 2 (1998): pp. 198–199.
126 For some recent statements on this issue see: Kishore Mahbubani, 'Lessons for the West from Asian Capitalism', *Financial Times*, 18 March 2009, Kishore Mahbubani, *The New Asian Hemisphere: The Irresistible Shift of Global Power to the East* (New York: PublicAffairs, 2008).
127 Tim Dunne, 'Liberalism', in *The Globalization of World Politics: An Introduction to International Relations*, ed. John Baylis, Steve Smith, and Patricia Owens (New York: Oxford University Press, 2008), pp. 112–113.
128 Barry Buzan, 'Security Architecture in Asia: The Interplay of Regional and Global Level', *The Pacific Review* 16, no. 2 (2003): pp. 143–173.

2 The rise of Southeast Asia and the search for regional order

1 Amitav Acharya, *The Quest for Identity: International Relations of Southeast Asia* (New York: Oxford University Press, 2001), p. 163. See also Anthony Reid, *Southeast Asia in the Age of Commerce, 1450–1680*, vol. 1 (New Haven, CT: Yale University Press, 1988), p. 6.
2 D.G.E. Hall, *A History of South-East Asia* (Hong Kong: Macmillan Press, 1981), p. 3.
3 Philip Charrier, 'ASEAN's Inheritance: The Regionalisation of Southeast Asia, 1941–61', *The Pacific Review* 14, no. 3 (2001): p. 317.
4 Mary Margaret Steedly, 'The State of Culture Theory in the Anthropology of Southeast Asia', *Annual Review of Anthropology* 28 (1999): p. 434.
5 Acharya, *The Quest for Identity: International Relations of Southeast Asia*, pp. 17, 163–164.
6 Milton Osborne, *Southeast Asia: An Introductory History* (Sydney and Boston: Allen and Unwin, 1983), p. 12. While Anthony Reid highlights that the Chinese had for centuries recognized the Southeast Asian states as the 'Nanyang' (Southern Ocean) region, he also highlights that this was largely a Chinese construct and not a perception widely held within the region. Reid, *Southeast Asia in the Age of Commerce, 1450–1680*, p. 6.
7 Michael Leifer, *Dictionary of the Modern Politics of South-East Asia* (London: Routledge, 2001), p. 29.
8 Interview with Ali Alatas, former Indonesian Foreign Minister (Jakarta), 3 May 2006. Bunn Nagara, in interview, also argues that 'all these countries in the original

ASEAN had very different colonial histories, and because of this each of them knew their colonial master better than they knew each other'. Interview with Bunn Nagara, Kuala Lumpur, 30 May 2006. See also: Thanat Khoman, 'ASEAN Conception and Evolution', Association of Southeast Asian Nations, 1992, www.aseansec.org/thanat.htm.

9 David Chandler, William R. Roff, David Joel Steinberg, Jean Gelman Taylor, Robert H. Taylor, Alexander Woodside and David K. Wyatt, *The Emergence of Modern Southeast Asia: A New History*, ed. Norman G. Owen (Singapore: Singapore University Press, 2005), pp. 272–273.

10 Donald E. Weatherbee, *International Relations in Southeast Asia: The Struggle for Autonomy* (Lanham, MD: Rowman & Littlefield Publishers, 2005), p. 6.

11 Jurgen Haacke, *ASEAN's Diplomatic and Security Culture* (London and New York: RoutledgeCurzon, 2003), p. 31.

12 Peter Church, *A Short History of Southeast Asia* (Singapore: John Wiley & Sons (Asia), 2006), p. 50.

13 Weatherbee, *International Relations in Southeast Asia: The Struggle for Autonomy*, p. 6.

14 Kusuma Snitwongse, 'Thirty Years of ASEAN: Achievements through Political Cooperation', *The Pacific Review* 11, no. 2 (1998): p. 183, Michael R.J. Vatikiotis, 'ASEAN 10: The Political and Cultural Dimensions of Southeast Asian Unity', *Southeast Asian Journal of Social Science* 27, no. 1 (1999): p. 77.

15 The term 'ASEAN-5' refers to the original members of ASEAN: Singapore, Malaysia, Indonesia, Thailand, and the Philippines.

16 Shaun Narine, *Explaining ASEAN: Regionalism in Southeast Asia* (Boulder, CO: Lynne Rienner, 2002), p. 10.

17 Yuen Foong Khong, 'ASEAN and the Southeast Asian Security Complex', in *Regional Orders: Building Security in the New World*, ed. David A. Lake and Patrick M. Morgan (Pennsylvania: Pennsylvania State University Press, 1997), p. 322.

18 Mely Caballero-Anthony, *Regional Security in Southeast Asia: Beyond the ASEAN Way* (Singapore: ISEAS, 2005), p. 6.

19 'Countering Threats to Internal Stability and Security', Singapore Ministry of Home Affairs: Internal Security Department, http://www2.mha.gov.sg/mha/isd/newisd_earlyyears.html.

20 Church, *A Short History of Southeast Asia*, p. 96.

21 Christopher Roberts, *ASEAN's Myanmar Crisis: Challenges to the Pursuit of a Security community* (Singapore: ISEAS, 2010), p. 55.

22 Church, *A Short History of Southeast Asia*, p. 94.

23 William R. Heaton, 'China and Southeast Asian Communist Movements: The Decline of Dual Track Diplomacy', *Asian Survey* 22, no. 8 (1982): pp. 797–798, Sheldon W. Simon, 'The Two Southeast Asias and China: Security Perspectives', *Asian Survey* 24, no. 5 (1984): p. 522.

24 Weatherbee, *International Relations in Southeast Asia: The Struggle for Autonomy*, p. 66.

25 Narine, *Explaining ASEAN: Regionalism in Southeast Asia*, p. 13. On the role of the Australian forces in Malaya during the 'Emergency' period see Peter Dennis and Jeffrey Grey, *Emergency and Confrontation: Australian Military Operations in Malaya and Borneo 1950–1966* (St Leonards: Allen & Unwin in association with the Australian War Memorial, 1996).

26 Gary A. Fuller, Alexander B. Murphy, Mark A. Ridgeley, and Richard Ulack, 'Measuring Potential Ethnic Conflict in Southeast Asia', *Growth and Change* 31, no. 2 (2000): p. 307.

27 Alex J. Bellamy, *Security Communities and Their Neighbours: Regional Fortresses or Global Integrators?* (Basingstoke: Palgrave MacMillan, 2004), p. 93.

28 Haacke, *ASEAN's Diplomatic and Security Culture*, p. 49.
29 C.M. Turnbull, 'Regionalism and Nationalism', in *The Cambridge History of Southeast Asia: From World War II to the Present*, ed. Nicholas Tarling (Cambridge: Cambridge University Press, 2005), pp. 275–276.
30 Leifer, *Dictionary of the Modern Politics of South-East Asia*, p. 178.
31 Donald G. McCloud, *Southeast Asia: Tradition and Modernity in the Contemporary World* (Oxford: Westview Press, 1995), p. 15.
32 Khong, 'ASEAN and the Southeast Asian Security Complex', p. 323.
33 Weatherbee, *International Relations in Southeast Asia: The Struggle for Autonomy*, pp. 57–58.
34 Haacke, *ASEAN's Diplomatic and Security Culture*, pp. 32–33.
35 Turnbull, 'Regionalism and Nationalism', p. 276.
36 Indonesia was one of five founding members. N. Ganesan, 'Thai-Myanmar-ASEAN Relations: The Politics of Face and Grace', *Asian Affairs: An American Review* 33, no. 3 (2006): p. 134.
37 Weatherbee, *International Relations in Southeast Asia: The Struggle for Autonomy*, p. 62.
38 Turnbull, 'Regionalism and Nationalism', p. 277.
39 Bellamy, *Security Communities and Their Neighbours: Regional Fortresses or Global Integrators?*, p. 89.
40 Martin Wight, *Systems of States* (Leicester: Leicester University Press, 1977), pp. 150–152.
41 Robert H. Jackson and Patricia Owens, 'The Evolution of International Society', in *The Globalisation of World Politics: An Introduction to International Relations*, ed. John Baylis and Steve Smith (Oxford: Oxford University Press, 2006), p. 54.
42 Amitav Acharya, *Constructing a Security community in Southeast Asia: ASEAN and the Problem of Regional Order* (London: Routledge, 2001), p. 63.
43 'Asian-African Conference, Bandung – Final Communique', Oxford University Press, 1955, http://fds.oup.com/www.oup.co.uk/pdf/bt/cassese/cases/part3/ch18/1702.pdf.
44 Haacke, *ASEAN's Diplomatic and Security Culture*, p. 19. The emergence of these norms was by no means a natural phenomenon. For some Southeast Asian rulers, sovereignty was traditionally conceived as a 'divinely sanctioned right to rule the universe' by the 'ruler or god-king' and, therefore, the notion of sovereign equality was a completely alien concept. Ibid. See also Steedly, 'The State of Culture Theory in the Anthropology of Southeast Asia', pp. 435–436.
45 Amitav Acharya, 'Bandung's 1955 Asia–Africa Conference and Indonesia', The Jakarta Post, 2005, http://global.factiva.com.
46 David M. Jones and Michael Smith, *ASEAN and East Asian International Relations: Regional Delusion* (Northhampton, MA: Edward Elgar, 2006), pp. 71–73.
47 Carlyle A. Thayer, 'The Five Power Defence Arrangements', *Security Challenges* 3, no. 1 (2007): p. 80. See also Chin Kin Wah, *The Five Power Defence Arrangements and Amda: Some Observations on the Nature of an Evolving Partnership* (Singapore: ISEAS, 1974).
48 Khoo How San, 'The Five Power Defence Arrangements: If It Ain't Broke…' Ministry of Defence (MINDEF), 2006, www.mindef.gov.sg/safti/pointer/back/journals/2000/Vol. 26_4/7.htm.
49 'Spreading Sunshine?', *Time*, 26 June 1972.
50 'A New Alliance, and More Help for Viet-Nam', *Time*, 24 June 1966.
51 Mya Than, *Myanmar in ASEAN: Regional Cooperation Experience* (Singapore: Institute of Southeast Asian Studies, 2005), p. 12.
52 Narine, *Explaining ASEAN: Regionalism in Southeast Asia*, p. 11.
53 Haacke, *ASEAN's Diplomatic and Security Culture*, p. 35.
54 As Joseph Liow states, '[c]entral to Jakarta's reaction to the Tunku's foreign policy initiatives was their dislike of what they saw as a newcomer taking the initiative in

an area where they considered themselves as rightful leaders; they also resented the fact that Malayan leaders could declare themselves to be 'neutral' while in effect showing benevolence to the West'. Joseph Chinyong Liow, 'Tunku Abdul Rahman and Malaya's Relations with Indonesia, 1957–1960', *Journal of Southeast Asian Studies* 36, no. 1 (2005): p. 101.

55 Arnfinn Jorgensen-Dahl, *Regional Organisation and Order in South-East Asia* (Basingstoke and London: Macmillan, 1982), p. 15.

56 Turnbull, 'Regionalism and Nationalism', p. 287.

57 'Thailand's Role in ASEAN: Historical Background', Thailand's Foreign Ministry, 2001, www.mfa.go.th/asean/thai/history.html.

58 Matthew Jones, *Conflict and Confrontation in Southeast Asia: 1961–1965* (Cambridge: Cambridge University Press, 2002), p. 158.

59 Weatherbee, *International Relations in Southeast Asia: The Struggle for Autonomy*, p. 69.

60 Ibid., pp. 65–66.

61 Ralf Emmers, *Cooperative Security and the Balance of Power in ASEAN and the ARF* (London and New York: RoutledgeCurzon, 2003), p. 11.

62 Turnbull, 'Regionalism and Nationalism', p. 285.

63 Jones, *Conflict and Confrontation in Southeast Asia: 1961–1965*, pp. 125–127.

64 These outcomes contradict Indonesia's policy of 'regional resilience' as outlined later.

65 James Cotton, 'The Domestic Sources of Regional Order in Michael Leifer's Analysis of Southeast Asia', in *Order and Security in Southeast Asia: Essays in Memory of Michael Leifer*, ed. Joseph Chinyong Liow and Ralf Emmers (London: Routledge, 2006), p. 211.

66 Turnbull, 'Regionalism and Nationalism', p. 285.

67 Alan Collins, *Security and Southeast Asia: Domestic, Regional, and Global Issues* (Boulder, CO: Lynne Rienner, 2003), p. 128.

68 Bellamy, *Security Communities and Their Neighbours: Regional Fortresses or Global Integrators?*, p. 92. See also Caballero-Anthony, *Regional Security in Southeast Asia: Beyond the ASEAN Way*, p. 53.

69 Weatherbee, *International Relations in Southeast Asia: The Struggle for Autonomy*, p. 69.

70 Michael Leifer, *Indonesia's Foreign Policy* (London: Allen & Unwin/Royal Institute of International Affairs, 1983), p. 99.

71 Michael Antolik, *ASEAN and the Diplomacy of Accommodation* (Armonke, NY: M.E. Sharpe, 1990), p. 19.

72 J.A.C. Mackie, *Konfrontasi: The Indonesia–Malaysia Dispute* (Kuala Lumpur, New York: Oxford University Press, 1974), pp. 256–260.

73 Ibid., pp. 256–260, 269.

74 The Philippines thought that this would be more acceptable to Sukarno because it provided an 'Asian solution to Asian problems' without the suspicions of a 'made in Washington' label that had been generated by Maphilindo. Further, and in the opinion of the Philippines, Malaysia could also be confident that the dispute would be resolved under the principles of consultation and by neutral participants. Ibid., pp. 269–270.

75 Mary Somers Heidhues, *Southeast Asia: A Concise History* (London: Thames and Hudson, 2000), p. 156.

76 Jurgen Haacke, '"Enhanced Interaction" with Myanmar and the Project of a Security community: Is ASEAN Refining or Breaking with its Diplomatic and Security Culture?', *Contemporary Southeast Asia* 27, no. 2 (2005): p. 42.

77 Karl Metcalf, 'Near Neighbours: Records on Australia's Relations with Indonesia', National Archives of Australia, 2001, www.naa.gov.au/Publications/research_guides/guides/neighbours/chapter1.htm.

78 Turnbull, 'Regionalism and Nationalism', p. 285. Sukarno died three years later on 21 June 1970.
79 'Foreign Relations 1964–1968, Volume Xxvi, Indonesia; Malaysia-Singapore; Philippines', U.S. Department of State, 1968, www.state.gov/r/pa/ho/frus/johnsonlb/xxvi/4433.htm. See also Dennis and Grey, *Emergency and Confrontation: Australian Military Operations in Malaya and Borneo 1950–1966*, p. 318.
80 Haacke, '"Enhanced Interaction" with Myanmar and the Project of a Security community: Is ASEAN Refining or Breaking with its Diplomatic and Security Culture?', p. 42.
81 'The Founding of ASEAN', ASEAN Secretariat, www.aseansec.org/7071.htm. For an alternative interpretation see: Santha Oorjitham, 'Being There: An ASEAN Architect Looks Back and Ahead', AsiaWeek, 1997, http://edition.cnn.com/ASIANOW/asiaweek/97/1212/cs3.html.
82 Emmers, *Cooperative Security and the Balance of Power in ASEAN and the ARF*, p. 12.
83 Narine, *Explaining ASEAN: Regionalism in Southeast Asia*, p. 13.
84 Jorgensen-Dahl, *Regional Organisation and Order in South-East Asia*, p. 36.
85 Narine, *Explaining ASEAN: Regionalism in Southeast Asia*, pp. 13–14.
86 'The ASEAN Declaration', ASEAN Secretariat, 1967, www.aseansec.org/1212.htm.
87 Ibid, pp. 42–43, Narine, *Explaining ASEAN: Regionalism in Southeast Asia*, p. 12.
88 Michael Leifer, *ASEAN and the Security of Southeast Asia* (London: Routledge, 1989), p. 24.
89 Emmers, *Cooperative Security and the Balance of Power in ASEAN and the ARF*, p. 13.
90 Turnbull, 'Regionalism and Nationalism', p. 288.
91 Haacke, *ASEAN's Diplomatic and Security Culture*, pp. 45–46.
92 For a detailed analysis of the event see Albert Lau, *A Moment of Anguish: Singapore in Malaysia and the Politics of Disengagement* (Singapore: Times Academic Press, 1998).
93 Leifer, *ASEAN and the Security of Southeast Asia*, pp. 17–18.
94 As Adam Malik also reflects, 'considerations of national and regional security ... figured largely in the minds of the founders of ASEAN'. Adam Malik, 'Regional Cooperation in International Politics', in *Regionalism in Southeast Asia: Papers Presented at the First Conference of ASEAN Students of Regional Affairs (ASEAN 1) Jakarta, October 22–25, 1974* (Jakarta: Centre for Strategic and International Studies, 1975), p. 162.
95 'The ASEAN Declaration.'
96 Ibid.
97 Emmers, *Cooperative Security and the Balance of Power in ASEAN and the ARF*, pp. 69–70.
98 Weatherbee, *International Relations in Southeast Asia: The Struggle for Autonomy*, p. 70.
99 Emmers, *Cooperative Security and the Balance of Power in ASEAN and the ARF*, p. 14.
100 Ralf Emmers, 'Regional Hegemonies and the Exercise of Power in Southeast Asia: A Study of Indonesia and Vietnam', *Asian Survey* 45, no. 4 (2005): p. 650.
101 Snitwongse, 'Thirty Years of ASEAN: Achievements through Political Cooperation', p. 183.
102 Vatikiotis, 'ASEAN 10: The Political and Cultural Dimensions of Southeast Asian Unity', p. 80.
103 Interview with the Directorate of Public Diplomacy, Ministry of Foreign Affairs, Jakarta, 26 April 2006.
104 Interview with MINDEF, Singapore, 27 July 2006.
105 Interview with Bunn Nagara, Kuala Lumpur, Tuesday 30 May 2006.

106 Weatherbee, *International Relations in Southeast Asia: The Struggle for Autonomy*, p. 68.
107 Leifer, *ASEAN and the Security of Southeast Asia*, p. 6.
108 Khong, 'ASEAN and the Southeast Asian Security Complex', p. 328.
109 Ibid., p. 325.
110 Marites Danguilan Vitug and Glenda M. Gloria, *Under the Crescent Moon: Rebellion in Mindanao* (Quezon City: Ateneo Center for Social Policy and Public Affairs, Institute for Popular Democracy, 1990), p. 97.
111 Andrew Tan, 'Intra-ASEAN Tensions', (London: Royal Institute of International Affairs, 2000), p. 27.
112 Emmers, *Cooperative Security and the Balance of Power in ASEAN and the ARF*, p. 16.
113 Narine, *Explaining ASEAN: Regionalism in Southeast Asia*, p. 19.
114 For example, in 2009 the Sulu Sultan reportedly said that he would 'assert his property rights over Sabah' and that he had entered into agreements with foreign companies to develop Sabah. 'Sulu Sultan Asserts Rights over Sabah', *Philippine Daily Inquirer*, 1 February 2009. In 2008, a member of Malaysia's parliament in Sabah asked why the Philippines had not dropped its claim to Sabah and in 2005 the Philippine government announced that it was planning to pursue its claim on Sabah in the International Court of Justice. 'RP Eyes Sabah Claim Revival', *Manila Standard*, 17 February 2005, 'Mp Asks Why Philippines Has Not Dropped Claim to Sabah', *Bernama Daily*, 27 May 2008.
115 'The ASEAN Declaration.'
116 Lau Teik Soon cited in Haacke, *ASEAN's Diplomatic and Security Culture*, p. 47.
117 N. Ganesan, *Bilateral Tensions in Post-Cold War ASEAN*, Pacific Strategic Papers (Singapore: Institute of Southeast Asia Studies, 1999), pp. 38–39, K.S. Nathan, 'Malaysia-Singapore Relations: Retrospect and Prospect', *Contemporary Southeast Asia* 24, no. 2 (2002): pp. 388–392, Tan, 'Intra-ASEAN Tensions', p. 10.
118 Ganesan, *Bilateral Tensions in Post-Cold War ASEAN*, p. 37.
119 Lee Kuan Yew, *The Singapore Story: Memoirs of Lee Kuan Yew* (Singapore: Times Editions, 1998), p. 23.
120 Turnbull, 'Regionalism and Nationalism', p. 287.
121 For example, a Deputy Vice Chancellor of one Malaysian university stated in relation to his perception of Singaporean government attitudes: '[the Singaporeans] must get what Malaysia is getting, this is the problem with the attitude … this is the *kiasu* mentality'. Interview by author, Malaysia, Friday 2 June 2006.
122 At another point in the interview the scholar stated 'they [Singapore] have this defence plan, you know, forward defence into Southern Malaysia, you have read about this right. And their idea of coming in would be to take things like water, you know probably as a resource, or if there is a Muslim government in Kuala Lumpur which is considered to be hostile to Singapore. It's that kind of thinking, I think no other country, in Southeast Asia, has any such defence plan … they have all these Israeli advisors, and all that which would bring this Israeli kind of mentality to them, like threat[s] everywhere … so that's why so many of them go through this military [training]. You know, even if they are in civilian life, all of them have to go through this national service, so they have this very strong military inclined way of thinking, even among the civilian government, and academia and all that, and they attract these kind of people who are inclined towards a rather, how should I put it, Christiangerian, Machiavellian, kind of thinking'. Interview with Senior Scholar, *ISIS Malaysia* (Kuala Lumpur, Malaysia), 13 December 2001. In response to this kind of sentiment, a former member of the PAP and Secret Police responds, 'so, of course, when the former Indonesian president, Habibie, calls us little red dots and the Malaysians try to threaten our water, that is for Singapore evidence that it must maintain a realist mode of thinking about the world'. Interview with Retired Singapore Official, Singapore, 5 December 2001.

123 Tun Razak and later Hussein Onn assumed the Premiership in Malaysia. Haacke, *ASEAN's Diplomatic and Security Culture*, pp. 47–48.
124 Narine, *Explaining ASEAN: Regionalism in Southeast Asia*, p. 19.
125 Weatherbee, *International Relations in Southeast Asia: The Struggle for Autonomy*, p. 70.
126 Interview with M.C. Abad, *ASEAN Secretariat* (Jakarta), 20 April 2006.
127 Sheldon W. Simon, *Asian Armed Forces: Internal and External Tasks and Capabilities* (Washington: The National Bureau of Asian Research, 2000), pp. 8, 19.
128 Jeannie Henderson, *Reassessing ASEAN* (London: The International Institute for Strategic Studies, 1999), p. 17. See also Narine, *Explaining ASEAN: Regionalism in Southeast Asia*, p. 19.
129 'Declaration of the Zone of Peace, Freedom and Neutrality', ASEAN Secretariat, 1971, www.aseansec.org/3629.htm.
130 Sheldon W. Simon, 'China, Vietnam, and ASEAN: The Politics of Polarization', *Asian Survey* 19, no. 12 (1979): p. 1172.
131 'Declaration of the Zone of Peace, Freedom and Neutrality.'
132 Leifer, *Dictionary of the Modern Politics of South-East Asia*, p. 199.
133 Acharya, *The Quest for Identity: International Relations of Southeast Asia*, pp. 110–111.
134 Collins, *Security and Southeast Asia: Domestic, Regional, and Global Issues*, pp. 129–130.
135 Markus Hund, 'The Development of ASEAN Norms between 1997 and 2000: A Paradigm Shift?', Centre for East Asian and Pacific Studies, Occasional Paper, no. 15, University of Trier, 2001, www.zops.uni-trier.de/op/OccasionalPapersNr15.pdf.
136 Emmers, *Cooperative Security and the Balance of Power in ASEAN and the ARF*, p. 15.
137 Donald E. Weatherbee, *International Relations in Southeast Asia: The Struggle for Regional Autonomy*, 2nd edn (Rowman and Littlefield: Plymouth, 2009), p. 73.
138 Narine, *Explaining ASEAN: Regionalism in Southeast Asia*, p. 15.
139 As Tun Abdul Razak then declared at the inaugural meeting of ASEAN, the 'vacuum left by the retreat of colonial rule must be filled by the growth and consideration of indigenous powers – otherwise our future, individually and jointly, will remain dangerously threatened'. Emmers, *Cooperative Security and the Balance of Power in ASEAN and the ARF*, p. 15.
140 Narine, *Explaining ASEAN: Regionalism in Southeast Asia*, p. 15.
141 Collins, *Security and Southeast Asia: Domestic, Regional, and Global Issues*, p. 128.

3 ASEAN through to the third decade: institutional responses and expansion

1 Shaun Narine, *Explaining ASEAN: Regionalism in Southeast Asia* (Boulder, CO: Lynne Rienner, 2002), p. 23.
2 'Joint Communique of the Seventh ASEAN Ministerial Meeting (Jakarta)', ASEAN Secretariat, 1974, www.aseansec.org/1237.htm.
3 James Cotton, *Crossing Borders in the Asia-Pacific: Essays on the Domestic-Foreign Policy Divide* (New York: Nova Science Publishers, 2002), p. 31.
4 'Declaration of ASEAN Concord', ASEAN Secretariat, 1976, www.aseansec.org/1649.htm.
5 Ibid.
6 Ralf Emmers, *Cooperative Security and the Balance of Power in ASEAN and the ARF* (London and New York: RoutledgeCurzon, 2003), p. 18.
7 Alex J. Bellamy, *Security Communities and Their Neighbours: Regional Fortresses or Global Integrators?* (Basingstoke: Palgrave MacMillan, 2004), p. 95.
8 'Treaty of Amity and Cooperation in Southeast Asia', ASEAN Secretariat, 1976, www.aseansec.org/1217.htm.

9 Ibid.

10 Jeannie Henderson, *Reassessing ASEAN* (London: The International Institute for Strategic Studies, 1999), p. 19.

11 Jurgen Haacke, *ASEAN's Diplomatic and Security Culture* (London and New York: RoutledgeCurzon, 2003), p. 39.

12 Ralf Emmers, 'The Indochinese Enlargement of ASEAN: Security Expectations and Outcomes', *Australian Journal of International Affairs* 59, no. 1 (2005): p. 72.

13 Narine, *Explaining ASEAN: Regionalism in Southeast Asia*, p. 40.

14 Sheldon W. Simon, 'China, Vietnam, and ASEAN: The Politics of Polarization', *Asian Survey* 19, no. 12 (1979): p. 1172.

15 Emphasis by author. Hentry Kamm, 'Concept of a Zone of Peace, Freedom and Neutrality (ZOPFAN), Originally Shunned by Communist Nations in Asia, Now Is Being Approved by China, Vietnam and the USSR', *New York Times*, 22 September 1978.

16 Ramses Amer, 'Regional Integration and Conflict Management. The Case of Vietnam', *Asia Europe Journal* 2, no. 4 (2004): p. 534.

17 Michael Leifer, *ASEAN and the Security of Southeast Asia* (London: Routledge, 1989), p. 85.

18 In relation to ASEAN, Carl Thayer contends that it was 'a sign of its growing political maturity … [that] ASEAN coordinated its response to Dong's visit, presented a united front, and collectively agreed to individually decline the offer of a non-aggression treaty'. Carlyle A. Thayer, 'ASEAN and Indochina: The Dialogue', in *ASEAN in the 1990s*, ed. Alison Broinowski (London: Macmillan, 1990), pp. 146–147.

19 'Joint Statement: The Special ASEAN Foreign Ministers Meeting on the Current Political Development in the Southeast Asia Region (Bangkok)', ASEAN Secretariat, 1979, www.aseansec.org/1257.htm.

20 Thus, it was no coincidence that Vietnam had formalized its alignment with the Soviet Union with the signing of the Treaty of Friendship and Cooperation on 3 November 1978 and later supported the establishment of the exiled Kampuchean National United Front for National Salvation that challenged the Pol Pot regime. Ralf Emmers, 'Security Cooperation in the Asia-Pacific: Evolution of Concepts and Practices', in *Asia-Pacific Security Cooperation: National Interests and Regional Order*, ed. See Seng Tan and Amitav Acharya (Armonk: M.E. Sharpe, 2004), p. 90.

21 Emmers, *Cooperative Security and the Balance of Power in ASEAN and the ARF*, p. 89.

22 While the Vietnamese government did not declare this as a motivation (in part or in whole) for its occupation of Cambodia (then Kampuchea), by 1979 the government did increasingly raise the issue of genocide for the purpose of arguing that the former Cambodian government had relinquished its moral right to rule. Vietnam further argued, somewhat less convincingly, that what was taking place within Cambodia was 'in fact' a revolutionary civil war against such a despotic and genocidal regime. Pao-Min Chang, 'Beijing Versus Hanoi: The Diplomacy over Kampuchea', *Asian Survey* 23, no. 5 (1983): p. 607.

23 Amitav Acharya, *Constructing a Security community in Southeast Asia: ASEAN and the Problem of Regional Order* (London: Routledge, 2001), p. 58.

24 Amer, 'Regional Integration and Conflict Management. The Case of Vietnam', p. 535.

25 Henderson, *Reassessing ASEAN*, p. 305.

26 Leifer, *ASEAN and the Security of Southeast Asia*, pp. viii, 83, 152.

27 Ibid, pp. 89–90.

28 Donald E. Weatherbee, *International Relations in Southeast Asia: The Struggle for Autonomy* (Lanham, MD: Rowman & Littlefield Publishers, 2005), p. 79.

29 Leifer, *ASEAN and the Security of Southeast Asia*, p. 107.

30 Vietnam claims that more than 20,000 Chinese were killed during the conflict. Further, military aid from the Soviet Union at the time meant that the Vietnamese military was superior in terms of logistics and weaponry. For example, fewer than 100,000 Vietnamese soldiers contained 200,000 Chinese troops. Grant Evans and Kelvin Rowley, *Red Brotherhood at War: Vietnam, Cambodia and Laos since 1975* (London: Verso, 1990), pp. 115–117.
31 Weatherbee, *International Relations in Southeast Asia: The Struggle for Autonomy*, p. 79.
32 Justus M. van der Kroef, 'ASEAN, Hanoi, and the Kampuchean Conflict: Between "Kuantan" and a "Third Alternative" ', *Asian Survey* 21, no. 5 (1981): p. 516.
33 Acharya, *Constructing a Security community in Southeast Asia: ASEAN and the Problem of Regional Order*, pp. 84–85.
34 'Joint Communique of the Thirteenth ASEAN Ministerial Meeting (Kuala Lumpur)', ASEAN Secretariat, 1980, www.aseansec.org/3679.htm.
35 Leifer, *ASEAN and the Security of Southeast Asia*, p. 127.
36 Acharya, *Constructing a Security community in Southeast Asia: ASEAN and the Problem of Regional Order*, p. 88.
37 Narine, *Explaining ASEAN: Regionalism in Southeast Asia*, p. 52.
38 Ibid., p. 53. Cf. Haacke, *ASEAN's Diplomatic and Security Culture*, pp. 93–110.
39 Khoo How San, 'ASEAN on Myanmar: Creative Damage Control', *Asia Times*, 2004, www.atimes.com/atimes/Southeast_Asia?EF27Ae04.html.
40 Emmers, *Cooperative Security and the Balance of Power in ASEAN and the ARF*, p. 106.
41 Kroef, 'ASEAN, Hanoi, and the Kampuchean Conflict: Between "Kuantan" and a "Third Alternative" ', p. 528.
42 Weatherbee, *International Relations in Southeast Asia: The Struggle for Autonomy*, p. 82.
43 'Singapore Declaration', ASEAN Secretariat, 1992, www.aseansec.org/5120.htm.
44 'Declaration of the Zone of Peace, Freedom and Neutrality', ASEAN Secretariat, 1971, www.aseansec.org/3629.htm.
45 'Treaty on the Southeast Asia Nuclear Weapon-Free Zone (Bangkok)', ASEAN Secretariat, 1995, www.aseansec.org/3636.htm.
46 Leifer, *ASEAN and the Security of Southeast Asia*, p. 255.
47 However, in recent years there has been some debatable evidence to suggest that Myanmar may have embarked on a nuclear weapons program.
48 The date for implementation by the ASEAN-6 (Singapore, Malaysia, Thailand, Indonesia, the Philippines and Brunei) was later advanced to 2003 and then to 2002.
49 Nattapong Thongpakde, 'ASEAN Free Trade Area: Progress and Challenges', in *ASEAN Beyond the Regional Crisis*, ed. Mya Than (Singapore: Institute of Southeast Asian Studies, 2001), p. 49. On the latter initiatives see Mya Than, *Myanmar in ASEAN: Regional Cooperation Experience* (Singapore: Institute of Southeast Asian Studies, 2005), pp. 26–29.
50 Weatherbee, *International Relations in Southeast Asia: The Struggle for Autonomy*, p. 96.
51 Consequently, and as a former Secretary-General to ASEAN writes: 'Wags had tagged it acerbically as "a caucus without Caucasians".' Rodolfo C. Severino, *Southeast Asia in Search of an ASEAN Community: Insights from the Former Secretary-General* (Singapore: Institute of Southeast Asian Studies, 2006), p. 266. An alternative retort was 'East Asia Except Caucasians'. Wolfgang Pape, *East Asia by the Year 2000 and Beyond: Shaping Factors* (New York: RoutledgeCurzon, 2000), p. 20.
52 For example, in November 1993, Malaysia's Prime Minister, Mahathir Mohamed, boycotted an informal summit meeting that had been arranged at the behest of US President Bill Clinton. This then led to a spat between the Malaysian and

Australian governments over a remark by the Australian Prime Minister, Paul Keating, that the Malaysian leader was recalcitrant for not attending the summit. Philip Bowring, 'A Spat for the Neighborhood to Watch', *International Herald Tribune*, 8 December 1993.

53 Michael Leifer, *Dictionary of the Modern Politics of South-East Asia* (London: Routledge, 2001), p. 109.

54 As the text of the AMM's communiqué states, *inter alia*, 'the Foreign Ministers consider that the ASEAN Economic Ministers Meeting (AEM) would be the appropriate body to provide support and direction for the EAEC, taking into account that the prospective members of EAEC are also members of APEC. Pursuant on this, the Foreign Ministers agreed that the EAEC is a caucus within APEC', 'Joint Communiqué of the Twenty-Sixth ASEAN Ministerial Meeting (Singapore)', ASEAN Secretariat, 1993, www.aseansec.org/3666.htm, Termsak Chalermpalanupap, 'Towards and East Asia Community: The Journey Has Begun', Association of Southeast Asian Nations, 2002, www.aseansec.org/13202.htm.

55 Donald E. Weatherbee, *International Relations in Southeast Asia: The Struggle for Regional Autonomy*, 2nd edn (Plymouth: Rowman and Littlefield, 2009), p. 209.

56 Than, *Myanmar in ASEAN: Regional Cooperation Experience*, p. 17.

57 Leifer, *ASEAN and the Security of Southeast Asia*, p. 152.

58 Emmers, *Cooperative Security and the Balance of Power in ASEAN and the ARF*, p. 24, Narine, *Explaining ASEAN: Regionalism in Southeast Asia.*

59 Aung Zaw, David Arnott, Kavi Chongkittavorn, Zunetta Liddell, Kaiser Morshed, Soe Myint, and Thin Thin Aung, 'Challenges to Democratization in Burma: Perspectives on Multilateral and Bilateral Responses', (Ottawa, Canada: International Institute for Democracy and Electoral Assistance, 2001), p. 39.

60 Emphasis by author. Kusuma Snitwongse, 'Thirty Years of ASEAN: Achievements through Political Cooperation', *The Pacific Review* 11, no. 2 (1998): p. 191.

61 Following a 1962 rebellion in Brunei, Malaysia had provided refuge for key leaders behind the rebellion whilst remaining publicly outspoken over Brunei's undemocratic system of government along with its continued reliance on Britain for security. C.M. Turnbull, 'Regionalism and Nationalism', in *The Cambridge History of Southeast Asia: From World War II to the Present*, ed. Nicholas Tarling (Cambridge: Cambridge University Press, 2005), p. 306.

62 Carolyn L. Gates, 'The ASEAN Economic Model and Vietnam's Economic Transformation: Adjustment, Adaption, and Convergence', in *ASEAN Enlargement: Impacts and Insights*, ed. Mya Than and Carolyn L. Gates (Singapore: ISEAS, 2001), pp. 322–323.

63 Bellamy, *Security Communities and Their Neighbours: Regional Fortresses or Global Integrators?*, p. 113.

64 David Chandler, William R. Roff, David Joel Steinberg, Jean Gelman Taylor, Robert H. Taylor, Alexander Woodside and David K. Wyatt, *The Emergence of Modern Southeast Asia: A New History*, ed. Norman G. Owen (Singapore: Singapore University Press, 2005), pp. 495–496.

65 Shaun Narine, 'ASEAN and the ARF: The Limits of the ASEAN Way', *Asian Survey* 37, no. 10 (1997): p. 117.

66 The surprise attack resulted in more than a hundred FUNCIPEC and security officials being killed. Chandler *et al.*, *The Emergence of Modern Southeast Asia: A New History*, p. 490. Further, Shaun Narine claims that until the 'public embarrassment' of the coup some of the ASEAN members were not particularly concerned about developments in the country as, either way, both of Cambodia's political parties had demonstrated their willingness to 'assist ASEAN businesses in getting licenses to exploit timber, textile manufacturing, and tourism, and they may even have facilitated illegal trade in weapons, drugs, and prostitution'. Narine, 'ASEAN and the ARF: The Limits of the ASEAN Way', p. 117.

67 Alan Collins, *Security and Southeast Asia: Domestic, Regional, and Global Issues* (Boulder, CO: Lynne Rienner, 2003), p. 145.
68 Narine, *Explaining ASEAN: Regionalism in Southeast Asia*, p. 118. In January 1998 Hun Sen added, 'other things, like economics, they can teach us, but on the subject of democracy and human rights, they must not teach us'. Sorpong Peou, 'Diplomatic Pragmatism: ASEAN's Response to the July 1997 Coup', Concilliation Resources, 1998, www.c-r.org/our-work/accord/cambodia/diplomatic-pragmatism.php.
69 Ibid.
70 On the issue of corruption the same interviewee stated, 'Corruption is in any country that is poor. You cannot live anywhere that is corrupt and live among corrupt leaders and not be corrupt yourself. A certain amount of corruption is ok as long as the country moves forward'. Interview with Chap Sotharith, Director CICP, Phnom Penh, 25 July 2005.
71 'Burma Prime Minister Arrives in Jakarta', *Reuters*, 29 June 1987.
72 Zaw *et al.*, 'Challenges to Democratization in Burma: Perspectives on Multilateral and Bilateral Responses', p. 38.
73 Derek Da Cunha, 'Renewed Military Buildups Post-Asian Crisis: The Effect on Two Key Southeast Asian Bilateral Military Balances', ISEAS, 2001, www.iseas.edu.sg/ipsi32001.pdf.
74 Mya Than and Tin Maung Maung Than, 'ASEAN Enlargement and Myanmar', in *ASEAN Enlargement: Impacts and Implications*, ed. Mya Than and Carolyn L. Gates (Singapore: Institute of Southeast Asian Studies, 2001), p. 252.
75 Interview with General Jose Almonte, *Former Presidential Advisor to Ramos* (Manila), 16 November 2005.
76 Ibid.
77 Gates, 'The ASEAN Economic Model and Vietnam's Economic Transformation: Adjustment, Adaption, and Convergence', p. 4.
78 Weatherbee, *International Relations in Southeast Asia: The Struggle for Autonomy*, p. 92.
79 Narine, *Explaining ASEAN: Regionalism in Southeast Asia*, p. 121.
80 Weatherbee, *International Relations in Southeast Asia: The Struggle for Autonomy*, p. 92.
81 Michael Leifer, 'The Political and Security Outlook for Southeast Asia' (paper presented at the 2000 Regional Outlook Forum, Singapore, January 2000), pp. 2–4.
82 Carolyn L. Gates and Mya Than, 'ASEAN Enlargement: An Introductory Overview', in *ASEAN Enlargement: Impacts and Implications*, ed. Mya Than and Carolyn L. Gates (Singapore: ISEAS, 2001), p. 11.
83 Weatherbee, *International Relations in Southeast Asia: The Struggle for Autonomy*, p. 100, 'Chairman's Press Statement for the ASEAN Post Ministerial Conferences (Kuala Lumpur)', ASEAN Secretariat, 2006, www.aseansec.org/18593.htm.
84 Moreover, by 2008 ASEM membership was formally enlarged to 45 countries. 'The ASEM Process', European Commission External Relations, 2010, http://ec.europa.eu/external_relations/asem/process/index_en.htm.
85 Yang Razali Kassim, 'Plan for Political, Security Dialogue Wins Support', *Business Times Singapore*, 24 July 1991.
86 Narine, *Explaining ASEAN: Regionalism in Southeast Asia*, p. 102.
87 Michael Leifer, *The ASEAN Regional Forum: A Model for Cooperative Security in the Middle East* (Canberra: Department of International Relations, ANU, 1998), p. 1.
88 Evelyn Goh, 'The ASEAN Regional Forum in the United States East Asian Strategy', *The Pacific Review* 17, no. 1 (2004): p. 47.
89 Jim Rolfe, 'Regional Security for the Asia-Pacific: Ends and Means', *Contemporary Southeast Asia* 30, no. 1 (2008): p. 100.
90 Kalimullah Hassan, 'Support for ASEAN Security Forum Plan', *The Straits Times*, 23 July 1991.

91 Yang Razali Kassim, 'Dialogue Partners Call for Forum on Regional Security', *Business Times Singapore*, 23 July 1991.
92 Michael Antolik, 'The ASEAN Regional Forum: The Spirit of Constructive Engagement', *Contemporary Southeast Asia* 16, no. 2 (1994): p. 120.
93 Statement by Philippines Foreign Secretary Raul Manglapus. See Kalimullah Hassan, 'ASEAN "Yes" to Talks on Regional Security', *Straits Times*, 24 July 1991.
94 'Chairman's Statement: The First Meeting of the ASEAN Regional Forum (Bangkok)', ASEAN Regional Forum, 1994, https://www.aseanregionalforum.org/PublicLibrary/ARFChairmansStatementsandReports/ChairmansStatementofthe1st-MeetingoftheASE/tabid/201/Default.aspx.
95 Paul Evans, 'Possibilities for Security Cooperation in the Asia-Pacific: Track 2 and Track 1', Pacific Symposium, 2001, www.ndu.edu/inss/symposia/pacific2001/evanspaper.htm, Michael Leifer, *The ASEAN Regional Forum* (London: The International Institute for Strategic Studies, 1996), p. 53.
96 Thailand's Deputy Foreign Minister, for example, pointedly declared that 'ASEAN will always have the driver's seat'. Meanwhile, Singapore's Foreign Minister, Shanmugam Jayakumar, contended that 'the process whereby ASEAN has developed gives valuable lessons for us when we [ASEAN] steer the ARF in subsequent years'. Leifer, *The ASEAN Regional Forum*, p. 36.
97 'The ASEAN Regional Forum: A Concept Paper', ASEAN Secretariat, 1995, www.aseansec.org/3693.htm.
98 This includes an abortive proposal by the Australian Prime Minister, Kevin Rudd, to establish an Asia Pacific Community. Andrew Carr and Christopher Roberts, 'Foreign Policy', in *The Rudd Government*, ed. Chris Aulich (Canberra: ANU, 2010).
99 'The ASEAN Regional Forum: A Concept Paper.'
100 Jorn Dosch, *PMC, ARF and CSCAP: Foundations for a Security Architecture in the Asia-Pacific* (Canberra: Strategic and Defence Studies Centre, 1997), p. 2.
101 'Confidence and Security Building Measures: ASEAN Regional Forum (ARF)', Bureau of Political-Military Affairs, 2000, www.state.gov/wwww/global/arms/bureau_pm/csbm/fs_000626_arf.html.
102 Dana R Dillon, 'Contemporary Security Challenges in Southeast Asia', Parameters, 1997, http://ptg.djnr.com.
103 'ASEAN Regional Forum (ARF)', Foreign Affairs and Trade: International Security Division, 2001, www.dfat.gov.au/arf/.
104 'Chairman's Statement: The Second Meeting of the ASEAN Regional Forum (Brunei Darussalam, 1 August 1995)', Association of Southeast Asian Nations, 1995, https://www.aseanregionalforum.org.
105 Narine, *Explaining ASEAN: Regionalism in Southeast Asia*, p. 106.
106 Ibid., p. 112.
107 Paul Dibb, 'Confidence Comes from Cooperation', *The Australian*, 5 June 2002. This issue was also raised by Stephen Leong. Interview with Stephen Leong, Deputy Director, *ISIS-Malaysia* (Kuala Lumpur), 13 December 2001.
108 'Joint Press Release of the Inaugural ASEAN Defence Ministers' Meeting (Kuala Lumpur, 9 May 2006)', Association of Southeast Asian Nations, 2006, www.aseansec.org/18414.htm.
109 Barry Desker, 'Is the ARF Obsolete? Three Moves to Avoid Irrelevance', Institute of Defence and Strategic Studies, 2006, www.rsis.edu.sg/publications/Perspective/IDSS0652006.pdf.
110 Tsuyoshi Kawasaki, 'Neither Skepticism nor Romanticism: The ASEAN Regional Forum as a Solution for the Asia-Pacific Assurance Game', *The Pacific Review* 19, no. 2 (2006): p. 224.
111 *The ASEAN Experience: Insights for Regional Political Cooperation* (Geneva, Switzerland: South Centre, 2007), p. 14, Dibb, 'Confidence Comes from Cooperation',

John Garofano, 'Power, Institutions, and the ASEAN Regional Forum: A Security community for Asia', *Asian Survey* 42, no. 3 (2002): p. 502.

112 Henderson, *Reassessing ASEAN*, p. 71.

113 David M. Jones and Michael Smith, 'The Changing Security Agenda in Southeast Asia: Globalization, New Terror, and the Delusions of Regionalism', *Studies in Conflict and Terrorism* 24 (2001): pp. 279–83, Shigekatsu Kondo, *East Asian Strategic Review* (Tokyo: National Institute for Defence Studies, 2000), pp. 32–34.

114 Cotton, *Crossing Borders in the Asia-Pacific: Essays on the Domestic-Foreign Policy Divide*, p. 33.

115 Performance legitimacy was a term originally coined by Amitav Acharya. See Amitav Acharya, 'Transnational Production and Security: Southeast Asia's "Growth Triangles"', *Contemporary Southeast Asia* 17, no. 12 (1995): p. 260.

116 Cotton, *Crossing Borders in the Asia-Pacific: Essays on the Domestic-Foreign Policy Divide*, p. 31.

117 Mark Beeson, 'ASEAN's Ways: Still Fit for Purpose?', *Cambridge Review of International Affairs* 22, no. 3 (2009): p. 337.

4 Testing ASEAN cohesion: security and economic challenges

1 *Conflict Barometer 2009* (Heidelberg: Heidelberg Institute for International Conflict Research, 2010), pp. 1, 51.

2 Milton Osborne, 'Temple of Gloom – Thai–Cambodian Relations Deteriorate', *Jane's Intelligence Review*, 9 December 2009.

3 Sokbunthoeun So, 'The Cambodia–Thailand Conflict: A Test for ASEAN', *East–West Center Asia Pacific Bulletin*, 10 December 2009.

4 Osborne, 'Temple of Gloom – Thai–Cambodian Relations Deteriorate.'

5 'Cambodian, Thai Troops in Shoot-Out', *Bangkok Post*, 25 January 2010.

6 'Thai–Cambodia Clashes "Damage Preah Vihear Temple"', BBC, 6 February 2011.

7 Indonesian president, Susilo Bambang Yudhoyono, held separate meetings with the Prime Ministers of both Thailand and Cambodia at the sidelines of the APEC Summit in 2009 but Indonesia did not achieve any tangible results. Michael R.J. Vatikiotis, 'Time for ASEAN to Resolve Spat', *Straits Times*, 28 January 2010.

8 May Kunmakara, 'Hun Sen Urges Leaders to Reduce Trade Deficit', *Phnom Penh Post*, 5 February 2010.

9 'Ambalat's Huge Oil and Gas Reserves', *Tempo*, 2 June 2009.

10 Clive Schofield and Ian Storey, 'Energy Security and Southeast Asia: The Impact on Maritime Boundary and Territorial Disputes', *Harvard Asia Quarterly* 9, no. 4 (2005): p. 36.

11 Donald K Emmerson, 'Security, Community, and Democracy in Southeast Asia: Analysing ASEAN', *Japanese Journal of Political Science* 6, no. 2 (2005): p. 175.

12 'Indonesian Navy Intensifying Security of Outermost Islands', *Antara News*, 31 August 2009.

13 E.g. K. Kesavapany, 'ASEAN Proves to Be a Regional Blessing', *The Straits Times*, 18 April 2005.

14 Jonathan Manthorpe, 'Southeast Asia's Deep Malaise', *Vancouver Sun*, 14 September 2009.

15 Emmerson, 'Security, Community, and Democracy in Southeast Asia: Analysing ASEAN', p. 175.

16 James Cotton, *Crossing Borders in the Asia-Pacific: Essays on the Domestic-Foreign Policy Divide* (New York: Nova Science Publishers, 2002), p. 34.

17 Tarique Niazi, 'The Ecology of Strategic Interests: China's Quest for Energy Security from the Indian Ocian and the South China Sea to the Caspian Sea Basin', *China and the Eurasia Forum Quarterly* 4, no. 4 (2006): p. 106.

18 Kuan-Hsiung Wang, 'Bridge over Troubled Waters: Fisheries Cooperation as a Resolution to the South China Sea Conflicts', *The Pacific Review* 14, no. 4 (2001): pp. 534–536.
19 Donald E. Weatherbee, *International Relations in Southeast Asia: The Struggle for Regional Autonomy*, 2nd edn (Rowman and Littlefield: Plymouth, 2009), p. 143.
20 Shaun Narine, *Explaining ASEAN: Regionalism in Southeast Asia* (Boulder, CO: Lynne Rienner, 2002), p. 85.
21 Ibid., p. 84, Christopher Roberts, 'China and the South China Sea: What Happened to ASEAN's Solidarity?', Institute of Defence and Strategic Studies, 2005, www.ntu.edu.sg/idss/.
22 'South China Sea Table and Maps', Energy Information Administration, 2002, www.eia.doe.gov/cabs/schinatab.html.
23 Rosemary Foot, 'Modes of Regional Conflict Management: Comparing Security Cooperation in the Korean Peninsula, China-Taiwan, and the South China Sea', in *Reassessing Security Cooperation in the Asia-Pacific: Competition, Congruence, and Transformation*, ed. Amitav Acharya and Evelyn Goh (Cambridge: MIT Press, 2007), p. 97.
24 Donald E. Weatherbee, *International Relations in Southeast Asia: The Struggle for Autonomy* (Lanham, MD: Rowman & Littlefield Publishers, 2005), p. 136.
25 'ASEAN Declaration on the South China Sea (Manila)', ASEAN Secretariat, 1992, www.aseansec.org/1196.htm.
26 Jeannie Henderson, *Reassessing ASEAN* (London: The International Institute for Strategic Studies, 1999), p. 59.
27 Zalmay Khalilzad D. Orletsky, Jonathan D. Pollack, Kevin Pollpeter, Angel Rabasa, David A. Shlapak, Abram N. Shulsky, and Ashley J. Tellis, *The United States and Asia: Toward a New US. Strategy and Force Posture* (Santa Monica, CA: RAND, 2001).
28 Ibid.
29 Henderson, *Reassessing ASEAN*, p. 61.
30 Cotton, *Crossing Borders in the Asia-Pacific: Essays on the Domestic–Foreign Policy Divide*, p. 34.
31 Email correspondence with Barry Wain, *Institute of Southeast Asian Studies* (Singapore), 22 March 2005.
32 Statistics based on raw data supplied by the Military Balance and the NBR Strategic Asia Database located at http://strategicasia.nbr.org. See also Jon Grevatt, 'China Unveils 18% Rise in Defence Budget', *Jane's Defence Industry*, 10 March 2007.
33 Greg Torode, 'A Diplomatic Victory for China', *South China Morning Post*, 31 October 2009, 'South China Sea Disputes Not on ASEAN Agenda', *Thai News Service*, 23 October 2009.
34 Interview with senior government official, Foreign Ministry (Hanoi), July 2005.
35 Christopher Roberts, 'The ASEAN Security community Project: The Prospects for Comprehensive Integration in Southeast Asia', *The Indonesian Quarterly* 34, no. 3 (2006): p. 286.
36 Christopher Roberts, *ASEAN's Myanmar Crisis: Challenges to the Pursuit of a Security community* (Singapore: ISEAS, 2010), pp. 93–96.
37 Ralf Emmers and Leonard C. Sebastian, 'Terrorism and Transnational Crime in Southeast Asian International Relations', in *International Relations in Southeast Asia: The Struggle for Autonomy*, ed. Donald E. Weatherbee (Lanham: Rowman and Littlefield Publishers, 2005), p. 156.
38 Ibid.
39 Recent speeches by both President Obama and the US Secretary of State, Hillary Clinton, have recognized the need for stroner reengagement. Ralph A. Cossa and Brad Glosserman, 'Regional Overview: They're Baaaack!', *Comparative Connections* 11, no. 4 (2010): pp. 1–14, Peter Alford, 'US Back in Asia to Stay: Hillary Clinton', *The Australian*, 14 January 2010.

40 This contention is based on substantial consultation with the major ethnic groups in both Singapore and Malaysia at both the elite and communal levels during the course of the past decade.
41 'DPM Najib Defends Crackdown', *Today*, 22 January 2010.
42 '"Allah" Issue Easing but Some Damage Done', *The Straits Times*, 19 January 2010.
43 'Speech by Senior Minister Lee Kuan Yew at the Chinese New Year Gathering at Cairnhill Community Club', Mita News, 2002, Lee Kuan Yew, 'Homegrown Islamic Terrorists', Ministry of Foreign Affairs, 2005, http://app.mfa.gov.sg/pr/read_script.asp?View,4361. However, according to Jones and Smith, Singapore's self-proclaimed discovery of this terrorist network was not discovered by the Singaporean intelligence services. On the contrary, the terrorist plots were only uncovered because of a 'fortuitous discovery of a video application for funding sent to Al Qaida found in Kabul rubble that once housed the jihadist equivalent of the Ford Foundation'. David M. Jones and Michael Smith, 'The Strange Death of the ASEAN Way', *Australian Financial Review*, 12 April 2002.
44 'Address by Senior Minister Lee Kuan Yew at the 1st International Institute for Strategic Studiesnasia Security Conference on Friday, 31 May 2002 at Shangrila Hotel', Mita News, 2002. Goh Chok Tong, Singapore's Prime Minister at the time, also raised such concerns and expressed, by way of an anecdotal example, how a family friend of a civil servant, having heard the news of various arrests of Islamic militants within Singapore, proclaimed that 'henceforth, she would not get into the same lift with a Malay'. 'Speech by Prime Minister Goh Chok Tong, a Dialogue with Community Leaders on Impact of Arrest of Jemaah Islamiah Operatives', Mita News, 2002.
45 Carolyn Hong, 'Muslims First, Malaysians Second', *The Straits Times*, 21 August 2006.
46 In the case of Malaysia, 27.16 per cent of the communal level respondents believed that terrorism is a concern that only affects 'the US and its allies'. In Indonesia, by contrast, just 2.78 per cent of Indonesian respondents believed that 'terrorism is a concern that affects the US and its allies only. The surveys in both countries were conducted on behalf of the author by citizens of each country and each of the surveyors was Muslim.
47 Joseph Chinyong Liow, 'Internal Conflicts in Southeast Asia: The Nature, Legitimacy, and (Changing) Role of the State', *Asian Security* 3, no. 2 (2007): pp. 73–74.
48 Damien Kingsbury, 'Southeast Asia: A Community of Diversity', *Politics and Policy* 35, no. 1 (2007): p. 11.
49 'Southeast Asia: Regional Overview', *Jane's Sentinel Security Assessment*, 10 March 2007.
50 Emmers and Sebastian, 'Terrorism and Transnational Crime in Southeast Asian International Relations', p. 165.
51 'Nine Charged over Laos 'Coup Plot'', Aljazeera.Net, 2007, http://english.aljazeera.net/NR/exeres/50EBCDC7-AF67–45D5–80BA-61918EAC8AB0.htm.
52 Shinworakornol Nakarin, 'South Militants Number 3,000', *The Nation*, 2006, www.nationalmultimedia.com/2006/06/23/national/national_30007121.
53 In Southern Thailand, Sharia law already has limited application in the context of family issues such as divorce. 'Thailand Considers Sharia Law in Troubled Muslim South', Channel News Asia, 2007, www.channelnewsasia.com/stories/afp_asiapacific/view/254544/1/.html.
54 'Thai King Intervenes to Ask Goverment to Soften Southern Approach', ChannelNewsAsia, 2004, www.channelnewsasia.com/stories/afp_asiapacific/view/114677/1/.html.
55 Interview with Dato' Mohd Annuar Bin Zaini, Malaysia National News Agency, Wednesday 24 May 2006.
56 Interview with James Wise, Australian High Commission (Kuala Lumpur), 23 May 2006.

57 Interview with Corrine Phuangkasem (Bangkok), 20 February 2006. Further, an eminent scholar, Kusuma Snitwongse, supports such sentiments and suggests that 'Malaysia would have no problem at all if Thaksin kept his mouth shut, I think that there is a latent distrust of Malaysia among some in the military'. Interview with Kusuma Snitwongse, Chulalongkorn University (Bangkok), 23 February 2006.

58 Thailand's then Deputy Interior Minister Sutham Saengprathum said 'there are pictures which are relatively clear and can be accepted as evidence in court. If the Malaysian government wants to see them, we can oblige'. 'Thai 'Proof' of Malaysia Camps', BBC, 2004, http://news.bbc.co.uk/go/pr/fr/-/hi/world/asia-pacific/4114091.stm.

59 Vaudine England, 'Malays Reject Accusations They Aid Thai Separatists', *International Herald Tribune*, 2005, www.iht.com/articles/2005/05/05/news/malaysia.php.

60 As D. Rajayah, Principle Assistant Secretary in the Policy Division of the Ministry of Defence, stated in interview, 'in the past there have been some media reports adverse to us and we have asked [the] Thais to provide us with some evidence … what they did have were old photos and not genuine and the Thais retracted … and I think the Thais understood our position'. Interview with D. Rajayah, Principle Assistant Secretary – Policy Division, *Ministry of Defence* (Putrajaya, Kuala Lumpur), 29 May 2006.

61 Interview with Major General, *Thai Police* (Bangkok), 22 February 2006.

62 'Diplomatic Stalemate: KL Says It Won't Release "Refugees"', *The Nation*, www.nationamultimedia.com.

63 Interview with Corrine Phuangkasem, *Thammasat University* (Bangkok), 20 February 2006. During the interview Corrine stated, '[e]very time that there is clash then [the] Thai government always blame[s] Malaysia. Last incident when 131 Thai Muslim went into exile into Kalimantan in Malaysia and at that time the relationship quite strained because the government blame Malaysia for accepting these people and that it was instigated by them to move over there by saying cannot live in Thailand because not safe and say might be executed by government. UNHCR tried to help 131 people who moved to Kalimantan, and the PM said interfering into Thai domestic problems. He said [they were] interfering, he shouldn't say that because their duty … People criticize that in the past Thailand accepted refugees because they come to Thailand to seek protection and we give them humanitarian assistance, when Thai people go to Kalimantan and get protection then say interfering, so people say he does not think about good reputation in the past. In terms of foreign affairs the PM intervene too much and sometimes he doesn't realize all the important factors, like Malaysia is now chairman of the organization of the Islamic conference and Indonesia chairman of the NAM group, and Malaysia might be the coming chairman and so should be on good terms with Malaysia because quite influential'.

64 'Diplomatic Stalemate: KL Says It Won't Release 'Refugees'.'

65 'Southern Unrest: PM: Spy Charge a Misunderstanding', *The Nation*, www.nationmultimedia.com.

66 In relation to this issue, a Major-General in the Thai Military states: 'when [you] talk conflict between Thailand and Malaysia, you know that we have dual nationality, when you make a problem you can go to Malaysia until it calms down. Thailand wants one nationality, but Malaysia doesn't agree. PAS has resisted this because they get the vote. They control the state along the border'. Interview with Major General, *Thai Military* (Bangkok), 18 February 2006.

67 'Six Malaysian Soldiers Detained in Southern Thai Province', Bernama, 2006, www.bernama.com/bernam/v3/printable.php?id=181570.

68 As Anthony Davis states, Southern Thailand 'is a domestic issue that is exacerbating long-standing bilateral tensions. It is opening up old wounds and rubbing salt in it. Six months ago Thai–Malaysia relations were worse than they ever had been. You can blame both sides [for this]'. Interview with Anthony Davis, *Jane's Intelligence* (Bangkok), 15 February 2006.

69 As a Major-General stated, '[e]very year we send officers to the national defence college [in Malaysia] on exchange. Last year we sent officers to it and we were greeted by only a Colonel and a Lieutenant Colonel. Worse, we were there for two hours and were not offered any refreshments. This was very bad. We had a bad feeling about how we were received. This year we did not send anyone. We did send one to Vietnam'. Interview with Major-General, Thai Military (Bangkok), 18 February 2006.

70 'Declaration on Joint Action to Counter Terrorism', ASEAN Secretariat, 2001, www.aseansec.org/5318.htm.

71 Emmers and Sebastian, 'Terrorism and Transnational Crime in Southeast Asian International Relations', pp. 165–166.

72 David Martin Jones and Michael L.R. Smith, 'Making Process, Not Progress', *International Security* 32, no. 1 (2007): p. 170.

73 'Vientiane Action Programme', ASEAN Secretariat, 2004, www.aseansec.org/VAP-10th%20ASEAN%20Summit.pdf.

74 As James Cotton adds, 'the "new ASEAN's" – Vietnam, Myanmar, Laos and Cambodia – were also absent from the accord'. James Cotton, 'Southeast Asia after 11 September', *Terrorism and Political Violence* 15, no. 1 (2003): p. 154.

75 Interview with Ju Hon, Singapore Ministry of Defence, 27 July 2007; interview with Dr. Chap Sotharith, Director CICP (Phnom Penh), 25 July 2005; interview with Kao Kim Hourn, Deputy Foreign Minister, 30 July 2005; interview with Kamarulnizam Abdullah, University Kebangsaan Malaysia, 29 May 2006; roundtable interview with The National Defence College of the Philippines (Manila), 24 November 2005.

76 Natasha Ogilvie-White, 'Non-Proliferation and Counter-Terrorism Cooperation in Southeast Asia: Meeting Global Obligations through Regional Security Architectures?', *Contemporary Southeast Asia* 28, no. 1 (2006): p. 4.

77 Damien Kingsbury and Clinton Fernandes, 'Terrorism in Archipelagic Southeast Asia', in *Violence in Between: Conflict and Security in Archipelagic Southeast Asia*, ed. Damien Kingsbury (Melbourne: Monash University Press and ISEAS, 2005), p. 49.

78 Kit Collier, 'Terrorism: Evolving Regional Alliances and State Failure in Mindanao', in *Southeast Asian Affairs 2006* (Singapore: ISEAS, 2006), p. 36.

79 For example, Professor Rolando Talampas argues that 'for a long time the Philippines was a sore thumb in the grouping because of US bases in the country'. Interview with Rolando Talampas, University of the Philippines (Manila), 14 November 2005.

80 James Cotton, 'The "Haze" over Southeast Asia: Challenging the ASEAN Mode of Regional Engagement', *Pacific Affairs* 72, no. 3 (1999): p. 332.

81 Cotton, *Crossing Borders in the Asia-Pacific: Essays on the Domestic-Foreign Policy Divide*, p. 3.

82 Mely Caballero-Anthony, *Regional Security in Southeast Asia: Beyond the ASEAN Way* (Singapore: ISEAS, 2005), p. 208.

83 Narine, *Explaining ASEAN: Regionalism in Southeast Asia*, p. 170.

84 Weatherbee, *International Relations in Southeast Asia: The Struggle for Autonomy*, p. 273.

85 Cotton, *Crossing Borders in the Asia-Pacific: Essays on the Domestic–Foreign Policy Divide*, p. 2.

86 Consequently, the issue was also addressed in the 1992 Singapore Resolution on the Environment and in the 1994 Bandar Seri Begawan Resolution on Environment and Development. 'ASEAN Cooperation Plan on Transboundary Pollution', ASEAN Secretariat, 1995, www.aseansec.org/8939.htm.

87 Ibid. A noteworthy limitation to the document however is seen by 'the avoidance of any mention of the promotion of foreign conservation or protection as a means of minimizing the generation of smoke'. Cotton, 'The "Haze" over Southeast Asia: Challenging the ASEAN Mode of Regional Engagement', p. 343.

88 Weatherbee, *International Relations in Southeast Asia: The Struggle for Autonomy*, p. 273.

89 Cotton, *Crossing Borders in the Asia-Pacific: Essays on the Domestic-Foreign Policy Divide*, p. 4.
90 Interview with C.P.F. Luhulima, Senior Fellow, Centre for Security and International Studies (Jakarta), 26 November 2001. James Cotton similarly argues that 'Indonesia, the pivotal actor in ASEAN, when forced to choose between regime solidarity and regional concern took the former option'. Cotton, 'The "Haze" over Southeast Asia: Challenging the ASEAN Mode of Regional Engagement', p. 342.
91 Cotton, *Crossing Borders in the Asia-Pacific: Essays on the Domestic-Foreign Policy Divide*. The Malaysian government was so alarmed by the public reaction to the haze that it also terminated 'routine air quality announcements'. Weatherbee, *International Relations in Southeast Asia: The Struggle for Autonomy*, p. 273.
92 The Singaporean Centre for Remote Imaging, Sensing and Processing (CRISP), through the Ministry of the Environment, had been providing Indonesia with satellite imagery of the fires in Sumatra and Kalimantan. Singapore directed CRISP to publish its imagery on the internet. Cotton, 'The "Haze" over Southeast Asia: Challenging the ASEAN Mode of Regional Engagement', p. 349.
93 Alan Collins, *Security and Southeast Asia: Domestic, Regional, and Global Issues* (Boulder, CO: Lynne Rienner, 2003), p. 142.
94 'ASEAN Ministers Endorse Draft Agreement on Forest Fire Handling in Ri', LKBN Antara, 2007, http://global.factiva.com.
95 Weatherbee, *International Relations in Southeast Asia: The Struggle for Autonomy*, p. 274.
96 Amitav Acharya, *Constructing a Security community in Southeast Asia: ASEAN and the Problem of Regional Order*, 2nd edn (London: Routledge, 2009), p. 254. See also 'Malaysia Hopes Indonesia Will Ratify Haze Agreement', *Bernama*, 29 June 2007.
97 Ardiansyah Fitrian, 'Climate Solutions: Clearing up the Region's Hazy Future', *The Jakarta Post*, 29 October 2010.
98 World Bank, 1993.
99 David M. Jones and Michael Smith, *ASEAN and East Asian International Relations: Regional Delusion* (Northhampton, MA: Edward Elgar, 2006), p. 225.
100 Collins, *Security and Southeast Asia: Domestic, Regional, and Global Issues*, p. 140.
101 M. Wesley, 'The Asian Crisis and the Adequacy of Regional Institutions', *Contemporary Southeast Asia* 21, no. 1 (1999): p. 55.
102 Gregory W. Noble and John Ravenhill, 'Causes and Consequences of the Asian Financial Crisis', in *The Asian Financial Crisis and the Architecture of Global Finance*, ed. Gregory W. Noble and John Ravenhill (Cambridge: Cambridge University Press, 2000), p. 3.
103 Garry Rodan, Kevin Hewison and Richard Robison, 'Theorising Markets in Southeast Asia: Power and Contestation', in *The Political Economy of Southeast Asia: Markets, Power and Contestation*, ed. Garry Rodan, Kevin Hewison and Richard Robison (New York: Oxford, 2006), p. 15.
104 *Environmental Implications of the Economic Crisis and Adjustment in East Asia* (East Asia Environment and Social Development Unity, World Bank, 1999), p. 2.
105 According to this perspective 'East Asia opened itself up to the free flow of international capital while lacking the proper instruments needed to regulate and control that capital. The Asian countries adopted the wrong domestic policies, but their greatest mistake was in allowing excessive financial liberalization, something they were encouraged to do by many of the same Western states and Western-based financial institutions that pinned responsibility for the economic collapse solidly on Asian business practices'. Narine, *Explaining ASEAN: Regionalism in Southeast Asia*, p. 140.

106 Weatherbee, for example, argues that '[t]hrough the advent of the economic crisis the structural inadequacies and institutional weaknesses that had been concealed by high growth rates were starkly revealed'. Weatherbee, *International Relations in Southeast Asia: The Struggle for Autonomy*, p. 96.

107 Jones and Smith, *ASEAN and East Asian International Relations: Regional Delusion*, p. 147.

108 Caballero-Anthony, *Regional Security in Southeast Asia: Beyond the ASEAN Way*, p. 204.

109 Jones and Smith, 'Making Process, Not Progress', p. 160.

110 Rodan, Hewison and Robison, 'Theorising Markets in Southeast Asia: Power and Contestation', p. 16.

111 Anthony L. Smith, *Strategic Centrality: Indonesia's Changing Role in ASEAN* (Singapore: ISEAS, 2000), p. 30.

112 Amitav Acharya, 'Transnational Production and Security: Southeast Asia's "Growth Triangles"', *Contemporary Southeast Asia* 17, no. 12 (1995): p. 260.

113 Such violence included the looting of Chinatown in Jakarta as a consequence, in part, of remarks by Indonesian Generals who publically blamed local Chinese for the flight of capital to destinations such as Singapore. 'Indonesia Alert: Economic Crisis Leads to Scapegoating of Ethnic Chinese', Human Rights Watch, 1999, www.hrw.org/press98/feb/indo-a11.htm. Since independence in 1949, there have been more anti-Chinese riots in Indonesia than in any other country in Southeast Asia. Nicholas Tarling, *Nations and States in Southeast Asia* (Cambridge: Cambridge University Press, 1998), p. 128.

114 Major General Agus was the Assistant for General Planning to the Commander-in-Chief of the Indonesian National Military (TNI) and the son of former Vice-President Umar Wirahadikusumah. Douglas Kammen, 'Akhir "Kedigdayaan" Abri?', University of Canterbury, 1999, www.infid.or.id/oldconf/1999/Douglas.htm.

115 Etel Solingen, 'ASEAN Cooperation: The Legacy of the Economic Crisis', *International Relations of the Asia-Pacific* 5, no. 1 (2005): p. 15.

116 Collins, *Security and Southeast Asia: Domestic, Regional, and Global Issues*, p. 145.

117 Narine, *Explaining ASEAN: Regionalism in Southeast Asia*, p. 169.

118 Solingen, 'ASEAN Cooperation: The Legacy of the Economic Crisis', p. 15.

119 'Be Calm over "Remarks", Surin Urges Malaysian Government', *The Nation*, 19 October 1998.

120 Jones and Smith, 'Making Process, Not Progress', p. 161.

121 Zakaria Haji Ahmad and Baladas Ghoshal, 'The Political Future of ASEAN after the Asian Crisis', *International Affairs* 75, no. 4 (1999): p. 763.

122 Narine, *Explaining ASEAN: Regionalism in Southeast Asia*, pp. 169–170.

123 Alan Dupont, 'Transnational Crime, Drugs, and Security in East Asia', *Asian Survey* 39, no. 3 (1999): p. 449.

124 Emmers and Sebastian, 'Terrorism and Transnational Crime in Southeast Asian International Relations', p. 172.

125 'ASEAN Vision 2020', ASEAN Secretariat, 1997, www.aseansec.org/5408.htm. The Vision 2020 originated from Mahathir's *Wawasan 2020* in 1991, which aimed to achieve development through the resolution of economic and social problems.

126 Richard Stubbs, 'ASEAN Plus Three: Emerging East Asian Regionalism', *Asian Survey* 32, no. 3 (2002): p. 450. In the context of such contentions Singapore's ambassador-at-large, Tommy Koh, suggested that the crisis 'stimulated a new sense of East Asian regionalism'. Cited in Dirk Nabers, 'The Social Construction of International Institutions: The Case of ASEAN + 3', *International Relations of the Asia-Pacific* 3, no. 1 (2003): p. 122.

127 'Hanoi Plan of Action', ASEAN Secretariat, 1998, www.aseansec.org/8754.htm.

128 Ibid.

129 Jones and Smith, 'Making Process, Not Progress', p. 156.

130 Discussion with Mr Rodolfo Severino, *Former ASEAN Secretary-General* (Singapore), 21 November 2007.

131 Narine, *Explaining ASEAN: Regionalism in Southeast Asia*, p. 166.

132 Interview with Ministry of Defence (Singapore), 27 July 2006. Furthermore, in relation to Myanmar, a former ambassador in the country explained that the country's leadership always seemed to learn the wrong lessons from major events in Southeast Asia and this was especially the case in relation to the economic crisis. Interview with Ministry of Foreign Affairs (Singapore), 5 September 2005.

133 N. Ganesan, 'ASEAN: A Community Stalled?', in *The Asia-Pacific: A Region in Transition*, ed. Jim Rolfe (Hawaii: Asia-Pacific Center for Security Studies, 2004), p. 122.

134 Kanishka Jayasuriya, 'Introduction: Governing the New Asia Pacific – Beyond the "New Regionalism" ', *Third Word Quarterly* 24, no. 2 (2003): p. 259.

135 Further, Singapore offers the most plausible non-liberal model of organization. David Martin Jones, 'Security and Democracy: The ASEAN Charter and the Dilemmas of Regionalism in South-East Asia', *International Affairs* 4 (2008): p. 741.

136 Siti Rahil Dollah, 'Asians Split on Ways to Revive Economies after Crisis', *Kyodo News*, 16 December 1997.

137 As former ASEAN Secretary-General Rodolfo Severino stated in interview, 'Singapore wants economies to be open because it itself is open. Meanwhile the Philippines and Indonesia are not confident in their economic competitiveness.' Interview with Rodolfo Severino, *ISEAS* (Singapore), 14 November 2005.

138 Jones and Smith, 'Making Process, Not Progress', p. 161.

139 Zulkifli Othman, 'Explain Talks with NZ, ASEAN Tells Singapore', *New Straits Times*, 9 September 1999.

140 'Welcome to Singapore FTA Network', Government of Singapore, 2010, www.fta.gov.sg.

141 Audrey Tan, 'Singapore Finds Multilateral Trade Talks Slow', *The Business Times*, 18 January 2000, 'Singapore Hopes for 'New Age' Model with Japan', *Straits Times*, 19 January 2000.

142 For example: 'Bilateral Trade Pacts a Threat to AFTA', *Bernama Daily Malaysian News*, 23 April 2002, Othman, 'Explain Talks with NZ, ASEAN Tells Singapore.', Muammar Kamurudin, 'Some Officials Show Concern over Singapore and New Zealand Trade Pact', *Bernama Daily Malaysian News* 2000.

143 'Free Trade Agreements Threaten to Undermine ASEAN', *Agence France-Presse*, 22 November 2000.

144 'Malaysia Denies Free Trade Plan, Slams Singapore', *Agence France-Presse*, 25 November 2000.

145 'Free Trade Agreements Threaten ASEAN Significance, Says Philippines', *Agence France-Presse*, 22 November 2000.

146 Naranart Phuangkanok, 'Thailand to Ink Bilateral Trade Pacts', *The Nation (Bangkok)*, 28 November 2000.

147 Reme Ahmad, 'Malaysia Changes Stance, Now Open to FTAs', *Straits Times*, 26 October 2002.

148 Praduma B. Rana, 'East Asian Regionalism', in *Regional Outlook: Southeast Asia 2007–08*, ed. Asad-ul Iqbal Latif and Poh Onn Lee (Singapore: Institute of Southeast Asian Studies, 2007), p. 73, Weatherbee, *International Relations in Southeast Asia: The Struggle for Autonomy*, p. 25.

149 Christopher M. Dent, 'The New Economic Bilateralism in Southeast Asia: Region-Convergent or Region-Divergent', *International Relations of the Asia-Pacific* 6, no. 1 (2006): p. 110. A respected trade economist from Malaysia, Mohammed Ariff, similarly suggests that by undermining the 'spirit of solidarity' in ASEAN the FTA will negatively influence ASEAN's goal to establish an economic community. 'Separate FTAs Undermine ASEAN Spirit of Unity: Scholar', People's Daily Online, 2007, http://english.peopledaily.com.cn/200607/12/print20060712_282121.html.

150 Tony Allison, 'Thailand, US Inch Ahead on Trade Accord', *Asia Times*, 2006, www.atimes.com.
151 Weatherbee, *International Relations in Southeast Asia: The Struggle for Regional Autonomy*, p. 206.
152 *Charting Progress Towards Regional Economic Integration: ASEAN Economic Community Scorecard* (Jakarta: ASEAN, 2010), p. 4.
153 In 1993 intra-ASEAN exports constituted 21.4 per cent and by 2005 they had reached 25 per cent. Jones and Smith, *ASEAN and East Asian International Relations: Regional Delusion*, p. 138.
154 Rodolfo C. Severino, 'Regional Economic Integration and the ASEAN Charter', in *Regional Outlook: Southeast Asia 2008/2009* (Singapore: ISEAS, 2009), p. 72.
155 John Ravenhill, 'Fighting Irrelevance: An Economic Community "with ASEAN Characteristics"', *The Pacific Review* 21, no. 4 (2008): pp. 472–473.
156 Hadi Soesastro, 'Accelerating ASEAN Economic Integration: Moving Beyond AFTA', in *CSIS Working Paper Series* (Jakarta: CSIS, 2005), p. 2.
157 Interview with senior official, Ministry of Foreign Affairs (Malaysia), May 2006.
158 Jones, 'Security and Democracy: The ASEAN Charter and the Dilemmas of Regionalism in South-East Asia', p. 742.
159 Statistics available from https://www.cia.gov/library/publications/the-world-factbook/. See also 'Indonesia 'Declines Debt Freeze'', BBC News, 2005, http://news.bbc.co.uk/2/hi/business/4204803.stm.
160 Ibid.
161 Mark Beeson, 'South-East Asia and the International Financial Institutions', in *The Political Economy of Southeast Asia: Markets, Power and Contestation*, ed. Garry Rodan, Kevin Hewison, and Richard Robison (South Melbourne: Oxford University Press, 2006), p. 252.
162 Jones, 'Security and Democracy: The ASEAN Charter and the Dilemmas of Regionalism in South-East Asia', p. 735.
163 Narine, *Explaining ASEAN: Regionalism in Southeast Asia*, p. 164.
164 Collins, *Security and Southeast Asia: Domestic, Regional, and Global Issues*, p. 150.
165 Ibid., p. 151.

5 Political transitions, changing values and visions for the future

1 Sukhumbhand Paribatra, 'Analysis – Is Burma Ready for Membership?', *Bangkok Post*, 22 May 1997.
2 David Martin Jones, 'Security and Democracy: The ASEAN Charter and the Dilemmas of Regionalism in South-East Asia', *International Affairs* 4 (2008): p. 746.
3 Ian Marsh, 'Democratization and State Capacity in East and Southeast Asia', *Taiwan Journal of Democracy* 2, no. 2 (2006): p. 77.
4 David Capie and Paul Evans, *The Asia-Pacific Security Lexicon*, 2nd edn (Singapore: Institute of Southeast Asian Studies, 2007), p. 120.
5 Leszek Buszynski, 'Thailand and Myanmar: The Perils of Constructive Engagement', *Pacific Review* 11, no. 2 (1998): pp. 290–291.
6 Christopher Roberts, *ASEAN's Myanmar Crisis: Challenges to the Pursuit of a Security community* (Singapore: ISEAS, 2010), p. 91.
7 Capie and Evans, *The Asia-Pacific Security Lexicon*, p. 124.
8 Neil Englehart, 'Democracy and the Thai Middle Class: Globalization, Modernization and Constitutional Change', *Asian Survey* 43, no. 2 (2003): pp. 253–279.
9 Jones, 'Security and Democracy: The ASEAN Charter and the Dilemmas of Regionalism in South-East Asia.'
10 Englehart, 'Democracy and the Thai Middle Class: Globalization, Modernization and Constitutional Change', p. 254.

11 Jorn Dosch, *The Changing Dynamics of Southeast Asian Politics* (London: Lynne Rienner, 2007), p. 40.
12 Jurgen Haacke, 'The Concept of Flexible Engagement and the Practice of Enhanced Interaction: Intramural Challenges to the "ASEAN Way"', *The Pacific Review* 12, no. 4 (1999): p. 588.
13 Amitav Acharya, 'Democratisation and the Prospects for Participatory Regionalism in Southeast Asia', *Third Word Quarterly* 24, no. 2 (2003): p. 383. For example, Chuan Leekpai had already tested the Thai military and the boundaries of the constructive engagement policy during his first term in office when he permitted a meeting of eight Nobel Prize laureates, including the Dalai Lama, to visit Thailand for the express purpose of pressuring Myanmar to adopt democratic reforms. While Thailand's military command objected because it wanted to maintain 'smooth relations' with Myanmar, the military silently accepted a decision on the matter by the Thai cabinet, thus demonstrating its obedience and subservience to the elected government. Dosch, *The Changing Dynamics of Southeast Asian Politics*, p. 41.
14 Haacke, 'The Concept of Flexible Engagement and the Practice of Enhanced Interaction: Intramural Challenges to the "ASEAN Way"', p. 585.
15 Cited in Ramcharan, 'ASEAN and Non-Interference: A Principle Maintained?', *Contemporary Southeast Asia* 22, no. 1 (2000): p. 75.
16 Marisa Chimprabha, 'End Sought to ASEAN's Main Policy', *The Nation*, 15 June 1998.
17 Haacke, 'The Concept of Flexible Engagement and the Practice of Enhanced Interaction: Intramural Challenges to the "ASEAN Way"', p. 586.
18 'Thailand's Non-Paper on Flexible Engagement', *Ministry of Foreign Affairs*, 25 July 1998.
19 Haacke, 'The Concept of Flexible Engagement and the Practice of Enhanced Interaction: Intramural Challenges to the "ASEAN Way"', p. 588.
20 Kusuma Snitwongse quoted in Dosch, *The Changing Dynamics of Southeast Asian Politics*, p. 63.
21 Roberts, *ASEAN's Myanmar Crisis: Challenges to the Pursuit of a Security community*, pp. 89–90.
22 Ruukan Katanyuu, 'Beyond Non-Interference in ASEAN: The Association's Role in Myanmar's National Reconcilliation and Democratization', *Asian Survey* 46, no. 6 (2006): p. 828.
23 N. Ganesan, 'Myanmar's Foreign Relations: Reaching out to the World', in *Myanmar: Beyond Politics to Societal Imperatives*, ed. Kyaw Yin Hlaing, Robert H. Taylor and Tin Maung Maung Than (Singapore: Institute of Southeast Asian Studies, 2005), p. 46.
24 Jewellord T. Nem Singh, 'Process of Institutionalisation and Democratisation in ASEAN: Features, Challenges and Prospects of Regionalism in Southeast Asia', *UNISCI Discussion Papers*, no. No. 16 (2008): pp. 157–158.
25 Shigekatsu Kondo, *East Asian Strategic Review* (Tokyo: National Institute for Defence Studies, 2000), p. 36. Additionally, in an interview with Dr. Kanala Khantaprab (Advisor to Deputy Prime Minister, Advisor to Defence Minister, Advisor to Deputy House Speaker), she also supported the utility of enhanced interaction stating that 'both sides must be able to exchange views … and be able to talk frankly'. Interview with Dr Kanala Khantaprab, Government of Thailand (Bangkok), 26 December 2001.
26 Katanyuu, 'Beyond Non-Interference in ASEAN: The Association's Role in Myanmar's National Reconcilliation and Democratization', p. 830.
27 Ibid., p. 830.
28 'EU, ASEM Talks Seek More Trade, Yuan May Not Help', *Europa*, 4 October 2010.

29 'ASEAN: Is Myanmar the First Crack in Solidarity?', Stratfor, 2004, www.stratfor.biz.

30 The SPDC did uphold its commitment to attend one meeting organized via the 'Bangkok Process' but other than to announce the reconvening of the national convention it made no concessions during this time. Jurgen Haacke, ' "Enhanced Interaction" with Myanmar and the Project of a Security community: Is ASEAN Refining or Breaking with Its Diplomatic and Security Culture?', *Contemporary Southeast Asia* 27, no. 2 (2005): p. 194.

31 'Burmese Border: Incursions Not Worth a War, Says Chavalit', *Bangkok Post*, 10 May 2001.

32 Dosch, *The Changing Dynamics of Southeast Asian Politics*, p. 53.

33 Interview with government officer, *Office of the National Security Council* (Bangkok), February 2006.

34 Dosch, *The Changing Dynamics of Southeast Asian Politics*, p. 63.

35 Ibid., pp. 12 and 46–47.

36 Cited in William Case, 'Low-Quality Democracy and Varied Authoritarianism: Elites and Regimes in Southeast Asia Today', *The Pacific Review* 22, no. 3 (2009): pp. 255–256.

37 In the case of Cambodia, it is important to note that while Prime Minister Hun Sen currently epitomizes the 'strongmen' tactics of earlier ASEAN rulers, the devolution of power to both regional and local governments has remained, leaving a significant component of democratic governance in place. Dosch, *The Changing Dynamics of Southeast Asian Politics*, p. 15. A fact reinforced by the continued freedom of the media within the country including the Phnom Penh Post. Meeting with Roger Mitton, *The Phnom Penh Post* (Hanoi), January 2010.

38 Amitav Acharya, *Asia Rising: Who Is Leading?* (Singapore: World Scientific, 2008), p. 145.

39 Jones, 'Security and Democracy: The ASEAN Charter and the Dilemmas of Regionalism in South-East Asia', p. 746.

40 Sandra Hamid and Douglas Ramage, 'Autonomy for Aceh', *The Wall Street Journal Asia*, 18 July 2006.

41 'Europe Forms 27 Million Euro Program for Aceh Peace Process', *Organanization of Asia-Pacific News Agencies*, 8 May 2007.

42 'Aceh: So Far, So Good', in *Asia Briefing No. 44* (Brussels: International Crisis Group, 2005), p. 2.

43 Jones, 'Security and Democracy: The ASEAN Charter and the Dilemmas of Regionalism in South-East Asia'.

44 Brian Bremner and Assif Shameen, 'Crisis Manager; Susilo Bambang Yudhoyono President, Indonesia', *BusinessWeek*, 11 July 2005.

45 'Tsunami Meeting to Discuss Aceh Aid', *The Age*, 17 March 2005.

46 Acharya, 'Democratisation and the Prospects for Participatory Regionalism in Southeast Asia', p. 251.

47 Dosch, *The Changing Dynamics of Southeast Asian Politics*, pp. 39–40.

48 Anthony L. Smith, 'Indonesia's Foreign Policy under Abdurrahman Wahid: Radical or Status Quo State?', *Contemporary Southeast Asia* 22, no. 3 (2000): p. 501.

49 Dosch, *The Changing Dynamics of Southeast Asian Politics*, pp. 12, 46–47.

50 Acharya, 'Democratisation and the Prospects for Participatory Regionalism in Southeast Asia', p. 381.

51 Ibid., p. 381.

52 Amitav Acharya, *Constructing a Security community in Southeast Asia: ASEAN and the Problem of Regional Order*, 2nd edn (London: Routledge, 2009), p. 254.

53 'Asia-Pacific', *Strategic Survey* 109, no. 1 (2009): pp. 345–346.

54 Acharya, 'Democratisation and the Prospects for Participatory Regionalism in Southeast Asia', p. 382.

55 Ibid., p. 382.
56 James Cotton, 'Regional Order and the over-Determination of Regional Institutions in the Asia-Pacific' (paper presented at the UTS–Guadalajara Workshop, Guadalajara, January 2004), p. 3.
57 'Solons Cross Party Lines', *ABS-CBN*, 11 December 2001.
58 'Suspend All Aid to Burma: Kraisak', *The Nation*, 21 October 2004.
59 These comments were made by Zaid Ibrahim, the Chair of the Malaysian Caucus. Zaid Ibrahim, 'ASEAN: Time to Interfere', *Irrawaddy*, April 2005.
60 'Malaysian MPs Launch Myanmar Democracy Push', *Reuters*, 8 June 2004.
61 Ibid.
62 'Malaysian Caucus Expresses Desire to Work with Burmese Opposition', *Democratic Voice of Burma*, 2004, http://english.dvb.no/print_news.php?id=1303.
63 'Myanmar – Suspend from ASEAN If No Progress in 12 Months', Democratic Action Party, 2004, www.dapmalaysia.org/english/2005/Sept05/lks/lks3650.htm.
64 'ASEAN: Is Myanmar the First Crack in Solidarity?'
65 Roberts, *ASEAN's Myanmar Crisis: Challenges to the Pursuit of a Security community*, p. 123.
66 Simon Montlake, 'Burma's "Black Friday" ', BBC, 2004, http://newsvote.bbc.co.uk.
67 ASEAN also reaffirmed its 'continued support for the efforts of the UNGA Special Representative Tan Sri Razali Ismail. 'Joint Communique of the 36th ASEAN Ministerial Meeting', ASEAN Secretariat, 2003, www.aseansec.org/14833.htm.
68 Mark Baker, 'Turmoil in Burma Splits ASEAN', *The Age*, 17 June 2003.
69 Soon after, in reflecting on the significance of the event, the Foreign Minister of Thailand asserted that 'ASEAN's willingness to talk about the matter showed it had reached another stage of maturity'. Bhanravee Tansubhapol, 'Rangoon Tackled over Suu Kyi', *Bangkok Post*, 17 June 2003.
70 Alan Collins, 'A People-Oriented ASEAN: A Door Ajar or Closed for Civil Society Organisations', *Contemporary Southeast Asia* 30, no. 2 (2008): p. 320.
71 'Report of the ASEAN Eminent Persons Group (EPG) on Vision 2020: The People's ASEAN', ASEAN Secretariat, 2000, www.aseansec.org/5304.htm.
72 Acharya, *Constructing a Security community in Southeast Asia: ASEAN and the Problem of Regional Order*, p. 274.
73 K.S. Balakrishnan, 'Malaysia's Foreign Policy and the Role of the Civil Society', *Asian Defence and Diplomacy* 10, no. 1 (2003): p. 44.
74 Stuart Harris, 'Policy Networks and Economic Cooperation: Policy Coordination in the Asia-Pacific Region', *Pacific Review* 7, no. 4 (1994): p. 390.
75 Collins, 'A People-Oriented ASEAN: A Door Ajar or Closed for Civil Society Organisations', pp. 315–316.
76 Meidyatama Suryodiningrat, 'Facing the People, ASEAN's Strategic Deficit', *The Jakarta Post*, 5 March 2009.
77 Collins, 'A People-Oriented ASEAN: A Door Ajar or Closed for Civil Society Organisations', p. 321.
78 Acharya, 'Democratisation and the Prospects for Participatory Regionalism in Southeast Asia', p. 282.
79 Similar problems had arisen in the context of the 2006 IMF–World Bank meeting where certain IMF–World Bank accredited civil society representatives were prevented from attending and Singapore's Home Affairs Minister, Wong Kan Seng, further stated that the actions of some civil society actions may 'attract severe punishment, including caning and imprisonment'. 'Singapore Ready to Cane World Bank/IMF Protestors', *Reuters*, 17 January 2006.
80 Acharya, 'Democratisation and the Prospects for Participatory Regionalism in Southeast Asia', p. 381.
81 Singh, 'Process of Institutionalisation and Democratisation in ASEAN: Features, Challenges and Prospects of Regionalism in Southeast Asia', pp. 160–161.

82 Collins, 'A People-Oriented ASEAN: A Door Ajar or Closed for Civil Society Organisations', p. 322.
83 'ARF Meeting Ends with No Progress on Myanmar Issue', *The Jakarta Post*, 2004, www.thejakartapost.com.
84 Kim Chew Lee, 'ASEAN and EU Thrash out Myanmar Problem', *The Straits Times*, 3 July 2004.
85 '10 ASEAN Nations Reject EU Effort on Myanmar', *International Herald Tribune*, 2004, www.iht.com/cgi/bin/generic.cgi?template=articleprint.tmplh&ArticleID=515631.
86 'ARF Meeting Ends with No Progress on Myanmar Issue'.
87 Ibid. ASEAN, 'Chairman's Statement: The Eleventh Meeting of ASEAN Regional Forum', Jakarta, 2 July, 2004, www.aseansec.org/16246.htm.
88 'Data Catalogue', World Bank, 2010, http://data.worldbank.org/data-catalog.
89 Moreover, Singapore's People's Action Party (PAP) has demonstrated that it is possible to adopt economic liberalisation whilst simultaneously maintaining regime authority. Jones, 'Security and Democracy: The ASEAN Charter and the Dilemmas of Regionalism in South-East Asia', p. 741.
90 For example, some ASEAN elite were concerned that ASEAN's silence on the violence in Timor Leste might be interpreted as a legitimization of those human rights violations. Singh, 'Process of Institutionalisation and Democratisation in ASEAN: Features, Challenges and Prospects of Regionalism in Southeast Asia', p. 156.
91 Various interviewees expressed concern about the presence of foreign forces in Southeast Asia as other ASEAN states are similarly struggling with the challenges of nation-building, ethnic tensions and separatist movements; a point also corroborated by Alan Dupont in his analysis of the issue. Alan Dupont, 'ASEAN's Response to the East Timor Crisis', *Australian Journal of International Affairs* 54, no. 2 (2000): p. 165.
92 Interview with Kwa Chong Guan, *RSIS* (Singapore), 5 December 2001.
93 Kusuma Snitwongse and Suchit Bunbongkarn, 'New Security Issues and Their Impact on ASEAN', in *A New ASEAN in a New Millenium*, ed. Simon Tay, Jesus Estanislao, and Hadi Soesastro (Jakarta: Centre for Strategic and International Studies, 2000), pp. 148–62. See also Alan Dupont, *East Asia Imperiled: Transnational Challenges to Security* (Cambridge: Cambridge University Press, 2001).
94 Interview with Pranee Thiparat, Chulalongkorn University (Bangkok), 22 February 2006.
95 The terms of reference for the ASEAN Troika were constituted in 2000. 'The ASEAN Troika', ASEAN Secretariat, 2000, www.aseansec.org/3637.htm. While the origins of the High Council are grounded in the TAC, its rules of procedure were finalized in 2001. 'Rules of Procedure of the High Council of the Treaty of Amity and Cooperation in Southeast Asia', ASEAN Secretariat, 2001, www.aseansec.org/print.asp?file=/amm/hanoi03.htm.
96 Interview with Umar Hadi, *Director of Public Diplomacy, Ministry of Foreign Affairs* (Jakarta), 26 May 2006.
97 Rizal Sukma, 'Towards an ASEAN Security community: Concept Paper', *Deplu*, 20 March 2003. This was the original paper circulated to the Indonesian Foreign Ministry. An almost exact replica was published on the Internet several months later. Rizal Sukma, 'The Future of ASEAN: Towards a Security community', Permanent Mission of the Republic of Indonesia to the United Nations, 2003, www.indonesiamission-ny.org/issuebaru/Mission/asean/paper_rizalsukma.PDF.
98 Interview with Umar Hadi, *Director of Public Diplomacy, Ministry of Foreign Affairs* (Jakarta), 26 May 2006.
99 Sukma, 'Towards an ASEAN Security community: Concept Paper'. As Sukma states in interview, the proposal 'owes a lot to the concept as developed by Deutsch and Amitav [Acharya], and after presenting it to the Foreign Minister here I

presented a modified version in New York. I have been working on this even though it has been watered down, massaged, but the intellectual rules had to be found, and I looked at Leifer who talked about a political community in the 80s'. Interview with Rizal Sukma, *CSIS* (Jakarta), 21 April 2006.

100 Interview with Rizal Sukma, *CSIS* (Jakarta), 21 April 2006. See also: 'Track 1 – Governmental Meetings', Dialogue and Research Monitor, 2003, www.jcie.or.jp/drm/2003/track1.html.

101 Interview with Pratap Parameswaren, *ASEAN Secretariat* (Jakarta), 25 April 2006. Interview with Chookiat Panaspornprasit, *Director, Institute of Security and International Studies* (Bangkok), 16 February 2006.

102 Cited in Acharya, *Constructing a Security community in Southeast Asia: ASEAN and the Problem of Regional Order*, p. 259.

103 Ibid., p. 259.

104 For example, a senior scholar at the Diplomatic Academy of Vietnam (Ministry of Foreign Affairs) stated that 'Indonesia's purpose was to try to regain the image of [being] ASEAN's leader.' Interview with the Diplomatic Academy of Vietnam (Hanoi), 7 July 2005.

105 Interview with Ministry of Foreign Affairs (Jakarta), May 2006.

106 In detail, the ASEAN Secretariat Official stated that 'and here the Secretariat was also a bit surprised when they saw the so-called draft, and we were having our debates trying to interpret the Indonesian initiative, because after having spent more than a decade here I more or less know what is feasible and what is not. I was the one asking the question, I asked myself, because either the drafter of the concept had no clue of what is possible in ASEAN or there were talks for some time of Indonesia leaving ASEAN out of frustration, we asked ourselves is this the excuse that Indonesia would use, if the rest reject, then it would leave ASEAN?' Interview with senior official, *ASEAN Secretariat* (Jakarta), April 2006.

107 Interview with Dr Chookiat Panaspornprasit, *Director of the Institute of Security and International Studies* (Bangkok, Thailand), 16 February 2006. Interview with M.C. Abad Jr., *ARF Unit Director* (ASEAN Secretariat, Jakarta), 20 April 2006. Interview with Luan Thuy Dong, Director of the Southeast Asian Studies Center, *Institute of International Relations* (Hanoi, Vietnam), 7 July 2005.

108 Various scholars and government officials from Indonesia, Thailand, and Vietnam suggested that the proposal did not originate from Indonesia.

109 'Cebu Declaration on the Acceleration of the Establishment of an ASEAN Community by 2015', ASEAN Secretariat, 2007, www.aseansec.org/19260.htm.

110 Donald E. Weatherbee, *International Relations in Southeast Asia: The Struggle for Autonomy* (Lanham, MD: Rowman & Littlefield Publishers, 2005), p. 108.

111 'ASEAN Security community Plan of Action', ASEAN Secretariat, 2004, www.aseansec.org/16827.htm.

112 Interview with Rizal Sukma, *CSIS* (Jakarta), 21 April 2006. M.C. Abad from the ASEAN Secretariat adds, 'the theoretical side, that is the heart of it, its building a community with a common identity, a common outlook, that is the heart of the theoretical basis of a security community'. Interview with M.C. Abad, ASEAN Secretariat (Jakarta), 20 April 2006.

113 Declaration of ASEAN Concord II (Bali Concord II), 2003. ASEAN Secretariat, http://www.aseansec.org/15159.htm. (accessed 14 October, 2003).

114 'ASEAN Security community Plan of Action', Draft, Deplu, 13 February 2004.

115 Christopher Roberts, 'ASEAN Charter: The Model Decision?', *The Straits Times*, 9 September 2005.

116 For details, see 'Vientiane Action Programme', ASEAN Secretariat, 2004, www.aseansec.org/VAP-10th%20ASEAN%20Summit.pdf.

117 Collins, 'A People-Oriented ASEAN: A Door Ajar or Closed for Civil Society Organisations', p. 321.

118 'Vientiane Action Programme.'
119 Interview with Songkane Luangmuninthone, *Ministry of Foreign Affairs* (Vientiane, Laos), 13 July 2007.
120 'South-East Asia's Jamboree: Fifth from the Right Is the Party-Pooper', *The Economist*, 2007, www.economist.com, Barry Desker, 'Where the ASEAN Charter Comes up Short', *The Straits Times*, 18 July 2008.
121 Roberts, *ASEAN's Myanmar Crisis: Challenges to the Pursuit of a Security community*, p. 184.
122 Acharya, *Constructing a Security community in Southeast Asia: ASEAN and the Problem of Regional Order*, p. 242.

6 Myanmar in ASEAN: the key challenge to cohesion and the ASEAN Way?

1 James Cotton, 'The ASEAN Dynamic – the Road to a 2020 Security community Passes through Yangon', ASEAN Focus Group, 2004, www.aseanfocus.com/asiananalysis/article.cfm?articleID=769.
2 Yukio Okamoto, 'Japan and the United States: The Essential Alliance', *The Washington Quarterly* 25, no. 2 (2002): p. 66.
3 Marwaan Macan-Markar, 'Malaysian MPs Criticise Burmese Junta', Mizzima News, 2004, www.mizzimma.com/archives/news-in-2004/news-in-jun/09-jun04–17.htm.
4 'A Regional Perspective on Burma: An Interview with M.R. Sukhumbhand Paribatra', *Irrawaddy*, July 2004.
5 Nick Cumming-Bruce, 'Malaysia Pressures Myanmar for Change', *International Herald Tribune*, 23 March 2005.
6 'ASEAN's Image Hurt by Shakeup in Myanmar, Malaysia Says', *Kyodo News*, 21 October 2004.
7 Jurgen Haacke, '"Enhanced Interaction" with Myanmar and the Project of a Security community: Is ASEAN Refining or Breaking with Its Diplomatic and Security Culture?', *Contemporary Southeast Asia* 27, no. 2 (2005): p. 195.
8 US Deputy Secretary of State, Robert Zoellick, stated, 'I did express our concern about how it would hinder our dealings with ASEAN if Burma were the chair, but I recognize that's a decision for the ASEAN countries to make.... Burma's role puts severe limitations on what the US can do, so I can't go beyond that at this point, we'll see what ASEAN decides to do'. 'ASEAN–US Ties at Risk If Myanmar Becomes Chair, Says Top US Official', *Agence France Presse*, 4 May 2005.
9 'Myanmar, Accountability to Top ASEAN Meeting in Laos: Diplomats', *Channel News Asia*, 22 July 2005.
10 Salim Osman, 'Myanmar May Not Chair ASEAN', *The Straits Times*, 24 April 2005.
11 In December 2004, through unofficial channels of communication, Myanmar was warned that any pledge towards democracy would only be considered credible when followed by the actual release of Aung San Suu Kyi from house arrest. Haacke, '"Enhanced Interaction" with Myanmar and the Project of a Security community: Is ASEAN Refining or Breaking with Its Diplomatic and Security Culture?', p. 196.
12 Progress in ASEAN will be dominated by a 'concern about what will happen if they were on the receiving end of such intervention'. Interview with Aileen Baviera, Department of Asian Studies (Dean), University of the Philippines (Manila), 17 November 2005.
13 'Myanmar, Accountability to Top ASEAN Meeting in Laos: Diplomats.'
14 'Malaysia to Press for Myanmar to Be Denied ASEAN Chair: Report', Channel News Asia, 2005, www.channelnewsasia.com/stories/afp_asiapacific/print/138635/1/.html.
15 Cumming-Bruce, 'Malaysia Pressures Myanmar for Change.'

16 'Malaysian Prime Minister Defends Blocking of Anti-Myanmar Motion in Parliament', Channel News Asia, 2005, www.channelnewsasia.com/stories/afp_asiapacific/view/145145/1/.html.
17 'Malaysian Parliament Delays ASEAN Chairmanship Debate', *Dow Jones International News*, 27 April 2005.
18 William Hollingworth, 'Myanmar Denies Using Chemical Weapons on Karen Soldiers', *Kyodo News*, 22 April 2005.
19 'Singapore PM in Talks with Myanmar Leaders', Bernama, 2005, www.bernama.com/bernama/v3/printable.php?id=126881.
20 'MFA Says What Happens in Myanmar Affects Whole of ASEAN', Channel News Asia, 2005, www.channelnewsasia.com/stories/singaporelocalnews/print/139115/1/.html.
21 'ASEAN to Discuss Myanmar's Political Situation Next Month', 4 March 2005.
22 Haacke, '"Enhanced Interaction" with Myanmar and the Project of a Security community: Is ASEAN Refining or Breaking with Its Diplomatic and Security Culture?', p. 196.
23 'Impasse over Myanmar at ASEAN's Minister's Retreat in Philippines', *Agence France Presse*, 11 April 2005.
24 'Myanmar May Give up ASEAN Chair to Uphold Common Interests: Singapore's Yeo', *Agence France Presse* 2005.
25 Osman, 'Myanmar May Not Chair ASEAN.'
26 'Philippines May Yet Assume 2006 Chairmanship of ASEAN', *Asia Pulse*, 26 June 2005.
27 'Myanmar May Give up ASEAN Chair to Uphold Common Interests: Singapore's Yeo.'
28 'Myanmar, Accountability to Top ASEAN Meeting in Laos: Diplomats.'
29 'Burma Will Not Take ASEAN Chair', BBC News, 2005, http://news.bbc.co.uk/go/pr/fr/-/2/hi/asia-pacific/4715283.stm, 'Myanmar Gives up ASEAN Chairmanship', Channel News Asia, 2005, www.channelnewsasia.com/stories/afp_asiapacific/view/159895/1/.html.
30 'ASEAN Leadership Uncertain after Myanmar Skips Turn', Reuters, 29 August 2005.
31 Teresa Kok, 'On the Occasion of the ASEAN Ministerial Meeting (Amm), Laos, 26–29 July 2005', ASEAN Inter-Parliamentary Caucus on Democracy in Myanmar, 2005, www.aseanmp.org/media/ps_260705.html.
32 Christopher Roberts, *ASEAN's Myanmar Crisis: Challenges to the Pursuit of a Security community* (Singapore: ISEAS, 2010), pp. 88–89.
33 These concerns were raised in interview by many policy makers and scholars throughout Southeast Asia.
34 'EU Unimpressed by Burma's ASEAN Move', *The Nation*, 15 September 2005, 'Bush Pressures ASEAN over Myanmar, Offers Bird Flu Help', *Agence France Press*, 18 November 2005.
35 'Expelling Myanmar from ASEAN Will Not Solve Problem: Singapore's Lee', *Agence France Presse*, 29 September 2005.
36 Singapore Foreign Minister George Yeo described the decision as 'sudden' and 'bizarre'. 'ASEAN Chides China, India for Inaction over Myanmar', *Agence France Presse*, 30 March 2006.
37 'Thai PM: Burma Never Informs ASEAN Neighbours of Political Developments', BBC, 14 December 2005.
38 Eileen Ng, 'Myanmar Told That Suu Kyi's Detention a Slap to ASEAN, Says Official', Associated Press, 11 December 2005.
39 Vaclav Havel and Bishop Desmond M. Tutu, *Threat to Peace: A Call for the UN Security Council to Act in Burma* (London: DLA Piper Rudnick Gray Cary, 2005), p. 7.

40 Lee Jones, 'ASEAN's Albatross: ASEAN's Burma Policy, from Constructive Engagement to Critical Disengagement', *Asian Security* 4, no. 3 (2008): p. 282.
41 Kavi Chongkittavorn, 'Record of ASEAN Discussion Reveals "Bitterness" with Burma', *The Nation*, 25 December 2005.
42 'UN's Burma Envoy Quits', SBS World News, 9 January 2006.
43 'Malaysian PM: ASEAN to Continue "Constructive" Engagement with Myanmar', BBC, 11 December 2005.
44 'Malaysian FM Says Myanmar Holding ASEAN Hostage', Dow Jones Newswires, 18 April 2006.
45 'Burma (Myanmar) Fact Sheet', Australian Department of Foreign Affairs, 2010, www.dfat.gov.au.
46 'ASEAN Chides China, India for Inaction over Myanmar.'
47 Nyan Win also refused to discuss the issue privately with his Thai and Malaysian counterparts, saying, 'the program is tight, we've got no time to meet bilaterally'. Sean Yoong, 'Myanmar Holds Firm on Suu Kyi Detention', *Washington Post*, 29 May 2006.
48 'Myanmar Dissident Healthy, U.N. Agent Says after Meeting', *The New York Times*, 21 May 2006.
49 'ASEAN Set to Wash Its Hands of Burma', *The Australian*, 22 June 2006.
50 'Transcript of Remarks by Minister for Foreign Affairs George Yeo in Parliament on 2 March 2006', Singapore Ministry of Foreign Affairs, 2006, http://app.mfa.gov.sg/2006/press/view_press.asp?post_id=1586.
51 Jones, 'ASEAN's Albatross: ASEAN's Burma Policy, from Constructive Engagement to Critical Disengagement', p. 283.
52 Hamid Albar Syed, 'It Is Not Possible to Defend Myanmar', *Wall Street Journal*, 24 July 2006.
53 Kavi Chongkittavorn, 'ASEAN Changes Tack to Call for UN Debate on Burma', *The Nation*, 4 July 2006.
54 Jones, 'ASEAN's Albatross: ASEAN's Burma Policy, from Constructive Engagement to Critical Disengagement', p. 283. Cuba officially protested through a letter to the UNSC (S/2006/780) on 19 September 2006. The UNSC did not receive any correspondence on the subject from ASEAN.
55 Ibid., p. 283.
56 'Summary Record of 52nd Meeting: A/C.3/61/Sr.52', A/C.3/61/SR.52 (New York: Third Committee, United Nations, 2007).
57 Indonesia's Foreign Minister, Hassan Wirajuda, stated that 'our view on Myanmar is that it should be more forthcoming in its interaction with its own ASEAN family, otherwise there is nothing much we can do when the United Nations through its Security Council decides to make its own moves on the question of Myanmar … As we are not well informed with what they are doing, we are not well-equipped to help defend Myanmar'. 'ASEAN Is Losing Patience with Myanmar', Reuters, 23 August 2006.
58 R. Ravichandran, 'Myanmar Does Not Pose Security Threat, Says Abdullah', *Bernama Daily Malaysian News*, 13 January 2007.
59 Abdul Khalik, 'RI Likely to Abstain on Myanmar', *The Jakarta Post*, 13 January 2007.
60 'ASEAN Says It Must Take Lead on Myanmar', *Agence France Presse*, 14 January 2007.
61 'ASEAN in a Better Position to Handle Myanmar Issue', Ministry of Foreign Affairs, Wisma Putra, 2007, www.kln.gov.my/?m_id=81&year=2007.
62 'ASEAN Should Not Be Held Hostage over Myanmar Issue: PM Lee', Channel News Asia, 2 June 2007.
63 'Malaysian Foreign Minister Urges Collective ASEAN Stance on Burma', Bernama Daily Malaysian News, 21 May 2007.

64 'Annan Speaks His Mind on ASEAN, Myanmar', Bernama Daily Malaysian News, 13 July 2007.
65 Mohd Azizaziz Noor, 'Better Not to Interfere; ASEAN Served Well by Its Non-Intervention in Myanmar's Affairs', *Today*, 19 July 2007.
66 Roberts, *ASEAN's Myanmar Crisis: Challenges to the Pursuit of a Security community*, p. 88.
67 The price of petrol had been as little as 14 cents just two years earlier. Christopher Roberts, 'Plight of Myanmar's People: Challenges for the International Community', S. Rajaratnam School of International Studies, 4 October 2007.
68 Andrew Selth, 'Burma's Saffron Revolution and the Limits of International Influence', *Australian Journal of International Affairs* 62, no. 3 (2008): p. 183.
69 Lily Zubaidah Rahim, 'Fragmented Community and Unconstructive Engagements: ASEAN and Burma's SPDC Regime', *Critical Asian Studies* 40, no. 1 (2008): p. 68.
70 Alan Collins, 'A People-Oriented ASEAN: A Door Ajar or Closed for Civil Society Organisations', *Contemporary Southeast Asia* 30, no. 2 (2008): p. 321.
71 'Statement by ASEAN Chair: Singapore's Minister for Foreign Affairs Geroge Yeo, New York', ASEAN Secretariat, 2007, www.aseansec.org/20974.htm.
72 Jurgen Haacke, 'ASEAN and the Situation in Myanmar/Burma', in *Myanmar/Burma: Challenges and Perspectives*, ed. Guo Xiaolin (Stockholm-Nacka, Sweden: Institute for Security and Development Study, 2008), p. 140.
73 Donald K Emmerson, 'ASEAN's "Black Swans"', *Journal of Democracy* 19, no. 3 (2008): p. 74.
74 Selth, 'Burma's Saffron Revolution and the Limits of International Influence', p. 285. See also Ardeth Maung Thawnghmung and Maung Aung Myoe, 'Myanmar in 2007: A Turning Point in the "Roadmap"?', *Asian Survey* XLVIII, no. 1 (2008): p. 19.
75 'Singapore Ministry of Foreign Affairs Spokesman's Comments on the Situation in Myanmar, September 27 2007', Ministry of Foreign Affairs, http://app.mfa.gov.sg/pr/read_content.asp?View,8314.
76 Haacke, 'ASEAN and the Situation in Myanmar/Burma', p. 139.
77 Selth, 'Burma's Saffron Revolution and the Limits of International Influence', p. 285.
78 Robert H. Taylor, 'Myanmar in 2007: Growing Pressure for Change but the Regime Remains Obdurate', in *Southeast Asian Affairs 2008*, ed. Daljit Singh and Tin Maung Maung Than (Singapore: ISEAS, 2008), p. 260.
79 Thawnghmung and Myoe, 'Myanmar in 2007: A Turning Point in the "Roadmap"?', p. 18.
80 For a concise summary of financial relations between the two countries see Rahim, 'Fragmented Community and Unconstructive Engagements: ASEAN and Burma's SPDC Regime', pp. 84–86. For information concerning certain military relations between Singapore and Myanmar see Jane's Intelligence Database.
81 Haacke, 'ASEAN and the Situation in Myanmar/Burma', p. 144.
82 Ibid., p. 147.
83 Jones, 'ASEAN's Albatross: ASEAN's Burma Policy, from Constructive Engagement to Critical Disengagement', p. 286.
84 Thawnghmung and Myoe, 'Myanmar in 2007: A Turning Point in the "Roadmap"?', p. 19.
85 Emmerson, 'ASEAN's "Black Swans"', p. 74.
86 'Security Council Told of 'Positive' Outcomes of Visit to Myanmar by Special Adviser, with Continuing Concerns over Human Rights Situation', US Fed News, 13 November 2007.
87 Vijay Joshi, 'ASEAN Cancels UN Myanmar Briefing, but Urges Move to Democracy', Dow Jones International News, 20 November 2007, Mergawati Zulfakar, 'Testing ASEAN's Patience', *The Star*, 21 November 2007.
88 Jones, 'ASEAN's Albatross: ASEAN's Burma Policy, from Constructive Engagement to Critical Disengagement', p. 286.

89 Velloor Ravi and Suk-Wai Cheong, 'Discord at the "Family Dinner"', *The Straits Times*, 21 November 2007.
90 Even Malaysia's Foreign Minister, Syed Hamid, blamed the outcome on Singapore's approach by stating 'the host country invited Gambari – it was not something that was done by ASEAN.' Benni Avni, 'Asian Nations Deal Blow to U.N. Efforts on Burma', *The New York Sun*, 20 November 2007.
91 'ASEAN Chairman Statement on Myanmar', ASEAN Secretariat, 2007, www.aseansec.org/21057.htm.
92 Varunee Torsricharoen, 'Singapore Miscalculates Balance of Power over Myanmar Issue', *Kyodo News*, 21 November 2007.
93 Zulfakar, 'Testing ASEAN's Patience'.
94 Haacke, 'ASEAN and the Situation in Myanmar/Burma', p. 154.
95 Vivian Ho, 'Malaysia Says ASEAN Will Prod Myanmar on Reform in 'Acceptable' Ways', *Kyodo News*, 16 January 2006.
96 Vivian Ho, 'ASEAN Has Made "Important Evolution" on Myanmar', *Kyodo News*, 28 July 2006.
97 Haacke, 'ASEAN and the Situation in Myanmar/Burma', p. 141.
98 'EU Shares ASEAN Frustration over Myanmar: Foreign Policy Chief', *Agence France Presse*, 21 April 2006.
99 Abdul Khalik, 'EU Says Talks with ASEAN Won't Be Derailed by Myanmar', *The Jakarta Post*, 8 August 2006.
100 'ASEAN, US Mull 1st Summit in November., but Differ over Myanmar', *Kyodo News*, 3 February 2006.
101 Eileen Ng, 'EU Trade Chief Says Myanmar's Poor Human Rights Record Could Hinder Trade Pact with ASEAN', Associated Press Newswires, 15 May 2006.
102 'EU Hopes for Creating FTA with ASEAN Countries', *Xinhua*, 20 November 2010.
103 'US Says Myanmar Sanctions Unaffected by ASEAN Trade Pact', *AFX Asia*, 24 August 2006.
104 Andrew Selth, 'Even Paranoids Have Enemies: Cyclone Nargis and Myanmar's Fears of Invasion', *Contemporary Southeast Asia* 30, no. No. 3 (2008): p. 386.
105 'Burma/Myanmar after Nargis: Time to Normalise Aid Relations' (Brussels: International Crisis Group, 2008), p. 3, Nga Pham, 'Burmese Still Struggling after Cyclone', BBC, 5 August 2008.
106 'Burma/Myanmar after Nargis: Time to Normalise Aid Relations', p. 7.
107 Selth, 'Even Paranoids Have Enemies: Cyclone Nargis and Myanmar's Fears of Invasion', p. 387.
108 'Burma/Myanmar after Nargis: Time to Normalise Aid Relations', pp. 2–3.
109 A second large-scale wave of deaths among survivors in the delta was thought to be a high possibility by the UN and relief agencies due to 'a lack of clean drinking water, water-borne diseases and malnutrition'. Jurgen Haacke, 'ASEAN and Political Change in Myanmar: Towards a Regional Initiative', *Contemporary Southeast Asia* 30, no. 3 (2008): p. 370. While these risks were largely averted, such an outcome was impossible to predict at the time and was largely due to the actions of ASEAN and the United Nations, as will be discussed later in the chapter. 'After Myanmar's Cyclone', Jane's Intelligence, 2008, www.janes.com.
110 Selth, 'Even Paranoids Have Enemies: Cyclone Nargis and Myanmar's Fears of Invasion', p. 388.
111 'Myanmar's Junta Says Referendum Voters Accepted New Constitution', *Kyodo News*, 30 May 2008.
112 'Burma/Myanmar after Nargis: Time to Normalise Aid Relations', p. 3.
113 Discussions with Burmese interlocutor, May 2008.
114 Ian Holiday, 'Burma: Beyond Burma Versus the World', *Far Eastern Economic Review*, 6 June 2008, p. 48.

115 Jonathan Pearlman, 'Rudd Says Donors Must Bash in Doors', *Sydney Morning Herald*, 10 May 2008.
116 Cited in Selth, 'Even Paranoids Have Enemies: Cyclone Nargis and Myanmar's Fears of Invasion', pp. 393–394.
117 'Transcript of Minister for Foreign Affairs George Yeo's Interview with Dow Jones on 16 July', Singapore Ministry of Foreign Affairs, 2008, http://app.mfa.gov.sg/2006/press/view_press.asp?post_id=4168.
118 'ASEAN Takes Charge in Myanmar Relief Effort', *AsiaInt*, 30 May 2008.
119 'French Naval Aid Ship Le Mistral Due Off Burma as Junta Refuses Help', *Sunday Business Post*, 18 May 2008. It is also important to note that most Western governments initially offered aid on the condition that it was delivered outside government structures. 'Burma/Myanmar after Nargis: Time to Normalise Aid Relations', p. 6.
120 Selth, 'Even Paranoids Have Enemies: Cyclone Nargis and Myanmar's Fears of Invasion.'
121 'ASEAN Emergency Rapid Assessment Team Mission Report' (Jakarta: ASEAN Secretariat, 2008).
122 Ibid.
123 Correspondence with official source from an Embassy in Singapore, 21 January 2009. See also 'Transcript of Minister for Foreign Affairs George Yeo's Interview with Dow Jones on 16 July.'
124 Emphasis by author. Haacke, 'ASEAN and Political Change in Myanmar: Towards a Regional Initiative', p. 371.
125 'Special ASEAN Foreign Ministers Meeting Chairman's Statement, Singapore', ASEAN Secretariat, 2008, www.aseansec.org/21557.htm.
126 For more information concerning these challenges see Roberts, *ASEAN's Myanmar Crisis: Challenges to the Pursuit of a Security community*, p. 193.
127 Donald K Emmerson, 'Critical Terms: Security, Democracy, and Regionalism in Southeast Asia', in *Hard Choices: Security, Democracy, and Regionalism in Southeast Asia*, ed. Donald K Emmerson (Stanford: Stanford University Press, 2008), p. 43.
128 'After Myanmar's Cyclone', 'Burma/Myanmar after Nargis: Time to Normalise Aid Relations', p. 9.
129 'Burma: Lawyer's Testimony Highlights Distorted Justice', *Human Rights Watch*, 16 December 2008.
130 Haacke, 'ASEAN and Political Change in Myanmar: Towards a Regional Initiative'.
131 Emmerson, 'Critical Terms: Security, Democracy, and Regionalism in Southeast Asia', p. 49.
132 Ibid., p. 47.
133 'Burma's Forgotten Prisoners', Human Rights Watch, 2009, www.hrw.org/node/84743.
134 Aside from the USDP, most of the the remaining votes went to another military aligned party – the National Unity Party. 'The New, Post-Election Landscape yet to Take Shape', *The Economist Intelligence Unit*, 1 January 2011.
135 Roberts, *ASEAN's Myanmar Crisis: Challenges to the Pursuit of a Security community*, p. 200.
136 Leslie Koh, 'George Yeo Gives ASEAN … C Grade for Its Handling of Myanmar Issues', *The Straits Times*, 18 July 2008.

7 Regionalism anew? Institutional outcomes and the limitations to change

1 These goals represent a small sample of the hundreds of goals contained in the *Bali Concord II* (2003), the *Plan of Action for a Security community* (2004), the *Vientiane Plan of Action* (2004), the *ASEAN Charter* (2007) and the *ASEAN Blueprint for a Security community* (2009).

2 David Martin Jones and Michael L.R. Smith, 'Making Process, Not Progress', *International Security* 32, no. 1 (2007): p. 163.
3 ASEAN, 'Memorandum of Understanding on the ASEAN Swap Arrangements', Kuala Lumpur, 5 August, 1977, www.aseansec.org/1388.htm.
4 Praduma B. Rana, 'East Asian Regionalism', in *Regional Outlook: Southeast Asia 2007–08*, ed. Asad-ul Iqbal Latif and Poh Onn Lee (Singapore: Institute of Southeast Asian Studies, 2007), pp. 73–74.
5 'Charting Progress Towards Regional Economic Integration: ASEAN Economic Community Scorecard' (Jakarta: ASEAN, 2010), p. 7.
6 Manu Bhaskaran, 'Review of Southeast Asian Economic Developments', in *Southeast Asian Affairs*, ed. Daljit Singh (Singapore: ISEAS, 2010), p. 43.
7 Adam Schwarz and Roland Villinger, 'Integrating Southeast Asia's Economies', *The McKinsey Quarterly*, Number 1 (2004): p. 40.
8 Rodolfo C. Severino, 'Regional Economic Integration and the ASEAN Charter', in *Regional Outlook: Southeast Asia 2008/2009* (Singapore: ISEAS, 2009), p. 73.
9 Vandoren, 'Regional Economic Integration in Southeast Asia', *Asia Europe Journal* 3, no. 4 (2005): pp. 521–525.
10 'Declaration of ASEAN Concord II (Bali Concord II)', ASEAN Secretariat, 2003, www.aseansec.org/15159.htm.
11 Chien-Huei Wu, 'The ASEAN Economic Community under the ASEAN Charter; Its External Economic Relations and Dispute Settlement Mechanisms', in *European Yearbook of International Law*, ed. C Herrmann and J.P Terhechte (Berlin, Heidelberg: Springer-Verlag, 2010), p. 336.
12 'ASEAN Economic Community Blueprint' (Jakarta: ASEAN, 2007), pp. 7–8.
13 Geoffrey B. Cockerman, 'Regional Integration in ASEAN: Institutional Design and the ASEAN Way', *East Asia: An International Quarterly* 27 (2010): p. 183. Carlyle A. Thayer, 'Background Briefing: ASEAN's Dispute Resolution Guidelines', *Thayer Consultancy*, 8 April 2010.
14 Jemy Gatdula, 'WTO Win on Cigarettes', *BusinessWorld*, 2 December 2010.
15 Here, Iwan Gunawan, from the ASEAN Secretariat, provides an example during interview of the impact of a strengthened ASEAN Secretariat complete with a legal personality: 'Let me talk about the approach of AusAid. Two out of ten ASEAN countries are not OECD eligible, this is Brunei and Singapore ... and so some of the people came up with the co-sharing formula of 80:20. This way they satisfy OECD rules. This way ASEAN can say it's for all ten but the other twenty per cent we have to come up with ourselves. This is a good model of how international assistance can be used to help empower the regional organization like ASEAN, to engage some of the countries to do things more directly. In practice this kind of approach has a different value to what bilateral aid can do, through ASEAN with things like customs harmonization, you can give aid bilaterally, but if you go through the ten it is more efficient and you can handle the ten all together without negotiating individually. So this is one good example and I'm sure in the area of non-economic aid the same logic could be explored. This way you could reach out to Myanmar without creating a difficult political problem.' Interview with Iwan Gunawan, ASEAN Secretariat, 27 April 2007.
16 John Ravenhill, 'Fighting Irrelevance: An Economic Community "with ASEAN Characteristics"', *The Pacific Review* 21, no. 4 (2008): p. 474. As Caballero-Anthony adds, the Charter would grant ASEAN status under international law and would, therefore, allow ASEAN to enter transactions in its own right'. Mely Caballero-Anthony, 'The ASEAN Charter: An Opportunity Missed or One That Cannot Be Missed?', in *Southeast Asian Affairs 2008*, ed. Daljit Singh and Tin Maung Maung Than (Singapore: ISEAS, 2008), p. 76.
17 Joseph Chinyong Liow, 'Southeast Asia in 2009: A Year Fraught with Challenges', in *Southeast Asian Affairs 2010*, ed. Daljit Singh (Singapore: ISEAS, 2010), p. 4.

18 Masahiro Kawai and Ganeshan Wignaraja, 'EAFTA or CEPEA: Which Way Forward?', *ASEAN Economic Bulletin* 25, no. 2 (2008): p. 113.
19 Ravenhill, 'Fighting Irrelevance: An Economic Community "with ASEAN Characteristics"', p. 476.
20 Donald E. Weatherbee, *International Relations in Southeast Asia: The Struggle for Regional Autonomy*, 2nd edn (Rowman and Littlefield: Plymouth, 2009), p. 213.
21 Raymond Atje and Kartika Pratiwi, 'A Bumpy Road toward ASEAN Economic Community 2015', in *The Global Economic Crisis* (Singapore: ISEAS, 2010), p. 138.
22 'ASEAN Chief Warns 2015 Single Market Goal in Peril', *Agence France Presse*, 29 November 2010.
23 'Singapore: ASEAN Selects Financial Office Site', Stratfor, 2010, www.stratfor.com.
24 Herbert Dieter, 'Changing Patterns of Regional Governance: From Security to Political Economy?', *The Pacific Review* 22, no. 1 (2009): p. 73.
25 Helen E.S. Nesadurai, 'Global Monitor: The Association of Southeast Asian Nations (ASEAN)', *New Political Economy* 13, no. 2 (2008): p. 375.
26 Liow, 'Southeast Asia in 2009: A Year Fraught with Challenges', p. 17.
27 Mari Pangestu, 'Southeast Asian Regional and International Economic Cooperation', in *International Relations in Southeast Asia: The Struggle for Regional Autonomy*, ed. Donald E. Weatherbee (Lanham: Rowman & Littlefield Publishers, 2005), p. 214.
28 Donald E. Weatherbee, 'Southeast Asia in 2006: Deja Vu All over Again', in *Southeast Asian Affairs 2007*, ed. Daljit Singh and Lorraine C. Salazar (Singapore: Institute of Southeast Asian Studies, 2007), p. 8.
29 Weatherbee, *International Relations in Southeast Asia: The Struggle for Regional Autonomy*, p. 113.
30 'Chairman's Statement of the East Asia Summit Foreign Ministers Informal Consultations', ASEAN, 2010, www.aseansec.org/24914.htm.
31 Christopher Roberts, 'ASEAN Charter: The Model Decision?', *The Straits Times*, 9 September 2005.
32 'Report of the Eminent Persons Group on the ASEAN Charter' (Jakarta: ASEAN, 2006).
33 Ibid., p. 6.
34 Ibid.
35 Ibid., p. 4.
36 Dario Agnote, 'ASEAN Foreign Ministers Agree to Create Human Rights Body', *Kyodo News*, 30 July 2007.
37 'ASEAN Overcomes Resistance, Will Set up Regional Human Rights Commission', *Associated Press Newswires*, 30 July 2007.
38 Jim Gomez, 'ASEAN Agrees to Human Rights Commission', The Irrawaddy, 2007, www.irrawaddy.org.
39 ASEAN, 'Charter of the Association of Southeast Asian Nations' (Jakarta: ASEAN Secretariat, 2007).
40 Ibid.
41 Ibid., p. 18.
42 Ibid., pp. 2, 4.
43 Barry Desker, 'Where the ASEAN Charter Comes up Short', *The Straits Times*, 18 July 2008.
44 Ibid.
45 Ravenhill, 'Fighting Irrelevance: An Economic Community "with ASEAN Characteristics"', p. 479.
46 ASEAN, 'Charter of the Association of Southeast Asian Nations', p. 14.
47 'ASEAN's 'Human-Rights' Council: Not Off to a Great Start', *The Wall Street Journal*, 25 October 2009.

48 Shaun Narine, 'ASEAN in the Twenty-First Century: A Sceptical Review', *Cambridge Review of International Affairs* 22, no. 3 (2009): p. 370.
49 Alan Collins, 'A People-Oriented ASEAN: A Door Ajar or Closed for Civil Society Organisations', *Contemporary Southeast Asia* 30, no. 2 (2008): p. 321.
50 Chalermpalanupap Termsak, 'Significance of the ASEAN Charter', *ASEAN Secretariat*, 24 May 2010.
51 For example, Hartfiel and Job contend that '[t]here are indeed competitive arms acquisition processes underway among Southeast Asian states, for sustaining technological dominance (on Singapore's part) and/or numerical equivalence'. Robert Hartfiel and Brian L. Job, 'Raising the Risks of War: Defence Spending Trends and Competitive Arms Processes in Southeast Asia', *The Pacific Review* 20, no. 1 (2007): p. 15.
52 Tim Huxley, 'Singapore and Malaysia: A Precarious Balance', *Pacific Review* 4, no. 3 (1991): p. 204.
53 'Singapore Risk: Security Risk', Economist Intellgience Unit, 25 July 2007. In 2008, the author attended a dinner at which the fomer Prime Minister and current Minister Mentor, Lee Kuan Yew, was the guest of honour. During his speech, it soon became apparent that the Senior Minister had not changed his perceptions about Malaysia as he argued that if Singapore did not keep up its guard Malaysia would walk right in and take over. Several retractions were issued the next day by the government.
54 Statistical information supplied by NBR Analysis, located at www.nbr.org and the 'Military Balance'. The figures for Myanmar for the years 2008 and 2009 were estimated as no data was available. The estimation was based on a conservative projection of the growth in military expenditure between the years 2006 and 2007.
55 Interview with Ekapong Rimcharone, Office of the National Security Council (Bangkok), 20 February 2006.
56 Interview with Major General Supaluck Suvarnajata, Army Specialist (Bangkok), 18 February 2006.
57 Interview with Lay Vannak, ASEAN Department, Office of the Council of Ministers (Phnom Penh), 29 July 2005. Interview with Sisowath Chanto and Ou Virak, Pannasastra University (Phnom Penh), 30 July 2005.
58 Interview with Rahmat Mohammed, Duty Vice Chancellor University Technology Mara (Kuala Lumpur), 2 June 2006.
59 Interview with Admiral Sunardi, (Jakarta), 4 May 2006. Interview with Interview with Ikrar Nusu Bakti, LIPI (Jakarta), 2 May 2006.
60 Interview with Ikrar Nusu Bakti, LIPI (Jakarta), 2 May 2006.
61 Interview with Aileen Baviera, University of the Philippines (Manila), 17 November 2005, Interview with Ross Quisao, Department of Labour and Employment (Manila, Philippines), 23 November 2005.
62 Interview with Ikrar Nusu Bakti, LIPI (Jakarta), 2 May 2006. Interview with Dick Sofjan, UNDP (Jakarta), 2 May 2006.
63 For example, Interview with Lay Vannak, ASEAN Department, Office of the Council of Ministers (Phnom Penh), 29 July 2005. Interview with Maj. General Krekphong Pukprayrura, Thai Police (Bangkok), 22 February 2006.
64 Interview with senior foreign affairs spokesperson, Ministry of Foreign Affairs (Cambodia), 30 July 2005.
65 On the issue of Cambodian workers, Chap Sotharith stated, 'ten Cambodian's have been shot by Thailand's border guard when trying to cross for work this year alone'. Interview with Chap Sotharith, Director of the Cambodian Institute of Cooperation and Peace (Phnom Penh), 25 July 2005.
66 Interview with Lay Vannak, ASEAN Department (Cambodian Council of Ministers) 29 July 2005.
67 Interview with Ministry of Defence, Singapore, 27 July 2007.
68 Interview with Admiral Sunardi (Jakarta), 4 May 2006.

69 Charles W. Jr. Kegley and Gregory A. Raymond, *When Trust Breaks Down: Alliance Norms and World Politics* (Columbia: University of South Carolina Press, 1990), p. 152.
70 Christopher Roberts, 'ASEAN Institutionalisation: The Function of Political Values and State Capacity', *RSIS Working Paper*, no. 217 (2010): pp. 6–10.
71 Mohammed Ayoob, *The Third World Security Predicament: State Making, Regional Conflict, and the International System* (Boulder, CO: Lynne Rienner, 1995), p. 13.
72 Robert E. Kelly cited in Roberts, 'ASEAN Institutionalisation: The Function of Political Values and State Capacity', p. 3.
73 Boaz Atzili, 'When Good Fences Make Bad Neighbours: Fixed Borders, State Weakness, and International Conflict', *International Security* 31, no. 3 (2007): p. 151.
74 Ibid., p. 150. In the case of the Preah Vihear Temple dispute, for example, 'Thailand's leaders responded to their weak state legitimacy by exploiting nationalist sentiments for domestic political gain'. Roberts, 'ASEAN Institutionalisation: The Function of Political Values and State Capacity', p. 7.
75 Benjamin Miller, 'Between the Revisionist and the Frontier State: Regional Variations in the State War-Propensity', *Review of International Studies* 35, no. S1 (2009): p. 244.
76 Discusions with Bangladeshi General, Asia-Pacific Rountable (Kuala Lumpur, Malaysia), June 2008.
77 Some scholars have examined economic factors in an attempt to quantify the necessary level of wealth within a state before a consolidated form of liberal democracy will be viable. Here, Paul Collier argues that a stable democracy will only emerge once the income level, on a *per capita* basis, exceeds approximately US$2,700 per annum – Myanmar, Cambodia and Laos all fall belwo this threshold. Paul Collier, *Wars, Guns and Votes: Democracy in Dangerous Places* (London: Vintage Books, 2010), p. 21. However, this figure is debateable as other factors such as cultural homgeneity and geography also affect the equation.
78 Karl W. Deutsch, Sidney A. Burrell and Robert A. Kann, *Political Community and the North Atlantic Area: International Organisation in the Light of Historical Experience* (New York: Greenwood Press, 1957), pp. 123–125.
79 Robert E. Kelly, 'Security Theory in the "New Regionalism"', *International Studies Review* 9, no. 2 (2007): p. 218.
80 Frank Schimmelfenning, 'The Normative Origins of Democracy in the European Union: Toward a Transformationlist Theory of Democratization', *European Political Science Review* 2, no. 2 (2010): pp. 211–233.
81 Ayoob, *The Third World Security Predicament: State Making, Regional Conflict, and the International System*, p. 4.
82 Sotharith adds that the security community 'proposal contained many sensitive issues such as democracy and human rights. It is difficult for a one-party country'. Interview with Chap Sotharith, Director of the Cambodian Institute of Cooperation and Peace (Phnom Penh, Cambodia), 25 July 2005.
83 Donald K. Emmerson, 'Security and Community in Southeast Asia: Will the Real ASEAN Please Stand Up?', *Southeast Asia Forum* (2005): p. 177. In a similar context, Etel Solingen has also argued that 'the growing gap between democracies and non-democracies' in the region 'has also brought issues of intervention to the fore'. Etel Solingen, 'ASEAN Cooperation: The Legacy of the Economic Crisis', *International Relations of the Asia-Pacific* 5, no. 1 (2005): p. 16.
84 Interview with M.C. Abad Jr., ARF Unit Director (ASEAN Secretariat, Jakarta), 20 April 2006.
85 Interview with Luan Thuy Dong, Director, Southeast Asian Studies Center (Diplomatic Academy of Vietnam, Hanoi), 7 July 2005. Another researcher within the DAV added the caveat that the 'Indonesian version of democracy has to be limited

to social harmony'. Interview with Nguyen Nam Duong, Diplomatic Academy of Vietnam (Hanoi), 7 July 2005.

86 Hajah Haji Saim Sainah is a professor at University Brunei Darussalam. Hajah Haji Saim Sainah, 'The ASEAN Socio-Culltural Community: How Best to Achieve It?', in *21st Asia Pacific Roundtable Conference: Strengthening Comprehensive and Cooperative Security in the Asia Pacific* (Kuala Lumpur: ISIS Malaysia, 2007), p. 3.

87 Interview with Noel Morada, University of the Philippines (Manila), 18 November 2005. A professor from Malaysia, Dato Zakaria Ahmad, raises another element of ambiguity within the ASEAN Security community project: 'So we know the ASEAN security community is not meant to be a defence pact or a defence alliance. But what we don't know is [what] ... it doesn't do. Where would the five power defence arrangement be allowable within the notion of a security community? Does it mean that they are free to have relationships with external governments like between the US and Singapore or between Myanmar and China?' Interview with Dato' Zakaria Ahmad, Help University College (Kuala Lumpur), 27 May 2006.

88 Narine, 'ASEAN in the Twenty-First Century: A Sceptical Review', p. 369.

89 Roberts, 'ASEAN Institutionalisation: The Function of Political Values and State Capacity', p. 19.

90 The ranks were calculated on the basis of total frequency for all three responses within the survey. Where there was more than one response with equal frequency then the rank was weighted against the respondent's preference for rank.

91 Donald E. Weatherbee, *International Relations in Southeast Asia: The Struggle for Autonomy* (Lanham, MD: Rowman & Littlefield Publishers, 2005), p. 11.

92 Tobias Nischalke, 'Does ASEAN Measure Up? Post Cold War Diplomacy and the Idea of Regional Community', *The Pacific Review* 15, no. 1 (2002): p. 109.

93 Jorn Dosch, *The Changing Dynamics of Southeast Asian Politics* (London: Lynne Rienner, 2007), pp. 21–22. In other words, '[f]oreign policy decision-makers are not simply agents of the national interest but political animals who must worry about their survival in office and the viability of their overall set of political goals, domestic and foreign'. David Skidmore and Valerie M. Hudson, *The Limits to State Autonomy: Societal Groups and Foeign Policy Formulation* (Boulder, CO: Westview, 1993), p. 3.

94 The validity of these figures is reinforced by the fact that they coincide with regional analysis concerning, for example, Thailand's 'war on drugs' and the proliferation of human trafficking in Cambodia and Vietnam. For an overview, see: Weatherbee, *International Relations in Southeast Asia: The Struggle for Regional Autonomy*, pp. 178–196.

95 Such contentions do not detract from the fact that sound economic performance also provides added legitimacy for democratic governments but such legitimacy is sought in the context of attaining viable competive gains through the electoral process – e.g. winning the next election.

96 'ASEAN-10', DFAT, 2010, www.dfat.gov.au/geo/fs/asean.pdf.

97 For example, see Leszek Buszynski, *Asia Pacific Security – Values and Identity* (New York: Routledge, 2004), Nischalke, 'Does ASEAN Measure Up? Post Cold War Diplomacy and the Idea of Region.al Community', pp. 89–117, Amitav Acharya, 'Imagined Proximities: The Making and Remaking of Southeast Asia as a Region', *Southeast Asian Journal of Social Science* 27, no. 1 (1999), Amitav Acharya, *The Quest for Identity: International Relations of Southeast Asia* (New York: Oxford University Press, 2001).

98 Acharya, 'Imagined Proximities: The Making and Remaking of Southeast Asia as a Region', p. 73.

99 Quoted in Acharya, *The Quest for Identity: International Relations of Southeast Asia*, p. 9.
100 Peh Shing Huei, 'Forge ASEAN Identity? Make Membership Worthwhile First', *The Straits Times*, 16 December 2005.
101 This problem was raised in interview by Noel Morada. Interview with Noel Morada, University of the Philippines (Manila), 18 November 2005.
102 Narine, 'ASEAN in the Twenty-First Century: A Sceptical Review', p. 369.

Conclusion: retrospect and prospects

1 Amitav Acharya, *The Quest for Identity: International Relations of Southeast Asia* (New York: Oxford University Press, 2001), pp. 110–111.
2 James R. Ferguson, 'ASEAN Concord II: Policy Prospects for Participant Regional "Development" ', *Contemporary Southeast Asia* 26, no. 3 (2004): pp. 399–400.
3 Boaz Atzili, 'When Good Fences Make Bad Neighbours: Fixed Borders, State Weakness, and International Conflict', *International Security* 31, no. 3 (2007): p. 140.
4 Donald K Emmerson, ' "Southeast Asia": What's in a Name?', *Journal of Southeast Asian Studies* 15, no. 1 (1984): p. 1.
5 Amitav Acharya, 'Collective Identity and Conflict Management in Southeast Asia', in *Security Communities*, ed. Emanuel Adler and Michael Barnett (Cambridge: Cambridge University Press, 1998), p. 219.
6 Amitav Acharya, *Constructing a Security community in Southeast Asia: ASEAN and the Problem of Regional Order* (London: Routledge, 2001), p. 208. In a subsequent 2009 edition of the same book, Acharya is even more circumspect where he states that '[a] lthough ASEAN's progress towards the ascendant phase level looked more promising in the early 1990s than in the latter part of that decade, such prospects appear somewhat better in recent years'. *Constructing a Security community in Southeast Asia: ASEAN and the Problem of Regional Order*, 2nd edn (London: Routledge, 2009), p. 298.
7 Yuen Foong Khong, 'ASEAN and the Southeast Asian Security Complex', in *Regional Orders: Building Security in the New World*, ed. David A. Lake and Patrick M. Morgan (Pennsylvania: Pennsylvania State University Press, 1997), p. 339.
8 Discussions with Rodolfo Severino (media interview, Channel News Asia, Singapore), 21 November 2007.
9 Yukiko Nishikawa, 'The "ASEAN Way" and Asian Regional Security', *Politics and Policy* 35, no. 1 (2007): p. 43.
10 Nicholas Khoo, 'Deconstructing the ASEAN Security community: A Review Essay', *International Relations of the Asia-Pacific* 4 (2004): p. 40.
11 Ibid.
12 Nishikawa, by contrast, argues that 'the idea of a security community can be illustrated, to a certain degree, by the region's dispute settlement mechanisms'. Nishikawa, 'The "ASEAN Way" and Asian Regional Security', p. 43.
13 Acharya, *Constructing a Security community in Southeast Asia: ASEAN and the Problem of Regional Order*, p. 216.
14 For a detailed assessment of why this is the case see Christopher Roberts, 'Region and Identity: The Many Faces of Southeast Asia', *Asian Politics and Policy* 3, no. 3 (2011, forthcoming).
15 While the level of integration in the political-security and socio-cultural spheres can be assessed as being low, the overall assessment concerning the level of complex integration is counter-balanced by a medium-low level of elite level socio-cultural integration and a medium to medium-low level of economic integration. The notion of a limited economic and security regime is adapted from Tim Huxley's assessment that ASEAN constitutes a 'limited security regime'. Tim Huxley, *Insecurity in the ASEAN Region* (London: Royal United Services Institute for Defence Studies, 1993), p. 81.

16 However, subsequent progress in terms of economic regionalization would be at a sub-ASEAN level (i.e. between a core group of ASEAN states) and unless appropriate mechanisms and support is offered to enable the remaining ASEAN members to join at a later date (e.g. along the lines of the AFTA process) then there is the risk that this process, if left unchecked, could exacerbate regional divides. Further, other than the AFTA example, the ASEAN members are in practice yet to demonstrate a significant willingness to proceed on a sub-ASEAN basis.

17 For example, the ASEAN scholarships offered by Singapore since 1999 to students from the remaining ASEAN member-states to obtain university degrees from the country's major tertiary institutions.

Select bibliography

Acharya, Amitav. *Asia Rising: Who Is Leading?* Singapore: World Scientific, 2008.

Acharya, Amitav. 'The Association of Southeast Asian Nations: "Security community" or "Defence Community"?' *Pacific Affairs* 64, no. 2 (1991): 159–177.

Acharya, Amitav. 'Collective Identity and Conflict Management in Southeast Asia'. In *Security Communities*, edited by Emanuel Adler and Michael Barnett, 198–227. Cambridge: Cambridge University Press, 1998.

Acharya, Amitav. *Constructing a Security community in Southeast Asia: ASEAN and the Problem of Regional Order*. London: Routledge, 2001.

Acharya, Amitav. *Constructing a Security community in Southeast Asia: ASEAN and the Problem of Regional Order*. 2nd edn London: Routledge, 2009.

Acharya, Amitav. *The Quest for Identity: International Relations of Southeast Asia*. New York: Oxford University Press, 2001.

Acharya, Amitav. 'A Regional Security community in Southeast Asia?' *Journal of Strategic Studies* 18, no. 3 (1995): 175–200.

Adler, Emanuel and Michael Barnett, eds. *Security Communities*. Cambridge: Cambridge University Press, 1998.

Ahmad, Zakaria Haji and Baladas Ghoshal. 'The Political Future of ASEAN after the Asian Crisis'. *International Affairs* 75, no. 4 (1999): 759–778.

Alagappa, Muthiah. 'Constructing Security Order in Asia: Conception and Issues'. In *Asian Security Order: Instrumental and Normative Features*, edited by Muthiah Alagappa, 70–105. Stanford, California: Stanford University Press, 2003.

Ashley, David W. 'The Failure of Conflict Resolution in Cambodia'. In *Cambodia and the International Community: The Quest for Peace, Development and Democracy*, edited by Frederick Z. Brown and David G. Timberman, 1–18. Singapore: ISEAS, 1998.

Atje, Raymond, and Kartika Pratiwi. 'A Bumpy Road toward ASEAN Economic Community 2015'. In *The Global Economic Crisis*, 125–143. Singapore: ISEAS, 2010.

Atzili, Boaz. 'When Good Fences Make Bad Neighbours: Fixed Borders, State Weakness, and International Conflict'. *International Security* 31, no. 3 (2007): 139–173.

Barnett, Michael. 'Social Constructivism'. In *The Globalisation of World Politics: An Introduction to International Relations*, edited by John Baylis and Steve Smith. Oxford: Oxford University Press, 2006.

Baylis, John, Steve Smith and Patricia Owens. *The Globalization of World Politics: An Introduction to International Relations*. Oxford: Oxford University Press, 2008.

Beeson, Mark. 'Asean's Ways: Still Fit for Purpose?' *Cambridge Review of International Affairs* 22, no. 3 (2009): 333–343.

Beeson, Mark. *Regionalism and Globalization in East Asia*. Basingstoke: Palgrave Macmillan, 2007.

Beeson, Mark. 'South-East Asia and the International Financial Institutions'. In *The Political Economy of Southeast Asia: Markets, Power and Contestation*, edited by Garry Rodan, Kevin Hewison and Richard Robison, 240–57. South Melbourne: Oxford University Press, 2006.

Beeson, Mark, and Alex J. Bellamy. *Securing Southeast Asia: The Politics of Security Sector Reform*. Abington, Oxon: Routledge, 2008.

Bellamy, Alex J. *Security Communities and Their Neighbours: Regional Fortresses or Global Integrators?* Basingstoke: Palgrave Macmillan, 2004.

Bengtsson, Rikard. 'The Cognitive Dimension of Stable Peace'. In *Stable Peace among Nations*, edited by Arie M. Kacowicz, Yaacov Bar-Simon-Tov, Ole Elgstrom and Alexander Jerneck, 92–107. Maryland: Rowman and Littlefield, 2000.

Breslin, Shaun. 'Theorising East Asian Regionalism(S): New Regionalism and Asia's Future(S)'. In *Advancing East Asian Regionalism*, edited by Melissa G. Curley and Nicholas Thomas, 26–51. Oxon: Routledge, 2007.

Bull, Hedley. *The Anarchical Society. A Study of Order in World Politics*. London: Macmillan, 1977.

Buszynski, Leszek. 'ASEAN, the Declaration on Conduct, and the South China Sea'. *Contemporary Southeast Asia* 25, no. 3 (2003): 343–362.

Buszynski, Leszek. *Asia Pacific Security – Values and Identity*. New York: Routledge, 2004.

Buszynski, Leszek. *SEATO – the Failure of an Alliance Strategy*. Singapore: Singapore University Press, 1983.

Buszynski, Leszek. 'Thailand and Myanmar: The Perils of Constructive Engagement'. *Pacific Review* 11, no. 2 (1998): 290–305.

Buzan, Barry. 'From International System to International Society: Structural Realism and Regime Theory Meet the English School'. *International Organization* 47, no. 3 (1993): 327–352.

Buzan, Barry. 'Security Architecture in Asia: The Interplay of Regional and Global Level'. *The Pacific Review* 16, no. 2 (2003): 143–173.

Buzan, Barry and Ole Waever. *Regions and Powers: The Structure of International Security*. Cambridge: Cambridge University Press, 2003.

Caballero-Anthony, Mely. 'The ASEAN Charter: An Opportunity Missed or One That Cannot Be Missed?' In *Southeast Asian Affairs 2008*, edited by Daljit Singh and Tin Maung Maung Than, 71–85. Singapore: ISEAS, 2008.

Caballero-Anthony, Mely. *Regional Security in Southeast Asia: Beyond the ASEAN Way*. Singapore: ISEAS, 2005.

Capie, David and Paul Evans. *The Asia-Pacific Security Lexicon*. 2nd edn. Singapore: ISEAS, 2007.

Case, William. 'Low-Quality Democracy and Varied Authoritarianism: Elites and Regimes in Southeast Asia Today'. *The Pacific Review* 22, no. 3 (2009): 255–269.

Cashman, Greg. *What Causes War? An Introduction to the Theories of International Conflicts*. New York: Lexington Books, 1993.

Chandler, David, Norman G. Owen, William R. Roff, David Joel Steinberg, Robert H. Taylor, Jean Gelman Taylor, Alexander Woodside and David K. Wyatt. *The Emergence of Modern Southeast Asia: A New History*. Edited by Norman G. Owen. Singapore: Singapore University Press, 2005.

Chang, Pao-Min. 'Beijing Versus Hanoi: The Diplomacy over Kampuchea'. *Asian Survey* 23, no. 5 (1983): 598–618.

Charon, Joel. *The Meaning of Sociology: A Reader*. Englewood, CA: Prentice Hall, 1987.

Charrier, Philip. 'Asean's Inheritance: The Regionalisation of Southeast Asia, 1941–61'. *The Pacific Review* 14, no. 3 (2001): 313–338.

Church, Peter. *A Short History of Southeast Asia*. Singapore: John Wiley & Sons (Asia), 2006.

Collier, Kit. 'Terrorism: Evolving Regional Alliances and State Failure in Mindanao'. In *Southeast Asian Affairs 2006*, 26–38. Singapore: ISEAS, 2006.

Collins, Alan. 'Forming a Security community: Lessons from ASEAN'. *International Relations of the Asia-Pacific* 7, no. 2 (2007): 203–227.

Collins, Alan. 'A People-Oriented ASEAN: A Door Ajar or Closed for Civil Society Organisations'. *Contemporary Southeast Asia* 30, no. 2 (2008).

Collins, Alan. *Security and Southeast Asia: Domestic, Regional, and Global Issues*. Boulder, CO: Lynne Rienner, 2003.

Cockerman, Geoffrey B. 'Regional Integration in ASEAN: Institutional Design and the ASEAN Way'. *East Asia: An International Quarterly* 27 (2010): 165–185.

Collier, Paul. *Wars, Guns and Votes: Democracy in Dangerous Places*. London: Vintage Books, 2010.

Cotton, James. *Crossing Borders in the Asia-Pacific: Essays on the Domestic-Foreign Policy Divide*. New York: Nova Science Publishers, 2002.

Cotton, James. 'The Domestic Sources of Regional Order in Michael Leifer's Analysis of Southeast Asia'. In *Order and Security in Southeast Asia: Essays in Memory of Michael Leifer*, edited by Joseph Chinyong Liow and Ralf Emmers, 210–225. London: Routledge, 2006.

Cotton, James. 'The "Haze" Over Southeast Asia: Challenging the ASEAN Mode of Regional Engagement'. *Pacific Affairs* 72, no. 3 (1999): 331–351.

Cotton, James. 'Regional Order and the over-Determination of Regional Institutions in the Asia-Pacific'. Paper presented at the UTS-Guadalajara Workshop, Guadalajara, January 2004.

Cotton, James. 'Southeast Asia after 11 September'. *Terrorism and Political Violence* 15, no. 1 (2003): 148–170.

Crocker, Jennifer and Riia Luhtanen. 'Collective Self-Esteem and Ingroup Bias'. *Journal of Personality and Social Psychology* 58, no. 1 (1990): 60–67.

Dauvergene, Peter. 'The Environment in Times of Crisis: Asia and Donors after the 1997 Crisis'. 53. Canberra: AusAid, 1999.

Dennis, Peter and Jeffrey Grey. *Emergency and Confrontation: Australian Military Operations in Malaya and Borneo 1950–1966*. St Leonards: Allen & Unwin in association with the Australian War Memorial, 1996.

Dent, Christopher M. 'The New Economic Bilateralism in Southeast Asia: Region-Convergent or Region-Divergent'. *International Relations of the Asia-Pacific* 6, no. 1 (2006): 81–111.

Desker, Barry and Christopher Roberts. 'Myanmar: Prospects and Challenges of Engagement'. In *Security through Cooperation: Cscap Regional Security Outlook (Crso)*, edited by Brian L. Job and Erin Williams, pp. 30–35. Singapore: CSCAP, 2008.

Deutsch, Karl W. *The Analysis of International Relations*. 2nd edn. New Jersey: Prentise Hall, Inc, 1981.

Deutsch, Karl W. *Nationalism and Social Communication: An Inquiry into the Foundations of Nationality*. 2nd edn. Cambridge: MIT Press, 1967.

Deutsch, Karl W., Sidney A. Burrell, Robert A. Kann, Jr., Maurice Lee, Martin Lichterman, Raymond E. Lindgren, Francis L. Loewenheim and Richard W. Van Wagenen.

Political Community and the North Atlantic Area: International Organisation in the Light of Historical Experience. New York: Greenwood Press, 1957.

Devine, Fiona. 'Methodological Questions – Qualitative Analysis'. In *Theory and Methods in Political Science*, edited by David Marsh and Gerry Stoker. Houndmills: Macmillan Press Ltd and St. Martins Press, 1995.

Dieter, Herbert. 'Changing Patterns of Regional Governance: From Security to Political Economy?' *The Pacific Review* 22, no. 1 (2009): 73–90.

Dosch, Jorn. *The Changing Dynamics of Southeast Asian Politics*. London: Lynne Rienner, 2007.

Dosch, Jorn. *PMC, ARF and CSCAP: Foundations for a Security Architecture in the Asia-Pacific*. Canberra: Strategic and Defence Studies Centre, 1997.

Dupont, Alan. 'Asean's Response to the East Timor Crisis'. *Australian Journal of International Affairs* 54, no. 2 (2000): 163–170.

Dupont, Alan. *East Asia Imperiled: Transnational Challenges to Security*. Cambridge: Cambridge University Press, 2001.

Dupont, Alan. 'Transnational Crime, Drugs, and Security in East Asia'. *Asian Survey* 39, no. 3 (1999): 433–455.

Eichengreen, Barry and J. Bradford DeLong. *Between Meltdown and Moral Hazard: The International Monetary and Financial Policies of the Clinton Adminstration*. Berkeley: University of California at Berkely and NBER, 2001.

Emmers, Ralf. *Cooperative Security and the Balance of Power in ASEAN and the ARF*. London and New York: RoutledgeCurzon, 2003.

Emmers, Ralf. 'The Indochinese Enlargement of ASEAN: Security Expectations and Outcomes'. *Australian Journal of International Affairs* 59, no. 1 (2005): 71–88.

Emmers, Ralf. 'Regional Hegemonies and the Exercise of Power in Southeast Asia: A Study of Indonesia and Vietnam'. *Asian Survey* 45, no. 4 (2005): 645–665.

Emmers, Ralf. 'Security Cooperation in the Asia-Pacific: Evolution of Concepts and Practices'. In *Asia-Pacific Security Cooperation: National Interests and Regional Order*, edited by See Seng Tan and Amitav Acharya, 1–18. Armonk: M. E. Sharpe, 2004.

Emmerson, Donald K. 'Asean's "Black Swans"'. *Journal of Democracy* 19, no. 3 (2008): 70–84.

Emmerson, Donald K. 'Critical Terms: Security, Democracy, and Regionalism in Southeast Asia'. In *Hard Choices: Security, Democracy, and Regionalism in Southeast Asia*, edited by Donald K Emmerson, 3–56. Stanford: Stanford University Press, 2008.

Emmerson, Donald K. 'Security, Community, and Democracy in Southeast Asia: Analysing ASEAN'. *Japanese Journal of Political Science* 6, no. 2 (2005): 165–185.

Emmerson, Donald K. 'What Do the Blind-Sided See? Reapproaching Regionalism in Southeast Asia'. *The Pacific Review* 18, no. 1 (2005): 1–21.

Emmerson, Donald K. '"Southeast Asia": What's in a Name?' *Journal of Southeast Asian Studies* 15, no. 1 (1984): 1–21.

Englehart, Neil. 'Democracy and the Thai Middle Class: Globalization, Modernization and Constitutional Change'. *Asian Survey* 43, no. 2 (2003): 253–279.

Evans, Grant and Kelvin Rowley. *Red Brotherhood at War: Vietnam, Cambodia and Laos since 1975*. London: Verso, 1990.

Farrell, Mary. 'The Global Politics of Regionalism: An Introduction'. In *Global Politics of Regionalism*, edited by Mary Farrell, Bjorn Hettne and Luk Van Langenhove. London: Pluto Press, 2005.

Fawcett, Louise. 'Regionalism from an Historical Perspective'. In *Global Politics of Regionalism: Theory and Practice*, edited by Mary Farrell, Bjorn Hettne and Luk Van Langenhove. London: Pluto Press, 2005.

Ferguson, Brian R. 'Anthropology of War: Theory, Politics and Ethics'. In *The Anthropology of War and Peace*, edited by David Pitt and Paul Turner, 141–159. South Hadley, MA: Bergin and Garvey, 1989.

Ferguson, James R. 'ASEAN Concord II: Policy Prospects for Participant Regional "Development"'. *Contemporary Southeast Asia* 26, no. 3 (2004): 393–415.

Flockhart, Trine. '"Complex Socialisation": A Framework for the Study of State Socialization'. *European Journal of International Relations* 12, no. 1 (2006): 89–118.

Foot, Rosemary. 'Modes of Regional Conflict Management: Comparing Security Cooperation in the Korean Peninsula, China-Taiwan, and the South China Sea'. In *Reassessing Security Cooperation in the Asia-Pacific: Competition, Congruence, and Transformation*, edited by Amitav Acharya and Evelyn Goh, 93–112. Cambridge: MIT Press, 2007.

Friedberg, Aaron L. 'Ripe for Rivalry: Prospects for Peace in a Multipolar Asia'. *International Security* 18, no. 3 (1993): 5–33.

Fuller, Gary A., Alexander B. Murphy, Mark A. Ridgeley and Richard Ulack. 'Measuring Potential Ethnic Conflict in Southeast Asia'. *Growth and Change* 31, no. 2 (2000): 305–331.

Funston, John. 'ASEAN and the Principles of Non-Intervention: Practice and Prospects'. In *Non-Intervention and State Sovereignty in the Asia-Pacific*, edited by David Dickens and Guy Wilson-Roberts, 9–22. Wellington: Centre for Strategic Studies, China Centre for International Studies, Institute of Strategic and International Studies, 2000.

Funston, John. 'ASEAN: Out of Its Depth?' *Contemporary Southeast Asia* 20, no. 1 (1998): 22–37.

Ganesan, N. 'ASEAN: A Community Stalled?' In *The Asia-Pacific: A Region in Transition*, edited by Jim Rolfe. Hawaii: Asia-Pacific Center for Security Studies, 2004.

Ganesan, N. *Bilateral Tensions in Post-Cold War ASEAN*, Pacific Strategic Papers. Singapore: Institute of Southeast Asia Studies, 1999.

Ganesan, N. 'Thai–Myanmar–ASEAN Relations: The Politics of Face and Grace'. *Asian Affairs: An American Review* 33, no. 3 (2006).

Garofano, John. 'Power, Institutions, and the ASEAN Regional Forum: A Security community for Asia'. *Asian Survey* 42, no. 3 (2002): 503–521.

Gates, Carolyn L. and Mya Than. 'ASEAN Enlargement: An Introductory Overview'. In *ASEAN Enlargement: Impacts and Implications*, edited by Mya Than and Carolyn L. Gates, 1–25. Singapore: ISEAS, 2001.

Giddens, Anthony. *The Nation-State and Violence*. London: University of California Press, 1987.

Goh, Evelyn. 'The ASEAN Regional Forum in the United States East Asian Strategy'. *The Pacific Review* 17, no. 1 (2004): 47–69.

Goldstein, Joshua S. and Jon C. Pevehouse. *International Relations: Brief Fifth Edition*. New York: Longman, 2010.

Green, December and Luehrmann. *Comparative Politics in the Third World: Linking Concepts and Cases*. Boulder, CO: Lynne Rienner, 2007.

Gries, Peter Hays. 'Social Psychology and the Identity-Conflict Debate: Is a "China Threat" Inevitable?' *European Journal of International Relations* 11, no. 2 (2005): 235–265.

Haacke, Jurgen. *Asean's Diplomatic and Security Culture*. London and New York: RoutledgeCurzon, 2003.

Haacke, Jurgen. 'ASEAN and Political Change in Myanmar: Towards a Regional Initiative'. *Contemporary Southeast Asia* 30, no. 3 (2008): 351–378.

Haacke, Jurgen. 'ASEAN and the Situation in Myanmar/Burma'. In *Myanmar/Burma: Challenges and Perspectives*, edited by Guo Xiaolin, 131–158. Stockholm-Nacka, Sweden: Institute for Security and Development Study, 2008.

Haacke, Jurgen. 'The Concept of Flexible Engagement and the Practice of Enhanced Interaction: Intramural Challenges to the "ASEAN Way"'. *The Pacific Review* 12, no. 4 (1999): 581–611.

Haacke, Jurgen. '"Enhanced Interaction" With Myanmar and the Project of a Security community: Is ASEAN Refining or Breaking with its Diplomatic and Security Culture?' *Contemporary Southeast Asia* 27, no. 2 (2005): 188–216.

Hall, D.G.E. *A History of South-East Asia*. Hong Kong: Macmillan Press, 1981.

Hartfiel, Robert and Brian L. Job. 'Raising the Risks of War: Defence Spending Trends and Competitive Arms Processes in Southeast Asia.' *The Pacific Review* 20, no. 1 (2007): 1–22.

Havel, Vaclav and Bishop Desmond M. Tutu. 'Threat to Peace: A Call for the Un Security Council to Act in Burma'. DLA Piper Rudnick Gray Cary, 2005.

He, Baogang. 'East Asian Ideas of Regionalism: A Normative Critique'. *Australian Journal of International Affairs* 58, no. 1 (2004): 105–125.

He, Kai. 'Indonesia's Foreign Policy after Soeharto: International Pressure, Democratization, and Policy Change'. *International Relations of the Asia-Pacific* 8, no. 1 (2008): 47–72.

Heidhues, Mary Somers. *Southeast Asia: A Concise History*. London: Thames and Hudson, 2000.

Heller, Dominik. 'The Relevance of the ASEAN Regional Forum (ARF) for Regional Security in the Asia-Pacific'. *Contemporary Southeast Asia* 27, no. 1 (2005): 123–145.

Hemmer, Christopher and Peter J. Katzenstein. 'Why Is There No Nato in Asia? Collective Identity, Regionalism, and the Origins of Multilateralism'. *International Organization* 56, no. 3 (2002): 575–607.

Henderson, Jeannie. *Reassessing ASEAN*. London: The International Institute for Strategic Studies, 1999.

Hettne, Bjorn. 'Globalisation and the New Regionalism'. In *Globalism and New Regionalism*, edited by Bjorn Hettne, Andras Inotai and Sunkel Osvaldo. New York: St. Martin's Press, 1999.

Hill, Monte H. 'Community Formation within ASEAN'. *International Organization* 32, no. 2 (1978): 569–575.

Howard, Michael. *The Causes of War and Other Essays*. Sussex: Temple Smith, 1983.

Hund, Markus. 'The Development of ASEAN Norms between 1997 and 2000: A Paradigm Shift?' Centre for East Asian and Pacific Studies, Occasional Paper, no. 15, University of Trier, www.zops.uni-trier.de/op/OccasionalPapersNr15.pdf.

Hurrell, Andrew. 'Norms and Ethics in International Relations'. In *Handbook of International Relations*, edited by Walter Carlsnaes, Thomas Risse and Beth Simmons, 137–154. London: Sage, 2005.

Jackson, Robert H. and Patricia Owens. 'The Evolution of International Society'. In *The Globalisation of World Politics: An Introduction to International Relations*, edited by John Baylis and Steve Smith, 45–62. Oxford: Oxford University Press, 2006.

Jayasuriya, Kanishka. 'Introduction: Governing the New Asia Pacific – Beyond the "New Regionalism"'. *Third Word Quarterly* 24, no. 2 (2003): 199–215.

Jayasuriya, Kanishka and Andrew Rosser. 'Pathways from the Crisis: Politics and Reform in Southeast Asia since 1997'. In *The Political Economic of South-East Asia: Markets, Power and Contestation*, edited by Garry Rodan, Kevin Hewison and Richard Robison, 258–282. Oxford: Oxford University Press, 2006.

Jepperson, Ronald L., Alexander Wendt and Peter J. Katzenstein. 'Norms, Identity and Culture in National Security'. In *The Cutlure of National Security: Norms and Identity in World Politics*, edited by Peter J. Katzenstein, pp. 33–75. New York: Columbia University Press, 1996.

Jones, David M. and Michael Smith. *ASEAN and East Asian International Relations: Regional Delusion*. Northhampton, MA: Edward Elgar, 2006.

Jones, David M. and Michael Smith. 'The Changing Security Agenda in Southeast Asia: Globalization, New Terror, and the Delusions of Regionalism'. *Studies in Conflict and Terrorism* 24 (2001): 271–288.

Jones, David M. and Michael Smith. 'Making Process, Not Progress'. *International Security* 32, no. 1 (2007): 148–184.

Jones, David M. and Michael Smith. 'Security and Democracy: The ASEAN Charter and the Dilemmas of Regionalism in South-East Asia'. *International Affairs* 4 (2008): 735–756.

Jones, Lee. 'Asean's Albatross: Asean's Burma Policy, from Constructive Engagement to Critical Disengagement'. *Asian Security* 4, no. 3 (2008): 271–293.

Jones, Matthew. *Conflict and Confrontation in Southeast Asia: 1961–1965*. Cambridge: Cambridge University Press, 2002.

Jones, Michael E. 'Forging an ASEAN Identity: The Challenge to Construct a Shared Identity'. *Contemporary Southeast Asia* 26, no. 1 (2004): 140–154.

Jorgensen-Dahl, Arnfinn. *Regional Organisation and Order in South-East Asia*. Basingstoke and London: Macmillan, 1982.

Kacowicz, Arie. 'Regionalization, Globalization, and Nationalism: Convergent, Divergent or Overlapping?' *Alternative: Social Transformation and Humane Governance* 24 (1999): 527–555.

Katanyuu, Ruukan. 'Beyond Non-Interference in ASEAN: The Association's Role in Myanmar's National Reconcilliation and Democratization'. *Asian Survey* 46, no. 6 (2006): 825–845.

Katzenstein, Peter J. *The Culture of National Security: Norms and Identity in World Politics*. New York: Columbia University Press, 1996.

Katzenstein, Peter J. and Rudra Sil. 'Rethinking Asian Security: A Case for Analytical Eclecticism'. In *Rethinking Security in East Asia: Identity, Power, and Efficiency*, edited by J. J. Suh, Peter J. Katzenstein and Allen Carlson, 1–34: Stanford University Press, 2004.

Kawai, Masahiro and Ganeshan Wignaraja. 'EAFTA or CEPEA: Which Way Forward?' *ASEAN Economic Bulletin* 25, no. 2 (2008): 113–139.

Kawasaki, Tsuyoshi. 'Neither Skepticism nor Romanticism: The ASEAN Regional Forum as a Solution for the Asia-Pacific Assurance Game'. *The Pacific Review* 19, no. 2 (2006): 219–237.

Kegley, Charles W. Jr. and Gregory A. Raymond. *The Global Future: A Brief Introduction to World Politics*. Belmont: Thompson, 2005.

Kegley, Charles W. Jr. and Gregory A. Raymond. *When Trust Breaks Down: Alliance Norms and World Politics* (Columbia: University of South Carolina Press, 1990).

Kelly, Robert E. 'Security Theory in The "New Regionalism"'. *International Studies Review* 9, no. 2 (2007): 197–229.

Keohane, Robert. 'Neoliberal Institutionalism: A Perspective on World Politics'. In *International Institutions and State Power: Essays in International Relations Theory*, edited by Robert Keohane. Boulder, CO: Westview Press, 1989.

Keohane, Robert and Lisa Martin. *Institutional Theory, Edongeneity and Delegation.* Cambridge: Harvard University, 1999.

Keohane, Robert O. and Joseph S. Nye Jr. *Transnational Relations and World Politics.* Cambridge: Harvard University Press, 1972.

Khong, Yuen Foong. 'ASEAN and the Southeast Asian Security Complex'. In *Regional Orders: Building Security in the New World*, edited by David A. Lake and Patrick M. Morgan, 318–342. Pennsylvania: Pennsylvania State University Press, 1997.

Khoo, Nicholas. 'Deconstructing the ASEAN Security community: A Review Essay'. *International Relations of the Asia-Pacific* 4 (2004): 35–46.

Kingsbury, Damien. 'Southeast Asia: A Community of Diversity'. *Politics and Policy* 35, no. 1 (2007): 6–25.

Kingsbury, Damien and Clinton Fernandes. 'Terrorism in Archipelagic Southeast Asia'. In *Violence in Between: Conflict and Security in Archipelagic Southeast Asia*, edited by Damien Kingsbury, 9–52. Melbourne: Monash University Press and ISEAS, 2005.

Kraft, Herman. 'The Principle of Non-Intervention: Evolution and Challenges for the Asia-Pacific Region'. In *Non-Intervention and State Sovereignty in the Asia-Pacific*, edited by David Dickens and Guy Wilson-Roberts, 23–41. Wellington: Center for Strategic Studies, 2000.

Kroef, Justus M. Van Der. 'ASEAN, Hanoi, and the Kampuchean Conflict: Between "Kuantan" and a "Third Alternative" '. *Asian Survey* 21, no. 5 (1981): 515–535.

Lake, David A. and Patrick M. Morgan. 'The New Regionalism in Security Affairs'. In *Regional Orders: Building Security in a New World*, edited by David A. Lake and Patrick M. Morgan, 3–19. Pennsylvania: Pennsylvania State University Press, 1997.

Lau, Albert. *A Moment of Anguish: Singapore in Malaysia and the Politics of Disengagement.* Singapore: Times Academic Press, 1998.

Lebow, Richard Ned. 'Reason, Emotion and Cooperation'. *International Politics* 42, no. 3 (2005): 283–313.

Lee, Yong Leng. *Southeast Asia: Essays in Political Geography*. Singapore: Singapore University Press, 1982.

Leifer, Michael. *ASEAN and the Security of Southeast Asia.* London: Routledge, 1989.

Leifer, Michael. *The ASEAN Regional Forum.* London: The International Institute for Strategic Studies, 1996.

Leifer, Michael. *The ASEAN Regional Forum: A Model for Cooperative Security in the Middle East.* Canberra: Department of International Relations, ANU, 1998.

Leifer, Michael. *Dictionary of the Modern Politics of South-East Asia.* London: Routledge, 2001.

Leifer, Michael. *Indonesia's Foreign Policy*. London: Allen & Unwin/Royal Institute of International Affairs, 1983.

Leifer, Michael. 'The Political and Security Outlook for Southeast Asia'. Paper presented at the 2000 Regional Outlook Forum, Singapore, January 2000.

Liow, Joseph Chinyong. 'Internal Conflicts in Southeast Asia: The Nature, Legitimacy, and (Changing) Role of the State'. *Asian Security* 3, no. 2 (2007): 73–79.

Liow, Joseph Chinyong. 'Tunku Abdul Rahman and Malaya's Relations with Indonesia, 1957–1960'. *Journal of Southeast Asian Studies* 36, no. 1 (2005): 87–109.

Liow, Joseph Chinyong. 'Southeast Asia in 2009: A Year Fraught with Challenges'. In *Southeast Asian Affairs 2010*, edited by Daljit Singh, 3–22. Singapore: ISEAS, 2010.

Mackie, J.A.C. *Konfrontasi: The Indonesia-Malaysia Dispute.* Kuala Lumpur, New York: Oxford University Press, 1974.

Mahbubani, Kishore. 'Lessons for the West from Asian Capitalism'. *Financial Times*, 18 March 2009.

Mahbubani, Kishore. *The New Asian Hemisphere: The Irresistible Shift of Global Power to the East.* New York: PublicAffairs, 2008.

Mansfield, Edward D. and Brian M. Pollins. 'The Study of Interdependence and Conflict: Recent Advances, Open Questions, and Directions for Future Research'. *Journal of Conflict Resolution* 45, no. 6 (2001): 834–859.

Marsh, Ian. 'Democratization and State Capacity in East and Southeast Asia'. *Taiwan Journal of Democracy* 2, no. 2 (2006): 69–92.

McCloud, Donald G. *Southeast Asia: Tradition and Modernity in the Contemporary World.* Oxford: Westview Press, 1995.

McFarlane, John. *Transnational Crime and Illegal Immigration in the Asia-Pacific Region: Background, Prospects and Countermeasures.* Canberra: Strategic and Defence Studies Centre, 1999.

Morgan, Patrick. 'Regional Security Complexes and Regional Orders'. In *Regional Orders: Building Security in the New World*, edited by David A. Lake and Patrick M. Morgan, 20–44. Pennsylvania: Pennsylvania State University Press, 1997.

Myoe, Maung Aung. *Neither Friend nor Foe: Myanmar's Relations with Thailand since 1988 – A View from Yangon.* Singapore: Institute of Defence and Strategic Studies, 2002.

Nabers, Dirk. 'The Social Construction of International Institutions: The Case of ASEAN + 3'. *International Relations of the Asia-Pacific* 3, no. 1 (2003): 113–136.

Narine, Shaun. 'ASEAN and the ARF: The Limits of the ASEAN Way'. *Asian Survey* 37, no. 10 (1997): 961–978.

Narine, Shaun. 'ASEAN in the Twenty-First Century: A Sceptical Review'. *Cambridge Review of International Affairs* 22, no. 3 (2009): 369–386.

Narine, Shaun. *Explaining ASEAN: Regionalism in Southeast Asia.* Boulder, CO: Lynne Rienner, 2002.

Narine, Shaun. 'Institutional Theory and Southeast Asia: The Case of ASEAN'. *World Affairs* 161, no. 1 (1998): 33–48.

Nathan, K S. 'Malaysia–Singapore Relations: Retrospect and Prospect'. *Contemporary Southeast Asia* 24, no. 2 (2002): 385–410.

Nathan, Laurie. 'Domestic Instability and Security Communities'. *European Journal of International Relations* 12, no. 2 (2006): 275–299.

Nischalke, Tobias. 'Does ASEAN Measure Up? Post Cold War Diplomacy and the Idea of Regional Community'. *The Pacific Review* 15, no. 1 (2002): 89–117.

Nishikawa, Yukiko. 'The "ASEAN Way" And Asian Regional Security'. *Politics and Policy* 35, no. 1 (2007): 42–56.

Noble, Gregory W. and John Ravenhill. 'Causes and Consequences of the Asian Financial Crisis'. In *The Asian Financial Crisis and the Architecture of Global Finance*, edited by Gregory W. Noble and John Ravenhill, 1–35. Cambridge: Cambridge University Press, 2000.

O'Neal, John R. and Bruce M. Russett. 'The Classic Liberals Were Right: Democracy, Interdependence, and Conflict, 1950–1985'. *International Studies Quarterly* 41 (1997): 267–294.

O'Neill, Kate, Jorg Balsiger and Stacy D. VanDeveer. 'Actors, Norms, and Impact: Recent International Cooperation Theory and the Influence of the Agent-Structure Debate'. *Annual Review of Political Science* 7 (2004): 149–175.

Osborne, Milton. *Southeast Asia: An Introductory History*. Sydney and Boston: Allen and Unwin, 1983.

Patty, John W. and Roberto A. Weber. 'Agreeing to Fight: An Explanation of the Democratic Peace'. *Politics, Philosophy & Economics* 5, no. 3 (2006): 305–320.

Pempel, T.J. *Remapping East Asia: The Construction of a Region*. Ithaca: Cornell University Press, 2005.

Putnam, Robert. 'Diplomacy and Domestic Politics: The Logic of Two Level Games'. *International Organization* 42, no. 3 (1988): 427–460.

'Quality of Partnership: Myanmar, ASEAN and the World Community'. Asian Dialogue Society, 2003.

Rahim, Lily Zubaidah. 'Fragmented Community and Unconstructive Engagements: ASEAN and Burma's SPDC Regime'. *Critical Asian Studies* 40, no. 1 (2008): 67–88.

Ramcharan, Robin. 'ASEAN and Non-Interference: A Principle Maintained?' *Contemporary Southeast Asia* 22, no. 1 (2000): 60–88.

Ravenhill, John. 'The New Bilateralism in the Asia Pacific'. *Third Word Quarterly* 24, no. 2 (2003): 299–317.

Ravenhill, John. 'Fighting Irrelevance: An Economic Community "with ASEAN Characteristics"'. *The Pacific Review* 21, no. 4 (2008): 469–488.

Ravenhill, John. 'East Asian Regionalism: Much Ado About Nothing?' *Review of International Studies* 35 (2009): 215–235.

Reid, Anthony. *Southeast Asia in the Age of Commerce, 1450–1680*. Vol. 1. New Haven, CT: Yale University Press, 1988.

Roberts, Christopher. 'The ASEAN Community: Trusting Thy Neighbour?' *The Nation*, 12 November 2007.

Roberts, Christopher. *ASEAN's Myanmar Crisis: Challenges to the Pursuit of a Security community*. Singapore: ISEAS, 2010.

Roberts, Christopher. 'ASEAN Institutionalisation: The Function of Political Values and State Capacity'. *RSIS Working Paper*, no. 217 (2010).

Roberts, Christopher. 'The ASEAN Security community Project: The Prospects for Comprehensive Integration in Southeast Asia'. *The Indonesian Quarterly* 34, no. 3 (2006): 270–293.

Roberts, Christopher. 'East Asian Regionalism: A Backgrounder on an Eclectic Alternative for Analaysis'. In *Do Institutions Matter? Regional Institutions and Regionalism in East Asia*, edited by See Seng Tan, 19–30. Singapore: S. Rajaratnam School of International Studies, 2008.

Roberts, Christopher. 'Myanmar and the Argument for Engagement: A Clash of Contending Moralities?' *East Asia: An International Quarterly* 23, no. 2 (2006): 33–62.

Rodan, Garry, Kevin Hewison and Richard Robison. 'Theorising Markets in Southeast Asia: Power and Contestation'. In *The Political Economy of Southeast Asia: Markets, Power and Contestation*, edited by Garry Rodan, Kevin Hewison and Richard Robison, 1–38. New York: Oxford, 2006.

Rolfe, Jim. 'Regional Security for the Asia-Pacific: Ends and Means'. *Contemporary Southeast Asia* 30, no. 1 (2008): 99–117.

Rumelili, Bahar. *Constructing Regional Community and Order in Europe and Southeast Asia*. New York: Palgrave Macmillan, 2007.

Sapolsky, Robert M. 'A Natural History of Peace'. *Foreign Affairs* 85 (2006): 104–120.

Schimmelfenning, Frank. 'The Normative Origins of Democracy in the European Union: Toward a Transformationlist Theory of Democratization'. *European Political Science Review* 2, no. 2 (2010): 211–233.

Schofield, Clive and Ian Storey. 'Energy Security and Southeast Asia: The Impact on Maritime Boundary and Territorial Disputes'. *Harvard Asia Quarterly* 9, no. 4 (2005): 36–39.

Selth, Andrew. *Burma's Muslims: Terrorists or Terrorised?* Vol. 150. Canberra: The Strategic and Defence Studies Centre, The Australian National University, 2003.

Selth, Andrew. 'Burma's Saffron Revolution and the Limits of International Influence'. *Australian Journal of International Affairs* 62, no. 3 (2008): 281–297.

Selth, Andrew. 'Even Paranoids Have Enemies: Cyclone Nargis and Myanmar's Fears of Invasion'. *Contemporary Southeast Asia* 30, no. 3 (2008): 379–402.

Severino, Rodolfo C. *Southeast Asia in Search of an ASEAN Community: Insights from the Former Secretary-General*. Singapore: ISEAS, 2006.

Severino, Rodolfo C. 'Regional Economic Integration and the ASEAN Charter'. In *Regional Outlook: Southeast Asia 2008/2009*. Singapore: ISEAS, 2009.

Simon, Sheldon W. 'Asian Armed Forces: Internal and External Tasks and Capabilities'. 1–28. Washington: The National Bureau of Asian Research, 2000.

Simon, Sheldon W. 'China, Vietnam, and ASEAN: The Politics of Polarization'. *Asian Survey* 19, no. 12 (1979): 1171–1188.

Simon, Sheldon W. 'Southeast Asia's Defense Needs: Change or Continuity?' In *Strategic Asia 2005–06: Military Modernisation in an Era of Uncertainty*, edited by Ashley J. Tellis and Michael Wills, 269–301. Seattle, Washington: National Bureau of Asian Research, 2005.

Simon, Sheldon W. 'The Two Southeast Asias and China: Security Perspectives'. *Asian Survey* 24, no. 5 (1984): 519–533.

Singh, Jewellord T. Nem. 'Process of Institutionalisation and Democratisation in ASEAN: Features, Challenges and Prospects of Regionalism in Southeast Asia'. *UNISCI Discussion Papers*, no. 16 (2008): 141–167.

Skidmore, David and Valerie M. Hudson. *The Limits to State Autonomy: Societal Groups and Foeign Policy Formulation*. Boulder, CO: Westview, 1993.

Slaughter, Anne Marie. *A New World Order*. Princeton NJ: Princeton University Press, 2004.

Slocum, Nikki and Luk Van Langenhove. 'Identity and Regional Integration'. In *Global Politics of Regionalism: Theory and Practice*, edited by Mary Farrell, Bjorn Hettne and Luk Van Langenhove, 137–151. London: Pluto Press, 2005.

Smith, Anthony L. 'Asean's Ninth Summit: Solidifying Regional Cohesion, Advancing External Linkages'. *Contemporary Southeast Asia* 26, no. 3 (2004): 416–433.

Smith, Anthony L. 'Indonesia's Foreign Policy under Abdurrahman Wahid: Radical or Status Quo State?' *Contemporary Southeast Asia* 22, no. 3 (2000): 498–527.

Smith, Anthony L. *Strategic Centrality: Indonesia's Changing Role in ASEAN*. Singapore: ISEAS, 2000.

Snitwongse, Kusuma. 'Thirty Years of ASEAN: Achievements through Political Cooperation'. *The Pacific Review* 11, no. 2 (1998): 183–194.

Snitwongse, Kusuma and Suchit Bunbongkarn. 'New Security Issues and Their Impact on ASEAN'. In *A New ASEAN in a New Millenium*, edited by Simon Tay, Jesus Estanislao and Hadi Soesastro, 148–162. Jakarta: Centre for Strategic and International Studies, 2000.

Soesastro, Hadi. 'Accelerating ASEAN Economic Integration: Moving Beyond AFTA'. In *CSIS Working Paper Series*. Jakarta: CSIS, 2005.

Solidum, Estrella. D. *The Politics of ASEAN: An Introduction to Southeast Asian Regionalism*. Singapore: Times Media, Eastern Universities Press, 2003.

Solingen, Etel. 'ASEAN Cooperation: The Legacy of the Economic Crisis'. *International Relations of the Asia-Pacific* 5, no. 1 (2005): 1–29.

Somit, Albert. 'Humans, Chimps, and Bonobos: The Biological Basis of Aggression, War, and Peace-Making'. *Journal of Conflict Resolution* 34, no. 3 (1990): 553–582.

Steedly, Mary Margaret. 'The State of Culture Theory in the Anthropology of Southeast Asia'. *Annual Review of Anthropology* 28 (1999): 431–454.

Stubbs, Richard. 'ASEAN Plus Three: Emerging East Asian Regionalism'. *Asian Survey* 32, no. 3 (2002): 440–456.

Sudo, Sueo. 'Forging an ASEAN Community: Its Significance, Problems and Prospects'. In *GSID Discussion Paper No. 146*. Nagoya: Nagoya University, 2006.

Sukma, Rizal. 'Towards an ASEAN Security community: Concept Paper'. *Deplu*, 20 March 2003.

Sukma, Rizal. 'The Future of ASEAN: Towards a Security community'. Permanent Mission of the Republic of Indonesia to the United Nations, www.indonesiamission-ny.org/issuebaru/Mission/asean/paper_rizalsukma.PDF.

Sutherland, Claire. 'Another Nation Building Bloc? Integrating National Ideology into the EU and ASEAN'. *Asia Europe Journal* 3 (2005): 141–157.

Syed, Hamid Albar. 'It is Not Possible to Defend Myanmar'. *Wall Street Journal*, 24 July 2006.

Tan, Andrew. 'Intra-ASEAN Tensions'. London: Royal Institute of International Affairs, 2000.

Tarling, Nicholas. *Nations and States in Southeast Asia*. Cambridge: Cambridge University Press, 1998.

Taylor, Robert H. 'Myanmar in 2007: Growing Pressure for Change but the Regime Remains Obdurate'. In *Southeast Asian Affairs 2008*, edited by Daljit Singh and Tin Maung Maung Than, 247–273. Singapore: ISEAS, 2008.

'Thailand's Non-Paper on Flexible Engagement'. *Ministry of Foreign Affairs*, 25 July 1998.

Than, Mya. *Myanmar in ASEAN: Regional Cooperation Experience*. Singapore: ISEAS, 2005.

Than, Mya and Tin Maung Maung Than. 'ASEAN Enlargement and Myanmar'. In *ASEAN Enlargement: Impacts and Implications*, edited by Mya Than and Carolyn L. Gates. Singapore: ISEAS, 2001.

Thawnghmung, Ardeth Maung and Maung Aung Myoe. 'Myanmar in 2007: A Turning Point in The "Roadmap"?' *Asian Survey* XLVIII, no. 1 (2008): 13–19.

Thayer, Carlyle A. 'ASEAN and Indochina: The Dialogue'. In *ASEAN in the 1990s*, edited by Alison Broinowski, pp. 139–61. London: Macmillan, 1990.

Thayer, Carlyle A. 'The Five Power Defence Arrangements'. *Security Challenges* 3, no. 1 (2007): 79–96.

Thayer, Carlyle A. 'New Terrorism in Southeast Asia'. In *Violence in Between: Conflict and Security in Archipelagic Southeast Asia*, edited by Damien Kingsbury, 53–74. Melbourne: Monash University Press and ISEAS, 2005.

Thayer, Carlyle A. 'Vietnam's Regional Integration: Domestic and External Challenges to State Sovereignty'. In *Vietnam's New Order: International Perspectives on the State and Reform in Vietnam*, edited by Stephanie Balme and Mark Side, 31–50. New York: Palgrave Macmillan, 2007.

Thongpakde, Nattapong. 'ASEAN Free Trade Area: Progress and Challenges'. In *ASEAN Beyond the Regional Crisis*, edited by Mya Than, 48–79. Singapore: ISEAS, 2001.

Tow, William T. *Asia-Pacific Security: US, Australia and Japan and the New Security Triangle*. London: Routledge, 2007.

Tow, William T. *Asia-Pacific Strategic Relations: Seeking Convergent Security*. Cambridge: Cambridge University Press, 2001.

Tow, William T. ed. *Security Politics in the Asia-Pacific: A Regional-Global Nexus?* Cambridge: Cambridge University Press, 2009.

Tow, William T., Ramesh Thakur and In-Taek Hyun, eds. *Asia's Emerging Regional Order: Reconciling Traditional and Human Security*. New York: United Nations University Press, 2000.

Tow, William T. and Chin Kin Wah, eds. *ASEAN, India, Australia: Towards Closer Engagement in a New Asia*. Singapore: ISEAS, 2009.

Turnbull, C.M. 'Regionalism and Nationalism'. In *The Cambridge History of Southeast Asia: From World War II to the Present*, edited by Nicholas Tarling, 257–318. Cambridge: Cambridge University Press, 2005.

Vatikiotis, Michael R.J. 'ASEAN 10: The Political and Cultural Dimensions of Southeast Asian Unity'. *Southeast Asian Journal of Social Science* 27, no. 1 (1999): 77–88.

Vayrynen, Raimo. 'Regionalism: Old and New'. *International Studies Review* 5 (2003): 25–51.

Vayrynen, Raimo. 'Stable Peace through Security Communities'. In *Stable Peace among Nations*, edited by Arie Kacowicz, Yaacov Bar-Simon-Tov, Ole Elgstrom and Alexander Jerneck, 108–129. Oxford: Rowman & Littlefield, 2000.

Vitug, Marites Danguilan and Glenda M. Gloria. *Under the Crescent Moon: Rebellion in Mindanao*. Quezon City: Ateneo Center for Social Policy and Public Affairs, Institute for Popular Democracy, 1990.

Wah, Chin Kin. *The Five Power Defence Arrangements and AMDA: Some Observations on the Nature of an Evolving Partnership*. Singapore: ISEAS, 1974.

Wallace, William, ed. *The Dynamics of European Integration*. London: Pinter, 1990.

Waltz, Kenneth. *Theory of International Politics*. Reading, MA: Addison-Wesley, 1979.

Waltz, Kenneth. 'Man, the State, and War'. In *War*, edited by Lawrence Freedman. Oxford: Oxford University Press, 1994.

Warleigh-Lack, Alex. 'Towards a Conceptual Framework for Regionalization: Bridging "New Regionalism" and "Integration Theory"'. *Review of International Political Economy* 15, no. 5 (2006): 750–771.

Weatherbee, Donald E. *International Relations in Southeast Asia: The Struggle for Autonomy*. Lanham, MD: Rowman & Littlefield, 2005.

Weatherbee, Donald E. *International Relations in Southeast Asia: The Struggle for Regional Autonomy*. 2nd edn. Plymouth: Rowman and Littlefield, 2009.

Weatherbee, Donald E. 'Southeast Asia in 2006: Deja Vu All over Again'. In *Southeast Asian Affairs 2007*, edited by Daljit Singh and Lorraine C. Salazar, 3–31. Singapore: ISEAS, 2007.

Wendt, Alexander. 'Anarchy is What States Make of it: The Social Construction of Power Politics'. *International Organization* 46, no. 2 (1992): 391–425.

Wendt, Alexander. 'Collective Identity Formation and the International State'. *American Political Science Review* 88, no. 2 (1994): 384–396.

Wendt, Alexander. *Social Theory of International Politics*. Cambridge: Cambridge University Press, 1999.

Wesley, M. 'The Asian Crisis and the Adequacy of Regional Institutions'. *Contemporary Southeast Asia* 21, no. 1 (1999).

Wight, Colin. 'State Agency: Social Action without Human Activity'. *Review of International Studies* 30, no. 2 (2004): 269–280.

Wight, Martin. *Systems of States*. Leicester: Leicester University Press, 1977.

Wu, Chien-Huei. 'The ASEAN Economic Community under the ASEAN Charter: Its External Economic Relations and Dispute Settlement Mechanisms'. In *European Yearbook of International Law*, edited by C Herrmann and J.P Terhechte, 331–357. Berlin, Heidelberg: Springer-Verlag, 2010.

Index

Page numbers in *italics* denote tables, those in **bold** denote figures.